Provence - August 15, 1944
DRAGOON
The other invasion of France

Paul GAUJAC

Translated from the French by Janice Lert and Philippe Charbonnier

Histoire & Collections - Paris

T a b l e   o f   C o n t e n t s

FOREWORD

On August 15, 1944, the American and French armies landed in Provence. Seventy days after the beginning of Operation Overlord in Normandy, they attacked the German forces from the rear. The Germans received orders to evacuate the territory south of the Loire River to avoid being caught in a trap.

The operation, initially called 'Anvil,' reached its initial goal, which was to catch the Wehrmacht between the Normandy sledgehammer and the anvil of Provence. But as the months passed other reasons had been found by the Americans to justify the operation and avoid being drawn by the British into a romantic push towards the Danube: the promises made to Stalin, the immediate landing of large French units instead of feeding them through the congested Atlantic ports, the need to seize an additional large harbor to support the offensive up north. Churchill grudgingly agreed, but declared that he was being 'dragooned' into the Riviera operation, hence its new codename.

The American divisions landed first: a regular division and two from the National Guard, originally made up of soldiers from the Southern states, as were most of those in the units of VI Corps or the Seventh Army.

These soldiers were veterans of the Italian campaign. Some had even fought in Morocco, Tunisia, and Sicily. It was the same for most shock troops, paratroopers and sailors — some had just fought in Normandy — and aircrews. The British, who com-

mitted only a single parachute brigade, nevertheless played an important role in the air and on the sea. Among the 861 ships composing the invasion fleet, 555 were American, 254 British, 34 French, seven Greek, four Dutch, three Norwegian, two Polish, one Belgian and one Italian.

The amphibious operation and the conquest of the beachhead were carried out by the Americans. But capturing the ports was the job of the French, who fielded three divisions and two-thirds of a fourth. And then it was every man for himself as the troops rushed north toward Lyons in a frantic pursuit of the Germans.

Of course Le Muy was not Sainte-Mère-l'Eglise, and the fighting in the Maures pine forests cannot be compared to hedgerow fighting in Normandy. But 'Anvil-Dragoon' was more subtle than Overlord, which encountered strong resistance. Its planning was more complex because of the use of ports and troops from all over the Mediterranean, and also taking into account the role of the special forces and the maquis.

The paradox of Dragoon is that the operation was so well organized and prepared and the Germans so weak, that it took place practically according to plans. Describing these plans in detail is thus almost the same thing as relating the operations themselves, and vice versa.

For this reason, part of the book is devoted to how the plans originated and how they were

During the first week of August 1944, part of the invasion fleet assembled in Naples Bay before proceeding toward the Provence coast.
Notice the heavy cruiser *Augusta* flanked by escort ships, troop transports and combat loaders.
This photograph has been taken from the Rione Amedeo hills toward the Castro dell'Ovo peninsula and Via Carracciolo whose trees may be seen along the riverside. *(ECPAD)*

prepared. Then comes the landing itself, between Cavalaire and Anthéor, in which aviators, sailors, commandos and paratroopers are not forgotten, with pages devoted to little-known or unknown episodes.

In preparing the book, we were able to consult numerous documents, studies and eye-witness accounts, published or unpublished, from essentially Anglo-Saxon or German sources. But the archives conserved by the French Navy and Air Force historical services were also a precious help.

Concerning the form, since it was an Allied operation against German forces, it was decided, to avoid a cumbersome and incomprehensible text, to print wherever possible unit names and technical terms in the original language, with translations whenever necessary. Likewise the times are indicated in the simplified form of four numerals from 0001 to 2400, corresponding to the German summer time which was the same in Italy at that period.

This book is a tribute to the American, British

Shoulder patches of the Sixth Army Group, AFHQ (Allied Force HQ in Algiers), the Seventh Army and French troops.
(Private collection)

On September 1, 1944 in Aix-en-Provence, the Allied high command for Dragoon discuss the progression of the troops toward Lyon. From left to right: Lieutenant General Alexander M. Patch, Seventh Army commander, Air Marshal Sir John C. Slessor, Lieutenant General Jacob L. Devers, commander of the 6th Army Group, General Sir Henry Maitland Wilson, Supreme Commander of the Allied Forces in the Mediterranean, and Major General Lowell W. Rooks.

Below.
General 'Jumbo' Wilson, between Generals Patch and Devers, arriving at Army B headquarters in Aix-en-Provence where he was met by General De Lattre. He insisted on shaking hands with General Carpentier, whom he had known when he was head of General Juin's staff in Italy.
(ECPAD)

and French sailors and soldiers who risked, and sometimes gave, their lives between August 15 and August 28, 1944, so that the inhabitants of Provence could be free.

It is also a tribute to the regretted Director of the British Naval Historical Branch, David Brown, who, in his preface to the anthology of amphibious operations in Europe, wrote:

"The sheer scale of the invasion of Normandy (Operation Neptune) which was the essential precursor of the liberation of north-west Europe (Operation Overlord), has tended to overshadow the significance of two other important amphibious assaults of that year, the invasion of the South of France (Operation Dragoon) in August 1944 and the seizure of the island of Walcheren (Operation Infatuate) in November.[1]"

---

1. Invasion of the South of France, Operation 'Dragoon,' 15th August 1944, *HMSO, London.*

IRONING OUT ANVIL

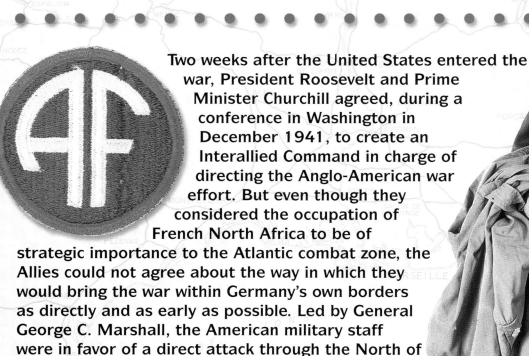

Two weeks after the United States entered the war, President Roosevelt and Prime Minister Churchill agreed, during a conference in Washington in December 1941, to create an Interallied Command in charge of directing the Anglo-American war effort. But even though they considered the occupation of French North Africa to be of strategic importance to the Atlantic combat zone, the Allies could not agree about the way in which they would bring the war within Germany's own borders as directly and as early as possible. Led by General George C. Marshall, the American military staff were in favor of a direct attack through the North of France, then to push east and toward Germany with all the means at their disposal. The British, on the other hand, preferred a 'peripheral' strategy, taking advantage of the superior Allied maritime mobility to hit and cripple the Axis forces at their weakest points before crossing the Channel and dealing the final blow.

An Eight Air Force officer in service uniform. The 8th, together with the 15th, flew long missions in preparation of 'Anvil.'
(Reconstruction, Militaria Magazine photo)

Top left.
Activated in England in September 1942, Allied Force Headquarters (AFHQ) moved to Algiers the following month. The shoulder patch in the colors of the Allied flags was approved on May 14, 1944.
(Le Poilu)

Left.
This convoy left the United States as part of Operation Torch and is traveling towards the coast of North Africa where the Anglo-American forces landed on November 8, 1942.
(US Army)

But forces for the 'great assault' were initially insufficient, so the Americans had to follow the British and intervene in French North Africa in November 1942. Then, caught up in the game, they accepted the invasion of Sicily, the landing at Salerno and the advance beyond Rome before finally putting an end to the British dream of an offensive towards the Danube by imposing an operation in the South of France.

BETWEEN SLEDGEHAMMER AND ANVIL

It was during the Quebec Interallied Conference in August 1943 that the idea of an operation in Southern France was first suggested by the Combined Chiefs of Staff [1]. Then at the end of November in Teheran, the project was analyzed in relationship to the invasion in the North of France. And since the Allies wanted to respond to the request by the Soviets that they open up a 'second front' as quickly as possible, priority over all other actions was given to the two operations, code-named 'Overlord' and 'Anvil' [2]. On December 6, the CCS informed General Dwight D. Eisenhower, the commander of Allied forces in Algiers who had already been chosen to lead Overlord, that the operation on the Southern coast of France was scheduled for May 1944. There would be sufficient shipping available for two divisions, since the amphibious operation programmed for the Bay of Bengal had been canceled. Eisenhower's command structure, Allied Force Headquarters (AFHQ), immedi-

Left.
The Supreme Headquarters, Allied Expeditionary Force (SHAEF), created in January 1944, adopted a shoulder patch showing the flamboyant sword of justice bringing liberty to the occupied countries.
(Private collection)

Right.
Vice Admiral Arthur K. Hewitt, commander of the Eighth Fleet, and Lieutenant General Jacob L. Devers, NATOUSA commander.

Activated in Algiers on February 4, 1943, U.S. Forces in the North African Theater of Operations (NATOUSA) chose in September a shoulder patch picturing the arch of a mosque.
(Private collection)

ately set to work to map out a first draft of a plan. This early estimate revealed the need for an American Corps composed of three divisions [3], including two assault divisions, to be reinforced subsequently by seven other formations, mostly French. Likewise, planning the operation and controlling field forces necessitated establishing an Army headquarters, and this was granted by CCS. An assault by three divisions having thus been agreed upon, it was decided to immediately undertake a study of the two possibilities. On December 19, AFHQ asked the Seventh Army in Palermo to estimate the needs

1. *The CCS or Allied Combined Chiefs of Staff, was composed of the British Chiefs of Staff (BCS) and the Joint Chiefs of Staff (JCS).*

2. *The Germans were supposed to be crushed between the 'Sledgehammer' (which became 'Overlord') and the 'Anvil.'*

3. *At first, it had been proposed to commit "one division or more, American or British."*

President Franklin D. Roosevelt and Prime Minister Winston Churchill in the gardens of the Hotel Anfa, during the Casablanca Interallied Conference in January 1943. Behind them, the members of the Combined Chiefs of Staff: Lieutenant General Henry H. Arnold, Admiral Ernest J. King, General George C. Marshall, Admiral of the Fleet Sir Dudley Pound, Air Chief Marshall Sir Charles F. A. Portal, Field Marshall Sir Alan Brooke.
(US Army)

The AFHQ Outline Plan

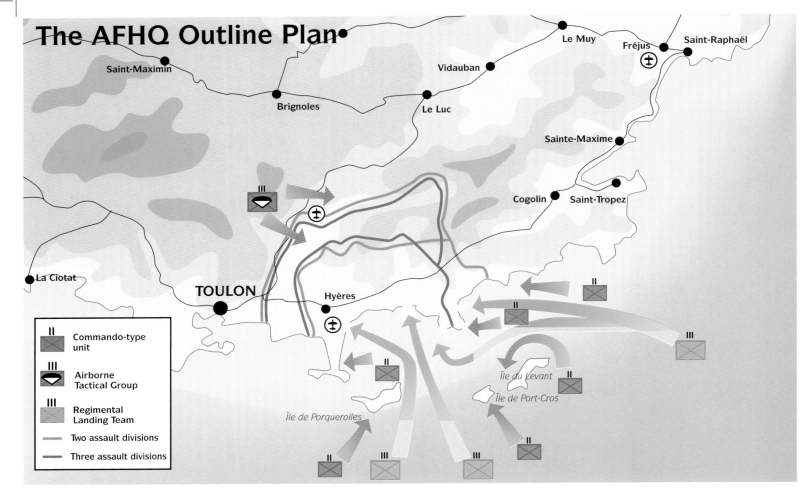

Saint-Raphaël
Fréjus
Le Muy
Vidauban
Saint-Maximin
Brignoles
Le Luc
Sainte-Maxime
Cogolin • Saint-Tropez
La Ciotat
TOULON
Hyères
Île du Levant
Île de Port-Cros
Île de Porquerolles

▦ II	Commando-type unit
▽ III	Airborne Tactical Group
▦ III	Regimental Landing Team
──	Two assault divisions
──	Three assault divisions

relating to a planning staff for an operation as important as the invasion of Sicily. Then, ten days later, the Army received information about the general objectives of a landing in Southern France code-named 'Anvil' and covered by the secret code 'Bigot' [4].

In the meantime, the AFHQ planners presented, on Christmas Eve, a draft project based on information received from the staff preparing for Overlord. First and foremost, considering the distance to be covered before reaching the objective, a line between Lyon and Vichy, it was clear that the sheer size of the operation required the rapid capture of a major port city. But which one? Sète and Toulon had insufficient capacity and were tactically vulnerable. However Marseilles answered the criteria, even though part of the city's artificial installations could be easily destroyed by the enemy.

The choice of an initial target thus fell on Marseilles, with, in consequence, the selection of the beaches east of Toulon for the assault. A preliminary order was issued on the 28th to Vice Admiral Henry K. Hewitt, naming him commander of naval operations with the title Western Task Force Naval Commander. At the same time, once information about earlier operations in the Mediterranean had been analyzed, the Mediterranean Allied Air Forces (MAAF) [5] issued a similar order to the units under their command which would be involved in the operation: Tactical and Coastal Air Forces, Troop Carrier and Air Ser-

Aerial photo from the port of Sète target file.
(Private collection)

SÈTE
ZÔNE INDUSTRIELLE NORD
Date de la photo : 10 Août 1943

---

4. *No one who was not authorized Bigot could receive messages concerning Anvil.*

5. *Created on December 10, 1943, by order of the CCS, MAAF controlled all the Allied, Italian and French air units within the theater of operations.*

tions [7] presented the respective points in the draft project that concerned them.

FORCE 163

Fifteen days later in Oran, a little group of logistics experts baptized 'Rear Force 163' set up their rear HQ next to Services of Supply headquarters, NATOUSA, and the main supply base of the 8th Fleet. The officers of Force 163 ran into problems immediately: the number of divisions had still not been decided upon, the final target was as yet unknown, and it was apparent that the future of the operation depended on developments in Italy and especially the planned invasion at Anzio. Another threat hovered over Anvil, this one coming from London. General Montgomery asked the CCS to approve reinforcements for Overlord at the expense of Anvil, which, according to this plan, was reduced to a mere diversionary operation mobilizing a single division. Eisenhower, in Washington at the time, approved the

---

6. North African Theater of Operations, US Army, or NATOUSA.

7. G-2 (Intelligence), G-3 (Operations), G-4 (Logistics), Transportation and Air Corps.

vice Commands. Hewitt left for Washington to submit his needs in men and equipment, particularly landing craft and escort ships. He also asked for the construction of additional installations for refueling in Corsica, where the landing craft would be forced to make a stopover.

On January 1, 1944, General Patton handed command of the Seventh Army over to Lieutenant General Mark W. Clark, who kept his Italian command while at the same time preparing for Anvil: it was planned that, after Rome was captured or during a pause in the campaign, Clark would leave the Fifth Army command and focus all his attention on Anvil. Then on the 8th, Eisenhower turned his command over to General Sir Henry Maitland Wilson and took the new title of Supreme Allied Commander, Mediterranean (SACMED), while Lieutenant General Jacob L. Devers took over the North African theater of operations [6], thus becoming the SACMED deputy.

The presence of the Seventh Army headquarters in Sicily might have misled the enemy as to the intentions of the Allies, but the fact that the other major commands involved were so far away was certainly not much of a help. So it was decided to discretely transfer a small team to Algiers, where they could work directly with the AFHQ, Navy and Air Force planners. Thus the planning group led by Brigadier General Garrison H. Davidson, the 7th Army Engineers commander, left Sicily and moved into the Bouzareah School. As soon as they arrived, on the morning of January 12, they were informed by Brigadier General Benjamin F. Caffey, AFHQ Special Operations Chief and Clark's planning deputy, that the team in charge of preparations had been named Force 163. Then a briefing was organized that same afternoon, at AFHQ, during which the different sec-

Aerial photo from the port of Marseilles target file.
(Private collection)

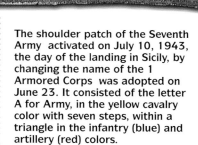

The shoulder patch of the Seventh Army activated on July 10, 1943, the day of the landing in Sicily, by changing the name of the 1 Armored Corps was adopted on June 23. It consisted of the letter A for Army, in the yellow cavalry color with seven steps, within a triangle in the infantry (blue) and artillery (red) colors.
(Le Poilu)

Lieutenant General Jacob L. Devers, SACMED deputy and commander of NATOUSA.
(US Army)

At one time assigned to Anvil, the 85th Infantry or Custer Division actually went to Naples in March 1944. Its shoulder patch is a reminder of its creation at Camp Custer, Michigan, in 1917.
(Private collection)

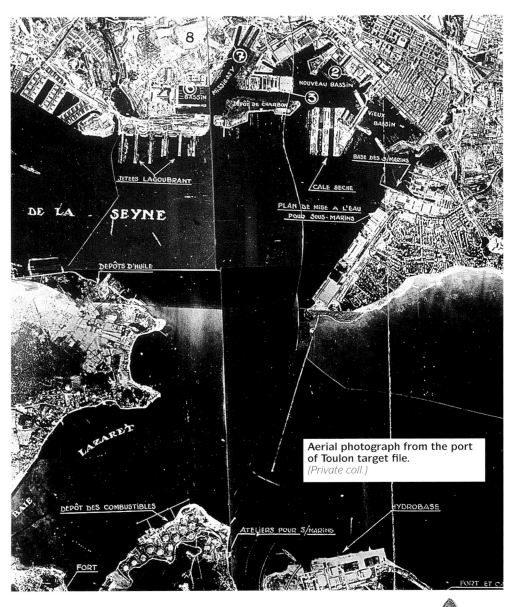

Aerial photograph from the port of Toulon target file.
(Private coll.)

increase from three to five divisions for Overlord, but at the same time warned against reducing Anvil "*both because of the promises given to the Russians at Teheran and because it would keep the French forces from playing a significant role*" in freeing their native soil.

Planning went forward nevertheless on the basis of one, two or three assault divisions with seven others making up the second echelon. The logistics experts prepared the requisitions for supplies so that the loading of the ships in the United States would not be delayed, and a troop list was written up. At the same time, beaches, coastal defence systems and the enemy positions were studied. But the draft project had not yet been approved by the CCS and no troops had as yet been pulled out of Italy to train in North Africa. However, on January 23, AFHQ notified Force 163 that three American divisions could be used for the invasion through Southern France [8], then reduced it the next day to a single assault division. On February 4, the planning teams of the three services met to compare their viewpoints: "*By the end of January, General Patton had left for the United Kingdom and had taken with him several of his key staff officers. There had been no selection of French troops, no withdrawal of divisions from Italy for training, no staging areas assigned, nor any designation of a Base Section Commander. The possibility occurred to those concerned with planning that Operation Anvil had been relegated to a 'Command Post Exercise' status. Actually the various sections were groping for something definite on which to plan. This was true not only in Force 163 itself, but also in the Naval and Air Planning Groups.* [9]"

The Ecole Normale of Bouzareah, Force 163 headquarters.
(Seventh Army)

The 91st Infantry Division was also at one time considered for Anvil, but was instead progressively engaged in Italy from June 1944 on. The fir tree symbolizes the state of Washington where the division was activated in 1917.
(Private collection)

On February 8, Wilson requested that the CCS make a decision rapidly about Anvil, since the date of the invasion and the importance of the assault troops would have a direct influence on the Italian campaign. At the same time, General Sir Harold Alexander, commander of the Allied forces in Italy, pleaded with Wilson not to take away any of his troops before the major offensive on Rome planned for the spring. Consequently Anvil could not take place before July. He even thought that the Anvil operation, with its limited means, would have no

---

8. These divisions at the time could have been the 3rd and 45th Divisions transferred from Italy, plus the 85th which had just arrived in Casablanca.
9. Seventh United States Army Report of Operations in France and Germany, 1944-1945, Aloys Graf, Heidelberg 1946.

Left.
Generals George S. Patton and Alexander M. Patch.
(Seventh Army)

Right.
Before heading for North Africa in March 1944, IV Corps oversaw stateside training in Atlanta, Georgia. Its shoulder patch, made up of four segments with the colors of the four corps, was created in 1918. *(Private collection)*

Unit patch of the 783rd Heavy Bombardment Squadron (USAAF 465th Bomb. Group), based at Pantanella, south-west of Taranto. *(Private collection)*

Below.
Even though no decision had been made about the fate of Anvil, the strategic airforces continued their attacks. On April 29, 1944, B-17s from the Fifteenth Air Force bombed the Toulon naval base. *(US Army Air Forces)*

Force 163 to select, before the meeting scheduled for March 1, the beaches which it considered to be the best choices for an assault. Davidson chose the sector between Cavalaire and Agay.

ANVIL SIDELINED

On March 2, Major General Alexander M. Patch was chosen to take command of the 7th Army, and AFHQ gave him command over the land forces participating in Anvil. The four principal leaders of the operation - all Americans - were now known: Patch (land forces), Hewitt (naval forces), Major General John K. Cannon (tactical air plans), Brigadier General Gordon P. Saville (fighter cover and close air support). The MATAF delegates came back to Algiers on the 5th to decide with Force 163 on a date when detailed study of the plans could start. But even though the 'footsloggers' were eager to have the aviators on their side, they couldn't actually come up with a date, since no firm decision had as yet been made concerning the number and types of ships assigned to the operation. However, the Air Force had decided that the time was ripe to join hands with Force 163. So the MATAF team, directed by Australian Group Captain R.B. Lees, settled in at Bouzareah, and were soon joined by representatives from the XII Tactical Air Command. Along with Captain Robert A.J. English, who had been detached with his group from Admiral Hewitt's headquarters and was already present on the spot, they constituted a true 'combined' command staff.

Force 163's structure was also reinforced: Davidson retained his position as director and Caffey supervised the entire group until he was reassigned to NATOUSA for medical reasons. The choice of Patch was particularly fortunate, and even though he was a newcomer in the Mediterranean, the change in command and cooperation among the different armed forces took place under the best possible conditions. The 7th Army staff had been badly

effect on the development of Overlord. In his opinion, no German force stationed in Northern France would risk its neck in the South unless Lyon were directly threatened, which meant that both Toulon and Marseilles would have to be captured. It then appeared clearly that the two Italian divisions would not be available for some time, and that the obligation to keep on supporting the Anzio beachhead, surrounded by Germans, would mean that the landing craft needed for the invasion were too busy elsewhere.

After this disappointing news came the CCS message, on February 10, indicating that Overlord had been postponed for three weeks, and ordering all LSTs (Landing ship, tank) that could be spared to sail for Great Britain. Force 163 did its best to attract AFHQ's attention to the fact that, if they were to continue working in an orderly manner, they needed clear orders concerning the composition of the forces to be engaged and the list of embarkation ports. The position of Force 163 was clear: either the Allies accept to simply hold the line in Italy while preparing Anvil, or Anvil would take place with so few forces that another Anzio would be inevitable.

AFHQ answered that the decision was to be made by the CCS, and in the meantime, preparation should continue on the basis of an assault led by two American divisions, coming from the area around Naples, followed by two divisions embarking in Sicily and North Africa. From February 17 to 20, planners from the Mediterranean Allied Tactical Air Force (MATAF) came to Algiers to meet their Army and Navy counterparts with the objective of elaborating a plan that the Air commander could approve. But everyone realized that it was impossible to count on an operation in May. And all the more so since no firm decision had yet been made by the CCS concerning the assignment of landing ships. This decision was needed in order to define the size of the assault echelon and thus to serve as a base for detailed plans.

On February 26, the CCS decided to delay its decision concerning Anvil until the situation could be reexamined on March 20, and gave the Italian campaign "*overriding priority over all existing or future operations in the Mediterranean.*" Two days later, Wilson, on Devers' recommendation, relieved Clark of his responsibility concerning Anvil so that he could concentrate on operations in Italy. While waiting for the arrival of a new Army commander, he asked

depleted after the departure of Patton; Patch chose to complete it with personnel from IV Corps that he had brought with him to Algeria; only the G-4 came from Sicily [10]. Likewise he bolstered the teams in Algiers and Oran [11]. As far as the Navy was concerned, the fact that Patch had participated in the battle of Guadalcanal in the Pacific, and understood naval issues, meant that he immediately won their esteem and trust. When Patch took over, the AFHQ draft project was still being used as a basis for Force 163's preparations, and the operation was scheduled for June along with Overlord. The first deadline to be met was April 15, when a draft plan elaborated with the Navy and Tactical Air Force commanders was to be submitted [12]. In the meantime, the first detailed plan concerning air operations was published on March 17 by the MAAF, and that same day, in a major report handed to Force 163, it was decided that the assault would take place at dawn.

On the 21st, after Wilson had reexamined the situation as had been decided upon the previous month, he recommended that Anvil be canceled in favor of the Italian campaign. The next day the BCS also voted to abandon the operation. But the Americans did not agree and supported Anvil unflinchingly, even though it was still impossible to guarantee the necessary number of transport ships. Thus they proposed not to undertake the two invasions simultaneously, and to tentatively set the deadline for Anvil to July 10, 1944. The outline plan was nevertheless submitted to the CCS by AFHQ on March 29. Patch was still in favor of June 1, and requested that the army corps, the assault divisions and the French units be designated as soon as possible, so that they could start their training. Wilson took his time answering, and finally on April 12 informed

Patch that he had decided not to launch Anvil before the end of July, because of the offensive in Italy scheduled for May 10 and the withdrawal from the Mediterranean of the landing ships needed for Overlord. During this time preparations continued, both by the naval forces completing the Planning Memoranda [13], and concerning the approval of the outline plan presented by the tactical air forces. They were informed on April 17 that "*the plan was not required until further notice, but that it was to be used as a basis for further planning* [14]."

The approval was nevertheless definite since the first phase of the landing rehearsals started on April 28. And the following day the combined Ground, Naval and Air outline plans were presented to the Supreme Allied Commander, Mediterranean, who arrived in Algiers with a group of high-ranking officers, including General Devers, Navy and Air Force delegates, and French officers.

10. The G-5 (civil affairs) was assigned in April.
11. In May the detachment that had remained in Sicily was disbanded.
12. Commander's Conference.
13. Especially ANPM No 12 of April 12, 1944 concerning the positions on the beaches.
14. MATAF Report on Operation Dragoon, November 1, 1944.

Right.
Generals Eaker, MAAF commander, Cannon, commander of the tactical air forces, Devers and Larkin. Larkin is wearing the shoulder patch of SOS NATOUSA, which he was commanding.

Above.
Activated in Algiers in July 1943, 15th Army Group directed Allied operations in Sicily and then in Italy, and was thus a direct rival of the Seventh Army. Its shoulder patch, adopted in May 1944, represents the waves of the Mediterranean Sea.
(Private collection)

Left.
Members of the Mediterranean Allied Air Forces (MAAF), created in January 1944, wore a shoulder patch whose symbol is evident: wings over the sea.
(Le Poilu)

Below.
Generals Wilson and Devers.
(Seventh Army)

The meeting took place in the Force 163 operations room and General Patch made some introductory statements. Then the G-2 briefly outlined conclusions concerning the terrain, enemy capabilities, defense plans and the order of battle. The plan - involving two or three assault divisions according to available means of shipping - was similar to the draft issued the month before. But in order to avoid an approach through the Hyères islands, the assault zone was moved to the east and the elements assigned to cover the beachhead thus designated: the 1er Régiment de Chasseurs Parachutistes to be dropped southeast of Le Luc during the night preceding the assault; four battalions from the First Special Service Force in Théoule and the Groupe de Commandos d'Afrique at Cap Cavalaire on D-Day; two battalions from the First Special Service Force on the Port-Cros and Levant islands, and two battalions of paratroopers at Le Lavandou the following night.

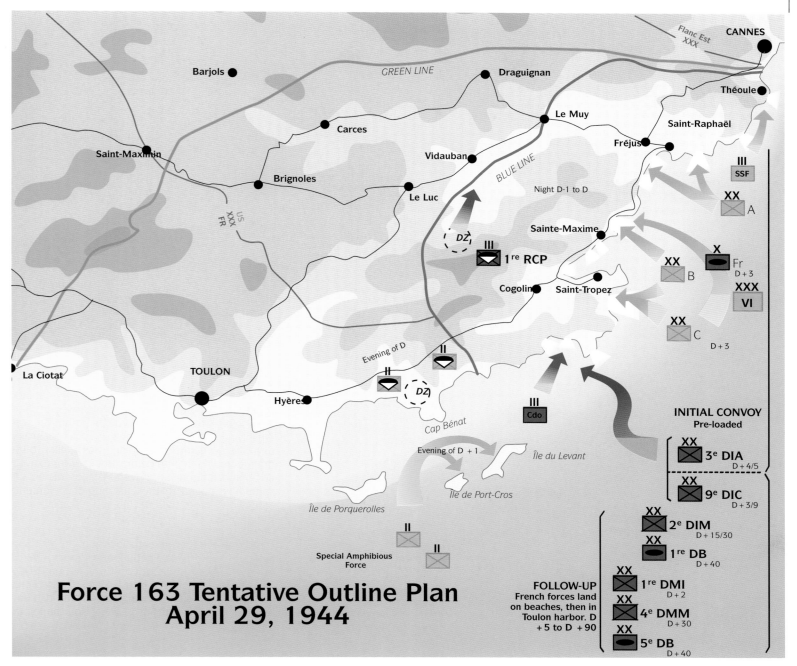

Force 163 Tentative Outline Plan
April 29, 1944

Map labels:
CANNES
Flanc Est XXX
Théoule
Saint-Raphaël
Fréjus
GREEN LINE
Barjols
Draguignan
Le Muy
Carces
Vidauban
BLUE LINE
Saint-Maximin
Brignoles
Le Luc
Night D-1 to D
III SSF
XX A
Sainte-Maxime
US XXX FR
DZ
III 1ᵉ RCP
X Fr D+3
XX B
XXX VI
Cogolin
Saint-Tropez
XX C D+3
Evening of D
II
La Ciotat
TOULON
II
DZ
Hyères
III Cdo
Cap Bénat
Evening of D+1
Île du Levant
INITIAL CONVOY
Pre-loaded
XX 3ᵉ DIA D+4/5
XX 9ᵉ DIC D+3/9
Île de Port-Cros
Île de Porquerolles
XX 2ᵉ DIM D+15/30
XX 1ʳᵉ DB D+40
II
Special Amphibious Force
II
FOLLOW-UP
French forces land on beaches, then in Toulon harbor. D+5 to D+90
XX 1ʳᵉ DMI D+2
XX 4ᵉ DMM D+30
XX 5ᵉ DB D+40

ANVIL WEIGHING IN

On May 5 SACMED informed Patch that, according to the War Office in London, no precise answer could be immediately given to the questions concerning the Anvil plans. Then it announced that a new order was to be sent out concerning a modified plan. And thus on the 13th, Force 163 received an order to 'cogitate' over three distinct plans corresponding to three hypotheses baptized 'Rankin A,' B and C. In the case that the Germans decided on a partial retreat, the invasion along the coast of France could take place before the proposed date for Overlord. The battle in Italy would continue and entry into France would take place according to the Anvil plan, in August.

A certain amount of resistance was expected on the beaches, followed by delaying actions in the lower Rhone River valley. If necessary, a second invasion could take place in the region around Sète, followed by a rapid advance toward the north. Plan A should be operational by June 10 at the latest. If the Germans decided to completely evacuate the South of France, leaving behind only foreign volun-

Below.
Contrary to Overlord, the Rankin C plan gave the FFI symbolized here by various armbands an important role in the liberation of the territory south of the Loire River.
(Musée des Troupes de Marine, Fréjus)

teers whose morale might be too low to make them efficient fighters, the plan was to harass the enemy and create confusion in back of the lines. In this case, *"the French Forces of the Interior would be called on to play a major part in carrying out sabotage and engaging in guerilla warfare to prevent German withdrawal. They were also to aid the military authority*

15 *Seventh United States Army Report of Operations in France and Germany, op. cit.*

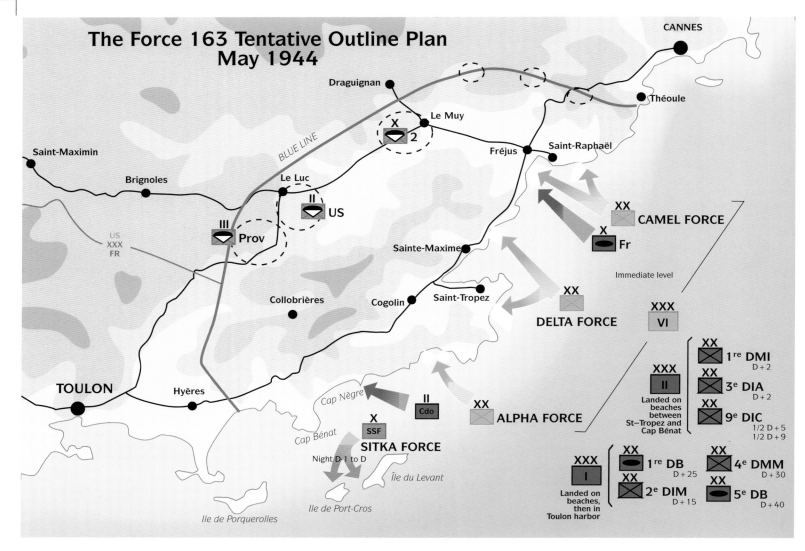

The Force 163 Tentative Outline Plan
May 1944

CANNES

Théoule

Draguignan

Saint-Raphaël

Le Muy

X 1 ▽ 2

BLUE LINE

Fréjus

Saint-Maximin

Brignoles

Le Luc

II ▽ US

III ▽ Prov

US XXX FR

XX CAMEL FORCE

X ● Fr

Immediate level

Sainte-Maxime

Collobrières

Cogolin

Saint-Tropez

XX

DELTA FORCE

XXX VI

XX ⊠ 1re DMI D+2

XXX II

XX ⊠ 3e DIA D+2

Landed on beaches between St–Tropez and Cap Bénat

XX ⊠ 9e DIC 1/2 D+5 1/2 D+9

TOULON

Hyères

Cap Nègre

II Cdo

XX ⊠ ALPHA FORCE

X SSF

SITKA FORCE

Cap Bénat

Night D-1 to D

Île du Levant

Île de Port-Cros

Île de Porquerolles

XXX I

XX ● 1re DB D+25

XX ⊠ 4e DMM D+30

XX ⊠ 2e DIM D+15

XX ● 5e DB D+40

Landed on beaches, then in Toulon harbor

---

in restoring order, setting up local administration, and initiating urgent relief measures [15]." In this case the invasion would take place near Sète and the advance would be in the direction of Bordeaux through the Carcassonne gap. Plan B should be presented by July 1st. Finally in the most favorable conditions, that is a German unconditional surrender and the end of all organized resistance, Plan C provided that the Seventh Army would enforce the clauses of the armistice, reestablish civilian authority and process prisoners of war. Thus to the initial scheme elaborated by Force 163 - including three divi-

Below.
This pamphlet was published in February 1943 by the Service of Supplies and contained information necessary for transportation and supply plans.
(Private collection)

sions in the first echelon from Cavalaire to Agay, covered from Gonfaron to Le Muy by paratroopers and on the Western flank by American and French commandos - three new alternatives were now added ... At the same time Wilson had asked the CCS on April 29 to reserve all possible land and amphibious potential to back up his May offensive in Italy. He was, for example, thinking about an invasion north of Rome or along the Pisa-Rimini line, and an intervention in Northern Yugoslavia designed to precipitate the fall of Hungary and allow the Allies to build air bases near Split. However Eisenhower was radically opposed to this plan, arguing that Allied resources were not sufficient to sustain two major battle theaters in Europe. He recommended that Anvil be launched on August 15 with enough forces to give the operation a chance of success. If not, all the French divisions, plus one or two American divisions, should be assigned to Overlord as soon as it would be possible to shuttle them to the battle zone.

From his stay in London and his discussions with Eisenhower during the month of May, Wilson was more and more convinced of the necessity of establishing a number of alternate plans, with the final choice being subject to the strategic situation after the Italian offensive and the progress of Overlord. Among the invasion sites, he preferred the area around Sète, the Riviera, the Gulf of Genoa or Civitavecchia. He had a new trump card - the 91st Division which had just arrived from the United States and was training in Arzew, plus two French armored divisions ready for battle - and was counting on the arrival from across the Atlantic of twenty-six LSTs. While Rankin A was being presented to SACMED,

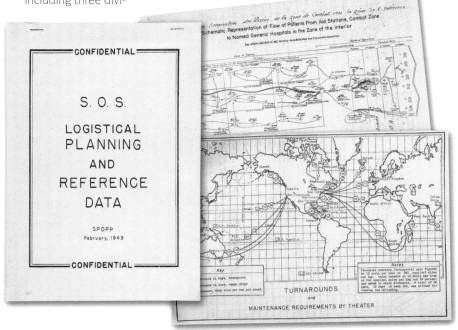

CONFIDENTIAL

S. O. S.

LOGISTICAL
PLANNING
AND
REFERENCE
DATA

SPOPP
February, 1943

CONFIDENTIAL

the BCS announced on May 29 that they gave their agreement to the CCS concerning priorities: first Italy, then Anvil. And Devers asked for the maximum possible quantities of supplies that could be transported on transatlantic ships, and warned the War Department that the deadline, fixed at the end of July or the beginning of August, would not be met if the most crucial supplies were not sent out on time. The problem was that, after the first deliveries to French North Africa starting April 15, the New York Port of embarkation received orders not to ship anything else for Anvil. Devers and Major General Thomas B. Larkin, commander of the NATOUSA Service of Supply, were nevertheless able to 'freeze' some supplies, in warehouses or on cargo ships, but it was a difficult task because these stocks were being tapped for the 5th Army in Italy.

But the outcome of the May offensive and the entry into Rome two days before the launching of Overlord changed the situation. And Wilson could finally inform the CCS that he was now able to undertake on August 15 an amphibious operation in the South of France, on the condition that additional troops, transportation and supplies be assigned to him. And he agreed on the short-term transfer of three American divisions and one French division from Italy. On June 14, Alexander therefore received orders to assign VI Corps, composed of the 3rd, 36th and 45th US Divisions and two large units of the French expeditionary forces, to the 7th Army. But still no final decision had been made concerning Anvil, and Wilson and Alexander had not abandoned their dream of reaching the Danube via the Ljubljana gap.

AN ADDITIONAL KEY PORT CITY

At the same time, Wilson, during a conversation with Marshall, made a new discovery concerning a factor vital to the Allied strategy: "*On June 17, I had the first of several conferences with General Marshall, General Arnold, and Major General Handy [16]. General Marshall informed me that General Eisenhower needed additional French ports in order that Allied formations might be deployed in France more rapidly and on a broader front, that there were between 40 and 50 divisions in the United States which could not be shipped to France as rapidly as desired or maintained there through the ports of Northwest France. General Marshall also expressed his opinion that General Eisenhower was likely to agree readily to the diversion of enough of his own resources to make possible our own assault on Southern France which would be designed to capture a major port. [17]*" More than ever logistics took supremacy over tactics; logistics were constantly at

16. *Major General Thomas T. Handy, head of the planning division of the War Department.*

17. *Report by the Supreme Allied Commander, Mediterranean, to the Combined Chiefs of Staff on the Operations in Southern France, August 1944.*

Shoulder patch of the Army Service Forces, created in March 1943 by changing the name of the Service of Supply (SOS). Its patch and its mission of administrative and logistics support remained the same.
(Private collection)

Right.
Unloading equipment on the Palermo docks.
(US Army)

The brick red and golden yellow shoulder patch of the Transportation Corps was worn by the personnel of the Ports of Embarkation, that is those working in the Atlantic ports, loading the Mediterranean-bound convoys.
(Le Poilu)

Below.
Protected by balloons, the port of Algiers - the Agha basin is pictured here - was bustling with activity at the beginning of 1944.
(Pierre Ichac)

the forefront of the minds of the Americans, and especially the planners of Force 163. During all of June 1944, once the divisions had been designated, the major preoccupation was how to assemble the means necessary to transport the troops and their equipment. The ships available in the theater of operations or promised from other sources were hardly sufficient to transport two divisions. AFHQ and the 7th Army had to find other means to insure transportation for the first echelon. Cargo ships were envisioned in greater quantities and sooner after the assault than planned, since Allied intelligence had insisted that the reaction of the German air force aviation would not be a problem. With these ships the landing plans were as follows:
- 84,000 men and 12,000 vehicles the first day,
- 33,500 men and 8,000 vehicles the next four days. The men would have seven days of supplies, as would the troops coming in with the six convoys planned from D +5 to D +30. At that time, the Coastal Base Section should take over control of operations on the beaches and in the port of Toulon which should be reopened by then.

Finally, on July 2, Wilson received orders from CCS to launch the operation on August 15 if possible. He consequently warned Alexander that Anvil had received top priority, but that the Italian theater would be losing only seven divisions. A final attempt was made by the British early in August to divert the forces assigned to the operation to land either in Brittany or Italy instead. But Eisenhower stuck to his guns with the Prime Minister.

Actually the project had been approved by SACMED on June 28, and AFHQ started carrying it out on July 7. But Wilson had to wait until August 11 to get the go-ahead from the British Chiefs of Staff. At that time 'Anvil' had become 'Dragoon' for security reasons.

AMPHIBIOUS OPERATIONS

Above:
The British 'Combined Operations' formation sign was worn as facing pair - with the submachine gun pointing to the front. It was worn, among others, by commandos and landing craft crews.

After World War I, no amphibious operations were included in British war plans: the bitter failure of the Dardanelles operation in 1915 was still present in their minds. However when the Italians attacked Abyssinia in 1935, an intervention in the Red Sea, or even in Italy, was considered. Then when the Japanese at Tientsin used four hundred barges associated with troop transports, the Admiralty sat up and paid attention. They finally obtained, during the summer of 1938, the creation of a combined forces structure to study the possibility of amphibious assault, to define methods and design the necessary equipment.

Sailor from a US Navy beach battalion.
(Reconstruction by Militaria Magazine)

(IWM)

Far left.
British Commandos and American Rangers coming back from Dieppe.
(IWM)

Left.
Off the coast of Morocco, the movement of the landing craft between the fleet and the Fedala beach is regulated by flags.
(US Army)

Thus the Inter-Service Training and Development Center, in charge of training and equipment design, first attempted to define the main characteristics of an amphibious assault. Tactical surprise was essential. To obtain results it was decided that the approach to the coast had to take place in the dark, with fast ships that would then launch the landing craft they were carrying. The troops would head for the shore hidden behind a smoke screen and protected by the guns of the fleet. Then the reserve units on board would enter action until both the beach and the anchoring area were out of range of the enemy artillery.

Once the 'beachhead' was secure, the rest of the personnel, vehicles and supplies carried on the anchored troop transports could then be unloaded by landing craft. At the same time, a method of ranging was developed in liaison with the Mobile Naval Base Development of the Royal Marines: the Army would control observation on land and the Navy would take charge of radio liaisons and fire direction, with the help of an artillery officer. This was the plan - approved by headquarters before the end of the year - that was used in North Africa and Sicily. However, after each invasion, the British and Americans studied the degree of success or failure and the lessons to be learned, then modified their tactical and technical plans in consequence.

FROM THE FIRST RAIDS TO THE INVASION OF SICILY

In February 1941, forty paratroopers from the 11th Special Air Service Battalion, under Major T.A.G. Pritchard, jumped southeast of Naples to blow up an aqueduct furnishing water for Campania. They did not do much damage, but the operation proved that it was possible to use paratroops in support of an invasion, on condition that the attack be minutely prepared.

Four months later, No 11 Commando landed on the Lebanese coast north of the Litani: 25%

American Ranger Infantry shoulder patch. *(Militaria Magazine)*

Above and below.
Commandos getting off an "R" craft. *(DR)*

Right.
British troops landing in Algeria in November 1942.

Below.
Landing exercise on an enemy coast executed by commandos in LCAs.

of the troops were lost, and there were grave deficiencies in navigation. Then in May 1942, the invasion of Madagascar brought to light the lack of a sufficient number of tank transport ships and lighters to unload the ships, as well as an absence of adequate beach organization. At the same time, during a raid on a radio station on the southeast coast of Crete, it was noted that a destroyer with a few small assault landing craft on board would have been a welcome addition. The next undertaking would the unfortunate Dieppe raid in

August. But this disaster yielded many valuable lessons:

1. An invasion should not take place at the most probable site.

2. If the coast is well defended, the troops on land must be supported at all times by naval fire.

3. The assault must go according to plan, the only alternate plan being the use of reserve units.

4. More than anything else, a command ship is indispensable.

Then, on November 8, American and British troops, sailing from British and American ports, landed in Casablanca, Oran and Algiers. The British had a command ship, but their allies stuck to a battleship off the coast of Morocco. Aboard the flagship *USS Augusta* thus cohabited General Patton, the commander of the Western Task Force, and Admiral Hewitt. As Patton was preparing to leave ship, the man-of-war opened fire and for the whole afternoon, the general was kept from reaching the shore. American paratroopers flying directly from England, who were supposed to take the

airfields south of Oran, were so scattered on landing that it was impossible for them to accomplish their mission.

The need for a command ship was thus confirmed - the British were now convinced that the commander of the land forces should not set foot on shore until his liaison and intelligence networks had been set up, because it was much easier to follow the situation from a ship. The exceptional performance of the three LSTs was also proved, as were the importance of training the landing craft crews and the need for efficient navigational assistance, precise technical information about the beaches and their surroundings, and the organization of salvaging teams to recover damaged landing craft.

Thus several measures were taken concerning future operations: landing craft would be provided to guide the assault waves, training of teams specializing in beach reconnaissance [1] would be accelerated, salvaging units [2] would be created. The next operation was 'Corkscrew,' the attack on Pantelleria Island in June 1943, with a daytime landing preceded by a hell-take-all air and naval bombardment. Actually the bombing did little serious damage to enemy defenses, but their com-

mand structure and communications were so upset that the garrison was unable to resist the assault.

Operation 'Husky' began on July 10 on the southern coast of Sicily. The operation involved elements from nine divisions, including two airborne. For the first time a landing took place using all the ships, landing craft and equipment designed and experimented over the last five years. And naval bombardment was accepted as part and parcel of amphibious assaults. From a technical point of view, Husky proved that the lessons learned from earlier attacks had been put to good use.

The many new American LSTs were invaluable additions, as were the DUKW amphibious trucks also used for the first time and which would prove

1. *Combined Operations Pilotage Parties or COPP.*
2. *Landing Craft Recovery Units.*

Above.
Even if the operation yielded many a valuable lesson, the Dieppe raid was a bitter failure for the British and Canadians. *(IWM)*

Above, right.
LCTs brought water and fuel to the elements of the VIIIth British Army progressing along the coast of Libya. *(DR)*

Shoulder patch of the US Navy Amphibious Forces, apparently inspired by the British Combined Operations sign. *(Private collection)*

Above, right.
The 3rd Infantry Division made an unopposed landing at Fedala in Nov. 1942. *(US Army)*

Left.
Western Task Force equipment is landed in the port of Fedala. *(US Army)*

Right.
The invasion of Pantelleria Island took place in broad daylight with massive support from battleships and bombers. *(DR)*

their worth in ferrying supplies between ships and shore depots. Their use allowed the near-elimination of the critical moment between the landing of the first infantry troops and the time when proper roads for moving artillery, anti-tank weapons and ammunition had been built on the beach. And pontoon barges proved to be very effective when they were put together by trained teams. Concerning logistics, the organization of the beach groups was satisfactory, with vehicles and weapons delivered to the invading units within twenty-four hours.

But it was decided that it was useless to try to unload the ships during the night: progress was too slow and enemy bombers could be present in the vicinity. Even though the first parachute drop was a success, reinforcements brought in for

the 82nd Airborne Division by air during the night proved fatal. The planes became targets for friendly anti-aircraft fire, and sixty were shot down or damaged[3].

Above.
July 11, 1944. American ships under enemy bombs off Gela, Sicily.
(US Army)

Left.
In the port of Bizerte, troops load into the LCI(L)s bound for Sicily.
(US Army)

Right.
On the Sicily shore, 90-mm AA guns towed by White trucks disembark from an LST on pontoon barges.
(US Army)

Below.
In Scoglitti, heavy equipment is unloaded from the LSTs with the help of pontoons built by the Seabees. *(US Army)*

Two nights later, more paratroopers, British this time, got the same treatment. These two tragic incidents demonstrated to the commanders the need for a fighter control ship[4] in charge of sounding the alarm if enemy planes approached. It also showed the necessity of installing a radar station on land as soon as possible. On the beaches things went relatively well. The US 3rd Infantry Division that landed near Licata undertook a reconnaissance mission three hours before the arrival of the assault waves. The men were then directed with the help of lamps.

Fire cover was excellent, with the first salvo well grouped on the water's edge. The shots were then directed further inland, but the parachute flares, intended to signal the destroyers to increase the range, lighted up the beach and attracted heavy artillery fire from the enemy. The only real prob-

3. *Out of 144, resulting in the loss of 300 American paratroopers or aviators.*
4. *Fighter Direction Ship.*

lem was the pile-up during unloading: equipment and supplies were dumped any- and everywhere to get them out of the way of the stranded landing craft.

THE SALERNO INVASION

After the Sicily campaign, the Allies were so optimistic that, under pressure from the Ameri-

Above.
In the port of Arzew, a regiment of French spahis is learning how to load its vehicles aboard an LST. *(ECPAD)*

Right.
Tirailleurs are training to transfer from a transport ship to a landing barge using a net hung alongside the hull.
(IWM IA 44453)

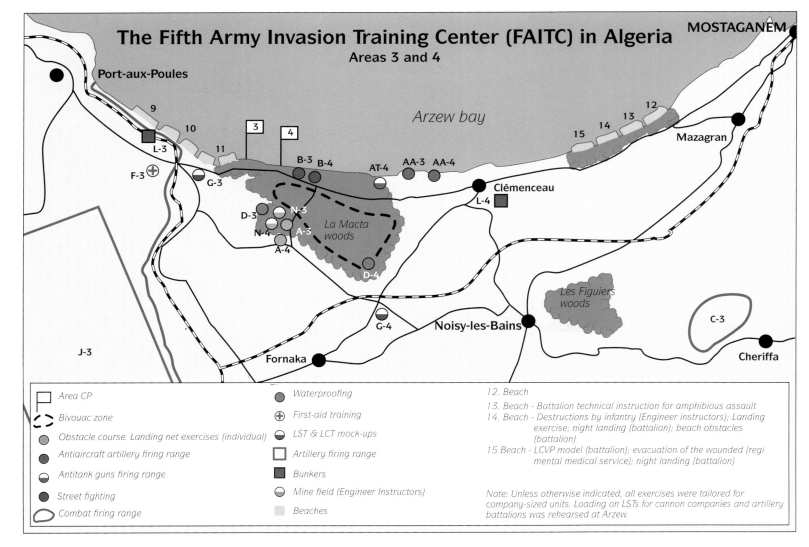

The Fifth Army Invasion Training Center (FAITC) in Algeria
Areas 3 and 4

MOSTAGANEM

Port-aux-Poules

Arzew bay

Mazagran

Clémenceau

La Macta woods

Les Figuiers woods

C-3

Noisy-les-Bains

Fornaka

Cheriffa

Symbol	Legend
Area CP	
Bivouac zone	
Obstacle course. Landing net exercises (individual)	
Antiaircraft artillery firing range	
Antitank guns firing range	
Street fighting	
Combat firing range	
Waterproofing	
First-aid training	
LST & LCT mock-ups	
Artillery firing range	
Bunkers	
Mine field (Engineer Instructors)	
Beaches	

12. Beach
13. Beach - Battalion technical instruction for amphibious assault
14. Beach - Destructions by infantry (Engineer instructors); Landing exercise; night landing (battalion); beach obstacles (battalion)
15 Beach - LCVP model (battalion); evacuation of the wounded (regimental medical service); night landing (battalion)

Note: Unless otherwise indicated, all exercises were tailored for company-sized units. Loading on LSTs for cannon companies and artillery battalions was rehearsed at Arzew.

TRAINING SCHEDULE FOR RIFLE COMPANIES AT THE FAITC

D 1	0830-1200	Boat team training	bivouac
	1300-1630	LCVP mock-up (battalion)	beach 15
D 2	0830-1200	Amphibious assault training at battalion level	beach 13
	1300-1630	Street fighting	B-4
D 3	0830-1200	Landing exercise (battalion)	beach 14
	1300-1630	Infantry demolitions	beach 14
D 4	0830-1630	Combat firing (battalion)	C-3
D 5	0830-1200	Instruction on landing net (btn)	A-4
	1300-2100	Free time (battalion)	
	2100-2400	Night landing (battalion)	beach 14
D 6	0000-1200	Final exercise (battalion)	
	1300	De-briefing	
D 7	0830-1630	Free time (battalion except anti-tank plat.)	
		Anti-tank Co. firing (anti-tank platoon)	AT-4
D 8	0830-1630	Combat firing (battalion except anti-tank plat.)	C-3
		Anti-tank Co. firing (anti-tank platoon)	AT-4
D 9	0830-1200	Bunkers	L-4
	1300-1630	Mine field	N-4
D 10	0830-1630	Beach obstacles (battalion)	beach 14
		Firing with anti-tank gun (AT platoon)	AT-4
D 11	0830-1630	Landing (combat team)	beaches 13, 14 & 15
D 12	0830-1030	De-briefing	
	130-2100	Free time	
	2100-2400	Night landing (combat team)	beaches 13, 14 &15
D 13	0000-1200	Final exercise 1300	Bivouac
		De-briefing	
D 14		Departure	

cans, landing ships were sent to India to participate in the war against the Japanese in Burma. But when the amphibious assault programed for Rangoon was canceled, they came back into the Mediterranean. Then came 'Avalanche' which took place at Salerno, south of Naples. Three Allied divisions landed there on September 9, 1943. This time, in spite of the approach taking place under cover of night, there was no surprise effect

dropped directly onto the beachhead. A battalion was also dropped behind the German lines during the night of September 14 to 15 to take crossroads and disorganize enemy communications lines. But once again they were scattered all over and unable to fulfill their mission.

Aircraft carriers played a vital role: their fighters took up where the Sicily-based planes ran out of gas. However, the lack of wind and the snail's pace of the carriers caused numerous accidents, which made the high command doubt whether carrier fighters alone would guarantee air superiority over beachheads.

And the Allied command noted that pinpoint accuracy from the naval guns was essential, and that it was dangerous to get too far inland without protecting one's flanks. Like Husky, Avalanche was nevertheless a success due in particular to the amphibious training centers in Egypt and near Oran. In Kabrit, Egypt, at the Combined Training Center, the British created five beach organiza-

Right.
After the assault phase, LCVPs are used to ferry supplies and baggage to the Salerno beachhead.
(National Archives)

tion units, using infantry or Royal Marines battalions. They were called "Bricks[5]" like those formed in England and numbered 31 to 35 to deceive the enemy.

They were committed for the first time in Sicily and then in Salerno. At the Fifth Army Invasion Training Center in Port-aux-Poules, Algeria, the divisions took a two-week course including various tactical exercises - street fighting, capturing blockhouses, crossing mine fields, destructions - or technical exercises - firing, waterproofing[6], loading the assault transport ships, day and night landings - either life-size or using scale models. It was

and the assault waves ran into determined defenders. It took a week of violent fighting to finally secure the beachhead, and the day was saved by the Navy's guns. Airborne troops, who had been reserved for a long time for a future operation on Rome, played only a minor role in Avalanche. Two regiments were sent in as reinforcements and

Above.
The anti-tank company of the 30th Infantry Regiment, 3rd Division, landing in Salerno.
(US Army)

5. The origin of the term 'brick' is unknown, except that beach organization was the 'base' on which any full force landing was to be 'built.

6. Some period documents speak of 'waterproofing' and 'dewaterproofing.'

also there that the tough job of embarkation officer[7] was taught, and that the personnel in charge of beach organization were schooled.

The process of amphibious assault on the enemy shore had now been perfected. It could be divided into three phases: the first two were studied at the FAITC. Through independent actions carried out by divisions (or similar groups) landing at regular distances from each other, the expeditionary corps tried first to get a foothold on the shore and to establish a certain number of beachheads providing shelter for landing the major part of the invading forces. Then, by converging actions fanning out from these beachheads, the corps tried to unite its forces. Finally, when all means had been gathered, it undertook complete destruction of the enemy forces.

During the first two phases, the landing, transport and maintenance of the invading forces were carried out for each division by a "beach base." The base was constituted little by little.

During the first phase of the assault, only one beach group per regimental combat team was landed. Its mission was to take care of unloading material, create exits from the beach, and supply arms and ammunition by creating the first depots on land. The mixed beach group was composed of elements from the Army and Navy, and commanded by an Army officer. His deputy was the Navy commander, known as 'Beachmaster.' He had a list of twenty-seven jobs to accomplish.

Six were done by the Naval Beach Battalions: marking non-navigable sectors, directing traffic, boat repairs, evacuation of the wounded, communication with the Naval command. The others were to be taken care of by ground personnel: marking beach limits and landing spots, remov-

Above.

In the bay of Arzew, French Tirailleurs are being initiated into the joys of landing from an LCVP.
(ECPAD)

Above.

French 1926-pattern steel helmet with device for the Zouaves, Spahis and North-African Tirailleurs.
(Private collection)

Right.
Tirailleurs have loaded into an LCVP which is about to be launched by the assault transport ship (APA 13) *Joseph T. Dickman*. The ship will later participate in the Provence operation as part of Task Unit 85.3.1
(ECPAD)

ing obstacles, unloading material, controlling movements beyond the beach zone, creating bivouacs and supply dumps, organizing depots, building roads to reach the highway system, beach security, communicating orders to invading units, updating their maps, repairing vehicles that had been damaged during landing, evacuation of prisoners. Only the command structure was mixed. The others were composed either of land personnel - transmissions, MPs, liaisons with the invading units, emergency vehicle repairs, security, engineering, workers, transportation, beach depots - or of navy men - medical, hydrographic, repairs. Finally it was decided that a control rescue boat would be

7. *Transport Quartermaster or TQM.*

available as close as possible to the beach, at anchor if necessary, ready to execute the orders of the Beachmaster, assisting him in directing traffic, transmitting orders to the landing craft and helping those in distress.

LANDING TECHNIQUES

The American amphibious doctrine was the result of the numerous experiments executed along the California and Florida shores, as well as the lessons learned from the operation in Europe by the British commandos and in the Pacific and North Africa by American troops.

Early in 1943, its main elements were:
- trying for total surprise, with absolute superiority on the sea and in the air;
- unified command of land, sea and air forces engaged in the same operation;
- rapid and brutal execution;
- methodical preparation, even in minute details.

Then, after the amphibious operations carried out in Italy, ideas evolved slightly.

Actually surprise was only a minor factor in Sicily and not at all in Salerno: "*There was a certain*

Right.
Shoulder patch of the US Army amphibious engineer units, approved on June 17, 1942.
(Private collection)

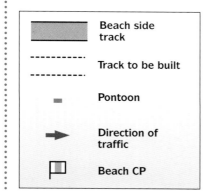

▭	Beach side track
-----	Track to be built

▬	Pontoon
➤	Direction of traffic
⚑	Beach CP

tendency among the executants to consider that, under present conditions of organization of defence along the coasts of Europe, a full force landing operation could be compared to an operation of breaking through a fortified front line, having the sea as a base. Thus landing troops on enemy beaches should be preceded by preparatory firing by naval artillery and an aerial bombardment designed to destroy the enemy's positions and open breaches in the secondary defence. This type of preparation would allow no possibility of strategic surprise. However the troops could benefit somewhat from tactical surprise by operating over a very wide front, by executing diverse actions designed to deceive the enemy as to the direction of the main action, and keep his reserves occupied. [8]"

When the commanding officer of a Regimental Combat Team was assigned an amphibious mis-

Below.
Transparent template showing the space needed by most vehicles and equipment, used by French Transport Quartermaster (TQM) officers to plan the loading of their unit on landing ships.

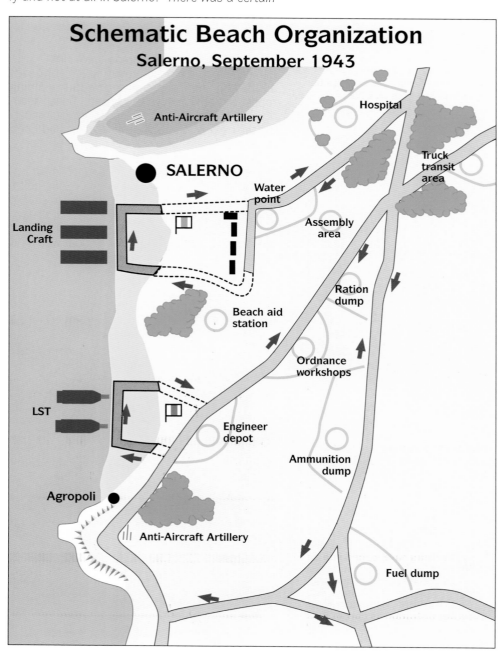

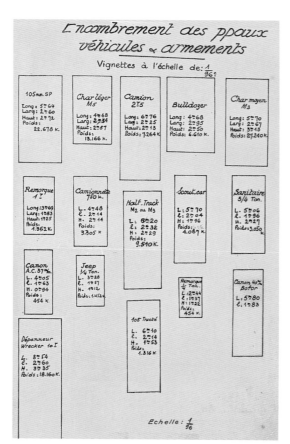

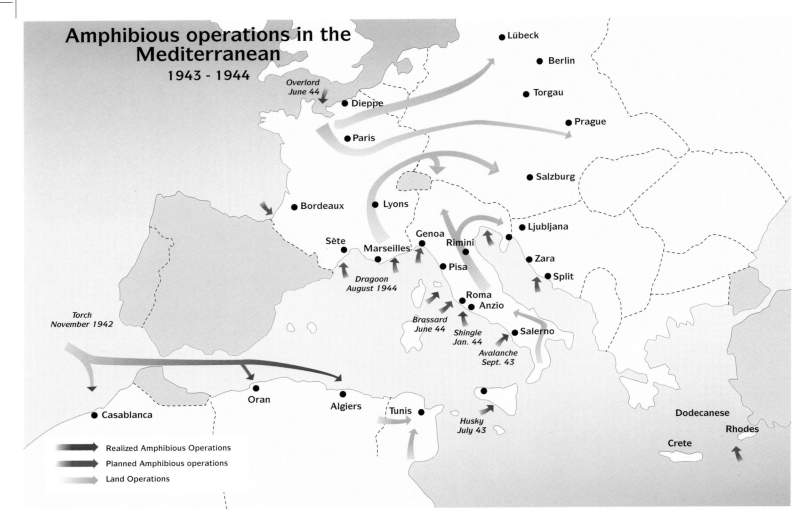

Amphibious operations in the Mediterranean
1943 - 1944

- Lübeck
- Berlin
- Torgau
- Prague
- Salzburg
- Dieppe
- Paris
- Bordeaux
- Lyons
- Ljubljana
- Genoa
- Rimini
- Sète
- Marseilles
- Zara
- Pisa
- Split
- Roma
- Anzio
- Salerno
- Oran
- Algiers
- Tunis
- Casablanca
- Dodecanese
- Rhodes
- Crete

Overlord June 44
Dragoon August 1944
Torch November 1942
Brassard June 44
Shingle Jan. 44
Avalanche Sept. 43
Husky July 43

→ Realized Amphibious Operations
→ Planned Amphibious operations
→ Land Operations

sion, his first job was, of course, to study the situation and define a plan of attack. He then had to take charge of the means - boats, men and guns - at his disposal and perfect all the details of the plan. In order to finalize preparations, he needed information about the units assigned to the regiment for the operation, and to know the number of boats available and their characteristics.

Once in possession of this information, his G-3 could then elaborate - in collaboration with the Navy - a first theoretical loading plan [9] allowing him to determine whether or not he would have to make changes in his original project. Once the plan was accepted by both services, it was sent to the Transport Quartermaster who checked its suitability. He had to decide if the prescribed loading plans could be carried out, and if not, the G–3 had to make the necessary changes. As soon as the RCT was notified that the loading was correct, the documents necessary for each of the elements involved could be drawn up. This was done in the presence of the commanders of all the assigned units and a Navy representative. The loading diagrams showed the position of each boat in the forthcoming operation: number of waves, position in the wave, landing time, and the assigned beaches. The unit loading tables indicated in detail the sites where the personnel and equipment were to board ship, the exact composition of the crews and the types of landing craft.. .

Several types of landings could take place, but in all cases the reconnaissance elements of the mixed detachment would need forty-five minutes to survey the beach [10]. The engineers would need

Above.
The Anzio beachhead was supplied either by LSTs carrying loaded trucks, or by freighters anchored at sea with DUKWs shuttling back and forth to the coast.
(US Army)

two hours to build tracks, mark the positions of the supply depots, and clear the exits of mines. In the case of a 'beach-to-beach' landing, the troops embarked on a friendly shore, then set foot on the far shore in the same boat. The advantage of this system was that the personnel did not have to be loaded and unloaded.

The craft used were standardized so that loading was easy and it was possible to combat-load a full battalion. But the craft were large and highly visible targets, and their draft was such that some required beaches with steep gradient. The infantry boat teams needed about ten minutes to land, and time had to be left for the last elements of the companies to evacuate the beach before the arrival of the support and reserve units.

During a 'mixed' operation, the assault waves came in smaller barges. The front was consequently wider than that offered by two Landing Craft Infantry (LCI), that is between 250 and 350 meters. But this system meant that the troops had to be transferred from larger craft to smaller boats, and that the LSTs had to remain two or three hours anchored off the beach, at the mercy of air attacks. Moreover, in order to free these ships rapidly, a large quantity of equipment and supplies had to be landed immediately, even though spreading it

8. *Etude sur les opérations de débarquement de vive force (Study on full force landing operations), by Major Cornet of the 2nd RTM, December 1943.*

9. *With the help of diagrams and loading plans drawn to the scale of the different boats that were distributed by FAITC.*

10. *A beach of approximately 1000 square meters was necessary for a first echelon battalion.*

out over several days would have been preferable. Timewise, the infantry barges could be unloaded and away from the shore in two to four minutes. It took a boat wave eight! minutes to clear the beach completely.

A 'ship-to-shore' operation allowed for transportation of the amphibious troops by the same route as the convoys; they thus reached the landing point more easily and discreetly. The major difficulty was that the small number of LCTs (Landing craft, tank) aboard the troop transports prevented an entire battalion from landing in a single wave.

The landed troops risked being deprived of their artillery at any given time. Normally each assault battalion was supported by its assigned destroyer and its fire was directed by a 'Naval Shore Fire Control Party' or (N)SFCP, including a Navy officer and an artillery officer [11].

"More than for any other form of operation, the fate of an amphibious operation depends on perfect execution, on close coordination of the forces engaged. It can only be undertaken with troops trained in this type of warfare, used to working together and giving each other mutual support during the different phases of combat. [12]"

'SHINGLE' AND THE FATE OF TWO EMPIRES

On January 22, 1944, a new invasion was undertaken, this time south of Rome in hopes of skirting the German defense at Cassino and reaching the Eternal City. 'Shingle' developed quietly and according to plan: the first waves reached on the beaches without any opposition and moved inland.

On the southern flank, the 3rd Division rapidly occupied its first objectives. On the left, paratroopers took Anzio town; Rangers captured Nettuno and were able to establish contact with the British to the north. The success of the operation was due to minute and careful planning, excellent weather, landing at the time and the place intended, but also to the absence of obstacles or of organized enemy defence and the fact that the enemy was taken completely by surprise.

However, memories of Salerno were vivid, so the Allies were cautious and did not immediately rush inland. And thus the two British and American divisions soon found themselves stuck on a beachhead surrounded by Germans. Moreover, bringing supplies in from Naples required keeping in Italy the LSTs that were due for England. For in the meantime these ships had been requested for Overlord.

Part of the naval and air fleet was later to come back to the Mediterranean for the invasion of southern France. This was one of the reasons why the southern invasion had been programed after the northern one instead of simultaneously.

The lack of LSTs resulted in several postponements and the operation was even almost canceled, because the Allies did not have enought ships to carry the two operations out at the same time. An exasperated Churchill even exclaimed: "*The fate of two great empires seems tied to a few cursed things called LSTs!*" Actually forty-one of these ships left the Mediterranean after Avalanche,

Top.
Since Husky, LSTs had been an essential element of amphibious operations. Here Royal Navy LST(2) 314 lowers her ramp onto the sand of the beach near the Pachino airfield, Sicily.
(National Archives)

Above.
'Two LSTs in the Mediterranean, the work horses of the Navy.'
(National Archives)

followed by fourteen others in February and March 1944 after Shingle.

In return, twenty-two were assigned after Overlord, in addition to the forty-eight delivered directly from the United States.

11. Plus 5 radio and 4 telephone operators.

12.'*Etude sur les opérations de débarquement de vive force*,' op. cit.

LANDING SHIPS AND CRAFT

After the evacuation of Dunkirk, the British, isolated in their island, realized that only land forces would be able to win a decisive victory on the continent, and that they would need a fleet especially designed for landing operations. Ships would have to be built to bring large armies to the enemy shore: they needed a shallow draft to land safely on a beach and then retract. Another necessity was a ramp at the bow, opening or lowering itself to allow vehicles and personnel to disembark rapidly. Three types of boats were thus progressively developed:
- small landing barges that would be transported to the zone of operations on the landing ships decks;
- larger landing craft that could sail to the landing area under their own power for a short trip, but could also be carried on larger ships for longer passages;
- ocean-going ships over sixty meters long.

Above.
Sailor from the 8th Naval Beach Battalion.
(Reconstruction, photo by Jonathan Gawne)

Above, left.
The unofficial 8th Naval Beach Battalion shoulder patch.
(Jonathan Gawne)

Left.
The port of Bizerte was damaged by the Allied bombs while it was occupied by the Axis forces. Here vehicles and tanks for Sicily are boarding fourteen LSTs and a dozen LCTs.
(National Archives)

There was thus a distinction between the ships able to transport whole units over long distances and even across the ocean, and the landing craft which would carry only a few men or tanks for the short trip to the beaches[1]. For the various arms and services, who had to choose the means most suited to their needs in any specific operation, it was the function that counted: transportation, support, command, navigational control, convoy police, repairs... Even though the British had the ideas, the Americans actually built the boats: more than 20,000 during WW I.

THE FIRST ASSAULT CRAFT

The beginnings were modest: the first motor landing craft was built for the British Admiralty in 1926 and there were only three in service four years later. Then six others were ordered in 1935. After these new craft were delivered in 1938, the Inter-Service Training and Development Center was set up to design the equipment necessary for amphibious assaults, especially craft that could land directly on or come very close to a hostile beach. For rapid transport ships equipped with davits capable of lowering craft filled with men, the merchant ships that were under construction at the time could be used. But nothing available answered the need for assault craft: silent, armored, capable of transporting a platoon in fighting gear, armed

Above.
Artist's drawing from an Abwehr study showing how the Germans envisioned an Allied invasion.

Above.
Royal Navy LCA 1063 was built in 1944. She could carry 35 men and 800 lbs of equipment. She was armed with a Bren LMG, two Lewis guns and two 50-mm mortars.
(Computer graphics by Christophe Camilotte)

Left.
LCA 1440. Notice the propeller guards and the ropes on the sides where a man who has fallen overboard can hang on.
(IWM A 9835)

Below.
Another artist's drawing from the same German intelligence study, this time featuring the landing ships and boats.
(Private collection)

with guns and machine guns capable of firing from the ship or from the ground, able to land vehicles, guns and tanks. The first designs involved a barge for forty men [1], the 'Landing craft, assault' (LCA). The Admiralty was not able to pursue the project at the time, so the ISTDC turned to civilian constructors: Fleming built an aluminum-alloy boat and Thornycroft a mahogany-hulled barge. During trials the Fleming boat was very stable on water and could 'beach' easily, but the thunderous noise from its two engines made it unacceptable. So Thornycroft won

the bid, and the fact that their prototype could be improved was also a decisive factor. Concerning the support landing craft, it appeared that this boat should be the same size as the preceding one and just as silent. The problem of weapons was resolved by adapting a mortar capable of firing a smoke shell that would explode when it hit the water. Thornycroft also won the right to build the prototype for a tank landing craft. Its load would be a 12-ton tank, which was considered at the time to be the heaviest machine capable of participating in an amphibious attack. At the same time, the ISTDC was studying various problems involved with amphibious assault: navigation to the beaches, crossing fields of shallow-water obstructions, landing supplies, control ships... Supplying the beachhead by air and the use of paratroopers were also under consideration [2]. Finally, after a report conclude that an operation was impossible under present conditions because of the lack of landing craft, thirty-two craft were ordered in April 1939: ten were used at Narvik in Norway in April 1940 and nine others at Dunkirk in June. A year later, orders totaled 262, of which almost all were designed for commando operations.

THE FIRST TANK LANDING SHIPS

In the first months of 1941, the main preoccupation of the ISTDC was to contribute to harassing raids along the coasts of occupied countries. However, it became increasingly evident that the decisive battle on the continent would begin by a cross-Channel crossing. In the meantime, operations could easily take place in the Mediterranean. There was a wide choice of targets: Sardinia, Sicily, Italy, Greece, Crete, Rhodes... But it was one thing to cross the Channel and quite

---

1. Four crew members, a section of 31 men and five sappers, transmitters or company CP personnel, as necessary.

2. Thus in Algeria members from the center attended an exercise drop by the French 602nd Air Infantry Group.

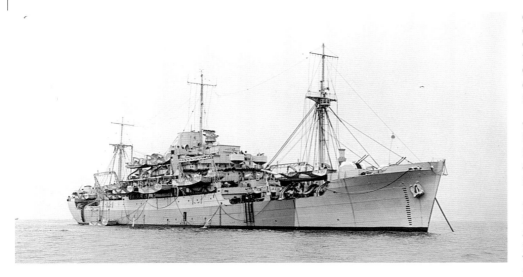

another to cross an ocean... In that case, only sea-going ships would be able to participate in the operation, and air cover would depend on aircraft carriers.

On the other hand, submarines would be less of a problem, and the possible attack zone was so wide that a landing point could be chosen that was lightly or not at all defended, and far enough away so that there would be no threat of counter-attack or of the immediate arrival of enemy reinforcements. It was thus evident that the ISTDC had to continue its work in providing ships and landing craft for an operation in the Mediterranean, which, it clearly seemed, would take place before the invasion of NW-Europe.

In June 1940 the first three *Glen*-class ships were modified to transport a battalion each. Then two idle steamships from the Dutch Continental line were sent to Belfast for alterations: the upper deck was removed to house the troops and enough landing craft were stowed on board to land almost all 450 men in a single wave. Then two ferries were converted into transports for landing craft, and three large Navy tankers were hijacked as they came out of the shipyards and equipped with rails and davits cranes for fifteen landing craft. All of this was accomplished during the summer of 1941. In the meantime the Army had entertained the idea of a 36-ton tank, so a landing craft capable of handling 40 tons was requested. Trials had taken place in November 1940 and

Above.
The *Gleneam*, one of the first *Glen*-class LSI(L)s. *(IWM A 25 302)*

Right.
The *Bachaquero*, an LST(1), one of two converted ferry boats. *(IWM A 20 037)*

Below.
GIs boarding LCVPs from the assault transport ship APA 13, *Joseph T. Dickman*, which participated in August 1944 in the landing on the coast north of Sainte-Maxime. *(IWM HV 63 557)*

Above.
LCVP 28 from APA 26, the *Samuel Chase*, was part of TU 84.3.1 (Alpha Yellow) in Provence. She was 11 m long, armed with two machineguns, and could carry 36 men and 3 tons of vehicles. *(Computer graphics by Christophe Camilotte)*

orders for thirty 'landing craft, tank' (LCT) were immediately sent out. These craft were sent to the Mid-East on cargo ships during the first semester of 1941. Twenty of them participated in operations in Greece, in Crete and at Tobruk. But this LCT Mark I had hardly come off the drawing boards when a faster boat was requested, adapted to the standard 16-ton tank.

So the LCT Mark I was built, larger than the first and with a second engine. Thirty five were shipped to the Middle East during the winter of 1941-42. Later the hull was lengthened and the engines improved to create the LCT Mark III[3] in April 1941. However all this progress was insufficient for a transatlantic crossing.

The failed operation in Dakar revealed the need for a control ship and especially ships able to navigate over a long distance and land their tanks from a ramp. A solution was found by adapting flat-bottomed tankers used on Lake Maracaibo in Venezuela. Another was to dream up a new ship traveling at a speed of 17 knots designed to follow the troop transports[4]. And thus was the 'landing ship, tank' (LST) born. Three were ordered from Belfast shipyards, with hopes of receiving American and Canadian orders for seven more.

THE AMERICAN ARSENAL

America's entry into the war in December 1941 profoundly changed the industrial capabilities of the Allies, and construction of landing craft soared. First the British sent a permanent mission in Washington. Then, from March 1942 on, a combined operations liaison officer resided there permanently, helping the Americans to benefit from the British past and future experience. But '*two years later, because of the rapid progress of the United States in equipment and tactics, the office of the Combined Operations Liaison Officer in Washington spent more time sending than receiving information from London.*[5]'

Even though the main naval commitment of the Americans was the Pacific, the other theaters naturally benefited from these technical and tactical breakthroughs. In the United States, actually, '*the start of the World War provoked intense research into all types of acceptable landing craft and their development, for the purpose of transporting various loads and different types of equipment.*[6]' The Higgins company in

---

3. *Moreover, in the Middle East the boats were equipped so that the crew could live on board.*

4. *The three infantry landing ships available at the time were in the Mediterranean preparing for the attack on Pantelleria.*

5. *Rear-Admiral L.E.H. Maund, Assault from the Sea, Methuen & Co, London, 1949.*

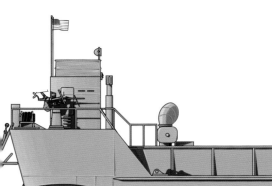

LCT(5) 268 belonged to TU 85.5.9 (Shallow Water Salvage Unit) operating off Delta Green in Provence. She was armed with three 20-mm AA gun, and could transport five medium tanks or nine trucks or 150 tons of cargo.
(Computer graphics by Christophe Camilotte)

New Orleans was a big help because of the experience it had acquired during the prohibition. At that time it produced eleven-meter-long boats, for bootlegging rum, that could outdistance coast guard motor-

Below.
An LSD loading trucks transported from the coast by an LCT.
(IWM)

LCP(L) and the LCV were put together in a single boat baptized 'Landing Craft, Vehicle, Personnel,' (LCVP) a typically American invention. For personnel, in April 1942 Admiral Mountbatten, Chief of Combined

Left.
LCV 829 manned by a crew of Royal Navy sailors.
(IWM A 27 986)

Top, right.
LCT(4) 1195, flying the Royal Navy flag, has just been launched at the Warrenpoint shipyards.

Above, right.
LCT(5) 2296 was one of the landing craft built in the United States and assigned to the Royal Navy, which added 2000 to the American serial number.
(IWM A 23 749)

Right.
This shot of US Navy LCT(6) 558 was published in a German intelligence document.
(Private collection)

boats and had sufficient armor to protect the crew from machine gun bullets.

Moreover, because of their shallow draft and their ribbed, flat-bottomed hull, they could land on beaches, unload and withdraw rapidly under their own power. At the request of the British, a motorboat built in New Orleans had already been used as a model for the manufacture of the 'Landing Craft, Personnel, Large,' which became, after adding a ramp for rapid unloading of the twenty-five soldiers aboard, the 'Landing Craft, Personnel, Ramped.' The next phase was the enlarging of the ramp so that it could take a truck or a Bren carrier, thus creating the 'Landing Craft, Vehicle.' Then the most interesting characteristics of the

Operations, requested a speed boat capable of transporting two hundred men to participate in a raid. Plans for the 'Landing Craft, Infantry, Large' came off the drawing boards immediately, and building the first one hundred began in record time. The first LCI(L)s crossed the Atlantic in December. For equipment, the craft proposed by Higgins and adopted by the two Navies became Landing Craft, Mechanized Mark III. It could carry a 30-ton Sherman tank and was entirely built in the United States and then transferred to the Royal Navy.

7. Embarcations for Amphibious Operations, lecture by Captain William K. Pflaum of the FAITC, Arzew.

As a result of the Lend-Lease Act, Great Britain – whose shipyards had reached their peak production– had already tapped the enormous capacities of American industry since the second semester of 1941. Moreover, three projects that had been brought up in London during the fall, finally came to fruition in January 1942. First of all, it was decided to build seven floating docks or 'Landing Ships, Dock' in the United Kingdom, replacing the LST(1)s originally planned. Secondly, for ferrying vehicles between the cargos and the beach, a fifth type of LCT was chosen. And the transatlantic landing craft known as the Atlantic Tank Landing Craft was adopted with the construction of a new type of LST. In all, eight hundred LCT(5)s and LST(2)s equally divided between the two Navies were built in America starting in May.

Then, using as a model the latest British LCT, the Americans developed the LCT(6), a landing craft with two ramps, one fore and one aft, to facilitate the unloading of the LSTs. And later on, a certain number of LST Mark IIIs where the elevator between the upper and main decks was replaced by a ramp were built in Canada and in Great Britain. On the other hand, the British kept their monopoly over support boats. These were generally derived from the assault craft and designed to accompany them to the beaches. The LCA, armed with a mortar and machine guns, became the Landing Craft, Support, Medium. And various models of LCIs or LCTs were developed into the Landing Craft, Support, Large and into other specialized craft: LCF (Flak) armed with 40-mm guns; LCG (gun) equipped with guns to take on coastal defenses; LCR (rocket) capable of raking nearly one thousand meters of beach. Finally the LCI(L) was adapted to become a Landing Craft, Headquarters.

In an effort at standardization, the names were codified, and an agreement was reached under which the landing craft would be defined according to their navigational capacity and their function. Thus the ocean-crossing landing ships [7] and the landing craft launched near the enemy shore were classified according to their functions: personnel transport, equipment transport, support and auxiliary boats. Actually there was a fundamental difference between the British and American attitudes concerning invasion operations and landing vessels. The British, even though they undertook raids along the coasts of the continent and in the Mediterranean, focused mainly on a great invasion in Normandy, and went all out in that direction, modifying and transforming the few craft at their disposal. The Americans, on the other hand, even

Above.
LCI(L) 195 was used as the TG 87.3 command ship for Delta Red beach in Provence. She was armed with four 20-mm guns and could carry 6 officers and 182 men or 75 tons of supplies.
(Computer graphics by Christophe Camilotte)

Left.
LSI(M) HMCS *Prince David* was armed with two 100-mm, one 40-mm and six 20-mm guns. It could transport 444 men, two LCM(1)s or (3)s, five LCAs and one LCS(M).
(IWM A 23 743)

Above right.
US Navy LCI(L) 235. In the background is a flotilla of LCI(L)s and an LST.

Right.
LCI(L) 368 during maneuvers along the American Atlantic coast. Sailors are preparing to lower the ramps while the 'landlubbers' calmly wait.
(National Archives)

Below.
A hundred British soldiers have left a luxurious ocean liner transformed into an LSI(L), and are heading for the shore in a LCM(1).

though they were latecomers to the war, used the total capacity of their exceptional industrial potential to create the best possible boats adapted to the war in the Pacific.

In 1943, ships designed for amphibious operations, or amphibious warfare ships, appeared for the first time on the American 'Navy List.'. There were mer-

7. The category was created in 1943 to include large ships like the LSTs and LSDs.

Above.
LCI(L) 98 was a Royal Navy vessel.
(IWM A 24 665)

was made up of six to eighteen boats, and three flotillas formed a section. More than two thousand LCAs were produced and used throughout the war.

Two support craft were derived from the LCA: the Landing Craft, Support (Medium) or LCS(M) and the Landing Craft, Assault (Hedgerow) or LCA(HR).

After these small assault craft had proven their mettle, the British realized in April 1942 that they would also need a sea-going ship, taht could accommodate 200 men in decent living conditions, and that could land them in 75 cm of water. At the end of the year the Americans came up with the Landing Craft, Infantry (Large). Its capacity of 180 to 200 men bunks could be increased to 250 over a short distance by housing the additional soldiers on the bow deck. For operations taking place over longer distances, units were loaded onto troop transport and then moved into the LCI(L)s 48 hours before arrival. These craft had been originally designed to land the first waves, but they proved to be too large and too vulnerable. So they were organized in flottillas of twelve and used to land reserve troops or reinforcements. For this they used gangplanks on either side of the bow, that could be lowered into the water.

From the LCI(L) were derived the British LCH and LCQ command boats, the LC(FF) or American flotilla

chant ships or destroyers turned into troop transports, and freighters used for supplies. There were also command ships, a sort of floating HQ for amphibious operations. All these vessels were classified as 'auxiliaries,' complements to the landing craft and landing ships. Thus by 1944 the Americans had a full range of complementary boats, completely standardized and used in all the seas around the globe, including the Mediterranean.

Right.
Off the Normandy shore coast, men in their assault uniforms climb down the net along the side of the transport ship to reach an LCT(6) that will carry them to the beach.
(IWM HU 87 101)

Below.
LCT(6) No 1144 was part of TU 84.1.5 off *Alpha Red* in Provence. She was armed with two 20-mm guns and could carry three 50-ton or four 30-ton tanks, or 150 tons of cargo.
(Computer graphics by Christophe Camilotte)

CRAFT AND SHIPS FOR TRANSPORTATION OF PERSONNEL

The 'Landing Craft, Assault' was a small boat designed and built by the British, with a hull made out of plywood. Its armor included sheet iron on the sides, an armored door at the back of the ramp and deck planking protecting the heads of the soldiers. It could be launched by a crane, derrick or davit and approached the beach discreetly. Its long silhouette meant that it was almost invisible at night, its two engines were very quiet and its wake was imperceptible when traveling at two or three knots. A flotilla

Photo taken from the German study of the Allied landing capabilities, showing from left to right: an LCM, an LCVP, an LCS and an LCP.
(Private collection)

Princess Beatrix, converted in 1942-43, and the LSI(S)es *Prince Baudoin* and *Prince Albert*, transformed in 1942. No LSI(HH) participated in Operation Dragoon.

During 1942, 58 traditional transport ships or APs[8] on the Navy List received the title 'APA' or attack transport for troops and vehicles to be used for the assault. The APs unloaded their cargo at bases far from the combat zone, but the APA were designed to operate within the zone limits. Actually, during Dragoon, seven of the eleven APs and the five APAs did the same missions and had the same title: combat loaders.

Another category of assault transport craft is the APD, whose prototype appeared in 1938. It was simply a destroyer in which two boilers and smokestacks had been removed to make room for troops and smaller landing boats. It was called a destroyer (fast) transport. This ship was also classified as high speed transport, and normally used for hit-and-run raids, with troops disembarking in landing boats. The five APDs that were engaged in Dragoon were destroyers of the flush-deck type, class 1916 to 1918, that had been transformed.

flagship, and the support craft, which were also American: LCI(R) for rockets, LCI(G) for gunboat, LCI(M) for mortars, and LCS(L). They all later fell in the category of 'landing craft'. The 'Landing Ships, Infantry' were British vessels, merchant ships turned into fast transports.

LSI were of four types: large, medium, small and hand-hoisting. The LSI(L)s, equivalent to the American APAs (Attack transports), were adaptations of mixed transatlantic liners, of which they retained the speed and the basic characteristics. For example, HMS *Keren*, the ex-RN *Hydra*, ex-*Kenya*, launched in 1930, first participated in the Dakar expedition, then was transformed in 1942. But most of the LSI(L)s engaged in Operation Dragoon were 12,000-ton capacity merchant ships temporarily equipped for a precise purpose. Among these was the *Ascania*, a large ocean liner, classified as a Landing Ship, Personnel or LSP, of which the American equivalent was the AP. LSI(M)s and (S)es were ships designed for coastal navigation and improved so that they could navigate in high seas. Off the coasts of Provence were present: the LSI(M)s *Prince David*, *Prince Henry* and

Above.
Royal Navy LCT(2) 130 on the beach with its ramp down. Notice the two 20-mm guns and the hoops designed to hold the canvas covers to protect the tanks in case of bad weather.
(IWM A 24 487)

CRAFT AND SHIPS TRANSPORTING VEHICLES AND EQUIPMENT

The Landing Craft, Vehicle, Personnel was built by the Americans and had a wooden hull with light armor on the ramp, the sides and the stations manned by the gunners and bosun. It could be loaded and

Above.
LCM(3) 1012, with two other landing craft, made up TU 87.6.5 (LCM Smokers) in the Delta sector. She could ferry a Sherman or 60 men or 30 t of cargo, once she had gotten rid of her smoke-making equipment.
(Computer graphics by Christophe Camilotte)

Left.
During an exercise in the eastern Mediterranean, an Royal Armoured Corps Sherman is unloading from LCT(3) 387.

Above.
LCM(3) 594 approaching the beach during Operation 'Torch' along the Algerian coast.

then lowered by davit into the water, and was normally used to transfer personnel and vehicles from the assault transport ships to the coast. After the British had perfected the Landing Craft, Mechanized, the Americans created a boat capable of carrying a 15-ton load. Then they produced, between 1942 and 1944, large quantities of LCM(3)s which could carry a 30-ton tank.

8. *A for fleet auxiliary ship and P for personnel.*

Left.
After participating in the landings in Sicily and Salerno, US Navy LST 317 sailed for England.
(IWM KY 26 363)

Below.
An LCT is being loaded onto the deck of an LST at the Quai du Sénégal in Oran harbor.
(DIHP)

only be transported by LSDs. But the Admiralty had discovered that the Mark III could not land on the Normandy beaches with their gentle slopes, and wanted a craft specially adapted for crossing the Channel. The LCT Mark IV was the answer, derived from models I and III but shorter and wider. The LCT(5) was built in three water-tight[9] sections by the Americans in 1942-43. It could carry five Shermans with their drivers only.

The following model, LCT(6) was derived from the preceding one, modified to allow loading from the rear and increase room for motor transport. It could be

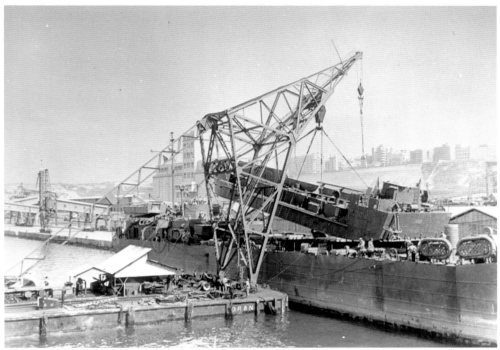

The difference with the LCM(1) was that the load was stowed below the water line, giving the boat better stability. On the other hand, it could not be hoisted, while loaded, onto a larger ship. The British prototype of a craft designed for transport and landing of tanks and vehicles on the beaches was the Landing Craft, Tank Mark I. It was built in 1940-41 but was progressively withdrawn and used for training. It was followed, from 1941 to 1943, by the LCT Mark I, better equipped: two generators, a radio, an electric cooker, ammunition compartments and a third screw. The LCT Mark III was built until 1944 on the same model as the Mark I, but with the addition of a ten-meter long section, making it larger and meaning that it could

Above.
US Navy LST 386 during a rehearsal with French troops in Arzew bay. Rhino pontoons are carried on the hull sides.
(IWM HV 87 101)

Below.
LST No 914 participated in the invasion of Provence as part of TU 84.1.1 (Alpha Red). She could carry eighteen Shermans and a LCT or 27 trucks and eight jeeps, plus 150 men.
(Computer graphics by Christophe Camilotte)

Above.
The ramp and front doors of an LST during an exercise in the United States.
(National Archives)

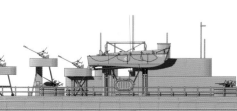

Above.
The AGC-5 *Catoctin*, ex-*Mary Whitbridge*, one of the seventeen command vessels of the US Navy amphibious force.
(National Archives)

used for direct landings of tanks and other vehicles, but could also be used as a pontoon to unload LSTs.

The Landing Ship, Tank was designed at the request of the British who needed a large sea-going vessel, capable of carrying a 2,100-ton load and of landing tanks and other vehicles during an amphibious assault. The ship had to reconcile two conflicting requisites: a deep draft for crossing the ocean and a shallow draft for landing on the beaches. The problem was solved by the Americans thanks to an ingenious system of ballast that could be filled with water on the high seas and emptied on arrival along the coast. After an initial draft accepted in November 1941, an 88-meter

were ordered before the project was finalized, and shipbuilding started even before a prototype had been completed. Moreover, since most of the coastal shipyards were at full capacity, more than half the ships had to be built inland, in the 'cornfield shipyards' of the American Middlewest, and floated along the navigable waterways to the sea. From 1943 on the construction time was reduced to four months and certain improvements the result of experience were added: the elevator was replaced by a ramp, the main deck was reinforced to be able to hold a fully-equipped LCT, the armament was increased, and a still was installed that could produce 15,200 liters of drinking water a day.

The LST(1) was thus a sea-going ship with a stern door that could be opened, designed for transporting and landing medium tanks, by ramp or by pontoon causeway, on beaches with a gradient superior to 1/37. The crew and the troops were accommodated on the first top deck, and the tanks parked on the second. A forty-ton crane was used to launch the small boats.

The American LST(2) had the same functions and the same unloading systems, plus being equipped to evacuate the wounded. They were used for the first

Below.
LCC 95 was part of TU 84.1.1 (Alpha Red). She was armed with two twin .50-mm MGs.
(Computer graphics by Christophe Camilotte)

A British fighter control ship.

long ship was proposed in January 1942. Then its length was increased to 99 meters with a width of 15 meters and a minimum draft of about one meter. This meant that the load could be balanced better and that the width of the stern door could be enlarged to more than four meters. Ventilation was added on the lower deck where the tanks were located, and an elevator was installed for the light vehicles on the upper deck.

Because of the urgency, all planning was done by telephone, telegram or air mail. The raw materials

Above, left.
Landing Craft, Control Mark 2, the latest model with a microfilm map projector on the radar screen.
(DR)

Above.
LSH(L) HMS *Bulolo*, a Royal Navy command ship fitted out in 1942 and able to transport six LCP(L)s and 258 men.
(IWM)

time in the Solomon Islands in June 1943, and proved very resilient. Even though their crews had nicknamed them 'Large Slow Targets,' very few were lost[10], considering the numbers built and the scope of the operations in which they took part. The versatile LST was used for a variety of other functions: for example as supply or depot ship with additional installations such

9. *An LST could carry five sections or an assembled LCT to be launched over the side; an LSD could carry three fully loaded LCTs.*

as two metal Quonset on the top deck to house forty officers, 196 bunks, a bakery, sixteen refrigerators for fresh food, four stills and fresh water in the ballast... Others were equipped for fire direction (FDTs) or aerial control (GCI). Some were even used as aircraft carriers for light artillery observation planes.

Finally, the AKA attack cargo ships or attack freighters, in association with APAs, constituted the hub of the American amphibious forces. They transported equipment and supplies to the beachheads, unloaded their loads directly on the beach with the help of the landing craft they carried, and could also be used for fire support.

COMMAND CRAFT AND SHIPS

The Landing Craft, Headquarters was an LCI(L) from the 1 to 350 series, specially equipped by the US Navy as a command craft. It had appropriate installations - message and operations center - and was principally used during the early phase of the assault for directing the assault waves. It also carried the assault battalion's CP until it could go ashore.

The Landing Craft, Control was used for piloting landing craft, as a marker for the departure line for the assault waves. Craft of this type controlled traffic and did preliminary hydrographic surveys. It had a steel hull and looked something like the Landing Craft, Support (Small), but could be recognized by its radio and radar antennae. The LCCs were usually carried by the assault transport ships, and were not designed to 'beach.' They were particularly well-equipped: gyro-compass, route tracer, sounding lines, SOradar, echo-sound receivers, goniometer, two TCS radio sets, two SCR-610 sets.

The importance of a Task Force headquarters, the room and communications required, were such that both navies soon gave up the idea of locating such a command structure on a battleship, especially since a fighting ship would also be assigned fire missions that were incompatible with the proper handling of a seaborne assault.

The Americans went further than the British and built floating CPs, known as Amphibious Force Flagships or AGCs. They had 49 remote-controlled radio transmitters, 95 receivers, three internal teletype circuits, pneumatic and loud-speaker systems. They were called Combined Operations Communications Headquarters Ships, and later Operations and Command Headquarters Ships. Because of all their signals equipment they were the ideal fleet command ship. They received no combat missions and their weapons were only defensive. Compared to the British Landing Ships, Headquarters, they could be recognized by their mast and radar antennae.

SUPPORT AND AUXILIARY CRAFT AND SHIPS

The British fitted some of their LCT(2)s and (3)s with rocket-launchers so as to prolong the possibility of naval

Right.
LCS(M)(3) No 47 with a 102-mm smoke mortar, two .50 and two .30 machineguns.
(IWM A 28757)

Right.
LCS(L)(2) No 251 armed with a 57 mm antitank gun in a turret, two Oerlikon 20-mm guns, twin .50 MGs, two Lewis guns and a 102—mm mortar.

Right.
LCT(R) 334 was a rebuilt LCT(3), armed with two 20-mm Oerlikon guns and from 800 to 1000 127 mm rockets, and equipped with SB RDF navigational aids.
(IWM

Right.
LCF(4) No 32 was an LCT(4) with impressive armament: four 40-mm 'pom-pom' guns and eight 20-mm turrets.
(IWM A 23 759)

Below.
LCF No 10 - armed with four 40 mm 'pom-pom' AA guns and eight 20-mm mounts - participated in the invasion of Provence with TU 85.12.5 (*Close Support Unit*) in the Delta sector.
(Computer graphics by Christophe Camilotte)

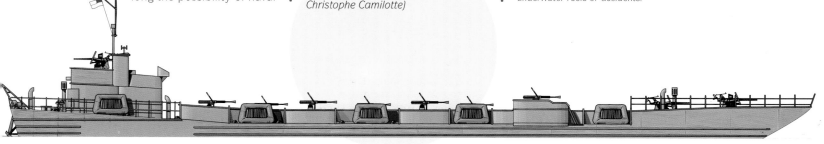

bombardment, which normally had to be suspended when the first waves approached the shore. The role of these support craft was to neutralize a portion of the enemy beach defenses by showering them with a huge concentration of exploding projectiles.

_____

10. 26 lost by enemy action and 13 victims of bad weather, underwater reefs or accidents.

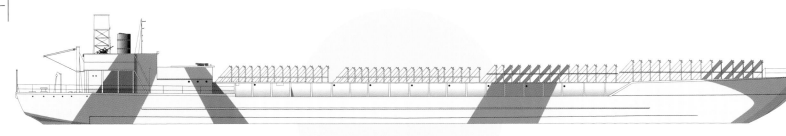

The Landing Craft, Tank (Rocket) could fire from a fixed distance and the rockets were ignited by an electric device, while a radar determined the precise range. All of the rockets could be fired in less than thirty seconds, and could cover a zone 700 meters long and 220 meters wide. As well as the physical destruction caused by the bombings, rockets also had a devastating effect on the enemy's nerves. The first six LCT(R)s were sent to the Mediterranean just in time to participate in the Sicily invasion.

On the LCT basis, the British also built the Landing Craft, Flak which had anti-aircraft weapons for both close protection and distance firing. It could protect the assault forces against low-level plane attacks, as well as against surface attacks before and after landing. It could also take on directly the enemy machine gun emplacements and pillboxes. The LCF(3), derived from the LCT(3), was the only one of these boats used during Operation Dragoon.

The LCT(3) also fostered another support boat

Above.
With five other rocket ships, an LCF, an LCG and eight LCM(R)s, LCT(R) No 136 made up TU 84.1.7 (*Red Close Support Craft Unit*), off Cavalaire beach.
(Computer graphics by Christophe Camilotte)

The different phases of an amphibious operation:
1. A Scout and Raiders team survey the beach during an exercise on the coast of Florida.
(National Archives)

2. The soldiers have boarded the LCVPs carried by APA-5 *Barnett* which participated in the invasion of Provence in the Delta sector.
(IWM EA 25 350)

armed with cannons from obsolete destroyers. This boat was also used for the first time in Sicily, and was in charge of short-range bombardment of the coastal defenses.

Finally the LSTs were also transformed into repair ships: the auxiliary repair ships or ARs were specialized in different jobs: B battle damage; L landing craft; V aircraft; ST salvage craft tender. The ARLs were supposed to repair, within the landing zone, a maximum number of damaged boats. Consequently the ramp and the stern doors were omitted.

Specific installations included booms, derricks, with one able to handle 50 tons, and winches designed to hoist the boats onto the ship for repairs. Mechanical and electrical repair shops were installed on the main and lower decks.

3. The vehicles are landed. This is LST(2) No 175 during an exercise in England.

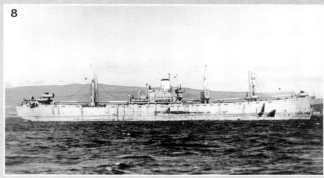

4. DUKWs rolling off from LSTs. LST 1 participated in operations in Sicily, Salerno, Anzio and Normandy. No 381 did the same, with the exception of Anzio.

5. The beachhead is secured as DUKWs move in equipment and supplies while the engineers are at work.
(IWM NA 6636)

8. Liberty ship *SS Saminver* during a refueling exercise off Greenock (Scotland) in April 1944.
(IWM A 23 033)

9. Seen from the destroyer *HMS Badsworth*, this Liberty ship of convoy UGS-6 B arrived in Algiers on April 14, 1943 with the first American equipment for the French army.
(IWM A 16 335)

Background photo.
The support craft are strafing the shore.
Here LCT(R) No 334 is letting fly a salvo of rockets.
(IWM A27942)

6. Reinforcements arrive. Here the 2^e division marocaine lands in Naples on Nov. 22, 1943 aboard Royal Navy LSTs 302 and 303 and US Navy LST 349, which broached on the reefs off Ponza island on Feb. 26, 1944.
(ECPAD)

7. LST(2) 80 was transferred to the Royal Navy on July 19, 1943.
(IWM A 23 745)

FROM ANVIL TO DRAGOON

While the future of Anvil was still uncertain, General Patch's staff continued to prepare and work out logistics plans. General Devers also played an important part, in his dual role as deputy to the Commander in Chief as well as NATOUSA commander. He was thus able to hoard supplies for Anvil which, without his interventions, would have been squandered elsewhere.

Lieutenant General Alexander M. Patch, the Seventh Army commander.
(Signal Corps)

Inset, above.
The Seventh Army shoulder patch, here an enameled variant for the coat lapels and the garrison cap.
(Le Poilu)

Major General Arthur A. White, the Seventh Army Chief of Staff.
(Signal Corps)

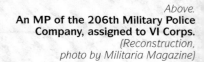

Above.
An MP of the 206th Military Police Company, assigned to VI Corps.
(Reconstruction, photo by Militaria Magazine)

PATCH PUTS DE LATTRE INTO THE PICTURE

On February 11, 1944, the AFHQ G-3 noted that, because of 'linguistic difficulties' it was impossible to create a Franco-American joint staff in the same vein as the Anglo-American structure. Instead, it was suggested to form a liaison section in charge of transmitting orders to the French formations who would be taking part in the invasion. However, for political reasons, the idea of attaching a French deputy with his limited personal staff to the American leader was considered.

General Wilson deemed it essential to inform the French command about the progress of preparations for Anvil, and he discussed them at length with General Giraud on March 7. The French Commander in Chief willingly accepted that his troops participate in the second wave, because the American divisions had better training in this type of operation, and a seaborne attack was complex enough without adding language problems. On the other hand, special French units [1] could be used as reinforcements for the assault divisions. And he also insisted on the significant aid that the Résistance could bring to the American troops once they had landed.

The question of command was a bit more delicate. Giraud thought that, since the majority of the divisions were French, it was only right that the leader of the ground forces be a Frenchman. Moreover, he felt that such a nomination would have an important psychological effect on the French resistance movements. The discussion was adjourned at the time, then resumed two days later. In the meantime, Giraud had consulted with General de Gaulle, President of the 'Comité de Libération Nationale.' Both men accepted Patch as leader of the first phase of

January 17, 1944 at the Summer Palace in Algiers. General Giraud is hosting General Sir Maitland Wilson, accompanied by General Devers, for the official ceremony of his inauguration as commander of the Allied Mediterranean theater of operations.
(ECPAD)

Below.
In the Palace gardens, the three generals salute the flag of the 1er régiment de tirailleurs algériens (RTA) before reviewing the honor guard.
(ECPAD)

Anvil, but insisted that a French Army, the equal of the Seventh Army, should then be created. While they were waiting for this point to be decided, Giraud accepted to discuss with Patch the possibility of adding a French team to Force 163, as suggested by General Davidson. And so, on March 19, Colonel Jean Petit and six French officers arrived at Bouzareah. They were assigned to the various sec-

1. Bataillon de choc, Commandos d'Afrique and 1er RCP.
2. G-2 Lieutenant Colonel Serre (Engineers); Major Le Hagre and Major Du Crest de Villeneuve (Colonial infantry); G-3 Lieutenant Colonels Agostini (Infantry) and Demetz (Armor); Second Lieutenant Barbecot; G-4 Commander Alix (Infantry).

to take place at the end of the landing phase. Wilson, on the other hand, preferred that, from the end of the assault phase to the creation of an army group, the seventh army control all three French and American corps.

De Gaulle now alone, after Giraud's ouster [5], was unhappy about what he considered to be an equivocal attitude on Wilson's part, and placed General de Lattre de Tassigny at the head "*of all the French ground forces participating in the invasion through the Southern coasts of France* [6]", authorizing him to undertake, alongside the Allied officers, preparations for the coming action. Wilson declared officially that he was completely satisfied. But when General Béthouart [7] informed him of the decision on April 15, he pointed out that De Lattre was also the commander of the French Armée B, and it would be difficult to integrate another high level staff into a system which was already top heavy with brass. Béthouart was therefore informed that, after discussion with Patch, a decision would be forthcoming.

The Allied leaders were not only upset about being faced with a fait accompli, they were also preoccupied by Giraud's dismissal. Wilson was particularly worried:

"*I was upset about this change because, for dealings concerning military operations, Giraud's staff was trustworthy and the security was good. I had serious doubts now that everything had to go through the Comité de la Défense Nationale* [8]."

Wilson and Patch nevertheless searched for a compromise that would put De Lattre 'in the picture' without upsetting the command structure. They suggested that, during the initial phase, De Lattre lead the first corps to be landed with as his deputy the corps commander and a mixed staff and take his orders from the Seventh Army. Then when the sec-

tions [2] as they arrived, and were soon joined by three second lieutenants assigned to beef up the team of translators. The presence of a single officer at G-4 undoubtedly surprised the Americans, who gave him such important prerogatives that he often commanded the planning of the other bureaus [3]. But even though Petit worked directly with the Seventh Army chief of staff, he actually had "*practically no power of decision and played the role of a liaison officer between Force 163 and the various French headquarters.* [4]"

In the meantime, the issue of who was to command had evolved. The French truly hoped that a national army could be created, even if it meant being part of an army group that was commanded by an American. However, they wanted this creation

General De Gaulle, president of the French Committee of National Liberation, leaving the Government Palace guarded by cavalrymen from the 1er régiment de spahis marocains.
(DR)

Canvas painting in memory of the victory of Massawa on April 8, 1941, signed by Captain Savey, commander of the 3rd Company of the 1st BIM, coming from Egypt to participate in the Eritrean campaign along side the Brigade Française Libre d'Orient.
(Musée des Troupes de Marine)

Right.
General De Lattre de Tassigny, Army B commander.
(DR)

Left.
"*General De Gaulle's vista from his window at the Villa des Glycines, his temporary residence.*"
(OFIC)

3. The plans were scheduled to be completed as follows: April 15, 1944 for the supply and transportation plan (G-4); June 14, 1944 estimation of the enemy capability (G-2); July 13, 1944 draft plan (G-3); July 18, 1944 troop strength and priorities (G-1); July 24, 1944 civilian affairs (G-5).
4. Riviera to the Rhine, op. cit.
5. Relieved from his functions as Commander in Chief after April 4, 1944.
6. Note No 210/3 TS dated April 18, 1944 forwarding a decision made by the CFLN.
7. Chief of staff for national defense since April 10, 1944.
8. Field Marshal Lord Wilson of Libya, Eight Years Overseas, 1939-1947, Hutchinson & Co., London. Anthony Cave Brown in Bodyguard of Lies, Harper & Row, New York 1975, notes that "the SHAEF security staff suspected that De Gaulle's headquarters in Algiers had been infiltrated by the German secret service, which was true."

The French Army national insignia, worn on the chest: a triumphant rooster against a rising sun.
(Private coll.)

ond corps had joined up with the first, he would take command of his army, under Patch's orders. The intentions of the Allies were clear: 'The aim of this arrangement was to keep control of important tactical decisions, troop priorities and supplies, and civilian affairs, in the hands of the top-

Above.
June 5, 1944 in Rome. Around General Clark, left to right: Generals Keyes (II Corps), Truscott (VI Corps), Juin (French Expeditionary Corps in Italy) and Gruenther (5 Army chief of staff).

Left.
General Béthouart, National Defense chief of staff and future commander of the 1er Corps in France.
(DR)

level Americans, while at the same time facilitating coordination with the Overlord forces. [9]' In any case this solution limited the authority of the French and once again placed a five-star general under the orders of a lieutenant general who only had three [10].

9. Riviera to the Rhine, *op. cit.*
10. The same thing had happened in Italy with Generals Juin and Clark.

Below.
"An honor guard of colonial troops saluting General De Gaulle as he arrives at the Fromentin Lycée, home of the French government."
(OFIC)

Nevertheless De Gaulle declared the solution satisfactory, as long as De Lattre maintained all his other prerogatives as Army Commander. But De Lattre hadn't waited for De Gaulle's signal: he had already spoken out against the outline plan produced by Force 163. On April 13 in a memorandum addressed to Colonel John S. Guthrie, the Seventh Army G-3, Lieutenant-Colonel Demetz, the 'Armée B' G-3, voiced his opposition to the solution adopted for Anvil: a single landing to take place about seventy kilometers from Toulon.

Not only was "*the distance between the landing site and the target city too great, but also the landing site was on the wrong side of the target, since the major part of the enemy reserve forces, stationed in the lower Rhone River valley, could easily move in from the West to reinforce those holding the port city. The enemy communications lines would neither be broken nor even endangered.*" He suggested "*a stranglehold surrounding Toulon on the East side (the region around Salins d'Hyères-Lavandou-Cavalaire) and on the West side (La Ciotat-Saint-Cyr-Bandol) with the goal of effectively allowing, right from the beginning, for:*
- *enough men to be landed to insure the success of the attack,*
- *the complete isolation of the city of Toulon.*"

On May 2 a seven-page note reaffirmed that a head-on attack on Toulon was to be avoided: the German defences were stronger there than anywhere

Above.
Colonel John S. Guthrie, the Seventh Army G-3.
(Seventh Army)

Below.
Hyères beach (Beach 256) looking northward.
(ISIS Report on Mediterranean France, Part VIII: Beaches, May 1943)

Bottom.
A pre-war photograph also included in the same Allied intelligence report: the seaside at le Lavandou (Beach 257).

order to carry out the complete stranglehold proposed above. Even though the invasion is to be prepared with an important attack force, it should not be forgotten that the operation may also take place against a weakened enemy, and thus all possibilities of rapid advance should also be analyzed right from the start."

THE 'DE LATTRE PLAN'

The question was raised again four days later in a note from the French staff. After regretting that the Allied Navy Commanders categorically refused to use the only wide beach available in the bay of Hyères "*before the coastline had been cleared by troops that had landed further away,*" the author spelled out the maneuver suggested by Armée B.

Toulon would be surrounded by troops disembarking on D-Day on the beaches of three zones "*with communications lines that could be used even in case of forest fires:*"
- in Bandol, a division with the goal of occupying Le Beausset and then Le Camp;
- in Le Lavandou, a division assigned to reducing enemy defenses in Hyères and the western hills, and a combat command to cover the northern flank and "*use its guns to prevent enemy movement around Solliès-Pont;*"
- in Cavalaire and Pampelonne, a division and a combat command heading for the Cogolin-Le Luc line, so as to gain control as rapidly as possible of the roads in the region of Le Luc-Flassans-Puget Ville.

Flanking cover would be ensured:
- to the West, around Saint-Cyr-sur-mer, by forces landed in Bandol, and around Le Camp and Méounes by two parachute regiments in liaison with "*elements of the Toulon resistance who had been evacuated to the Méounes region.*"
- to the East, by a commando put ashore along the coast between Sainte-Maxime and Saint-Tropez.

On D + 3 at Salins d'Hyères and Le Lavandou would land two other French divisions and a combat command which would be launched through Solliès-Pont to the North of Toulon and used for the direct attack on the city in liaison with the Hyères division and perhaps the one in Le Beausset.

Once these troops were in place, the assault on Toulon could be launched on D + 5 or D + 6 and the city captured on D + 7.

When De Lattre came to see Patch at Bouzareah

else along the coast, and it would be impossible to take advantage of the suprise effect.

On the other hand, the idea of outflanking was a possibility, fanning out from a beachhead located as close as possible to the port. Moreover, "*the capture of Toulon by outflanking would be immensely helped by an action against those enemy communications lines that could be used to move reinforcements in to defend the port. A landing in the Bandol-La Ciotat region, at the same time as the one near Lavandou-Hyères, would mean that the city would be surrounded and thus more easily captured. Moreover in these areas forest fires, particularly frequent in summer along the coasts of Provence, could not be used by the enemy to hinder the progression of the Allied troops. If this strategy was approved, the invasion forces, using the closest acceptable beaches to Toulon, on both the East and West sides, could number, at the end of D + 1, four infantry divisions.*' And the note concluded: '*it would appear that the operational plan must be completely overhauled, and that additional means must be approved, in*

orders to study Operation 'Rankin' that was pro-gramed in the case of 'substantial' weakening of the German forces in France or of German evacuation of occupied territories. Under optimal conditions, Wilson hoped to land in France via Marseilles, and Toulon if possible, with the Anvil forces, then occupy the regions South of the Loire River and put two 'mobile' divisions at Eisenhower's disposal. Armée B consequently assigned territory to its seven divisions, a plan which was completed by a symbolic British brigade group in Marseilles and an American division attached to the 3e division algérienne.

At the end of May, the Force 163 plan confirmed the following points: the participation of a third division, the assault foreseen between Cavalaire and La Napoule, within the framework of an American corps, and the initial phase taking place in four steps:

during the first week of May 11, he presented his propositions before an assembly of officers gathered in the operations room. At that time he must have supported the conclusion reached in the May 6th note from his G-3:

"*To succeed within the time frame specified for the landing operations, the capture of Toulon will require the use of major ground forces on communications lines through difficult terrain. This implies, during the first days of the operation, that the enemy will no longer be able to maneuver freely and especially to move up relatively important reserve units. This situation could result from a weakening of the German forces accomplished by operations launched on other fronts, by guerilla action and by aerial bombings. Consequently, Operation Anvil should only be attempted within the context of taking advantage of a weakened enemy.*"

Then on May 13, Armée B headquarters received

Above.
Western part of Cavalaire Bay (Beach 259) looking towards the Southwest
(ISIS Report on Mediterranean France, Part VIII Beaches, May 1943)

Right.
'Invasion money' handed out to Allied soldiers.
(H.P. Enjames collection, GI Collector Guide)

- capture of a beachhead marked out by a Blue Line, completed by the assault echelon by D + 3 at the latest;
- capture of Toulon around D + 25 by a French corps landing as far West as possible and fighting along the Hyères-Toulon road;
- extension of the beachhead to the Green Line beyond Toulon, effective by D + 40;
- assault on Marseilles starting on D + 40, probably necessitating the use of the whole French 2nd Corps, which should be available by D + 90.

On May 31, in a Note on the landing operations scheduled in the Western Mediterranean Theater, the 3e bureau of Armée B repeated the objections which had already been raised: the lengthy distance between the beaches and Toulon, the forced delays in ground operations and arrival of the larger units. In fact "*the capture of Toulon, which is the only way for Allied forces to arrive at a satisfactory rate, must result from the initial phase of landing operations. It must take place as soon as possible, around D + 7.*"

But the Allied planners had already rejected the French proposals. On May 16, the naval section of Force 163 wrote up a very severe criticism of the 'De Lattre plan:' the French proposal went far beyond the capabilities of the Allies in shipping for the assault troops; the beaches were not acceptable for an

Operation RANKIN C
Assigned occupation areas for the French 'Armée B' divisions

XX 1re DB

Metz

Paris

Strasbourg

Nancy

XX 5e DB

Orléans

Mulhouse

Tours

Dijon

XX 3e DIA

XX 4e DMM

XX

Limoges

Vichy

Lyon

XX 2e DIM

Bordeaux

XX 1re DMI

X

XX 9e DIC

Toulouse

Marseilles

Toulon

11. As indicated by the Seventh Army Report of Operations. On the other hand, the Armée B war diary (Journal des marches et opérations) makes no mention of it.

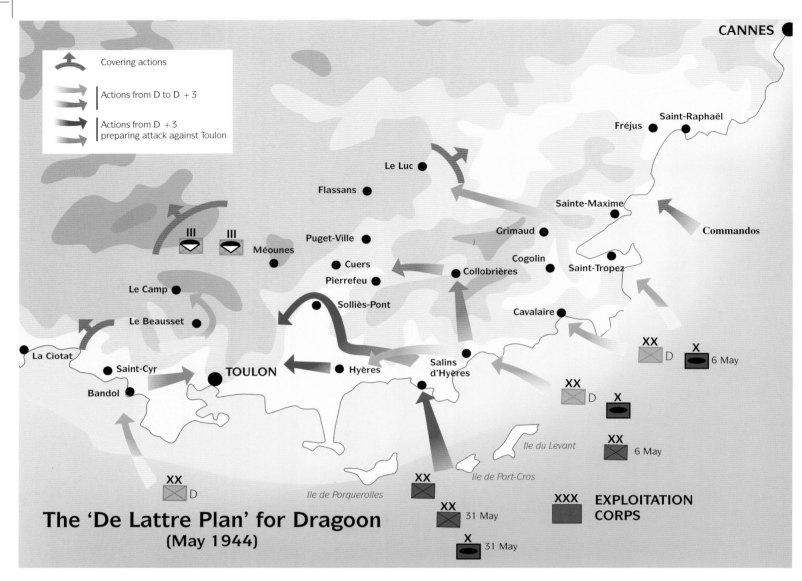

Covering actions

Actions from D to D + 3

Actions from D + 3 preparing attack against Toulon

The 'De Lattre Plan' for Dragoon
(May 1944)

assault from the sea, and the necessity of supporting two different landing zones weakened air and naval cover. The note concluded: "*because existing naval and air forces find it impossible to completely support ground operations, the plan in question is not considered either satisfactory, possible or acceptable.*"

Patch repeated these conclusions in a letter to De Lattre: even if the Toulon attack was launched from one side only, thus making a rapid capture of the city impossible, the advantages of a narrow beachhead and more favorable terrain outweighed all other considerations. Even though the plan was considered "*innovative and original* [12]", the proposed maneuver - very different in spirit and in letter from the one produced by Force 163 -

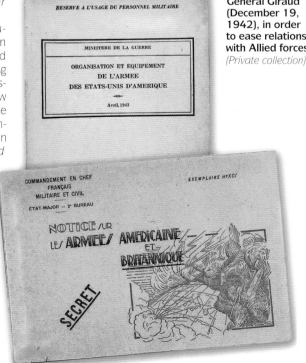

A Manual on the US Army published in April 1943 by the American War Department for French soldiers, and a French handbook on the American and British Armies, produced by the 2ᵉ bureau on orders from General Giraud (December 19, 1942), in order to ease relations with Allied forces. *(Private collection)*

had no chance of being acceptable to the methodical and experienced American planners.

LAST DITCH ATTEMPTS

The first objections to the Force 163 G-3 outline plan actually came from its own G-4 who didn't like the way the initial phase was to be carried out and especially the excessive delays concerning the capture of Toulon. They were considered unrealistic, because they held up the redeployment of the support units who would have to work from the beaches at least until D + 40. Its conclusion was clear: "*G–3 must revise the project… Rapid seizure of Toulon is essential to the following operations.*"

On June 17, elements of Armée B came ashore on the island of Elba with the support of the Allied Mediterranean naval and air forces. Operation 'Brassard' — whose primary objective was to assist the Fifth Army in its Northward progression resulted in violent fighting on the shore and heavy losses among the troops and the landing craft. This was a bad omen for the Provence invasion…

While preparations had been under way for an operation scheduled on May 25, De Gaulle had insisted that De Lattre control General Henri Martin, the 1st Corps commander. This was not to Wilson's liking. He considered this piling on of generals to be superfluous for such a little island, as well as a source of potential problems. In spite of this, Brigadier General Henry C. Wolfe traveled specially from Salerno

---
12. *La planification Anvil, op. cit.*

The invasion of Elba, on June 17, 1944
(From top to bottom)

The landing craft under fire from the coastal batteries.
(IWM A24382)

The British for the first time used smoke-laying barges, to shield the landing craft from enemy coastal batteries.
(IWM A24379)

The American LCT(5) 140 heading for the beach.
(IWM A24383)

British LCT(3) 356 nearing the beach.
(IWM A24381)

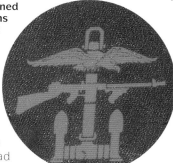

Armée B, and the French mission had integrated its G-3 section [14]. On June 22, G-3 presented a new plan, mentioning for the first time the VI Corps coming from Italy, and differing from the previous plans essentially by the increase in airborne troops, as well as the earlier commitment of the exploitation forces: D + 4 to D + 10 instead of D + 40 for the first corps, D + 15 to D + 40 instead of D + 90 for the second. Moreover the capture of the islands of Hyères was advanced to the night

Below:
Marina di Campo. After the conquest of the island, British commandos retrieve their dead on the quayside.
(Signal Corps)

13. Eight Years Overseas, *op. cit.*

14. *Lieutenant-Colonel Agostini had been the Armée B Assistant Chief of Staff since May 5, 1944, Colonel Demetz had taken over command of the 2e Dragons on June 1, 1944, and Colonel Petit was military governor of the island of Elba.*

to advise the French 9e division coloniale in amphibious training and Wilson promised the necessary planes to drop the 1er régiment de chasseurs parachutistes, even though "*it was likely that the paratroopers would miss the narrow peninsula where they were supposed to land and end up in the brine* [13]." Then the French requested and obtained that the operation be delayed until June 17. Wilson could no longer guarantee the necessary number of planes as they were now being used to move the tactical aviation units towards Rome.

Operation 'Brassard' finally took place as scheduled, but with no paratroopers.

A few days before, Force 163 had received the representatives of the French Air Force, Navy and

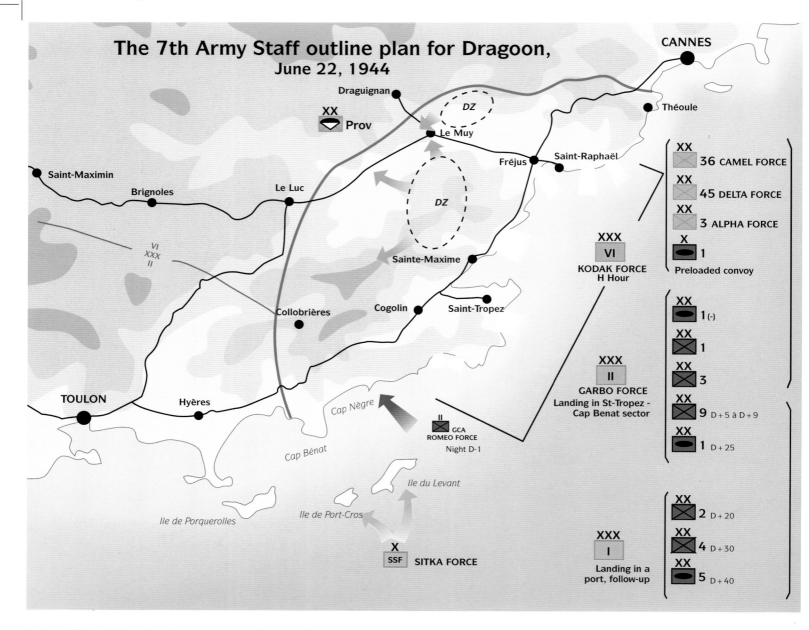

The 7th Army Staff outline plan for Dragoon, June 22, 1944

CANNES

Draguignan

DZ

XX Prov

Théoule

Le Muy

Fréjus Saint-Raphaël

Saint-Maximin

Brignoles

Le Luc

DZ

XX	36 CAMEL FORCE
XX	45 DELTA FORCE
XX	3 ALPHA FORCE
X	1

Preloaded convoy

VI
XXX
II

Sainte-Maxime

XXX
VI
KODAK FORCE
H Hour

Collobrières

Cogolin Saint-Tropez

XX	1 (-)
XX	1
XX	3

XXX
II
GARBO FORCE
Landing in St-Tropez -
Cap Benat sector

| XX | 9 D+5 à D+9 |
| XX | 1 D+25 |

TOULON Hyères

Cap Nègre

GCA
ROMEO FORCE
Night D-1

Cap Bénat

Ile du Levant

XX	2 D+20
XX	4 D+30
XX	5 D+40

XXX
I
Landing in a
port, follow-up

Ile de Porquerolles Ile de Port-Cros

X
SSF SITKA FORCE

---

between D-1 and D, and western cover was no longer ensured along the coastline.

The French Resistance movements, supported by the 1er RCP paratroopers were now tasked with "*harassing the enemy to the north and west of the assault zone and thus block any predictable movement of German armored reserves toward the beachhead on D-Day.*"

Like previous plans, this one was sent to the various commands for study and criticism. At VI Corps, Truscott thought that the scheduling should be revised. For 'Armée B,' the plan "*differs considerably from the first Anvil plan and concurs, in numerous instances, the plan proposed by the Commanding General of Armée B... In this plan, the idea of covering the assault on Toulon on the west side was not included because of the objections raised by the U.S. Navy about creating a new landing zone west of Toulon: the Seventh Army estimated that, to execute this cover under optimal conditions, it would need an airborne division which the Supreme Commander had refused to grant for the operation.*" [15]

The modified project - De Lattre finally obtained the requested west-side cover - after all was submitted to SACMED on June 28 and approved. Then on July 2, SACMED chief of staff Lieutenant General A.H. Gammell broke the news to Patch and suggested that the use of the airborne soldiers be reexamined in order to determine especially whether

Activated in August 1940 at Fort Sheridan, Illinois, VI Corps fought for the first time at Paestum on September 9, 1943. Then it took part in the Anzio landings in January 1944 and was the first to enter Rome in June.
(Le Poilu)

they should all jump as a group or spread out over three zones as had been planned.

Two days later, Force 163 started moving into Naples, occupying the Flambeau Building on the waterfront, which became Seventh Army headquarters.

On the 10th, "*the decision was made to transfer the [Armée B] headquarters to Naples where the Force 163 staff was settling. The move was to take place in four echelons: the 1st was scheduled to leave Algeria around July 12 and the 4th echelon was to leave about twenty days after the first* [16]." The first echelon boarded the *Arundel Castle* as planned and some of the officers reached Italy by plane the next day. Then on the 15th, the echelon moved into the Institut de France, via Francesco Crispi [17] at the foot of the Posilipo. All the command structures were now located in Naples (Seventh Army, Armée B and VI Corps [18]) a half-hour ride from the royal palace of Caserta where AFQH was based. The Seventh Army rear echelon, which had moved back from

---

15. Note on the Anvil plan, June 22, probably from the Armée B 3e bureau.
16. Armée B war diary.
17. According to the Armée B diary. In his memoirs, De Lattre situated his HQ in Caivano.
18. Their planning staff had been working since June 23, 1944 in the former barracks of Naples, while the headquarters were in Bagnoli.

Palermo to Mostaganem in May, was also present.

On July 21, after the complicated planning of the Toulon operation had been approved by General De Larminat, commander of the French 2nd Corps, De Lattre asked Patch to turn the French units originally placed under VI Corps or Seventh Army over to himself as soon as the Blue Line had been crossed [19].

Then, seven days later, during a conference in Naples attended by Admiral Lemonnier, the Navy chief of staff, De Lattre, counseled by Lemonnier, raised the question of forest fires in the wooded sections of the Maures massif:

"Forest fires are inevitable, whether they result from aerial bombings, artillery 'softening' or enemy action... [they] could compromise the success of the operation and even be an absolute obstacle to landings on some beaches. Therefore it seems necessary

to eliminate this risk by having all the areas vital to the invasion and the maneuvers burned over. [20]"

In spite of Larminat's hesitations who was *"not sure that the smoke would cause any more bother to the defenders than to the attackers, and that the main problem was the wind, which could not be predicted [21],"* De Lattre suggested lighting fires along the coast between the Rhône River and Genoa, close to military targets and in areas where the fires would easily spread. American aviators dutifully calculated the number of planes necessary to treat those areas with incendiary bombs, and then deemed the operation impossible. Then Wilson spoke up and politely dismissed the project [22].

On July 27, AFHQ changed the name of the operation from 'Anvil' to 'Dragoon,' and on August 1, 6th Army Group headquarters was activated in Bastia

19. Letter written by the 3rd bureau, corrected by the general and "probably dispatched with the cabinet seal ".

20. July 29 note, typewritten and unsigned, conserved without the blueprint of the regions to be burned mentioned in the text.
21. Chroniques irrévérencieuses, Plon 1962. Truscott was informed and admitted he was puzzled.
22. The decision forbidding forest fires was transmitted by the Seventh Army on August 2, 1944.
23. Study concerning a rapid advance toward the North through the Alps Mountains, August 12, 1944.
24. Hyères-Giens, Toulon, Sanary-Bandol, La Ciotat, Marseilles.
25. General De Lattre de Tassigny, Histoire de la Première Armée Française, Rhin et Danube, Plon, 1949.

The personnel of the Sixth Army Group received on October 23, 1944 a shoulder patch with six crossed bars on a red Army-color background.
(Le Poilu)

Left.
General De Larminat, commander of the 2e Corps d'Armée scheduled to lead the French forces for the invasion.
(DR)

(Corsica), for overall control of American and French forces in the South of France.

On August 7, Colonel Henri Zeller arrived from France by plane with information that, considering the perceptible weakness of the enemy defense along the coast, prompted the Army B G-3 to dream up *"a daring maneuver based on rapid action, local initiative and the dynamism of the French troops [23]."* He had noticed that the Dragoon Plan funneled the French in the corridor between the coast and the Rhône river, where they would have to tackle very strong German coastal strongholds one after the other [24], then move north in the Rhône valley where the enemy was entrenched and where invading armies could be slowed down for a considerable time. On the other hand, the VI Corps had received *"a relatively easy mission"* once the beachhead had been captured. So it was suggested that Armée B be steered *"in a bold advance through the Alps of Provence and Dauphiné or through the lower Alps in the Vaucluse and the Vercors toward the Isère River valley."*

The most realistic solution retained the Allied plan under its previous form but suggested *"as soon as possible after the landing, moving a group of armored units and mountain troops to the Durance River at Meyrargues, to begin their progression North through the lower Alps, trying to keep constantly one step ahead of the Americans"* in liaison with the FFI. It would thus be logical that this maneuver be assigned to Armée B, the FFI being its *"ardent advance guard."* This project was exposed to the Seventh Army commander, who rejected it outright. According to De Lattre, Patch *"seemed to think that my plan reflected a hidden desire to spare my troops from attacking Toulon and Marseilles [25]."*

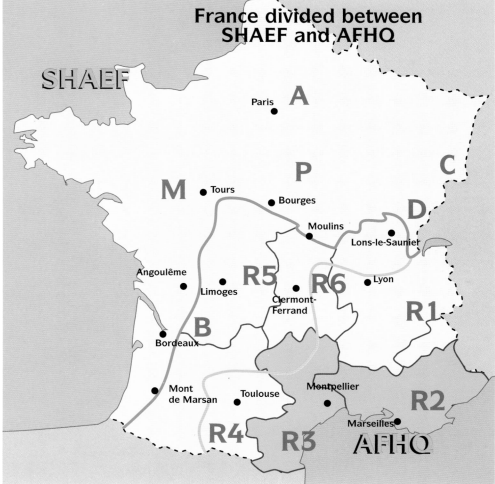

France divided between SHAEF and AFHQ

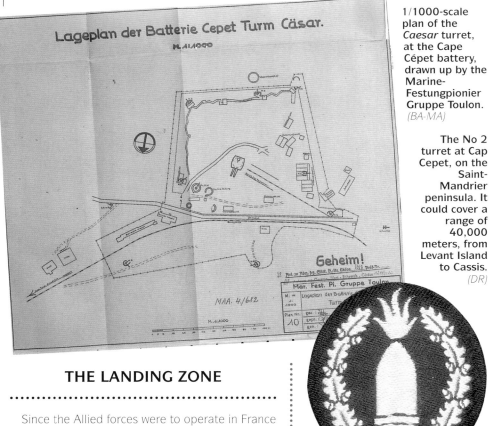

1/1000-scale plan of the *Caesar* turret, at the Cape Cépet battery, drawn up by the Marine-Festungpionier Gruppe Toulon. (BA-MA)

The No 2 turret at Cap Cepet, on the Saint-Mandrier peninsula. It could cover a range of 40,000 meters, from Levant Island to Cassis. (DR)

THE LANDING ZONE

Since the Allied forces were to operate in France under different supreme commanders, two zones were defined for airborne operations, the commitment of special forces, and future land operations. The 'borderline' between the London-based SHAEF and the Algiers-based AFHQ passed through the city of Lyons, then continued around the Eastern side of the Massif Central, and finally included much of the region around Toulouse. In the Southeast, the target area of Anvil was limited to the Rhône River valley, the Hautes-Alpes and the Italian border, while the landing area stretched from the Maures to the Esterel massifs.

During the early stages of planning, the Allied headquarters had rejected the coastline between Marseilles and Sète for a number of reasons: swamps, risks of flooding, poor landing possibilities, absence of important ports... The beaches west of Toulon were out of range for planes based in Corsica and those between Cannes and Nice were rejected as well, because there was no possibility of advancing directly inland. The choice was thus limited to the coastline between Cannes and Toulon.

The consequence was that the latter port became the primary target and would be the only logistics base before the capture of Marseilles. But the beaches of Hyères which were ideal in all other respects were in the direct line of fire of the coastal batteries on the Giens peninsula and the adjoining islands, and especially within range of the heavy artillery of the fortress of Toulon, particularly the 340s in Saint-Mandrier. Moreover, the narrowness of the roadstead would make naval bombing and mine dredging between the continent and the islands difficult.

So the choice available to the planners of the Seventh Army and the Eighth Fleet was finally reduced to the sector comprised between the bay of Cavalaire and Anthéor cove.

This area could be easily approached from the sea and had acceptable beaches with low tide variations, an abundance of little port towns that could be used for unloading supplies, and space for building airstrips. However these beaches were often isolated and separated from each other by rocky terrain with diffi-

German artillery proficiency badge. (PS Collection)

Below.
Vertical view of the port of Toulon.
(ISIS Report on Mediterranean France, Part VIII Ports, September 1943)

cult exits. And most importantly, they were dominated by high cliffs that would absolutely have to be taken if the Allies didn't want another Anzio, and that the troops holding the beachhead be counter-attacked or, worse, prevented from advancing further inland.

In spite of all this, eighteen beaches were selected in the assault zone: five from the Cavalaire bay to the Salins cape, six from the gulf of Saint-Tropez to the Pointe des Issambres, two in Fréjus-Saint-Raphaël, three from the Drammont to Anthéor and two in Théoule. In this region the road system was reduced to two highways between Saint-Raphaël and Toulon, rather narrow and easy to block: one hugged the coastline and the other the valley of the Argens River and then the corridor between Le Luc and Solliès-Pont. None of the other roads, narrow and poorly maintained, could be used for heavy military traffic:

"*Secondary and minor roads connect and supplement the main highways but these roads pass through mountainous terrain in most areas. Weakness of the road system, apart from its canalization and susceptibility to blocking by demolition, lies in its bridges, some of which are of extremely limited capacity. Traffic delays may also be caused by the fact that roads run through small towns and villages and become quite narrow at these points* [26]." And

there were only two railroad tracks: the main line between Saint-Raphaël and Toulon running inland beside the state highway, and the single-track line along the coast. Then there was the climate: mistral wind, sudden storms coming from the gulf of Genoa, intense heat and thunderstorms.

The Americans seemed to be especially worried about sanitary conditions and were afraid they would hamper the operational capacity of the landing troops. One of their major fears was venereal disease and prostitution which was widespread and uncontrolled. Next on the list was intestinal sickness diarrhea and dysentery caused by water pollution: "*Raw sewage is disposed of in streams and rivers and is also used as a ground fertilizer. Hence all sources of water are contaminated. Where water purification is attempted by slow sand filtration and chlorination the results obtained do not meet the United States Army standards [27].*" And finally malaria or dengue were endemic all along the coast and spread by the swamp mosquitoes.

THE DRAGOON PLAN

During July, while units along the Tuscany front had been relieved one by one and were getting back into shape in the South of Italy, preparations increased. Amphibious operations training began again for the three assault divisions, and the commander of the airborne task force began to assemble his units which were spread out all over the theater of operations.

The French units in Corsica and Italy recouped their losses in troops and materiel, and in North Africa the final touches were put on the equipment of the two armored divisions. But "*although equipping the French almost uniformly from American sources greatly simplified Anvil logistics, De Lattre's dependence on primarily non-French-speaking soldiers from France's overseas empire greatly limited the capabilities of his forces. The French white cadre who could handle colonial combat troops was stretched exceedingly thin and his staff and technical capabilities remained weak. Once ashore, more troops could be recruited over time, but for now he would have to make do with what manpower was available [28].*"

Early in August, the directives for ground, naval and air forces were settled and field orders written up [29]. On the tactical side, the need to rapidly capture the hills dominating the landing zones and build airstrips, compelled Seventh Army to define a wide beachhead that would have to be occupied as soon as possible. The Blue Line bordering this zone thus stretched from Cape Léoube curving North to La Napoule.

Between these two points there were around seventy kilometers of landing beaches. The selected beachhead was deep enough (thirty kilometers) to put the landing beaches out of reach of German long range guns, and wide enough to build airstrips and spread out supply dumps. It also allowed the first and second landing echelons to maneuver freely and prepare their defense in case of an enemy counter-

26. VI Corps Field Order No 1, Operation Anvil, dated July 30, 1944.
27. Ibid.
28. Jeffrey J. Clarke, Southern France, 15 August-14 September 1944, US Army Center of Military History, Washington 1992.
29. Seventh Army on July 29, 1944; Armée B on August 8, 1944; VI Corps on July 30, 1944; 3rd and 36th divs on August 1, 1944; 45th div. on August 2, 1944; 1st ABTF on August 5, 1944.

More photos from the ISIS Report on Mediterranean France, Part VIII Beaches, May 1943

From top to bottom:
The Porquerolles bay and wharf seen from Fort Sainte-Agathe looking west.

Western part of Cavalaire Beach (Beach 259), showing the sand dikes protecting the road and railway.

The village of Anthéor between the sea and the Esterel massif.

attack.

During the night preceding the actual landing, paratroopers and special units would be committed to protect the invasion area flank:
- the 1st Special Service Force in the Hyères islands;
- the Groupe de Commandos d'Afrique at Cap Nègre, west of Cavalaire;
- the First Airborne Task Force, including nine parachute or glider infantry battalions, in the Argens River valley, around Le Muy;
- the Groupe naval d'assaut de Corse at Le Trayas, near Théoule.

VI Corps was to land on three different beaches between Cavalaire and Pampelonne, northeast of

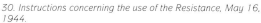

REGION SUD-EST

Situation des FFI au 1er Aout 44

force General Cochet, the military representative for the French government in the Southern theater of operations since April 22, but whose command would only become effective once the invasion had started.

In the meantime, Cochet would act as liaison, as well as buffer between the unhappy French civilian leaders and the equally disgruntled Allied leaders, since he had to at the same time execute the orders of the provisional government in Algiers [30] and do his best to satisfy the requests of the Allied command in Caserta [31].

Wilson particularly hoped that the FFI could furnish as much help as possible in upsetting the German troop movements and assisting the progression of the Allied landing forces.

The missions assigned to the FFI were, in order:

Sainte-Maxime, and between Saint-Raphaël and Anthéor each assigned to a different division: 3rd, 45th and 36th.

The entire assault echelon was to embark in the area around Naples or take off by plane from the Rome area, excepting the special troops leaving from Corsica. General Aimé Sudre's Combat Command No 1 would embark in Oran and was to land with the first waves and assemble near Fréjus to prepare to attack toward the west up the Argens River valley.

Two French infantry divisions (1re division de marche d'infanterie - DMI - and the 3e division d'in-

Above.
Excerpt taken from the 1/1,000,000-scale map showing the positions of the FFI in the Southeast regions on August 1, 1944.
(Private collection)

Right.
Gathering weapons containers dropped to the maquis.
(OFIC)

Left.
Wings worn by Allied 'Special Forces' advisors to the Résistance.
(Private collection)

Below.
Dropping arms and supplies to the maquis from American heavy bombers.
(OFIC)

30. *Instructions concerning the use of the Resistance, May 16, 1944.*
31. *AFHQ directive issued on July 29, 1944 and SPOC employment plan of August 1, 1944.*

fanterie algérienne - DIA, sailing from Taranto) and the rest of the 1re division blindée (DB, 1st French armored division, sailing from Oran minus one combat command), were scheduled to reach the Alpha sector beaches on D + 1.

Coming from Corsica, the 9e division d'infanterie coloniale (DIC) and the two groups of Moroccan Tabors would be the next to land, on D + 9. But the rest of the 2nd French Corps, including the 1re DB's third Combat Command would not rally before D + 25.

The capture of Toulon by the French was scheduled for September 3 (D + 20), and that of Marseilles around September 25 (D + 40 to D + 45).

And the armed 'Maquis' whose numbers in the target area were estimated on August 1 at 8,000, were relied upon in the plans. The FFI had been originally directed from London because Anvil was conceived as support for Overlord, but then they came under the control of AFHQ from July 8 on. At that time their action was controlled by the Special Project Operations Center, an Interallied organization associated with the AFHQ G-3, with an attached French section and a liaison with the Seventh Army.

The FFI were also under the orders of French air

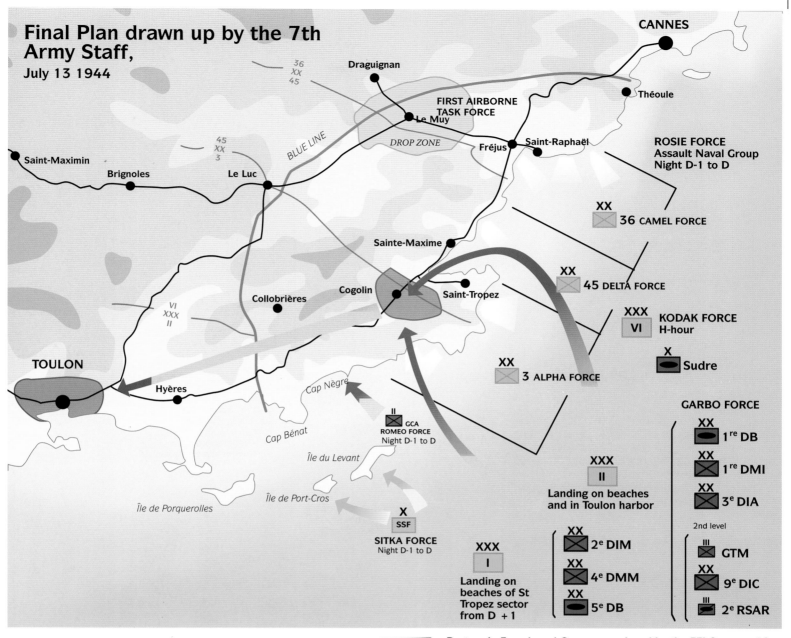

Final Plan drawn up by the 7th Army Staff,
July 13 1944

CANNES

Draguignan

36
XX
45

Théoule

FIRST AIRBORNE
TASK FORCE

Le Muy

DROP ZONE

BLUE LINE

45
XX
3

Fréjus

Saint-Raphaël

ROSIE FORCE
Assault Naval Group
Night D-1 to D

Saint-Maximin

Brignoles

Le Luc

XX
36 CAMEL FORCE

Sainte-Maxime

Collobrières

Cogolin

Saint-Tropez

XX
45 DELTA FORCE

VI
XXX
II

XXX
VI
KODAK FORCE
H-hour

TOULON

Hyères

Cap Nègre

XX
3 ALPHA FORCE

X
Sudre

Cap Bénat

II
GCA
ROMEO FORCE
Night D-1 to D

GARBO FORCE

Île du Levant

XXX
II

Landing on beaches
and in Toulon harbor

XX
1re DB

XX
1re DMI

XX
3e DIA

Île de Port-Cros

Île de Porquerolles

X
SSF

SITKA FORCE
Night D-1 to D

XXX
I

Landing on
beaches of St
Tropez sector
from D + 1

XX
2e DIM

XX
4e DMM

XX
5e DB

2nd level

III
GTM

XX
9e DIC

III
2e RSAR

- destroy bridges, cut rail lines and block roads;

- initiate diversionary actions to lure German forces away from the Allied beachhead;

- cut telephone and telegraph wires in all of the South of France;

- attack fuel and ammunition depots, sabotage airstrips and harass isolated garrisons;

- be prepared to undertake actions on the regular units' flanks.

To accomplish these missions, the FFI were assisted by various Special Forces teams - Interallied missions, Jedburgh teams, Operational groups, counter-sabotage groups [32] - and had received important arms drops from Blida in Algeria or from England.

On August 10, SACMED received orders to execute Operation Dragoon as planned and the commander of Armée B "*arrived in Taranto by plane from Naples. He immediately boarded the* Batory *where he met Admiral Guéguard [sic], leader of the* Montcalm *and* Georges Leygues *cruiser division* [33]." Two convoys ferrying French troops had already set to sea, one from Oran, the other from Taranto, and the first attack force from Salerno had just crossed the Bonifacio straits heading for Ajaccio.

PROVISORISCHE REGIERUNG
DER FRANZÖSISCHEN REPUBLIK

AN ALLE ANGEHÖRIGEN
Der Deutschen Wehrmacht Und Gestapo!

GOUVERNEMENT PROVISOIRE
DE LA RÉPUBLIQUE FRANÇAISE

A tous les membres
de la Wehrmacht et de la Gestapo!

Posters in French and German produced by the FFI Command for "members of the Wehrmacht and the Gestapo," threatening them with retaliation should they harm the civilian population.
(Private collection)

In the air, the first phase of the preparatory operations was just being completed: the Mediterranean Allied Air Forces had dropped more than 12,500 tons of bombs.

After months of hemming and hawing, the signal for the 'other invasion,' the Provence landings, was finally on.

---

32. See Paul Gaujac, Special Forces in the Invasion of France, Histoire & Collections, *1999.*
33. Armée B war diary. He is referring to Vice-amiral Jaujard, commander of the 4th Cruiser Division.

MEANWHILE IN PROVENCE

On November 11, 1942, the German and Italian forces had crossed the demarcation line and invaded the southern half of France. Then, on September 8, 1943, the Germans took the place of the Italians, and the whole Mediterranean shore came under Wehrmacht control, which set about improving its defense.

The soldiers from across the Rhine would live *"wie Gott im Frankreich* [1]*"* a little longer but the threat of an invasion became imminent: Allied bombers started to appear more frequently and the French resistance fighters increased the tempo of their ambushes, while at the same time the disposition of German forces in the South was weakened in favor of the Normandy front after June 6, 1944.

Top, left.
The German navy U-Boot crew badge.
(Reconstruction by Militaria Magazine)

Above.
Gunner of an Army GHQ coast artillery battalion.
(Provence 44)

Left.
Vehicles from the SS Panzer Corps Signal Battalion 101 parked under the palm trees on the Place de la Liberté in Toulon.
(DR)

DIE WACHT AM MITTELMEER [2]

The German 19th Army was in charge of defending the Mediterranean coastline. It originated as a 'for special employment' HQ created in Königsberg in March 1940 and which, after guarding the demarcation line, became the LXXXII Corps at the end of May 1942. Also called Armeegruppe Felber [3], it participated in the invasion of the unoccupied zone of France and then settled in Marseilles to take charge of the four divisions assigned to coastal defense.

On August 5, 1943, General der Infanterie Georg von Sodenstern took over command of what was to become, three weeks later, the 19th Army. Then a Gruppe Kniess [4] was created to head the three divisions on the East side of the Rhone River and a liaison staff was set up in each 'Département' major town [5].

For the Germans, Southern France was naturally just about the last of their worries. But when the Allies landed at Anzio on January 22, 1944, they took notice, because that could be the first of a series of actions designed to compel them to disperse their forces. Consequently, the seven French départements along the Mediterranean coast were placed entirely under military administration [6]. Then, on March 20, Marshall Erwin Rommel was tasked with improving the defenses along the Southern coast.

At the beginning of April, the 19th Army received the staff of the LXII Reserve Corps who, on arrival in Draguignan, were given charge of the 148th and 242nd divisions while the Gruppe Kniess headed the 338th, detached from the Luftwaffe 4th Corps. Then to insure the coordination of all the forces South of the Loire River, Army Group G was activated on May 3. But it was only an Armeegruppe - a temporary command less important in the hierarchy than a Heeresgruppe - assigned to Generaloberst Johannes Blaskowitz [7] who installed his headquarters on May 12 in Rouffiac, near Toulouse.

At that time the amphibious capacities of the Allies had been more correctly appraised and the fear of a major operation - to be launched in liaison with an attack in the North and using the numerous forces remaining in North Africa after the landing in Anzio - vanished. The Oberkommando der Wehrmacht was convinced that any action in the South of France would be nothing more significant than a bit of saber-rattling.

However no specific strategy in case of an offensive against 'Fortress Europe' had been defined. Field Marshal Gerd von Runstedt, commander on the Western front, was in favor of keeping the reserves back from the coastline in order to be able to counter-attack any landing forces. Blaskowitz and Sodenstern agreed: rather than defending a static front, they preferred moving inland and waging a battle of movement there. But Rommel, who had experienced the Allied superiority in air power, wanted to assign heavier forces to the defense of the coastline. This solution, implying that not an inch of territory would be lost, was naturally the one which won Adolf Hitler's approval.

---

1. "Like God in France," the German equivalent of "the life of Riley."
2. Watch on the Mediterranean, the German 19th Army news sheet.
3. Named for General der Infanterie Hans Felber, who later left for Serbia.
4. Named for General der Infanterie Baptist Kniess, former commander of the LXVI. Reserve-Korps in Clermont-Ferrand.
5. Verbindungsstäbe 747 in Nîmes, 761 in Avignon and 497 in Marseilles, 792 in Digne, 800 in Toulon and then Draguignan, 994 in Nice, and Hauptverbindungsstab 894 in Marseilles, then in Eguilles.
6. On February 15, 1944, each liaison staff took the title and prerogatives of a Feldkommandantur.
7. He fell out of favor after opposing the German occupation policy in Poland. He had commanded the 1st Army in Bordeaux since October 24, 1940.

Above.
Breast badge of Heer Flak crews.
(Private Collection)

Above.
Living 'like God in France' in the Riviera sunshine, soldiers take a break under parasols while waiting to resume work near a 'Tobruk' - a French Somua tank turret in a concrete pit - built at the base of the north wharf at La Ciotat.
(ECPAD)

But the 19th Army had trouble enforcing the Führer's orders fixing the line of resistance on the coast. Blaskowitz was to witness this when he inspected the sector east of the Rhône at the end of May: the only organized areas were Marseilles, Toulon, La Ciotat, Fréjus and Cannes.

Right.
Documents published by the Kommandant des Heeresgebiets Südfrankreich. War diary (Verordnungsblatt) dated February 15, 1944 and "execution" (Vollstreckungsplan) plan of July 12, 1944 listing detention conditions for German or French delinquents, men and women.
(Private Collection)

Soldiers from Arbeitsabteilung 7/284 of the Reichsarbeitsdienst (RAD) building a camouflaged shelter beside the Californie airfield in Nice.
(ECPAD)

Organization Todt collar patch.
(Private collection)

Below.
Important construction projects (blockhouses, antitank walls, etc.) were controlled by the Organization Todt which subcontracted to French companies, as seen here in the construction of a submarine base at Cap Janet in Marseilles.
(ECPAD)

ers was very dangerous. Not only could the enemy thus gain information about the position, the type and the size of the constructions, but there was considerable risk of sabotage, for example in the quality of the concrete used. The will and the aptitude of these workers were not as good as those of the Germans. The same thing could be said of the Italian soldiers, because of the despondency that characterized their officers and their reticence to actually consider themselves part of our common cause... The cases of venereal disease were extremely numerous in their ranks, and this was also true of the Madagascans and the Senegalese, who were not very efficient either. And the Indochinese were even worse. [11"]

In addition to these difficulties, there was the crying lack of materials and means of transportation, which led the O.T. to give preference to jobs that were located near railway lines. The organization also had other work that took priority, such as surveillance of the bauxite mines and construction of pens in Toulon or Marseilles for the subs operating in the Western Mediterranean. This base was never built, but nevertheless it attracted American bombers, which meant that Flak units were reinforced in these sectors to the detriment of certain others. The Flak was also protecting the Anthéor viaduct and the Saint-Laurent-du-Var bridge supporting the railway line to Italy [12].

Finally, the defensive system was lacking in density and depth. Thus Navy regulations, specifying that all guns be

Each division was responsible for its sector. But their limited resources were hardly sufficient for day-to-day activities, so major projects were controlled by the corps of fortress engineers [8] who took charge of overseeing construction work. Since the Festungs-Pionier-Kommandeur I attached to the 19th Army had no construction units at his disposal, the Organization Todt took charge of recruiting a workforce. The OT worked with German firms and used French companies, Italian pioneers [9], French colonial soldiers or French civilians, volunteers or not. Theoretically, coastal defences were built according to defined models, and the Engineers' job was to certify that the work was done correctly and was well suited to the type of terrain [10]. Once completed, the works had to be camouflaged. This was an important task but sometimes completely wasted, since the O.T. - usually more interested in efficiency than in discretion - may not have bothered to screen the work site from land or airborne observers.

"*Even though it was necessary, the use of French work-*

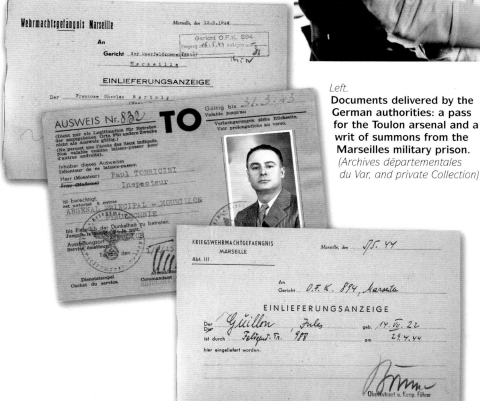

Left.
Documents delivered by the German authorities: a pass for the Toulon arsenal and a writ of summons from the Marseilles military prison.
(Archives départementales du Var, and private Collection)

turned toward the sea, meant that firing inland was impossible, and the Germans only began strengthening their gun pits with concrete after January 1944. And even though a second line of defense, inland from the coast, had been reconnoitred, there were neither men nor materials available to build it.

In June 1944, 300 defensive works had been finished or were being built along the coast:

---

8. Three companies between Sanary and the Italian border before August 6, 1944.
9. In the sector controlled by the 242. ID, six companies - 86 Germans and 1,300 Italians - working for the OT, and one in Sainte-Maxime working for the fortress engineers.
10. There were 320 different types of constructions: strongpoints (24), pillboxes (38), gun (71) or machine gun (99) pits, shelters (88).
11. Interview with Generalmajor Wilhelm Ullersperger, in Allendorf on March 26, 1947.
12. Flak-Abteilung 481, a mixed semi-mobile group with three 88-mm batteries and three 20s, positioned in Agay, Anthéor and Théoule. The bridge on the Var was protected by Flak-Abteilung 391 with four 88-mm batteries, one 37 and one 20.

Generaloberst Johannes Blaskowitz was in disgrace since he had opposed the German occupation methods in Poland in 1939. He shared command south of the Loire River with the *Kommandant des Heeresgebiets Südfrankreich* in Lyons.

● in the Toulon defense sector (111 km-long): 41 finished, including 9 for the Kriegsmarine; 36 under construction;

● between Cavalaire and Agay (154 km): 61 finished including 8 for the Kriegsmarine; 35 under construction;

● between Agay and the Italian border (131 km): 93 finished including 3 for the Luftwaffe; 22 under construction;

● the Lerins islands (11 km): 6 finished.

Concerning land mines and obstacles, Marshall Rommel, during his inspection, prescribed planting them on the beaches at low tide. But there were not enough mines to go around and most of the signs warning of land mines put up by the Germans were lures, signaling mine fields that did not exist. However regularly spaced wooden stakes were planted upright in wide empty tracts that could be used for landing gliders.

When the Allies landed in Normandy, all of the coastal sectors in Southern France were put on alert, and the OKW was also afraid of an operation on the Ligurian coast or the Riviera in support of the Allied progression through Italy. When they realized that they had nothing to fear from that area, the Western command borrowed some units from Army Group G.

Thus two of the three German armored divisions stationed in the Southwest moved up to the Normandy front, and were soon followed by one of the two tank battalions belonging to the third. The 1st Army and then the 19th were also asked to contribute. The latter lost an infantry

So not only did the 19th Army have to reinforce the front North of the Loire River and prepare to resist an Allied amphibious action in the South, but it also had to face increasing 'terrorist' activity, notably by the Maquis. Therefore, in order to step up the fight against the partisans and better coordinate the preparations for any future invasion, eleven French Départements, including the seven along the Mediterranean coast, were declared 'combat zones' on June 17. From then on, the 19th Army commander had total control in these zones [14] and all territorial services, including security forces, came under his orders.

On June 29, General der Infanterie Friedrich Wiese [15] replaced Sodenstern, who had been dismissed, as head of the 19th Army.

13. Reserve-Division, whose main mission was training personnel sent as reinforcements to the field divisions.
14. Corresponding exactly to FFI regions R.2 and R.3.
15. Since August 5, 1943, commander of the XXXV. AK which was annihilated at Bobruisk in June 1944.

A 2 cm Flak gun during an exercise on the northern wharf of La Ciotat harbor.
(ECPAD)

regiment, artillery battalions and the antitank companies attached to four divisions. In Languedoc, the three divisions were replaced by others in the process of being reconstituted or called in from the Massif Central [13]. Then the Flak protecting the bridges over the Rhone left. In compensation, the Gruppe Kniess was raised to the level of a corps on July 10, but that was not much of a consolation. The German deployment was at that time:

	Sector	Length	HQ
LXXXV. AK			*Taillades*
338. ID	*Petit Rhône-Sausset-les-Pins*	*95 km*	*Barbegal*
244.ID	*Carry-le-Rouet-Bandol*	*80 km*	*Marseilles*
LXII. Res.K			*Draguignan*
242. ID	*Sanary - Anthéor*	*150 km*	*Brignoles*
148. RD13	*Le Trayas-Italian border*	*100 km*	*Grasse*

GERMAN BEACH OBSTACLES

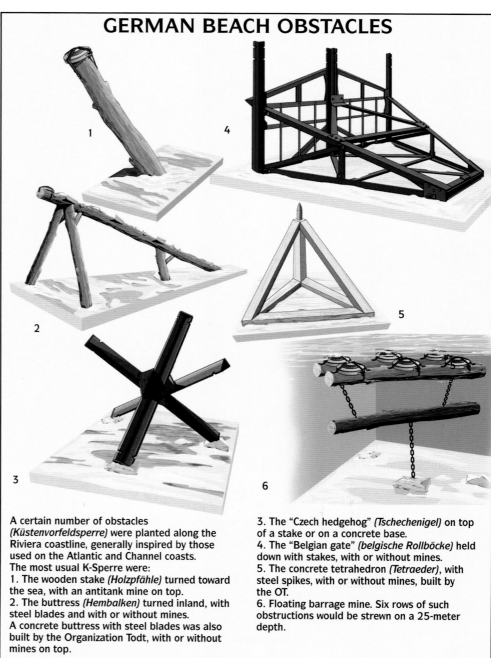

A certain number of obstacles *(Küstenvorfeldsperre)* were planted along the Riviera coastline, generally inspired by those used on the Atlantic and Channel coasts. The most usual K-Sperre were:
1. The wooden stake *(Holzpfähle)* turned toward the sea, with an antitank mine on top.
2. The buttress *(Hembalken)* turned inland, with steel blades and with or without mines.
A concrete buttress with steel blades was also built by the Organization Todt, with or without mines on top.

3. The "Czech hedgehog" *(Tschechenigel)* on top of a stake or on a concrete base.
4. The "Belgian gate" *(belgische Rollböcke)* held down with stakes, with or without mines.
5. The concrete tetrahedron *(Tetraeder)*, with steel spikes, with or without mines, built by the OT.
6. Floating barrage mine. Six rows of such obstructions would be strewn on a 25-meter depth.

BETWEEN SANARY AND ANTHÉOR

••

The shore stretching from Toulon to the Italian border was placed under the responsibility of the LXII. Reserve-Korps, which had been activated in September 1942 to lead the reserve divisions stationed in Ukraine. It had been commanded since its creation by Generalleutnant Ferdinand Neuling, and was transferred to France in January 1944. After a short stay in Bourg-en-Bresse, the corps moved to Draguignan on April 8 [16], where it was located together with other Army ancillary services in the city proper [17] or its vicinity [18].

In Toulon the German Navy was everywhere: submarines, coastal patrol boats, coastal artillery, antiaircraft batteries, signal, port protection, smoke screens, arsenals... Naval detachments were also present in every port along the coast: Saint-Tropez [19], Sainte-Maxime and Saint-Raphael.

The Luftwaffe was also represented by Flak batteries, of which two-thirds were located around Toulon and the remainder divided up among the Anthéor viaduct and the Le Luc and Cuers airfields [20]. Cuers also harbored a tactical reconnaissance flight, and a maritime reconnaissance flight was operating out of Saint-Mandrier and the Etang de Berre [21]. And the entire defense network depended heavily on numerous signals units: technical in Vidauban [22], monitoring at Cap Sicié, Pierrefeu and Mont-Agel [23], detection in Carqueiranne, Agay and Collobrières[24].

The defense of the coast from Sanary to Anthéor was assigned to the 242. Infanterie-Division, led by General-major Hans Baessler. This division had been activated in July 1943 at the Gross-Born camp in Pomerania, by changing the name of a month-old formation, on the basis of what was left of a Silesian division that had been annihilated in Ukraine. On August 3rd, it was assigned to the OB West, and left for Liège (Belgium), then moved into Southern France in September. It was first assigned as a reserve unit for the 19th Army while finishing its activa-

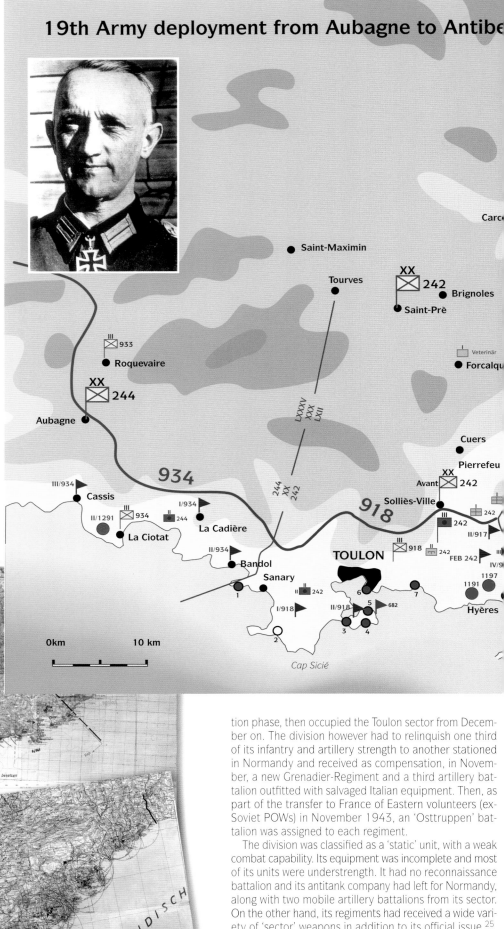

tion phase, then occupied the Toulon sector from December on. The division however had to relinquish one third of its infantry and artillery strength to another stationed in Normandy and received as compensation, in November, a new Grenadier-Regiment and a third artillery battalion outfitted with salvaged Italian equipment. Then, as part of the transfer to France of Eastern volunteers (ex-Soviet POWs) in November 1943, an 'Osttruppen' battalion was assigned to each regiment.

The division was classified as a 'static' unit, with a weak combat capability. Its equipment was incomplete and most of its units were understrength. It had no reconnaissance battalion and its antitank company had left for Normandy, along with two mobile artillery battalions from its sector. On the other hand, its regiments had received a wide variety of 'sector' weapons in addition to its official issue [25].

The division had inherited from the Italians a sketchy defensive organization that it tried to improve as best it could. For this, the fortress engineers gave precious technical assistance as the coastal works which were to bear the brunt of the assault were concerned. However, at the

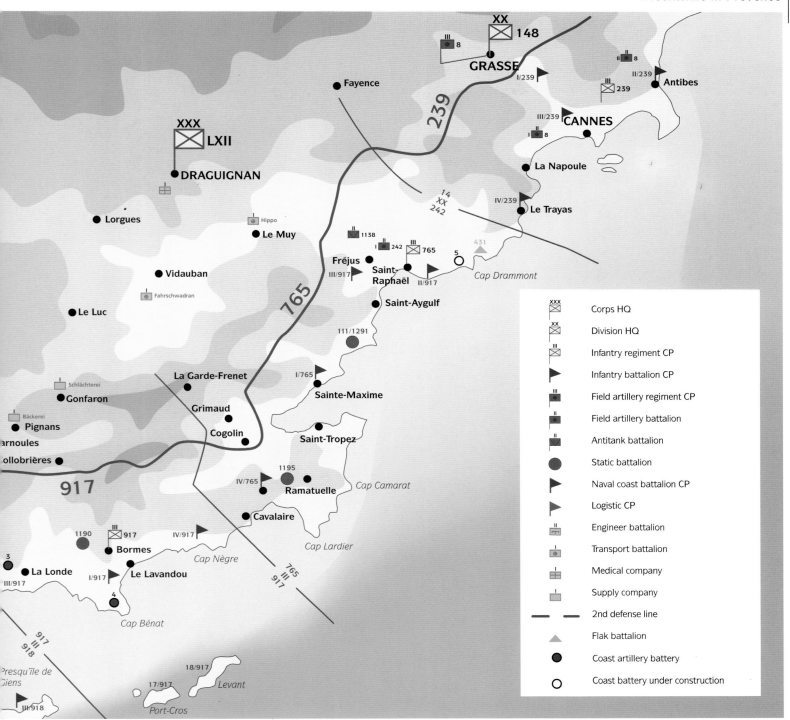

	918. GR	917. GR	765. GR	Tot.
Light MGs	92	31	53	176
Heavy MGs	87	62	93	242
Flame Throwers	106	111	138	195
50-mm Mortars	73	9	18	100
81-mm Mortars	27	-	21	48
20-mm Guns	21	24	-	45
88-mm Rocket Launchers	3	2	3	8
French 25-mm AT guns	1	1	-	2
French 37-mm AT guns	-	3	-	3
Russian 45-mm AT guns	5	5	2	12
Czech 47-mm AT guns	-	3	1	4
French 47-mm AT guns	7	-	-	7
Italian 47-mm AT guns	8	-	-	8
7,5 PaK Guns	5	1	3	9
8,8 PaK Guns	4	1	1	6
French AA 75-mm guns	-	-	12	12
German 65-mm CA guns	12	3	5	20
French 75-mm CA guns	14	-	4	18
Italian 75-mm CA guns	5	21	3	29
Russian 76,2-mm CA guns	9	8	-	17
Czech 80-mm CA guns	-	2	-	2
Czech 100-mm CA guns	-	1	-	1
French 105-mm CA guns	-	-	2	2

Previous page, inset
General der Infanterie Freidrich Wiese,
nine years younger than his immediate
superior, served in the Freikorps in
1919. He was rapidly promoted, and
was a fervent Nazi
in the eyes of the Americans.
(DR)

Previous page, bottom
**German map indicating artillery units
in the LXII. Reserve-Korps sector on
July 25,1944, including information
about the range of their guns.**
(BA-MA)

Previous page, far left.
**A May 25, 1944 map of the Fréjus
strongpoint.**
(BA-MA)

16. Accompanied by motorized signal company 462, and Artillery
Commander (Arko) 219, that is 400 men including 30 officers.
17. Nachschubstab zbV 281, supply company 1/609, transport
company 4/989, field hospital 217, medical transportation company
1/591 and ammunition depot.
18. Transport company 5/995 at Les Arcs, fuel dump near La Motte,
traffic control center, army postal service, bakery, supply center,
horse-drawn train squadron at Le Muy, stables at Puget-sur-Argens.
19. 125 sailors armed with 5 light anti-aircraft guns and 7 machine
guns.
20. Each one protected by a battery of 20-mm guns and a company
from the 3rd Battalion Flieger-Regiment 90.
21. 2./Nahaufklärhiten 13 and 2./ Seeaufklärungsstaffel 128.
22. 2nd company from the Luftnachrichten-Betriebs-Abteilung zbV 16,
attached to the territorial regiment in charge of the South of France.
23. Platoons from the 9th company of the Luftnachrichten-
Funkhorch-Regiment West.
24. 4th and 8th companies of the Ln-Rgt 51, 20th company from
the Ln-Rgt 52 (Laquina summit) all three assigned to the
II. Jagdkorps in Chantilly through the Jagdführer Süd-Frankreich in
Aix-en-Provence.
25. Numbers as of July 25, 1944: AT - antitank, AA - anti-aircraft,
CA - coastal artillery.

Breast badge for Kriegsmarine Flak gun crews.
(Private Collection)

One of the two 75-mm French guns in concrete pits for the close defense of the coastal battery emplaced on the Plateau des Plaines Marines. Its 130-mm gun covered the bay of La Ciotat between the Deffend point and the Bec de l'Aigle.
(DR)

Right.
One of the six 88-mm guns of the antiaircraft battery on the cliffs of Cap Janet, overlooking the Remisage or winter docking basin in Marseilles.
(DR)

beginning there had been no cooperation whatsoever with the Kriegsmarine, who made up the major part of the German forces in Toulon, and thus the shore batteries where neither capable of firing inland nor were they protected on this side. And the Flak, which was part of another command system, manifested its independence and refused to cooperate.

At first the 202nd division staff was located in Solliès-Pont, along with the forward CP, but then headquarters had been transferred to the Château de Saint-Pré, near Brignoles. The support units were spread out among a number of inland towns - Vidauban, Pignans, Carnoules, Gonfaron, Forcalquier - and the Gapeau River valley.

Each of the three infantry regiments had been assigned a portion of the coastline. On the west side, Grenadier-Regiment 918 occupied the sector between Sanary and the Gapeau River. GR 918 actually formed the infantry component of the Toulon defenses, and was involved with the numerous coastal [26] and antiaircraft [27] batteries in position around the port. Its elements were stationed as follows: CP in La Valette, 1st battalion near Six-Fours, 2nd between Saint-Mandrier and Le Pradet, part of the 3rd on the island of Porquerolles, the 4th, the Armenian battalion [28], held the positions around Hyeres. The two companies of the combat engineer battalion in La Farlède worked for this regiment. In its sector could also be found Feld-Ersatz-Bataillon [29], which was finally composed of two rifle companies and one of engineers, split between La Crau and Solliès-Pont.

Artillerie-Regiment 242 was garrisoned near La Farlède and was the command post of the field artillery in this defensive sector, with four battalions - two from the regiment and two from the GHQ reserve [30] - turned towards the bay of Sanary and Hyères harbor.

In the center GR 917 had its CP at Bormes-les-Mimosas and three battalions along the coastal strip: the 3rd near La Londe-les-Maures, the 1st at Le Lavandou and the Armenian 4th battalion [31] around Cap Nègre and on the Port-Cros and Levant islands, off Hyères. Its 2nd battalion, stationed near La Farlède, was the only reserve of the division. In its sector, the two coastal batteries of Mauvanne and Cap Bénat covered the Hyères roadstead, and a field battalion was positioned near Bormes [32].

To the east was positioned GR 765, created on November 12, 1943, from elements of a battalion of the 319th Division garrisoning the Channel islands. At first it was supposed to be part of the 715. ID, in the Nice region, but was finally assigned to the 242nd and beefed up by personnel from the two other regiments. Its 4th (Osttruppen) battalion, made up of Azerbaijanis [33], protected the beaches of the Saint-Tropez peninsula, and the 1st battalion was billeted on both sides of Sainte-Maxime. The rest of the regiment was holding the outlet of the Argens River valley: CP in Valescure, 3rd battalion between Fréjus and Saint-Raphaël, and 2nd at the eastern end of the sector. It was reinforced there by two batteries from a recently-formed antitank battalion [34], its third being assigned to the field artillery in Ramatuelle. Four battalions or batteries were spread out along the coast: Ramatuelle, San Peire-sur Mer, Le Drammont. At Anthéor, the Flak 88s covered the viaduct approaches.

Of the three Grenadier units, GR 765 was the most vulnerable:

"It had recently been formed during the spring of 1944 and had only partially completed its basic training. Its 4th battalion, the 807th Azerbaijani Bn., was a unit from the Eastern front, of doubtful reliability, whereas the three oth-

Previous page.
One of the six 88-mm guns of the antiaircraft battery installed in the old Endoume fort, across from the Château d'If, visible at the back of the picture between Ratonneau and Pomègues Islands.
(ECPAD)

Right, from top to bottom.
In Sanary bay, access to the small port of La Coudoulière is barred by an antitank wall of concrete pyramids built by the Italians.

South of Le Pradet, on the Garonne bay, a Tobruk (tank turret on a concrete base) defending the little port of Bonnettes.
(DR)

On the Pointe des Ponchettes in Nice, a 75-mm gun is able to fire down the beach's length.

Kriegsmarine coastal artillery NCO shoulder strap.
(Private Collection)

The *Pescagel*, a fishing trawler transformed into a submarine chaser in the Toulon arsenal. It is fitted here with a dual 37-mm antiaircraft mount.
(ECPAD)

ers had in their ranks a large proportion of Germans coming from Sudetenland, Poland, Russia or the Baltic countries. How long would these forces be able to resist an important attack? That was the question. [35]"

WHAT DID THE ALLIES REALLY KNOW?

Thanks to aerial photography, to intelligence relayed by the French Resistance, to information furnished by pris-

26. 9 manned by the Navy, including 4 105-mm guns, 4 120s, 11 138s, 4 150s, 7 164s and 2 340s.
27. 7 manned by the Navy and 8 by the Air Force, including a total of 46 88-mm guns and 18 100s or 105s.
28. Ex-armenisches Feld-Btl I/198.
29. Divisional training and reinforcement unit.
30. II and III/AR 242, Heeres-Artillerie-Abteilungen 1191 and 1197, including 14 batteries of Czech 105-mm howitzers and Italian 100s or 146s.
31. Ex-armenisches Feld-Btl II/9.
32. 3. and 4./Marine-Artillerie Abteilung 627 and Heeres-Artillerie-Abteilung 1190 including two batteries of 105s or 150s and three batteries of Italian 100-mm howitzers.
33. Ex-aserbeidschanisches Feld-Btl 807, CP in Ramatuelle.
34. Artillerie-Pak-Abteilung 1038 (bodenständig) created in Prussia in June, 1944. CP at Camp Galliéni.
35. Riviera to the Rhine, op. cit.

ZAC 5. LXTB. 40325/3 - P

1

Left, below, and opposite page.
Photographs taken in Nice from February 12 to 17, 1944 by French Agent ZAC 5 and sent to Algiers.
(Private Collection)

1. Wooden footbridge over the Var above Saint-Laurent.
2. The *Le Condé*, a freighter which had been bombed the night before in Villefranche-sur-Mer by the Allied air forces and towed to the Commerce port to be used as a barrage.
3. Kriegsmarine gunboats tied up at the Commerce wharf.
4. Construction of a wall barring the Avenue des Phocéens and a blockhaus in the Albert 1er Gardens.
5. The Promenade des Anglais looking toward the west and the Palais de la Jetée on the pier that was demolished on March 2 to clear fields of fire.

tions. He declared them to be clearly improper. Since that date, the German staff has been busy improving the Southern defense network." [37]

"*It results from the declarations of a high-level German officer that the 19th army, composed of officers and soldiers of different nationalities, is completely disorganized. It does not have sufficient means of transportation available to ensure*

2

oners in Normandy or in Italy and to intercepted and decoded messages, the Allies had good knowledge of the 19th Army order of battle and installations. They had pinpointed coastal batteries on the maps and accumulated an impressive amount of data about the beaches and their surroundings, thus compounding precious documentation for the landing forces. However these various means had their limits. Aerial photographs thus pinpointed all enemy positions without distinguishing between the real ones and the fakes, which had of course been built to fool the reconnaissance planes. For example, the Titan battery situated on the eastern point of Levant Island and protecting the Cavalaire beaches represented a major threat for the Allied Navy until they learned that it was a dummy.

As the French artillerymen had noticed in Italy, the Allies had a tendency to add intelligence information together and obtain impressive but unrealistic totals. Thus they had tallied more than 200 medium and heavy guns in the Toulon sector and 150 guns, of 75-mm or heavier caliber to the sector between Cavalaire and Agay.

This was three times the real number in the sector controlled by the 242nd division [36]:

Cal.	Division	Army	Coastal	Total
75	12	—	4	16
100	12	—	12	24
120	—	—	4	4
138	—	—	10	10
150	12	24	4	40
164	—	—	8	8
340	—	—	4	4
Total	36	24	46	106

And Allied agents, occasional or otherwise, naturally had no access to the German positions and therefore could not base their reports on direct observation. Although some may have had the chance to have a closer peek, they did not necessarily have the competence to appreciate the importance or the accuracy of what they saw.

"*During the week between February 14 and 20, 1944, Marshall Rommel inspected the Southern France fortifica-*

ZAC5 LXTK 40362I

3

---

36. *According to Generalmajor Walther Vogel, 19th Army artillery commander, questioned in 1947.*
37. *Synthesis note from 'Caesar' to 'Stéphane,' dated March 3, 1944, and 'from secure sources.'*

sustenance." [38]

Certain intelligence reports were imprecise and even surprising, such as the presence of Waffen SS units or Tiger tanks. On the other hand, and in spite of transmission delays, a drawing of a road sign or a symbol painted on a vehicle, a sketch or a photo, could be of precious assistance in identifying a new unit, keeping up-to-date on battle order, or following the evolution of the enemy defense system.

As to the use of deciphered 'Ultra' messages, they completed and confirmed information received from other sources and helped understand the enemy, but gave no indications about its intentions. Likewise the deception operations that the Allies dreamed up to try to hide their projects from the Germans were limited and only partially successful.

The first mission assigned to Force A, in charge of deception operations, was to create such an important threat that the German forces south of the Loire River would not be able to move north to reinforce the Normandy front before D + 25, that is, in July. Operation 'Vendetta' thus consisted in making the Germans believe in a landing in Narbonne followed by a push toward Toulouse. But the Germans were quick to see that the Allied naval fleet was insufficient for such an operation, and that, in any case, that type of action would be more useful in the southeast of France or the north of Italy. This feeling continued to dominate their thinking even after the Normandy invasion, and they refused to consider the possibility of imminent action in the South. But even though OBWest did not believe in any threat from that direction, it nevertheless arranged to be able to ward off any possible action. Thus the armored divisions would move northward during the first days of Overlord, but large infantry formations would not until July.

Concerning the 242nd division, the Allied intelligence services knew quite a bit about its past and its organization, but believed at the beginning that is was composed of "*young Nazis, probably enthusiastic, but lacking experience.*" Two months later, in March 1944, it was noted "*that many soldiers are aged from 34 to 40 and some have fought on the Eastern front.*" The division was at the time considered to be at full strength with, in some cases, ex-Soviet personnel which had been temporarily put under their orders. But, it was added: "*the division should not be underrated.*" In July more precise information was obtained: a division of limited use, at 85% of its theoretical strength (14,000), 95% of artillery, 90% of fire power, 11 months of training [39].

As far as the Luftwaffe was concerned, the Allies realized that it was not a serious threat. They estimated

Above.
German coastal artillery artificer NCO (*Feuerwerker*) sleeve badge.
(Private collection)

Below.
Map legends of the German defensive positions drawn up by the Armée B intelligence staff section.

Bottom.
Allied intelligence worksheets on German coastal guns: Le Drammont (Gulf of Fréjus - P-63), Les Issambres (Pte. Issambre - P-34, P-52), Titan (Levant Island - M-20, 26, 27), Saint-Tropez (Cap Saint-Tropez - P-39, 47, 48). Titan (Levant Island - M-20, 26, 27).
(Private collection)

the number of planes that could be used against their forces at 100 maximum [40]. Their activity was thus limited to 155 daily sorties, reduced to 90 in case of an intense effort over a period of four or five days. That meant a few bomber attacks during the day, mine-dropping at night and fighter planes on the defensive:

"*It should be borne in mind that a large proportion of enemy sorties would be ineffective owing to the poor quality of the crews. This applies particularly to anti-shipping bombers.* [41]"

The naval forces were deemed insignificant. The only danger could come from submarines, but the Allies knew that there were no longer any seaworthy German submarines in the Western Mediterranean. They also knew that they would not be able to count on any surprise effect, because German reconnaissance planes would easily spot the ships gathering for the invasion. The best they could do would be to keep the time and place secret, even though the repeated aerial bombings and the increase in guerilla activities might give the game away.

The problem for the Allies was to guess how the German command would react once the invasion had started. They thought that Army Group G would first try to keep them pinned down in the Maures massif. Then, once they realized that they could not stop the Allied advance, they would pull their troops back to the main ports where they could attack communication lines and cut off any spearheads toward the Rhône River. As long as Marseilles and Toulon remained in their hands, it would be difficult for the Seventh Army to make any headway beyond the beachhead. But once the ports had fallen and the defensive potential along the coast was exhausted, Army Group G would order a retreat via the Rhône River valley.

On the coast, two regiments from the 242nd Division and elements of the 148th would take the first blows. When the enemy realized - in the evening of the first day at the latest - the scope of the attack, it would decide to move in the 11th Panzer Division against the beachhead, unless they had already left for Normandy. Then, the next morn-

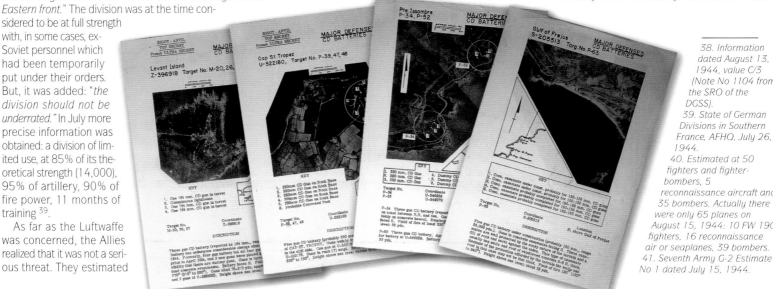

38. Information dated August 13, 1944, value C/3 (Note No 1104 from the SRO of the DGSS).
39. State of German Divisions in Southern France, AFHQ, July 26, 1944.
40. Estimated at 50 fighters and fighter-bombers, 5 reconnaissance aircraft and 35 bombers. Actually there were only 65 planes on August 15, 1944: 10 FW 190 fighters, 16 reconnaissance air or seaplanes, 39 bombers.
41. Seventh Army G-2 Estimate No 1 dated July 15, 1944.

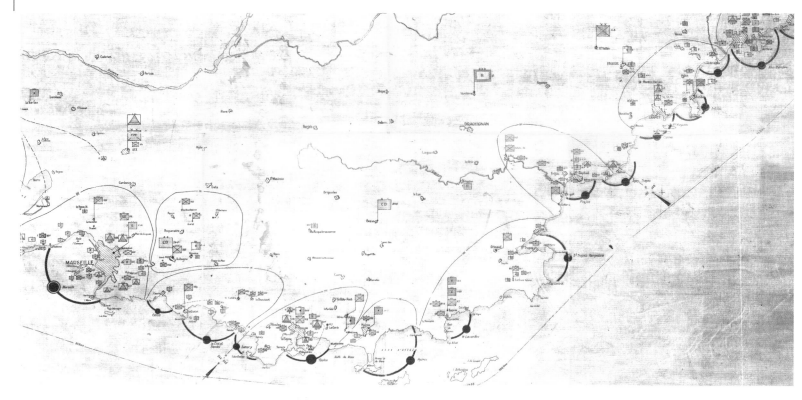

ing, the units on the line of contact would be assisted by the reserve regiments from the nearby 148th and 244th Divisions. Next, the 338th Division would probably send over a regimental combat team on D + 1 or 2, followed by its other elements two days later. This would be about the time when the 11. Panzer-division, having crossed the Rhône, would appear in the invasion stage.

The remaining forces, probably two of the three divisions stationed in Languedoc, would be requisitioned and committed in Provence: the first on D +5 and the second on D +9. Consequently, the Allies counted on the air forces and the FFI to delay their move. Likewise, the role of the maquis would be essential in keeping the 157th Division in the area around Lyon-Grenoble-Valence to protect the communica-

An August 1943 pamphlet from the Oberkommando der Kriegsmarine on amphibious operations conducted by the Allies and the lessons to be learned from them.
(Private Collection)

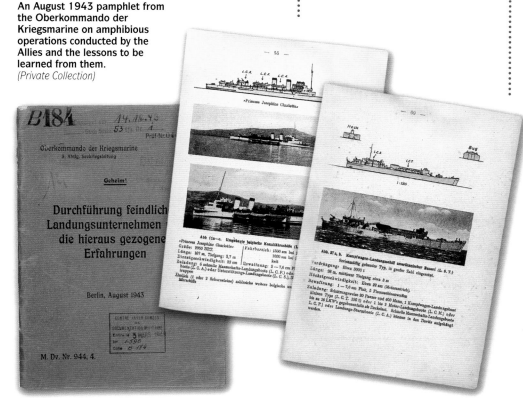

Opposite page.
Excerpts from various AFHQ intelligence bulletins.

1, 2, 3, 4, 5. These photographs of Monaco and Nice, collated by a secret agent, had been published in a Swiss magazine: a 75-mm gun at the foot of the staircase from Rauba Capeu to the Nice Castle.
6, 7, 8 and 9. Drawings sent to Algiers by agents in France: defensive positions on the coastline between Nice and Toulon, deployment in the Basses-Alpes, the SNCASE aircraft factory in Marignane, the coast between Le Lavandou and Dattier, road signs in Frejus and Saint-Raphael.
(Private Collection)

Above.
Excerpt from a map of German positions, from Nice to Marseilles, drawn up by the intelligence section of the French General Staff in Algiers.
(Private Collection)

tions lines. And the possibility of reinforcements coming in from Italy could not be excluded.

AND WHAT DID THE GERMANS REALLY KNOW?

Since American and French units had been engaged in Italy, the German intelligence service [42] had been generally well informed. They knew everything about the organization and the equipment of the Americans, and paid particular attention to the armored formations and the airborne and special forces.

Concerning their future opponents, the OB West intelligence section noted that: "*the American soldier is naively persuaded that he will win, but he is lacking in discipline, materialistic, and prefers avoiding violent attacks. For him, victory will be won by the equipment he is using and not by hand-to-hand combat. The officer corps does not make a very good impression, generally speaking* [43]." This severe sentence dated from the period after Salerno and was nevertheless slightly hedged because "*according to new information received, the American combat spirit and experience of the troops fighting in Italy has considerably improved.*"

As for the French, their "*colored troops have little combat value. The white soldiers, particularly the officers, are only interested in taking revenge on all the German people.*"

A study circulating in April 1944 stated that "*the French expeditionary forces are composed of 3/4 of foreigners*" and that "*there are hardly any units left composed entirely of whites, except for the Foreign Legion, which has lost a lot of men.*"

---

42. *Generalstab des Heeres, Abteilung Fremde Heere West.*
43. *Note on the comportment in captivity of the Western command dated November 17, 1943.*

DEFENSE INSTALLATIONS AT NICE

75mm PAK 97/38 - ADOPTED FRENCH 75 WITH MUZZLE BRAKE - ABOUT TO BE EMPLACED BELOW ESCALIER LESAGE AT 982668.

6

THE SAME GUN AS ABOVE ABOUT TO BE CAMOUFLAGED.

2-2/1762(a)

75mm GUN IN OPEN EMPLACEMENT AT ROAD FORK AT CARRAS 943649

3-6-2/1762

DEFENSE POSITIONS IN NICE

Four photographs from the "Muenchener Illustrierte Presse," reprinted in an (unidentified) Swiss review dated 4 May 44

Obstacles anti-chars devant une pharmacie.

Dans les jardins Albert 1er, à Nice.

A/Tk obstacles in front of a drug store
(See Report No. SS/SP/23, B,I,1,a,xxiii)

In the Gardens of Albert I, in NICE
(For a similar position, see Report No. SS/SP/23, B,I,1,a,xxi)

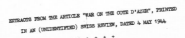

Barrage antichars érigé en pleine ville.

Positions de combat sur la plage.
(Quatre photos de la "Munchener Illustrierte Presse.)

A/Tk obstacles in the heart of town

Defense positions on the beach.

4

EXTRACTS FROM THE ARTICLE "WAR ON THE COTE D'AZUR", PRINTED IN AN (UNIDENTIFIED) SWISS REVIEW, DATED 4 MAY 1944

+ + + + + + + +

Les soldats allemands et l'organisation Todt ont transformé les quais de Nice en un front fortifié dont la vision attristerait le cœur des millions d'hivernants de jadis s'ils pouvaient contempler cette étrange transformation.

German soldiers and the TODT organization have transformed the quays of NICE into a fortified front, the sight of which would grieve the heart of millions of former winter tourists if they could but see this weird transformation.

Soldats masqués-- 0 il y en a peut-être cent au tout -- et patrouille allemande.

Vision de paix et de guerre telle qu'on pouvait la voir jusqu'à l'an dernier.

Soldiers of MONACO-- there are about 100 of them all together, - and a German patrol.

A vision of peace and war, such as could be seen up to last year.

5

ANNEX - B

ANNEXE-II-
Echelle: 1/20.000

Etang de Berre

Base Aérienne de Marignane

Usine S.N.C.A.S.E.

G.C. n° 15

ANNEXE-I-
Echelle: 1/300.000

Légende:
Voie ferrée ordinaire
Voie ferrée à voie étroite
Routes
R.N ou N.559 - Route Nationale n° 559
Rivière

Toulon
Hyères
La Londe-les-Maures
Rade de Bormes
Cap Bénat
Rade d'Hyères
Golfe de Giens
Presqu'île de Giens
ILES D'HYÈRES
Ile de Port Cros
Ile du Levant
Ile de Porquerolles

8

148.R

D/193 V

9

Each category was studied in turn:

"*The officers and the whites in the North African units are highly trained. Their defeat did not deal them as severe a moral blow as it did to the Metropolitan soldiers, but the reserve white formations are less ready to fight than were the home population. Troop morale has been influenced by heavy losses and the lack of successful campaigns, insufficient pay and supply problems, the Allies' apparent contempt of French interests, and political differences existing between Mainland France and the Dissidents. But their confidence in themselves could be improved by rearming them and the prospect of a coming victory. Then, in the case of initial victories in France, the French could become very enthusiastic and show a new spirit that they have been lacking up to now.*"

The North Africans, "*who make up most of the expeditionary forces, are noted for their warlike nature, particularly those of Berber origin. They are stubborn and resistant, and can be used in Europe during the cold season. But, considering how much prestige the French have lost, resulting from their defeat and the attitude of the Allies in North Africa, it is uncertain whether the Arabs and Berbers will be willing to sacrifice themselves once again for France.*"

The Senegalese were considered to be "*docile soldiers who endure well in warm climates, but who were not as successful as expected in 1940 because they were not familiar with the new weapons.*" Finally "*the irregular foreign troops (Goums) who were originally intended for police and guerilla operations in Africa, have apparently been successful in mountain warfare, in Tunisia, Sicily and Southern Italy. Nevertheless they are of limited use.*" [44]

The 'Bataillon de Choc' and the 'Commandos d'Afrique' had been identified, probably because of their presence in Corsica. And of course the composition of the three North African divisions and the Free French division was known, even though the Germans were not too sure about the mountain division and the Free French Division. On the other hand, they had little information about the 1re division blindée [45].

As to the Allies' intentions, the commander of the 19th Army was convinced during the month of July that, because of the Allied problems in Normandy, a landing in the Golfe du Lion was out of the question. He thought an action on one bank of the Rhône or the other, or between Toulon and

Above.
Released on June 5 in Paris, this German press photo, probably taken between Grasse and Nice, is captioned: "*Red Cross nurses from Nice with cakes and reading material come to visit an isolated post where engineers are busy planting mines.*"
(Private Collection)

Below.
Enameled insignia of the 6860th Headquarters Detachment or 'T' Force, in charge of intelligence gathering for the Seventh Army.
(Le Poilu)

Cannes, heading toward the Rhône Valley or the Route Napoléon, more likely. In the second case, it was sufficient for the Allies to penetrate about thirty kilometers inland through the Maures massif to find good roads and hook up with the maquisards in the Alps. Consequently, General Wiese sped up the work going on in the sector between Toulon and Cannes, and requested that the 148th Division be transformed into an infantry division. He was also anxious to husband the maximum of its forces on the left bank of the Rhône, and so asked that the 9th armored division be sent over, and ordered his engineer chief to organize contingency crossing points south of Avignon.

When the 9th Panzer left for Normandy, Wiese requested, unsuccessfully, that the 11th Panzer-Div. be sent to Aix. He was upset by this because it was clear from the intense bombings of the Rhône and Var bridges at the beginning of August,

---

44. *Army study by the Comité Français de Libération (French Liberation Committee) dated April 25, 1944.*
45. *3e Chasseurs d'Afrique mistaken for the 5e; 7e and 8e Chasseurs d'Afrique identified whereas they were actually committed in Italy.*

Excerpt from a map annex to Seventh Army Weekly G-2 Estimate No 8, dated August 8, 1944.
(Private Collection)

CARTE JOINTE
AU "WEEKLY G-2 ESTIMATE" No 8

day, "*the Army has received aerial intelligence reports concerning the concentration of important invasion forces in Corsica, the Italian ports and North Africa. It remains to determine where these forces are to land: Southern France or Gulf of Genoa? Graziani's Ligurian Army is preparing for the second hypothesis.*

Around noon on August 14, the Army was informed that the Corsican fleet had set sail in a northwesterly direction. Thus the dies were cast. On August 15, the question of the landing zones would be answered." [47]

One of the 2-cm Flak guns of the Endoume antiaircraft battery in Marseilles.
(©ECPAD)

that the Allies intended to isolate the region east of the river and prevent reinforcements from crossing over from the west bank or coming from Italy, this last opportunity he never counted on.

At the same time, the division commanders and all concerned formations of the Wehrmacht participated in map war games: the scenario being an enemy landing in the delta of the Rhône River or on either side of Saint-Raphaël, along with paratroopers being dropped in Le Muy. As a result of the exercise that took place in Draguignan on August 8, Wiese ordered Neuling to place native German companies among the Ost battalions positioned in the sector between Hyères and Saint-Raphaël. He also requested that the antitank artillery battalion be positioned near Saint-Raphaël, and that one regiment be pulled out of the 148th Division to constitute reserves in the area of Le Muy, in order to oppose any threat on his rear.

Of the 285,000 to 300,000 Germans, from all the different services, stationed in the 19th Army area, about one third, around 85,000, were in or near the landing zone [46]. The others were on the West bank of the Rhône or fighting the maquis, or part of various formations - naval, air, administrative, logistics - under separate commands.

On August 10, although Wiese had been constantly warned for the last three weeks about an imminent invasion, the synthesis received from Berlin concluded that no major landing was being considered by the Allies at that time. But the next

Above.
Map showing German positions on the Western front as of August 14, 1944, drawn up by the operations staff of the Oberkommando des Heeres.
(BA-MA)

Below.
Excerpts from OKH information bulletin No 34 dated April 26, 1944, devoted to the American Army (First Special Service Force), and from the OKL January 1944 bulletin featuring Allied airborne troops.
(Private collection)

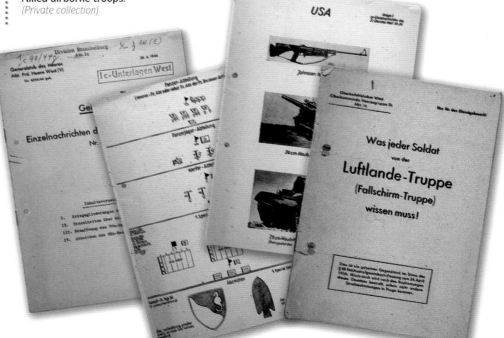

46. *Jeffrey J. Clarke and Robert Ross Smith,* Riviera to the Rhine, *OCMH, Washington DC, 1993.*
47. *Testimony by Generalleutnant Walter Botsch, 19th Army Chief of Staff, interrogated on July 10, 1946.*

THE FIRST ONSLAUGHT COMES FROM THE SEA

VI Corps had been withdrawn from the front after the fall of Rome and assigned to the Seventh Army on June 15. Two days later, its commander, Major General Lucian K. Truscott Jr., was called to Bouzareah to be briefed on Operation Anvil. Then in Salerno he attended a presentation of the procedures used in Normandy, before returning to Rome to study the plans with his staff.

Top left.
The brass enameled insignia of the 'Groupe de Commandos d'Afrique.'
(Private Collection)

Above.
A French Commando d'Afrique.
(Reconstruction by Provence 44)

Left.
Aboard *USS Catoctin*, listening to the explanations of Captain R.A.J. English, USN, leaning over the sponge model made in U.S.A., from left to right: Contre-Amiral Lemonnier (French Navy Chief of Staff), Vice-Admiral Kent Hewitt, USN (CNWTF), General Sir Henry Maitland Wilson (SACMED) and Admiral Sir John Cunningham RN (CincMed).
(US Navy)

At the beginning, Truscott stressed to Patch the necessity of grouping all of the planners involved in Naples and creating a single command structure for the assault phase. In particular, he suggested that all the participating units be under his command as leader of the land forces and that his rank be equal to that of the chief of the naval forces. But VI Corps was a latecomer, and the seventh Army with its partners had already finalized their plans. The introduction of a new level of command would be a source of confusion. Beyond that, Patch believed that, during the assault, VI Corps could not cope with directing the special units and airborne troops, on top of its three assigned assault divisions.

Truscott let himself be convinced and it was only natural that the Navy would direct the operations until the ground units CPs could be established on the shore. So the Navy planning group came to Naples on July 8 and was joined two days later by Admiral Hewitt, who was thus nearby the other command structures: Seventh Army, Armée B and XII Tactical Air Command.

THE WESTERN NAVAL TASK FORCE

Thanks to the wealth of experience gained during previous invasions in the Mediterranean, the Force 163 Navy planners were able, on April 15, 1944, to present a draft plan exposing the broad lines of action and the various tasks of the naval forces.

However, the incertitude about Anvil was a problem in defining the final details of the Navy plan. For example, additional landing ships coming from across the Atlantic were only assigned in May, and the exact number of those that SHAEF could spare was not known until June. And the composition of the first wave was not decided until July 2. Consequently, the final version of plan No 4-44 and its eighteen annexes did not appear until July 24.

The Western Naval Task Force actually called for three attack task forces, one for each of the assault zones - Alpha TF 84, Delta TF 85 and Camel TF 87 - and three specialized task forces:

● TF 80 or Control Force, for convoy protection and then support on the landing beaches;

April 14, 1944. General Wilson salutes the invasion fleet from the bridge of HMS *Kimberley*:
"John Cunningham carried me out on a destroyer to see the boats heading for the assault zone. What an astonishing sight to see the various convoys with their escorts led by the LCIs, followed by the LCTs then the LSTs further back, and finally the bombarding fleet, the troop transport ships and the freighters loaded with supplies." **(Eight Years Overseas)**
(IWM A25261)

Below.
Admiral Cunningham with General Wilson and two Royal Navy officers, reading the latest messages.
(IWM A25230)

● TF 86 or Support Force, in charge of landing the Sitka and Romeo forces, then supporting the progression of the ground troops;

● TF 88 or Aircraft Carrier Force, with planes assigned to protect the beachhead and the landed troops.

Ships and craft were assigned as follows:

The Control Force, or Task Force 80, was placed under direct orders of Admiral Hewitt, whose flag was raised on the *Catoctin*, which had arrived in

	TF 80	TF 84	TF 85	TF 87	T F 86	TF 88	Total
Battleships	-	1	2	1	1	-	5
Aircr. carr.	-	-	-	-	-	9	9
Cruisers	-	6	3	6	3	4	22
Destroyers	42	6	11	11	3	14	87
Escort ships	23	--	-	-	-	-	23
Patrol boats	-	24	14	16	-	-	54
Mine sweepers	32	30	30	23	8	-	123
Torpedo boats	26	-	-	-	16	-	42
Landing craft	-	155	118	120	-	-	393
Trans. ship	-	6	10	12	10	-	38
Other	57	17	18	15	6	-	113
Total	180	245	206	204	47	27	909[1]

1. Plus 1370 craft transported or towed to the landing zone.

Algiers on March 19. The ship was heavily outfitted with signals and communications gear, photo labs, reproduction facilities - allowing his staff to work under excellent conditions:

"The Catoctin *was a strange ship, sent from the United States for the occasion. She was one of those newly-built vessels, specially designed for use as a command ship for important amphibious operations. Outside she looked like a big transport ship, but her decks were bristling with antennae: the* Catoctin *had no less than 40 radio transmitters and could receive 70 different wavelengths at the same time. The main receiving station looked like the offices of a large bank at rush hour. Fifty sailors with earphones were busy teletyping the messages they were receiving, which were thus sent out simultaneously to all concerned and posted at the central command station where they were projected onto a screen; messages were*

also usually repeated over the loudspeaker on the decks." [2]

Besides the Admiral's group which included the US destroyer *Plunkett* [3], TF 80 had eight other task groups:
- TG 80.2 Beach control, organized around the 124th Beach Battalion;
- TG 80.3 Refueling in the assault zone, with secondary bases in Ajaccio, Porticcio, Propriano, Calvi and Ile Rousse;
- TG 80.4 Marking out the air corridor that was to be used by the transport planes, and diversions in the bay of La Ciotat and the region around Nice-Cannes;
- TG 80.5 Cover for the rest of the naval forces and protection against enemy surface vessels in the assault zone [4];
- TG 80.6 Control and escort of the assault and reinforcements convoys, then organization of convoys leaving the landing zones;
- TG 80.7 Fleet support trains: repair ships, ammunition transports, tankers, water ships;
- TG 80.8 Control of secure French ports;
- TG 80.9 Control of movement, loading, and departure in and from the Corsican ports [5].

As usual with the Americans, the operation was characterized by a gigantic logistics effort and remarkable organization of the convoys. Two bases were thus fitted out for the Eighth Fleet in Oran and the 8th Amphibious Force in Bizerte. In Palermo the dry docks and repair installations served as the naval shipyard, and La Maddalena and Bastia were used as bases for the torpedo boats.

A shuttle service was imagined between Corsica and the beachhead. But no less than five different ports were necessary to accommodate all the ships. So, starting in April 1944, fuel depots were built there [6]. For drinking

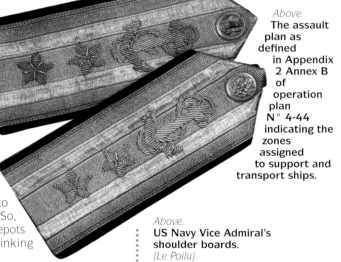

Above.
The assault plan as defined in Appendix 2 Annex B of operation plan N° 4-44 indicating the zones assigned to support and transport ships.

Above.
US Navy Vice Admiral's shoulder boards.
(Le Poilu)

water, which was at a premium on the island, reservoirs and distillation stations were added (see table above).

Construction and repair ships were waiting in Naples, Oran, Corsica and Sardinia, ready to leave for the landing zone. Two 350-ton pontoon causeways were to follow with two British LSDs [7]. Also three LSTs and four LCIs were equipped as mother ships for the smaller vessels. And additional LCMs [8] were assigned to speed up the important task of unloading the freighters, normally done by Navy LCTs and Army DUKWs.

Requisitions for Army supplies were sent to Washington starting in January 1944, and stocks progressively built up until April. But since the operation was repeatedly put off, the stockpiles were inevitably tapped for the Italian campaign and the levels diminished. So when Anvil was back on the planning table in June, General Devers - who had already 'frozen' certain supplies in the dumps during the period of uncertainty - ordered SOS NATOUSA to give priority to the operation. But this was not enforced until July 2, when the loaded convoys were finally allowed to leave the U.S. ports. At

PETROLEUM AND WATER STORAGE IN CORSICA

	Fuel oil	Diesel	Gasoline		Water	
			80 oct.	100 oct.	Tank	Distil./day
Ajaccio	36 000 t	3 150 t	2 700 t	3 900 t	450 t	95 t
Calvi	-	2 800 t	1 500 t	2 700 t	300 t	35 t
Ile Rousse	-	1 400 t	-	-	150 t	35 t
Bastia	-	-	1 500 t	4 000 t	-	-
Porto-Vecchio	-	-	1 500 t	4 000 t	-	-

The HMS Kimberley gunners watch the LSTs in Convoy SM-1 disappear beyond the horizon.
(IWM A.25 231)

2. Admiral Lemonnier, «Cap sur la Provence», France-Empire, Paris 1954.
3. Relief Flagship.
4. To this effect, the PT boats had been assigned to TF 86 for the night preceding the invasion and to TF 84 for cover on the west flank, then for night patrol in the zone around Cannes-Nice.
5. The 90 and 95 mine-sweepers were among them.
6. The work was done by the 1045th Seabee Detachment composed of 300 specialists who later worked in Toulon and Marseilles.
7. On the other hand, the two assigned LSEs (Landing Ship Emergency Repair) arrived long after D-Day.
8. 218, including 170 loaded on freighters and 48 on two LSGs and one LSC.

At the end of July, as usual before a major operation, King George VI visited the forces participating in Anvil. First the admirals were presented to him by Admiral Cunningham (on the left Admiral Hewitt and on the right Admiral Troubridge, CTG 88). Then he toured Naples harbor on a British motor boat flying the King's Colours. Leaving the shore, he passed in front of HMS *Zetland*, a TG 80.6 destroyer, with in the background the city overshadowed by the Vomero, San Elmo castle and the San Martino museum. *(IWM A24996, 24 999, 25 001)*

Top, right and above.
On the morning of August 15, 1944, Winston Churchill boarded HMS *Kimberley* to observe the invasion. But because of the possibility of mines, the destroyer was not allowed to go any closer than the 100-fathom line, which displeased the Prime Minister, as his personal physician confirmed in his memoirs: *"16 August 1944. The P.M. returned from his trip in bad spirits. He had not been able to get closer than six kilometers from the beaches. He did not hear a single shot."* He is shown here on the *Kimberley* deck surrounded by members of the crew *(IWM A 25 246 & 25 256)*

the end a three-month supply for ten divisions was available, that is the amount that could be carried in one hundred freighters for the assault itself, plus another hundred freighters for reinforcements.

On the first day, it had been planned to land 84,000 men and 12,000 vehicles from VI Corps. They were to be followed from D + 1 to D + 4 by 33,500 men and 8,000 vehicles including the first French elements. Then, from D + 5 to D + 30, a convoy loaded with seven days of rations, equipment, clothing and fuel for the units that had landed would arrive every five days. But since G-2 predicted strong resistance and therefore rather slow progress, it was decided to give priority to ammunition during the first five days. Consequently the amount of fuel transported was reduced by 20% and rations by 30%, not to mention motor transport.

As to the naval convoys, every precaution was taken so that they would arrive at destination in good condition. Thus routes, schedules and speed were calculated so as to avoid intersecting routes and traffic congestion, and to allow the ships to reach in the assault zone under cover of the night. In addition, the Coastal Air Force insured aerial protection during the passage, and the Straits of Bonifacio were checked for mines.

The Germans could not help but notice such a large number of boats in the Naples harbor. *(DR)*

Left.
Soldiers of the 3rd Infantry Division gathered on the beach in Pozzuoli, near Naples, waiting to board the LCIs and transport ships anchored in the gulf.
(IWM EA33704)

Badge
worn the US Navy Construction Battalions. The letters CB gave them their appropriate nickname 'Seabees.' They were the men who assembled, floated and handled the pontoon causeways leading to the beaches.
(Le Poilu)

Below.
Bird's-eye view of the assault zone as shown on each of the twelve maps of the invasion beaches.
(Private Collection)

- land the First Special Service Force on the Levant and Port-Cros islands;
- land the groupe des commandos d'Afrique, who were to neutralize the Cap Nègre defenses and block the coastal road:
- destroy the Cap Nègre battery if it was still battleworthy, and the Cap Bénat guns, covering Cavalaire Bay.

The force would then take control of all the support ships and assign them as needed with new missions as needed by the situation.

For this, Hewitt requested larger ships than the light cruisers he had. And thus five battleships and three heavy cruisers sailed from the English Channel at the end of June and the beginning of July.

The rehearsals aimed mainly at improving procedures for firing on land targets, especially for the teams [10] that had already been involved in May and June when the Fleet supported the Fifth Army along the Italian coast. For aerial observation, it was decided to bolster the planes on the aircraft carriers with the addition of Mustang fighters, piloted by naval aviators. Pilots from the *Brooklyn* thus trained in Berteaux, Algeria, then in Pomigliano, where they were joined in April by others from the *Philadelphia* who had trained in the United States on Wildcats, and, in July, by mechanics from the battleships. However these ten pilots - too few to really make a difference - were later returned to their ships or assigned to light cruisers. Instead it was decided that if the carriers were forced to leave the assault zone, the seaplanes from the battleships and from two cruis-

TASK FORCE 86

During the assault phase, the task of the Support Force, under Vice Admiral Lyal A. Davidson [9], was to:

9. *Commander Cruiser Division Eight on the* Augusta, *on which he had participated in the invasion of Sicily with Hewitt.*
10. *Shore Fire Control Party or SFCP.*

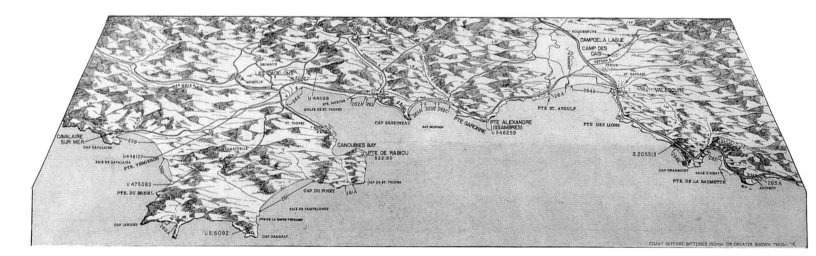

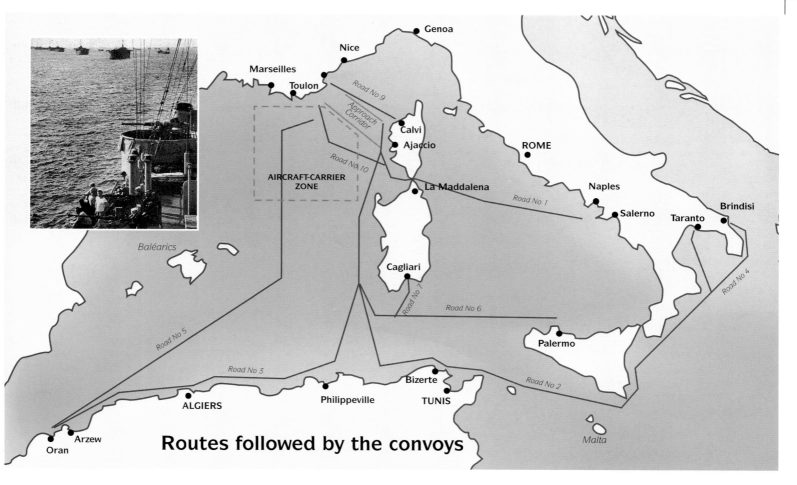

Routes followed by the convoys

ers would be based in Ajaccio. In that case, the *Texas* would be anchored within range of the coast and used as an intermediate floating airbase for refueling and catapulting.

And the French sailors had to be taught the ways of the Allies. In order to reassure a somewhat worried Admiral Davidson, the French Navy Chief of Staff organized a sortie off Oran and in Arzew Bay, with training fire on land targets under the direction of an Allied team. It was such a success that, speaking of a cruiser that had not been refurbished in the United States, one expert declared:

"*Your* Duguay-Trouin *is pretty old and her firing system is archaic: we wonder how your gunners manage with such out-dated material. But they fired excellent shots…*" [11]

Inset, above.
LSTs from convoy SM-1 heading towards the coast of Provence.
US Army)

Below.
One of the convoy SM-1 Liberty ships towing her barrage balloon.
(IWM A 25 271)

On June 16, Davidson visited the Normandy beaches and was impressed "*by the strength of the defensive concrete gun emplacements, the ingenuity exercised in their location and concealment; the lack of dependability of aerial bombing in pre-landing neutralization; the demand naval gunfire; and*

ROUTES BETWEEN THE PORTS AND THE ASSAULT ZONE

Distances in nautical miles.
1 nm = 1 852 m

	Ajaccio	Assault Area	Naples	Bonifacio
Naples	315	430	-	250
Oran	685	810	880	700
Algiers	485	610	680	500
Ajaccio	-	145	315	85
Calvi	65	105	o	140
Bastia	120	160	280	115

Time necessary to reach the assault zone in hours and according to speed in knots, to which must be added the time necessary for loading, for waiting to leave port and for stationing, without taking into account weather conditions

	5	51/2	71/2	8	10	11	12
Naples	86	79	58	54	43	40	36
Oran	162	148	108	102	81	75	68
Algiers	122	111	82	77	61	56	51
Ajaccio	30	27	20	18	15	13.5	12
Calvi	21	19	14	13	10.5	9.7	8.8
Bastia	32	29	22	20	16	14.7	13.4
Taranto			144				91

the absolute necessity for maintaining naval gun-fire until the last moment before the landing with aerial or offshore observation from a landing craft." [12]

Davidson also realized that the problem of underwater obstacles was more delicate in the Mediterranean because the low tide amplitudes meant that they would never become visible above water. He thus suggested using pontoon causeways, on the provision that a sufficient number were available and that some could be lost.

On July 1, TF 86 received orders to prepare a draft plan for artillery support in case Overlord ships became available. Then it was given control over the Sitka operation on the 6th. At that time, Davidson decided to assign about twenty officers to the Seventh Army HQ. Liaisons with Armée B were carried out by Commander Bataille who had previously been commanding the cruiser *Emile Bertin* off the Italian

Above.
French cruisers training in the bay of Oran for the invasion of Provence. Notice the cruiser *Gloire*, No 2 in the line, recognizable because of her camouflage scheme.

Above, right.
Cruiser *Gloire*'s insignia.
(SHM)

Right & below.
On D-1, gunners on the light cruiser USS *Philadelphia*, are test firing antiaircraft guns. Along with the *Montcalm* and the *Georges Leygues*, CL-41 made up Task Unit 85.12.2 commanded by French Contre-Amiral Jaujard
(National Archives)

coast.

The Eighth Fleet's flagship was the *Augusta*, and Hewitt took charge of the training program for the American ships arriving in the theater, which included, for example, a signal exercise involving air control units, with a naval bombing observed by the SFCPs and the fighter pilots. However the British and French ships - whose programs were only approved on August 3 - had to train with their own task force.

The final assignment of vessels was pronounced on July 27, and from then on preparation of the support plans for each assault force could start, in liaison with CTF 86. However the Cruiser Division Two ships were involved so late in the game that only the *Marblehead* participated in the operation, the *Omaha* - like the *Jeanne d'Arc* - was kept in reserve and the *Cincinnati* remained in Oran for engine repairs. The battleship *HMS Ramillies* joined the fleet as it was already on its way to Provence; she had received plans and operations orders coming through the Straits of Gibraltar.

Preparation for assault transports was also shortened because of the late arrival of certain ships. Thus the *Osmond Ingram* arrived on August 1 without ever having participated in a sea invasion and with inappropriate landing craft. And the landing crews of the four LSIs coming from Great Britain had been replaced at the last minute by novices from the Royal Marines.

Vice Admiral Theodore Chandler, commander of CruDiv 2, arrived on August 2, without any staff and with no experience of amphibious operations or of ground troops support. He was nevertheless welcome as coordinator of the various operations in the Hyères islands and on Cap Nègre, and to smooth things over between the commander of the Special Service Force and Captain Maynard, Commander Transport Division Five. That allowed Admiral Hewitt to focus with General De Lattre on the attack on Toulon and Marseilles.

In spite of these drawbacks and the little time available for training, the rehearsal on the 8th was a success. Then on the 9th at 0930, orders went out to execute the Dragoon plan, with H-hour set at 0800 on the 15th. A half hour later, the first convoy left Naples for Ajaccio.

THE SPECIAL OPERATIONS GROUP AND THE DECEPTIONS

Task Group 80.4 was to simulate landings near Antibes and La Ciotat with the goal of confusing the enemy as to the exact point where the operation was to take place.

Lieutenant Commander Douglas E. Fairbanks Jr's

11. Cap sur la Provence, op. cit.
12. Operations and action of the Support Force Eighth Fleet during Invasion of Southern France, CruDiv 8 report dated October 21, 1944.

'Beachjumpers' group [13] - two gunboats and two fighter-director ships - left Ajaccio at 1030 on the 14th, accompanied by fighter planes designed to intimidate any reconnaissance aircraft that might try to discover the flotilla. They were joined in the evening by four motor torpedo boats from Bastia. Three of these sped off to lay a protective screen against the German gunboats in the vicinity of Nice. Four others were to land French marines of the 'Groupe naval d'assaut de Corse' in Théoule.

The main group continued its way north, as if heading for Genoa, imitating an important armada with the help of intense radio activity, radar jamming and

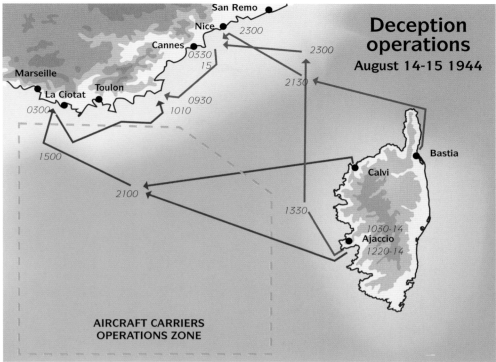

Deception operations
August 14-15 1944

Left, top to bottom.
Views of the coastline: Pointe de l'Ilette point, the light AA battery in the old Graillon battery at Cap d'Antibes, Théoule machine-gun blockhaus, port of Cannes and Napoule gulf (Beach 266), photos taken from La Californie.

TASK GROUP 80.4 SPECIAL OPERATIONS GROUP
(Captain Henry C. Johnson, USN)

TU 80.4.1 Western Diversionary Unit
(Captain Henry C. Johnson, USN)
- DD 495 *Endicott*.
- ML 299, 337, 451 et 581 (29th Minelayer Flottilla.)
- PT 552 to 559 (Motor Torpedo Squadron 291).
- Beach Jumper Unit 3 - Lieutenant Commander A.G. Stanford, USNR.
- ASRC 21 to 24, 27, 31 to 37 (Air Sea Rescue Boat Squadron 1).
- ASRC 11, 12, 25, 28.
- Beach Jumper Unit 5 - Lieutenant Commander Artie L. Williams, USNR.

TU 80.4.2 Eastern Diversionay Unit Lieutenant
(Commander Douglas E. Fairbanks Jr, USNR)
- HMS *Aphis*.
- HMS *Scarab*.
- HMS *Stuart Prince* - Commander W.A. Moens, RSN.
- HMS *Antwerp* - Lieutenant Commander J.F.R. Rand, RN.
- ML 456, 461, 478 and 575 (22rd Minelayer Flottilla).
- PT 302 to 313 (Motor Torpedo Squadron 223).
- Beach Jumper Unit 1 - Lieutenant Commander C.B. Osborne, USNR.
- Scout and Raider team.
- Groupe naval d'assaut de Corse.

echoes created by windows dropped from planes, and balloon reflectors. At 2230, HMS *Antwerp* and *Stuart Prince* left the group and took up position at the points which had been decided on to mark out the corridor for the transport planes. An hour later Task Unit 80.4.2 turned west and the gunboats coming back from Théoule provided protection to the east.

At 0420, the gunboats HMS *Aphis* and *Scarab* arrived off Antibes. Covered by the other ships, they started to fire on the coastline up to the mouth of the Var River. After shelling the shore for about an hour, the whole flotilla went to Briande Bay and joined up with the Western group.

Twenty-five miles south of the Hyères islands, destroyer *Endicott* under Captain Henry C. Johnson, and the four gunboats of the Western group which had left from Ajaccio, were joined by eight PT boats and twelve rescue ships [14] based in Calvi. The flotilla simulated a convoy thirty kilometers long and thirteen wide, more imposing than that of the Sitka Force that was getting ready to land at that time. It headed north for La Ciotat, making sure that it had been spotted on the Cap Sicié radar that Allied aviation had taken pains not to destroy.

In spite of the fog, the *Endicott* and two gunboats opened fire against the coast while the ASRCs produced a smoke screen, and prepared to enter the bay for a make-believe landing: actually only one gunboat made it. And, at 0400 in the surrounding countryside, a fleet of Dakotas dropped dummy paratroopers, laden with firecrackers triggered when they hit the ground.

Then Task Unit 80.4.1 withdrew to Briande Bay at 1100.

SITKA FORCE IN THE ISLANDS

The First Special Service Force was a very special unit made up of American and Canadian volunteers, activated in August 1942 for the purpose of attack-

15. Hollywood film celebrity, reserve officer, British disciple in matters of deception and creater of the Beach Jumper units in charge of it.
16. Air Sea Rescue Craft or ASRC.

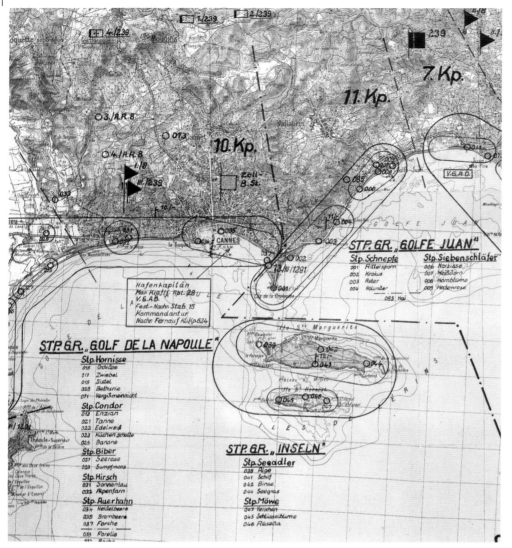

Above. **Brigadier General Frederick speaking with Lieutenant Colonel S. Moore, commander of the 2nd Regiment, during the attack on Ceretto Alto, January 15, 1944.**
(NARA)

for counter-attacks, selection and preparation of beaches for the landing of supplies.

Combined exercise 'Bruno,' the final rehearsal, took place during the night of August 7-8 off Gaeta on two islands with characteristics similar to those of the Hyères islands. In spite of a gusty wind, two regiments landed on Zannone and the third at Ponza without a hitch. The mock 'enemy' was rapidly skirted and the islands taken.

Then on the 11th, the five APDs and two LSIs of the assault group left Castelabate for Propriano, in Corsica. There, in their bivouac, the Forcemen rested and cleaned their guns and equipment. It was at this time that they finally learned of their mission: cleaning out the Port-Cros and Levant Islands and neutralizing the Titan battery. The destruction of this battery was essential to the Alpha sector. The aerial photo specialists and the G-2 were sure that three 164-mm guns were emplaced there. Only Commander Le Hagre, the Seventh Army liaison officer, insisted that they had been sabotaged in November 1942 and that those visible on the photos were dummies. He was all the more certain because on June 8 the French submarine *Casabianca* had been within range and the battery had not reacted. The Navy suggested sending in a sub to try to find out the truth. If that did not work a team could be landed to get a closer look.

Consequently the Force intelligence officer went to Corsica to learn how to handle the folding kayak

---

ing electric plants in Norway. 'Forcemen' received special training in parachuting, skiing, mountaineering and demolitions. When the Norway plan was scuttled, the SSF moved to the North Pacific and then to Italy in December 1943. It was committed on the Anzio beachhead [15] with heavy losses, replaced by reinforcements from Canada and disbanded Ranger battalions.

The Force was relieved on June 7th on the Tiber and left for Lake Albano, near the Moroccan goumiers and the Papal residence at Castel Gandolfo. Rumor had it that its leader, Brigadier General Robert T. Frederick, was to command the 36th Infantry Division. And on June 23, during an awards ceremony, he announced his departure for a new command. He was followed by Colonel Edwin M. Walker, replaced as CO of the Third Regiment by Canadian Lieutenant Colonel R.W. Beckett. Lieutenant Colonel Robert S. Moore took over the Second Regiment which had been led by Jack F.R. Akehurst, the senior Canadian officer, who left for the First Regiment.

On July 4 the SSF took up quarters at Santa Maria di Castelabate, on the seashore south of Salerno. Individual and collective training resumed. A thousand volunteers were rejected after a rigorous selection process and partially replaced by convalescing veterans [16]. Then training started in conjunction with the Invasion Training Center and with the help of the SFCP and the beach marking teams. Generally speaking, each exercise was made up of the different nighttime phases of the operation: beach marking, landing in rubber boats, cliff-climbing in full combat gear, spontaneous attacks on inland targets, preparation

Above
Map dated July 25, 1944, indicating the three strongholds in the Cannes sector: Golfe-Juan, the Lérins islands and the Napoule gulf.
(Private Collection)

Parachute wings and oval worn by Forcemen.
(Private collection)

Staff Sergeant Cyril V. Krotzer, from the Headquarters Detachment, 2nd Regiment, on April 15, 1944, during the raid on Ceretto Alto in the Anzio beachhead.
(National Archives)

---

15. It received the nickname Black Devils Brigade from an officer of the 'Hermann Göring' Division.
16. Effectives at the end of July: 2,515 including 159 officers.

east of Levant Island. Through binoculars, the islands outlined against the sky could be seen despite the ground haze. The convoy then broke up, each ship heading for her transport or firing zone. To the west, the eight PT boats of the Screening Group continued their patrols, while to the north four others from TG 86.5 followed the Romeo group, ready to create a diversion if the enemy showed up.

When it reached its assembly area, LSI *Prince Baudoin* launched her LCAs while the APDs let the LCP(R)s slide stealthily along their hulls. Beside them the motor boats were waiting with their engines idling. At 23.17 the first landing craft, towing behind them rubber boats filled with a dozen men, set out for the coast at four knots. The torpedo boats ahead of them stopped about three thousand meters from the landing sites to check their radars and set the LCAs on their final course. Then, when they were one thousand meters from the shore, the LCAs let the rubber boats go, and the LCP(R)s did the same two hundred and fifty meters further on. The scouts preceded the first boats on kayaks or electric-powered surfboats, marking the approach lane with electric buoys. Then the rest of the team [19] marked the beach and took up positions on the cliffs.

There were delays. The *Osmond Ingram* was overladen and one of its landing boats had to tow thirteen

used by the British Special Boat Section [17]. Then on July 28, the HMS *Unicorn* carried him in close to the archipelago so he could reconnoitre landing sites and the elusive battery.

Even though the French Naval officers who knew the islands had insisted that it was unrealistic to want to invade from the south, Colonel Walker nevertheless chose the rocky coast on the seaward side. He thought, correctly, that the northern beaches were well defended and that it would be impossible to

Above.
Present-day view of the Valinco gulf and Propriano in Corsica.
(Private Collection)

Below.
Task Group 86.3 ships anchored off Propriano.
(Musée de l'Armée, Paris)

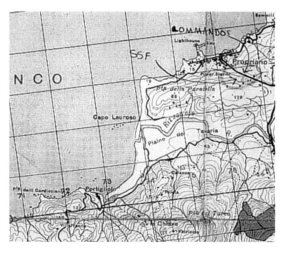

land there without being spotted. And he was confident that his men would be able to scale the cliffs and cut their way through the thick maquis so as to occupy the islands two hours before H-hour.

While the commandos were camping on the banks of the Gulf of Valinco, the ships that had remained in Italy or Sardinia were heading for Propriano where TF 86 assembled on the 13th [18]. At that date Admiral Davidson called for a last-minute briefing on the *Augusta* for final details.

The Task Force left Corsica late in the morning of Aug. 14th. The sun was shining, the sea was calm and the wind, blowing from the south at four or five knots, and it looked like nothing would go wrong. Along the way the destroyer HMS *Kimberley*, flagship of Admiral Sir John Cunningham, commander of the naval forces in the Mediterranean, came up to the line of ships and saluted the *Prince Henry*, carrying Admiral Chandler and Captain Maynard, commander of Task Unit 86.3.2, with a "*Good luck to all!*". Even though German reconnaissance planes had spotted the convoy there was no attack. The radars near Toulon had been jammed by the counter-measures units on the ships or in Corsica.

At 21.56 the convoy was twenty kilometers south-

Above.
Section from a map used by the Commandos d'Afrique African during a combined exercise with the Special Service Force on the beaches of Propriano.
(Private Collection)

The shoulder patch of the First Special Service Force in the shape of an Indian arrowhead, was approved on September 14, 1942.
(Le Poilu)

dinghies. The LCP(R)s proved to be noisier and more difficult to handle than the LCAs, and marking the beaches took quite a bit of time. The scouts preceding the fourteen hundred Forcemen from the 2nd and 3rd Regiments arrived on Levant Island at 0135 and the seven hundred men from the 1st Regiment landed on Port-Cros at 0200.

The Canadians from the 1st Battalion 2nd Regiment led by Major Edward H. Thomas [20] silently scaled the cliffs and crept to the Titan battery, only to discover that the dreaded 164s were nothing but stovepipes... Likewise the landing on Port-Cros met with no opposition [21]. So

---

17. British unit of canoeists operating in the Adriatic Sea and around Rhodes.
18. Except the Lorraine, a net-layer, and the group of torpedo boats.
19. The team in charge of beach marking and protection included 27 men from the Army and two Navy scouts
20. He was 24 years-old and had been commanding the batallion since December 1943.

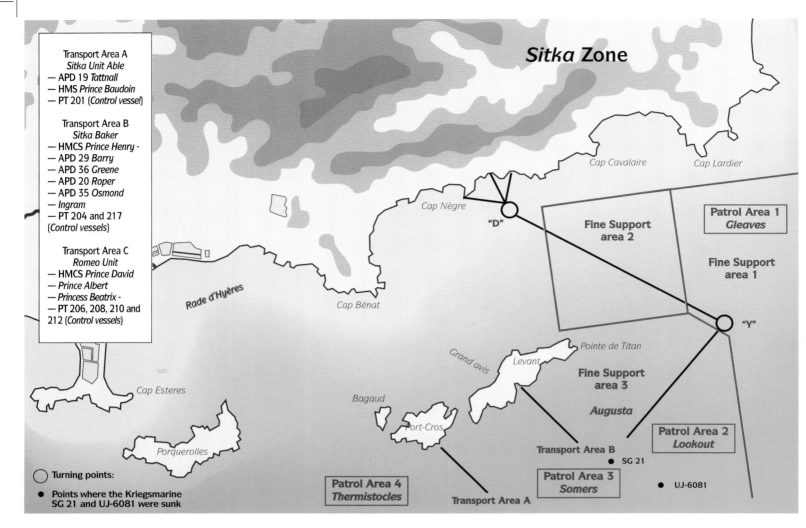

Sitka Zone

Transport Area A
Sitka Unit Able
— APD 19 *Tattnall*
— HMS *Prince Baudoin*
— PT 201 (*Control vessel*)

Transport Area B
Sitka Baker
— HMCS *Prince Henry* -
— APD 29 *Barry*
— APD 36 *Greene*
— APD 20 *Roper*
— APD 35 *Osmond*
— *Ingram*
— PT 204 and 217
(*Control vessels*)

Transport Area C
Romeo Unit
— HMCS *Prince David*
— *Prince Albert*
— *Princess Beatrix* -
— PT 206, 208, 210 and
212 (*Control vessels*)

○ **Turning points:**

● **Points where the Kriegsmarine
SG 21 and UJ-6081 were sunk**

Cap Cavalaire   *Cap Lardier*

Cap Nègre

Patrol Area 1
Gleaves

"D"

**Fine Support
area 2**

**Fine Support
area 1**

"Y"

Cap Bénat

Rade d'Hyères

Pointe de Titan

Grand avis   *Levant*

**Fine Support
area 3**

Augusta

Bagaud

Cap Esteres

Port-Cros

Porquerolles

Patrol Area 2
Lookout

Transport Area B

● SG 21

Patrol Area 4
Thermistocles

Transport Area A

Patrol Area 3
Somers

● UJ-6081

Left.
PT-212 carrying survivors from the German coastal cutter *Escaburt*.
(US Navy)

Below.
Cliffs on the southern coast of Levant Island.
(Private Collection)

The *Somers* closed in and used light signals to request that the boats identify themselves. But no answer to the blinking projector was forthcoming, so DD 381 opened fire at 5,000 meters and broke radio silence to report. SG 21 was hit and heaved over. Another broadside and the ship was afire. The flames lit up the zone and alerted the Germans on the shore. It was 04.40.

Two minutes later the *Somers* fired on UJ 6081, heading southeast. The chaser was finally hit at 05.08 and her crew abandoned ship. A capture crew climbed aboard and the survivors were picked up in lifeboats.

Meanwhile on Levant Island Colonel Walker [23] was raving: the intelligence was wrong and all his men had

the exhausted Forcemen took up positions on the heights and most of them fell right to sleep.

But as the transport ships were moving back to the withdrawal zone, a salvo from the destroyer *Somers*, patrolling in zone No 3, suddenly crackled through the quiet night. For an hour DD 381 had been following on the radar screen two boats coming from the west. They were SG 21 and UJ 6081 [22] from the German 6th Security Fleet, sent out from Marseilles to reconnoitre the invasion fleet which had been spotted by a German plane further east than had been expected. At 04.28 the SG 21 captain radioed the presence of the fleet south of Saint-Tropez.

21. *Prisoners declared that they had seen boats approaching, but they had disappeared out of range before the Port-Man battery had been able to get them in its sights.*
22. *Schnelle Geleitfahrzeuge: rapid escort boat. U-Boot-Jäger: submarine chaser.*

captured were dummy guns and a few Germans hiding in caves, whereas they would have been much more useful on the continent. He began by reporting to Admiral Davidson that the Titan battery had been occupied. Then he detailed the situation in a message to the *Augusta*:

"*Two useless islands. Suggest immediate evacuation. 240 prisoners. Enemy battery decoy. Request permission to leave immediately*"

General Patch, to whom the request was relayed,

Right.
The moorings at the foot of the Titan lighthouse.
(Private Collection)

Below.
Port-Cros, Landing 311 and the fort on pointe de Saint-Moulin with its two destroyed German guns, photographed on September 12, 1944.
(National Archives)

quickly answered:

"*Stay where you are for the time being.*"

However the islands were not as deserted as they thought. On Port-Cros equipment had been landed in the Port Man bay and the Vigie fort had been occupied, but the garrison had escaped through a tunnel and joined up with those defending the other two forts.

The *Augusta*'s help was requested by the SFCP and at 16.00 the first 203-mm shells fell on the forts without really doing much damage. On Le Levant the patrols were now confronted with stiff resistance from a strongpoint that had gone unnoticed in the dark. The destroyer *Lookout* had to intervene to convince its occupants to surrender. Then radio contact was lost. Patch was no longer receiving any report and opted to send his aide-de-camp to the island. James Forrestal, the secretary for the Navy, decided to go along. They landed on Yellow Beach during the last minutes of twilight and came back with good news: there were only a few snipers or pockets of resistance left, and the prisoners and wounded had left for Cavalaire. Finally at 22.34 resistance on the island ceased. During the night it was sporadically shelled by the shore batteries. Then in the afternoon of the 16th, the SSF were relieved by Senegalese and the 2nd Regiment moved to Cavalaire.

On the other hand, Port-Cros was being shelled every night by the Cap Bénat battery. It was the last fortress that had managed to resist the Navy guns and the bombs dropped from Wildcats fighters. The *Ramillies* finally had to be borrowed from TF 84: twelve direct hits with 381-mm shells followed by a company-sized assault from the 1st Regiment

LEGEND

1. Scarlet Beach
2. Emerald Beach
3. Red Beach
4. Blue Beach
5. Green Beach
6. Amber Beach
7. Yellow Beach (equipment)

◯

⬅ Battalion line of advance

prompted the last diehards to surrender on the 17th. Immediately LST 32 entered Port-Cros bay and laboriously unloaded a radar that was set up on the western point of the island [24]. On the same afternoon, Colonel Walker and the two regiments that had remained in the islands moved to the continent and the Force was grouped at Sylvabelle.

ROMEO FORCE ON CAP NEGRE

The 'Groupe de Commandos d'Afrique' originat-

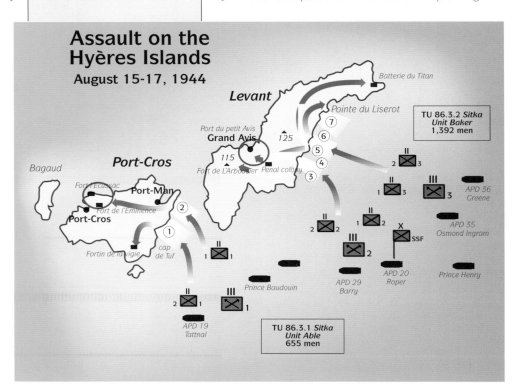

Assault on the Hyères Islands
August 15-17, 1944

23. Accompanied by Enseigne de Vaisseau Lasserre, from *Casabianca*. A dispute with Commandant Lherminier and his knowledge of English and special operations resulted in his being chosen for this liaison job.

24. GCI (Ground Control Interceptor) station.

(sailing, parachuting, demolitions) had been completed, the group arrived in Saint-Florent, Corsica. It was then that the idea of a raid of Cap Nègre or Cavalaire was hatched.

In June the group participated in the invasion of Elba island. Then on July 1 its orders were cut for Dragoon: attached to VI Corps, the group would make a nocturnal landing between D-1 and D near Cap Nègre to neutralize the German defenses and block the coast road as well as the one leading inland. That mission was slightly modified on the 17th with the addition of a new objective "*the cliffs situated 3.200 m north of Cap Nègre.*"

Lieutenant-Colonel Bouvet planned a surprise attack against the battery by a small group landing around midnight before the moon came up [25]. At the same time the main body would land near Le Rayol to help reduce the German resistance and secure the flanks around Mont Biscarre, La Môle and Bormes. For this, Bouvet did not request naval artillery support, but he did need precise information about landing sites, and liaisons "*with maquis elements on the beaches,*" as well as a parachute drop of water and ammunition during the day.

For the Americans the actions on the continent and in the islands were inter-dependent, and an interval of one and a half hours between the landing at Cap Nègre and that of the rest of the forces

ed as an irregular unit ('Corps franc d'Afrique' - CFA) created in November 1942 on the fringes of the French African Army. After the Tunisian campaign the CFA was disbanded and its men were allowed to choose whether they wanted to join up with the Free French forces or form a group of commandos attached to the Algerian Division. Seven hundred volunteers were finally accepted and, with sound regular officers, four commandos were organised and trained in amphibious operations.

On January 25, 1944, once advanced training

Top.
POWS from the Levant Islands help Forcemen unload the barges.
(National Archives)
Above.
**August 14, 1944.
On USS *Greene* (APD-36), Lt-Col. Bourne, CO of the SSF 2/3rd Regiment, gives his last instructions. Then each officer assembles his men to explain the mission details.**
(National Archives)

was unjustified. Consequently the time allowed for the preliminary attack on the battery was set earlier. Then the discovery of pillboxes flanking the Rayol beach meant that a destruction group had to be organised and landed along with the assault detachment. Even though a preliminary fire to burn over the maquis[26] and a submarine reconnaissance were denied by General Wilson, Bouvet was able to obtain two food and ammunition re-supplies:

25. On August 15, 1944 the moon rose at 0315.
26. Requested because of fear of the mistral wind and the consequences if the Germans set the maquis afire.
27. Accomplished by an American unit based in Corsica, with whom he secretly accompanied on a bombing mission over Cap Negre.
28. Lieutenant-Colonel Vernier (surgeon), Captain Juberry (anesthesia and transfusions), Lieutenant Mergier (assistant pharmacist), David Rowlands (operating room nurse), Miss Joan Fryke (nurse), Miss Rachel Howell Evans (nurse's assistant), Adjudant-Chef Noceto (administration and supplies).

The Groupe de commandos d'Afrique aboard Royal Navy LSIs

	LCA	LCM	Rubber boats	Men	Vehicles	Equipment
Prince David	6	2	8	268	4	5 t
Prince Albert	8	-	8	320	-	-
Princess Beatrix	6	2	8	245	4	5 t

Above.
General De Lattre de Tassigny decorates three Commandos d'Afrique officers who had shown valor during the heavy fighting on Elba.
(ECPAD)

one by sea at 09.00 and another at 11.00 by parachute [27]. Moreover, the Group was reinforced with a medical team led by Lieutenant-Colonel Vernier from the 1re DMI [28].

Meanwhile the Group had left Saint-Florent for Porto Vecchio, and from there the LSTs carried them to Civita Vecchia. The men enjoyed Bastille Day in Rome, but were furious at being kept away from France. Strange rumors were making the rounds; some even mentioned a departure for Yugoslavia... Once in Agropoli, near Salerno, though, things calmed down. Then on August 12, sailors and commandos left for Propriano where they were briefed aboard the *Augusta*. Bouvet learned that Cap Nègre harbored several 75-mm guns and a battery of four 155s, plus an antitank gun covering the coastal road[29]. He was finally allowed to reveal the secret plans to his men and was able to announce that the attack would begin in France on August 14 at midnight. The Group was divided up among the three LSIs, with Bouvet on the *Prince David* with Captain SH Norris, commanding the *Romeo Unit*; the group was divided on the three LSI as indicated on the table below.

At 1800, the file of ships reached the rendez-vous with the five American PT boats serving as control ships. Then at 2200 the 'Princes' anchored in the transfer zone, eleven nautical miles from the coast. Three LCAs were launched from the *Princess Beatrix*. The night was dark and the sea as flat as a pancake. Lieutenant Spencer from the Royal Navy and Captain Ducournau's commandos bound for Cap Nègre climbed down the nets into the landing boats, each taken in tow by a PT boat. PTs 210 and 208 then left for the coast, pulling the LCAs, each trailing an empty lifeboat [30]. The LCAs carried twenty-three men and the PT boats fifteen. Later the men were to be divided up with twenty-eight per LCA and ten in each rubber boat. Three miles from the coast the men in the PT boats thus transferred to the LCAs and rubber boats, and they headed off alone, with the captain in the lead.

The third landing craft, carrying the surfboat and

Above.
August 13, 1944 on the Punta di Balconcelli, facing the gulf of Valinco where the Sitka Force boats are anchored, Lieutenant-Colonel Bouvet is telling his men that they are going to land in France.
(Private Collection)

Below.
The commandos listen attentively to Lieutenant Colonel Bouvet's speech announcing the landing in France. In the first row of the command commando: Warrant Officer Olive, Chief WO Giuseppi, platoon leader, and Second Lieutnant Bonin of the signal platoon.
(Private collection)

Right.
The Commandos d'Afrique guidon (late-war pattern).

two rubber boats, hitched on behind PT 206. At five hundred meters from the shoreline, the surf boat was launched. Commander Rigaud and USN Lieutenant Johnston were tasked with reconnoitering the Rayol beach and the two sites where the blockhouse

29. Information annexed to the TF 86 operation plan, August 10, 1944.
30. Using gunboats to tow the LCAs made it possible to shorten the length of time necessary to cover the 18 km between the marshaling zone and the cape.

DAY

DAWN

1

2

DAY

DAWN

Shoulder title for the Commandos d'Afrique, in red letters on a grey-blue, then dark blue background.
(Private collection)

3

4

PHOTO OF MODEL NO. 7

PHOTO OF MODEL NO. 8

5

6

7

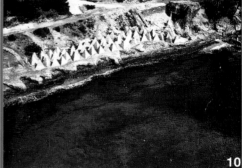

8

9

10

11

12

13

14

15

5. Landing 317. The western part of Rayol beach, with the staircases leading inland. *(Private Collection)*
6. Aerial view of the countryside around Cap Nègre. *(USAAF.)*
7. 77-mm gun blockhaus on the east slope of Cap Nègre.
8. 77-mm gun blockhaus on the west side of Cap Nègre, facing Cavalière Bay.
9. Aerial photograph of the coast between the Bormes roadstead and Cap Nègre. *(Private Collection)*
10. 77-mm gun blockhaus and dragon teeth obstructions on the small beach west of Cap Nègre.

1 to 4. Photos of the relief model used to prepare the operation, representing the daytime and nighttime views of the coastline, at sea level and at a distance of 10 km: No 9 - from Cavalière (Beach 258) to Cavalaire (Beach 259), No 7 - The Bormes roadstead (Beach 257). *(Private Collection)*

12. Cap Nègre and the Pramousquier beach. *(Private Collection)*
13. Le Canadel, landing beach. *(Private Collection)*
14. Aerial view of part of the Cap Nègre western shoreline.
15. Landing 316. Aiguebelle, looking northeast. *(Private collection)*

The raid at Cap Nègre
August 15, 1944

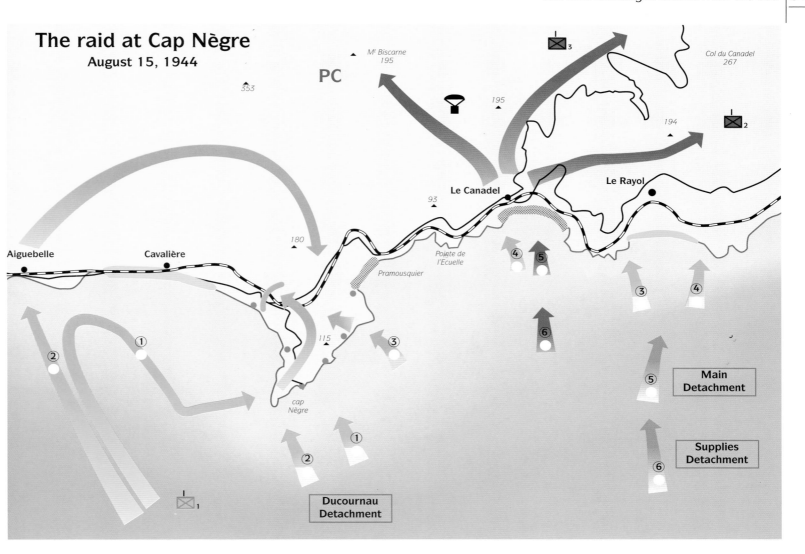

PC

▲ Mt Biscarne
195

353

195 ▲

Col du Canadel
267

194 ▲

Le Canadel

Le Rayol

93

Main
Detachment

180 ▲

Pointe de
l'Ecuelle

Supplies
Detachment

Pramousquier

Aiguebelle

Cavalière

115 ▲

cap
Nègre

Ducournau
Detachment

Right.
Right.
**The veterans of the 1er Commando
d'Afrique pose in front of their
bivouac tents in Civita Vecchia.**
(Musée de l'Armée, Paris)

Left.
**American PT Boats in the port
of Bastia.**
(National Archives)

Below
**August 14, 1944. A PT boat
carrying commandos leaves the
gulf of Valinco.**
(Musée de l'Armée, Paris)

raiding party were to land.

All of the other LCAs, towing their loaded rubberboats, advanced in flotilla formation behind PT 212.
Two detachments of forward artillery observers (FOB)
[31] accompanied the group CP. After waiting for the
final information from PT 210, the flotilla was to
spread out and prepare to land the troops at H-hour.
And the LCMs were to line up behind PT 218 who

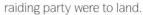

34. *Forward Observer Bombardment, the British equivalent of
the American SFCPs.*

Left.
The cliff-side path on Cap Nègre.*(DR)*

Right.
During a later stay in Le Lavandou, the African commandos reenact - in daytime for the French Army Cinema Service - the night landing on the rocks around Cap Negre.
(ECPAD)

Left.
The Cavalière inlet (Beach 258) seen looking east towards Cap Nègre.
(Private Collection)

Below.
Present-day view of Cavalière beach.
(Private Collection)

was to sheperd them.

But the best laid plans could go awry. Three men from the Ducournau group fell overboard and the second LCA had to stop to fish them out. Then the first two landing craft drifted off course to the west. When Ducournau realized his mistake, he ordered an about-turn. But Second Lieutenant Jeannerot thought he had just beached. A flare lit up the bay and the craft broached on rocks with its ramp ajar. A machine-gun opened fire from the mainland. It was 00.43. The commandos waded to a small wood from which they were soon dislodged by a forest fire lit by flares. They came across a railway station and thus learned that they were at Aiguebelle, three kilometers west of Cap Nègre. Jeannerot then decided

Below.
August 14, 1944 on board HMCS *Prince David*. Lieutenant-Colonel Bouvet is posing with his commandos and the Spears ambulance surgical team.
(Musée de l'Armée, Paris)

to move into the maquis and try to join up with Ducournau. At 0400 they stopped behind Cavalière: all his men were exhausted. A few rifle shots and machine-gun bursts could be heard in the distance, then a flare lit up the Rayol beach.

By this time Ducournau had been able to reach the foot of the cliffs. Sergeant Daboussy was climbing to tie to a tree the cable that would allow the men, loaded with 40 pounds of guns and equipment, to reach the crest eighty meters above. At that spot, instead of the expected 155s there were actually two 76-mm Russian guns which were soon taken care of with a bengalore torpedo. At 01.45 the position was secure [32].

Unknowingly the Ducournau commandos had actually been able to take advantage of an unexpected diversion! The ten commandos from the Texier group who were supposed to land on the left side of the Rayol beach, actually ended up at the foot of the eastern side of the cape. The senior NCO was killed by a grenade as he was scaling the cliff, and the defenders were tricked into shooting at each other in the dark. To the right, Sergeant Du Bellocq's group also got lost and their boat landed at Canadel.

At that time Bouvet found himself at the head of the main body:

32. The sector was occupied by the GR 917 4th Armenian batalion and some fortress engineers.

"*We approached the coast silently: we smelled the pines, the fragrance of France. But then suddenly, just as we were starting to make out the dark hulk of Cap Nègre, German double star flares started going off to the west of us. Again and again. We could clearly distinguish the grenades exploding and the spurt of tracer bullets on the other side of Cap Nègre, far off to the*

Above, from left to right
Canadel beach just after the war. Cap Nègre and the Bénat peninsula at the same time, seen from the road going up to the col du Canadel. Present-day view of Cap Negre. *(Private Collection)*

to climb up through the gardens to the Provence railway line and the Canadel station. By 0400, taking advantage of the confusion among the enemy, the strip of coastline had been crossed with no problems.

As planned, the LCMs carrying the jeeps arrived on the beach at 0300. But since this beach was completely cut off from the hinterland, the boats had to be reloaded and sent to Rayol, where there was a road leading inland from the shore. As the sun was rising the equipment was unloaded and the CP group with the mortars climbed up Mont Biscarre.

The artillery liaison team connected with the fleet at 07.42 and ranged the first fire from the *Dido*. Then a German counter-attack on the neck of Cap Nègre was repelled with the help of the *Augusta* guns. At 1000 the units could finally take a breather: Cap Nègre was occupied by the 1st commando, the 3rd was reaching the La Mole intersection and the 2nd had cleaned out the village of Rayol. An hour later, on Biscarre, at a spot signaled by yellow smoke, twin-engine Bostons parachuted containers that were picked up and manhandled by prisoners.

At one o'clock in the afternoon, Lieutenant Colonel Bouvet could report to Admiral Davidson that the shore road was blocked and that contact had been established with the American patrols coming from Cavalaire.

Then La Mole was captured. Finally at 1800 the first motorized elements from the 7th Infantry Regiment met up with the 1st Commando.

Two hours later, the Group received orders to start marching toward Le Lavandou [35].

west. Then a few flares went off over the shorefront. But the green light that Major Rigaud was supposed to show could not be seen. It was half past one. Suddenly we got a sickening feeling. Could the enemy have learned our intentions? The memory of the fireworks when we landed on Elba gripped us. [33]"

Bouvet also realized that Cap Nègre was right near him on the left. He had the LCA flotilla veer to starboard to reach the Rayol beach that was supposed to have been identified by Rigaud's signal light [34]. Time was running out and the craft could not remain long thus two hundred meters from the shore: the sailors therefore received orders to disembark. And so at 01.53, the flotilla moved to the shoreline, in correct order and without the men getting their feet wet. But it was not the right beach, it was the one two kilometers to the west that Bouvet had refused during preparations! No matter now, the men had

Above.
Frisking prisoners on the slopes of Mont Biscarre.
(Musée de l'Armée, Paris)

Below.
The first Sherman DD from the 756th Tank Bn. appears early in the afternoon on August 15.
(Musée de l'Armée, Paris)

---

33. *Lieutenant-Colonel Bouvet,* Une opération amphibie: le débarquement de Provence, *unpublished.*
34. *Actually the narrowness of the bay where the two officers had landed prevented surface vessels from seeing the light.*
35. *It lost 11 killed and 50 wounded.*

CROWDED SKYLANES

On August 10, 1944, when the British Chiefs of Staff relayed to General Wilson the order to execute 'Dragoon,' the air forces had already been working for months on the possibility of an invasion through the South of France. Of course their action was indirect, because it took place within the framework of the general operations program in support of Overlord. And their effort was limited since the Mediterranean Allied Air Forces gave priority to support of ground operations in Italy and to attacking targets that were out of range for the England-based bombers. To these missions were soon added sorties in support of the French guerrillas.

In spite of the uncertainty surrounding Anvil, the MAAF, under Major then Lieutenant General Ira C. Eaker, seconded by Air Marshal Sir John C. Slessor, nevertheless continued planning. The result was the air outline plan dated July 12 assigning the MAAF its various tasks.

And so, in preparation to the ground units' landings, the strategic air forces intensified their attacks.

Above.
P-38 fighter pilot.
(Reconstruction by Militaria Magazine)

Top, left.
The Mediterranean Allied Air Forces shoulder patch, with its evident symbolism, was worn well before General Marshall finally authorized it on August 12, 1944.
(Private collection)

Left.
August 6, 1944. Fifteenth Air Force Liberators attacking the railroad bridge across the Rhône below Avignon. In this oblique photo, taken from the north, one can see two B-24s in flight, the city and its famous bridge, with the Durance river in the background.
(National Archives)

STRATEGIC BOMBINGS

Since the invasion of Morocco, the Twelfth Air Force [1] had been tasked with supporting American ground forces. Later, on November 1, 1943, its heavy bombers became the core of the Fifteenth Air Force, commanded by Major General Nathan F. Twining [2], who was also leader of the Mediterranean Allied Strategic Air Force (MASAF). During the winter, while headquarters were being installed in Bari, the Liberator and Flying Fortress groups reached the Foggia airfields to participate in the aerial offensive against the Reich. And thus, from January 5, 1944 on, operations of the two air forces fighting Germany - the 8th in England and the 15th in Italy - were coordinated from London.

The first Fortresses appeared in the sky of Provence on August 17, 1943 over the Istres-le-Tube and Salon airfields. But then, since most of the missions at the time were directed toward Germany or the Balkans, continuing attacks were only irregular and aimed at specific targets: airfields south of Avignon, the Anthéor viaduct and bridge over the Var, ports of Marseilles and Toulon.

In April 1944 the 15th had four hundred airworthy B-24s and B-17s. One month later, there were near-

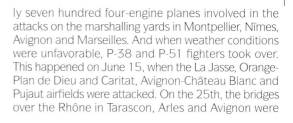

Above.
The Fifteenth Air Force was activated on November 1, 1943 in Tunis, and authorized to wear its own shoulder patch on February 19, 1944.
(Le Poilu)

Below.
A B-24 from the 460th Bomb. Group over Capri. The tail markings were chosen on arrival in Italy: a white circle inscribed in a square, with the numeral 1 (for the first unit of the 55th Wing).
(Private collection)

ly seven hundred four-engine planes involved in the attacks on the marshalling yards in Montpellier, Nîmes, Avignon and Marseilles. And when weather conditions were unfavorable, P-38 and P-51 fighters took over. This happened on June 15, when the La Jasse, Orange-Plan de Dieu and Caritat, Avignon-Château Blanc and Pujaut airfields were attacked. On the 25th, the bridges over the Rhône in Tarascon, Arles and Avignon were

'Section 8' was a 465th Bomb. Group Liberator.
(Private collection)

attacked by 650 bombers, as well as depots in Sète, Balaruc and Le Pontet. On July 11, Toulon was bombed again. The next day over four hundred Liberators attacked a variety of targets: Nîmes, Miramas, Théoule, Saint-Laurent-du-Var... On the 17th, 162 B-24s came back over Arles and Tarascon. Then, after a period of bad weather and missions over Hungary and the Balkans that were part of a program of shuttle flights between Italy and the USSR, the air raids continued on August 2 against Le Pouzin, Portes-les-Valence, Le Pontet and Avignon, while the railroad lines were cut in ten spots between Lyon and the Rhône River delta.

Nevertheless, compared to the air offensive preceding the invasion of Normandy, this one was limited in scope. This was "*in large part due to the actions of the French Resistance forces. The guerilla fighters blew up bridges and trains, killed German soldiers, destroyed their installations. For these jobs, they received unusual support from the 15th Air Force B-24s* [3]. Indeed, as soon as Eaker took command of the MAAF in December 1943, he increased 'Carpetbagger' missions for supplying the Maquis, which were flown by B-24s of the 859th [4] and 885th [5] Bombardment Squadrons based in Bari and Blida [6].

Late in July 1944, priority was finally given to Dragoon: Corsica had been transformed into a giant

Opposite.
The 'Section 8' crew photographed on the Pantanella airfield.
(Private collection)

---

1. Activated on August 20, 1942 at Bolling Field, near Washington, DC for the North African theater, it was made up of units withdrawn from Great Britain or assigned from the U.S.
2. Previously commander of the Thirteenth Air Force in the Southwest Pacific.
3. Steve Birdsall, Log of the Liberators, Doubleday & Co., New York, 1973.
4. Also flying C-47s, and decorated with the French Croix de Guerre.
5 Distinguished Unit Citation for Southern France, August 12, 1944.
6. A big effort was organized on August 12, 1944, with eleven B-24s undertaking separate drops involving 30 tons of weapons and equipment, 18 paratroopers and 225,000 leaflets.

Corsica
The Carrier-Island

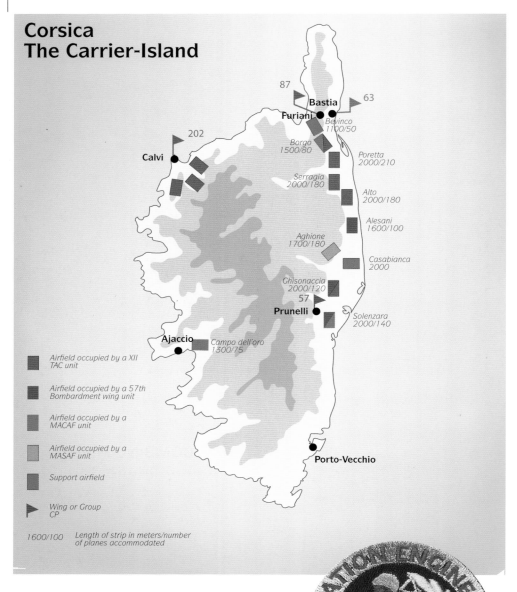

87

Bastia

63

Furiani

Bevinco
1100/50

202

Calvi

Borgo
1500/80

Poretta
2000/210

Serragia
2000/180

Alto
2000/180

Alesani
1600/100

Aghione
1700/180

Casabianca
2000

Ghisonaccia
2000/120

57

Prunelli

Solenzara
2000/140

Ajaccio

Campo dell'oro
1300/75

▪ Airfield occupied by a XII TAC unit

▪ Airfield occupied by a 57th Bombardment wing unit

▪ Airfield occupied by a MACAF unit

▪ Airfield occupied by a MASAF unit

▪ Support airfield

▶ Wing or Group CP

1600/100 — Length of strip in meters/number of planes accommodated

Porto-Vecchio

The electrical mechanics of the 488th Bombardment Squadron, 340th Group, found their tent riddled with shrapnel after the raid on the Alesani airfield carried out by German bombers on May 16, 1944.
(National Archives)

---

aircraft carrier from which the Twelfth Air Force fighter-bombers took off to attack targets in southeastern France.

CORSICA, THE CARRIER-ISLAND

From the beginning it was apparent that, to strike in the south of France without weakening air support in Italy, the air forces would have to be redeployed, making of 'backward and swampy' Corsica a spring-board for the invasion.

In December 1943 this mission was assigned to Vice Marshal Sir Hugh P. Lloyd, commander of the Mediterranean Allied Coastal Air Force (MACAF), who delegated coordination to Brigadier General D.D. Graves, Air Commander, Corsica, in Bastia. He was commander of the 63rd Fighter Wing responsible for air defense of Corsica and Sardinia. The first reconnaissance in October, when Corsica had been secured by the French, proved that only the eastern side of the island was suitable for airfields. But it was bristling with mines and isolated from the western side by destructions.

Moreover there were only two ports on the island: Ajaccio, with a capacity of 3,000 tons per day and which could only accept one Liberty ship at a time, and Bastia, with only 2,000 tons per day and whose roadstead was regularly mined by the Germans.

The first job was thus to restore communications between the two halves of the island and along the

eastern plain where more than fifty bridges had been blown. At first the work was done by Italians supervised by Frenchmen, but difficult relations between the two, along with the lack of tools and construction materials, meant that progress was slow. And once the roads and bridges had finally been repaired by the American engineers [7] in February 1944, they had to be maintained in spite of bad weather and heavy traffic.

An artificial port with a capacity of 200 tons per day was built in Porto-Vecchio, and material and supplies stored in Ajaccio were carried to the east coast on LCTs, where they were unloaded at first directly on the beaches, then in the port of Bastia as soon as the Navy gave permission.

For fuel, a pipeline with a daily capacity of 7,200 tons was built between Porto-Vecchio and Bastia with a reversible pumping system allowing pumping from both ends. And in addition there were 17,600 tons in reserve tanks on the island and 9,400 more on Maddalena, with another 16,000 on tankers which were on call ready to sail.

7. *Two General Service Regiments: the 41st (Colored) from North Carolina arrived on December 14, 1943 via Liberia and Algeria, the 335th arrived on January 10, 1944.*

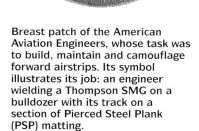

Breast patch of the American Aviation Engineers, whose task was to build, maintain and camouflage forward airstrips. Its symbol illustrates its job: an engineer wielding a Thompson SMG on a bulldozer with its track on a section of Pierced Steel Plank (PSP) matting.
(Le Poilu)

Right.
Aviation engineers unrolling a roll of tarred felt known as 'Hessian Matting' which will become the runway of a new airstrip.
(National Archives)

A Martin B-26-B-40 Marauder belonging to the 444th Squadron, 320th Bombardment Group.
(Computer graphics by André Jouineau)

Bombs, with an estimated demand of 52,000 tons, were loaded on Liberty ships to Cagliari (Sardinia), then transshipped onto coastal lighters to be landed on the east coast.

As was the case for supplies, the arrival of personnel was also staggered over a period of about three months. The elements of the Coastal Air Force and the Twelfth Air Force bombardment wings were in Corsica from May 15 on, but it was July 26 before the units of the XII Tactical Air Command reinforced by British and French squadrons started to move, and even then their regular operations were not interrupted. Actually the transfer took only eight days:

Right.
An A-20 Havoc bomber from the 47th Bombardment Group (Light) on the Poretta airfield preparing to leave for a mission.
(USAAF)

Below.
A Spitfire from Royal Air Force Squadron 242, 322 Wing, has just landed at Calenzana after patrolling over the beachhead, and is heading toward the refuelling point.
(IWM - CL 880)

more than one permanent American battalion [9] assigned to this task.

At the end, when work was completed, the air forces had at their disposal a state-of-the-art communications network and fourteen operational strips capable of accommodating forty-six Allied squadrons [10].

THE BOMBING PLAN

The Coastal Air Force was not only in charge of construction and defense of Corsican air bases, it also had to protect convoys within a forty mile radius around the beaches, and participate in anti-submarine warfare and sea rescue outside the assault zone.

The Strategic Air Force also had to be ready to satisfy requests from the ground tactical forces and

8. 71st and 72nd Companies, which became I/71 and II/71 on April 1, 1944.
9. including elements from three Engineer Aviation Battalions: the 812th which had arrived from Sicily on January 11, 1944 after a long trip from Florida via Kenya, Egypt, Libya, Algeria and Sicily and whose 'colored' engineers remained on the island to maintain the airfields; the 845th arriving from Italy on February 16, 1944, and the 817th from Italy which stayed from March 16 to June 20, 1944, then returned on July 17, 1944.
10. Including 2,156 aircraft.

each squadron was divided into two waves transported on LSTs.

As to the airfields, at first it was decided to simply upgrade the existing sites - Ajaccio, Calvi, Ghisonaccia and Bastia - to American standards. Then two new airfields were built for the coastal aviation, followed by more sites for the tactical forces. Once the roads had been repaired, construction work began with Italian workers and French machines driven by Spaniards. The Italian troops that were available between November 1943 and May 1944 were used for a variety of tasks: mine-clearing, construction of buildings or radar stations, access roads for fresh water supplies and depots, bush-cutting... Two companies from the French aviation engineers [8] were also employed in Ajaccio and Ghisonaccia. But because of priorities in Italy and French North Africa, there was never much

Right.
April 23, 1944. The 340th Bombardment Group ground echelon arrives in Porto-Vecchio aboard one of the two Royal Navy LST (1)s.
(USAAF)

A North American B-25-J-1 Mitchell,
part of the 489th Squadron, 340th
Bombardment Group.
(Computer graphics by André Jouineau)

Top.
The crew of B-26 *Zero Four*, 319th Bomb. Group, based in Decimomannu, Sardinia, then at Serragia from September 20, 1944 on. The group received the French Croix de Guerre for its action in Italy between April and June. *(USAAF)*
Above.
A B-25J used by the 319th Bomb. Group after their Marauders had been withdrawn.
(USAAF)

Above.
Picture taken on August 6, 1944 at 1003 from a French B-2 of Groupe I/22 'Maroc,' showing bombs falling around the railroad bridge crossing the Rhone at Arles.
The Roman arena is clearly visible.
(Private collection)

the new bases in Corsica before the beginning of operations.

Thus Cannon decided to assign support of the 15th Army Group to the Desert Air Force and to move the XII Tactical Air Command [11] on the island. Two squadrons of medium bombers were kept in reserve ready to assist one or the other. And since most of the transport units had been sent to Normandy, requests went out to send the groups need-

intervene in the fighting when necessary. Eaker was not in favor of this since the bombing of Cassino. But memories of Pantelleria and Salerno were still vivid and the aviators had to abide.

The choice of the best time to attack the coastal batteries was also subject to discussion. On July 12, Major General John K. Cannon, commander of the Tactical Air Force, pronounced in favor of massive action on D-1. Admiral Cunningham and General Patch did not agree. They argued that the experience gained in Normandy, where aerial bombing had failed to obliterate enemy positions, meant that such a short period of preparation was unrealistic, considering that the batteries were numerous and protected by the jagged coast line. In the end the MATAF Bombing Plan disclosed on August 4 was a compromise: preparation would begin on D-10, and the coastal batteries would be targeted starting on D-6.

Responsibility for the planification of the assault phase fell entirely on MATAF, which was forced to shuffle its forces - American Twelfth Air Force and British Desert Air Force - in order to support the troops both in Italy and in Provence, and settle in

**Twelfth Air Force shoulder patch,
authorized on December 1, 1943.**
(Le Poilu)

Right.
**Flight gear in a French
Marauder unit in 1944-1945:
parachute, Flak vest and
steel helmet.**

ed for an airborne operation on to the Mediterranean theater.

Considering how uncertain Anvil was, planning was of course difficult. The first orders went out from MATAF on January 31, 1944, but the planners had to wait until July 8 - when the decision was finally made - for the teams to assemble in Naples. On the

11. Activated on April 15, 1944 by changing the name of the XII Air Support Command.

• Destruction of airfields in southern France and northern Italy, the ones between Toulouse and Marseilles being taken out by the heavy bombers;

• Isolating the invasion zone by destroying communications lines in the Rhône valley and between Cannes and Genoa by the tactical forces, between Valence and Modane by the strategic air forces if it could not be done by the Résistance;

• Attacking any enemy submarines around Toulon that may have been reported.

The second phase, or Operation 'Nutmeg,' would last from August 10 to 03.50 on August 15. This phase targeted the assault area where coast batteries, radar stations and troops along the coastline had to be neutralized. So that a tactical element of surprise could be preserved, and that the secret of the Allied intentions would not be revealed until sixteen hours before H-hour [14], it was decided to order the same type of action alternatively on the three other coastal sections, between Béziers and Viareggio.

The third phase, or Operation 'Yokum,' would occur in the time remaining until H-hour, its aim being to destroy as much of the enemy defenses as possible along the coast as well as the airfields within the invasion area. All available forces were to be committed. Yokum also involved a diversion around La Ciotat, and a massive parachute operation north of Le Muy involving the elements of the airborne division.

The air forces's assignments during Operation 'Ducrot,' the last phase, were typical: destruction of defenses in the assault area, isolating the battlefield

14th, Brigadier General Gordon Saville, who had been named commander of the Anvil air forces three days before, submitted his outline plan concerning bombing support for the ground troops. The MATAF team then left Naples for Algiers, leaving the XII TAC to finalize plans in liaison with the Seventh Army. A stream of orders and instructions flowed until August 8 and all the subordinate officers were briefed about the operation on the 12th and 13th.

For Operation Dragoon, MATAF fielded in Corsica thirty-nine squadrons [12] from the XII TAC, whose CP was coupled with that of the Seventh Army, and from the 87th Fighter Wing installed at Furiani, plus twelve squadrons of B-25s from the 57th Bombardment Wing. There were also sixteen squadrons of B-26s from the 42nd Wing based in Sardinia, the C-47s being grouped around Rome. Allocation by squadron and nationality was as follows:

	USAAF	RAF	FAF
Fighters & reconnaissance planes	26	12	4
Bombers	24	—	4
Transport planes	32	—	—

Six fighter squadrons from the Fifteenth Air Force based in Corsica and the planes on the aircraft carriers belonging to Task Force 88 were also placed under Cannon's orders. He also had between four and six MACAF night fighters, which would be useful for escorting the air transport fleet, and the Desert Air Force could if necessary bring in twenty-five squadrons for reinforcement [13].

The MATAF Bombing Plan involved four phases. During the first, staged from August 5 to 9, priority would be given to preparing the invasion, while at the same time continuing to assist the offensive in Italy and Normandy, by:

Above.
August 6, 1944. B-26s from the 319th Bombardment Group strike the railroad bridge in Tarascon. It was hit by several bombs that destroyed two spans, opened a 56-meter-wide breach and weakened the structure.
(MATAF via SHAA)

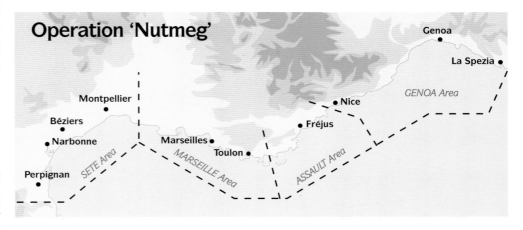

Operation 'Nutmeg'

by insuring that all bridges were cut, harassment of enemy troops trying to move in the Rhône valley and the Alps.

Below.
17th Bombardment Group B-26s on their base at Villacidro, Sardinia. On June 4, 1944 the group received the French Croix de Guerre for its action in Italy.
(SHAA)

12. 29 fighter (18 P-47s and 11 Spitfires), 5 recce, one night fighter, four light bomber squadrons.
13. 13 fighter, 5 recce, one night fighter, six bomber squadrons.
14. August 14 at 1600.

sion of Normandy had demonstrated the effectiveness of the fighters against this type of target.

The sorties [16] were staggered timewise, and divided up over the four coastal sectors between the bombers and fighters of the Twelfth and Fifteenth Air Forces:

	Sète	Marseilles	Dragoon	Genoa
August 11	batteries (MB)	batteries (FB)		
August 12	batteries (HB)	batteries (HB)	batteries (MB)	batteries (HB)
	radars (F)	radars (F)	batteries (FB)	radars (F)
August 13[17]	batteries (HB)	batteries (HB)	radars (F)	batteries (HB)
	radars (F)	batteries (MB)	batteries (F-FB)	radars (F-FB)
August 14	batteries (HB)	batteries (MB)	batteries (HB)	radars (F)
		radars (FB)	radars (F)	radars (FB)

Phase III lasted four hours and ten minutes before H-Hour. Twelve heavy bomber groups and their escort, the two Marauder wings and all of the XII TAC fighter-bombers were thus committed:
- Between 0550 and 0610, patrols by four Thunderbolts flying over the invasion area, ready to silence any battery that might open fire;
- From 0610 to 0730, small groups of all types of

FROM NUTMEG TO YOKUM

During the preliminary phase, the air forces thus intervened as planned in the skies of Provence in support of the Normandy invasion and in preparation for Anvil-Dragoon [15]. In addition to the important damage resulting from this action, the long series of sporadic attacks had the effect of bewildering the Germans as to the execution of the Bombing Plan and the location of the future invading zone.

On and after August 6, the sun came out after a several days of bad weather, and the bombers undertook the systematic destruction of the bridges over the Rhône, Drôme, Isère and Var Rivers, while the fighter-bombers strafed railway lines and rolling stock as well as airports. On D-Day communications with Italy and Lyons had been completely destroyed, and the only bridge left over the Rhône was the railroad bridge in Avignon, which had been cut off during a raid but rebuilt with a single track by the Germans.

Phase II was to begin on August 10. But because of inclement weather, only the fighters could take off to attack the Genoa and Marseilles batteries. So the program had to be spread out over the next four days. The heavy bombers concentrated on the batteries while the enemy radars were assigned to their escort planes, since a study done during the inva-

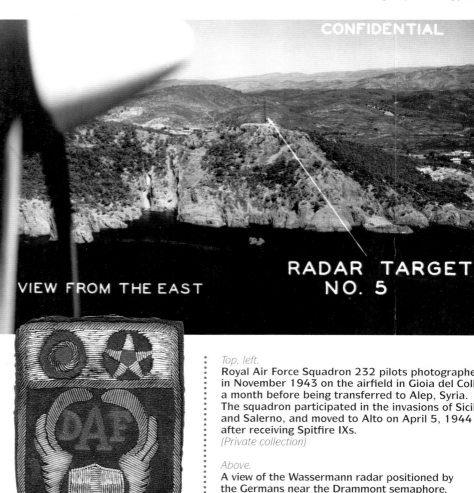

VIEW FROM THE EAST

RADAR TARGET NO. 5

Top, left.
Royal Air Force Squadron 232 pilots photographed in November 1943 on the airfield in Gioia del Colle, a month before being transferred to Alep, Syria. The squadron participated in the invasions of Sicily and Salerno, and moved to Alto on April 5, 1944 after receiving Spitfire IXs.
(Private collection)

Above.
A view of the Wassermann radar positioned by the Germans near the Drammont semaphore.
(SHAA)

Desert Air Force **shoulder patch showing the Allied roundel and the insignia of the British 8th Army which the DAF supported.**
(Private collection)

Left.
A French Marauder pilot in his steel helmet and Flak vest.

15. This involved one quarter of the 6,000 sorties accomplished by the MAAF planes since April 28, 1944, 12,500 tons of bombs dropped including 67% on communications lines, 17% on ports, 9% on plants and 7% on airstrips.
16. 5,408 equally divided between the MASAF and the MATAF, 6,740 tons of bombs including 4,450 for MASAF, 70 missions for the bombardment group (42 with B-17s and B-24s under escort; 28 with B-25s and B-26s), 32 night bomber sorties, 512 with fighter-bombers. 50 planes were lost, including 15 heavy bombers, 4 medium, one maritime patrol plane and 29 fighters or fighter-bombers.
17. Moreover various airfields were also struck that day: Les Chanoines, La Jasse, Istres-le-Tube, Salon-de-Provence, Valence-La Trésorerie and Toulouse-Blagnac.

**Lockheed P-38
(F-4) photo plane from the
French Air Force Reconnaissance Group 2/33.**
(Computer graphics by André Jouineau)

**Vertical photo of the coastal sector
from Agay to Drammont, taken
from 7,000 meters up on January
3, 1944 at 1230 by the 60th
Photo Reconnaissance Squadron.**
(SHAA)

Right, insert.
**XII Tactical Air Command shoulder
patch, authorized only locally. The
upside-down broadsword
symbolizes the power of
destruction coming from the sky.**
(Private collection)

aircraft attacking specific targets;
• From 0635 to 0730, bomber formations releasing a deluge of bombs over the beaches to annihilate defenses and underwater obstacles;
• From 0800 on, thirty-two fighter-bombers [18] ready to intervene on call.

On August 15 at dawn the weather forecast [19] confirmed and overcast sky over the beaches. Consequently, and according to the agreement with the land forces who did not want any air attack to take place without visual contact with the target, thus eliminating any risk to troops on the ground, instructions were given to limit 'blind' bombing. Some four-engine planes were able to take advantage of a hole in the cloud layer to drop their bombs, but by and large the others failed, as did most of the medium bombers [20].

The beaches were targeted along their total length and along a width of four hundred meters, starting seventy-five meters from the shore. In order to avoid hitting any of the boats, no attack could be executed at an angle of more than 45° with respect to the beach. Likewise, approaches were to take place along precisely defined corridors, in order to avoid another Sicily mishap. In spite of all these difficulties and constraints, the result was nevertheless considered satisfactory, since the assault troops met almost no resistance.

THE FOURTH PHASE

When the first waves reached the beaches, Phase IV began. All the air forces were initially involved in this phase. This included the Navy carrier planes, their job being to insure protection of the carriers themselves, to observe the ships' fire [21], and combat support missions by rocket-firing fighters. Actually the number of operational aircraft remained higher than expected.

The estimation had been based on the experience of Salerno, but here the number of available planes did not decrease rapidly in proportion to the number of sorties undertaken.

Thus the nature of the support missions changed

18. 16 carrier planes including 8 with rockets, and 16 from the XII TAC.
19. Clear weather until the island of Elba, then 3/10 to 6/10 low stratus clouds along the Provence coast, visibility six to ten kilometers.
20. Of the 959 sorties, 610 were successful, with 774 tons of bombs dropped; losses included two heavy, three medium and one fighter-bomber.
21. Divided among Task Group 88.1 for the Sitka and Alpha sectors, TG 88.2 for Delta and the XII TAC for Camel.

**P-47 Thunderbolts of the 86th Fighter
Squadron (79th Fighter Group).**
(USAAF)

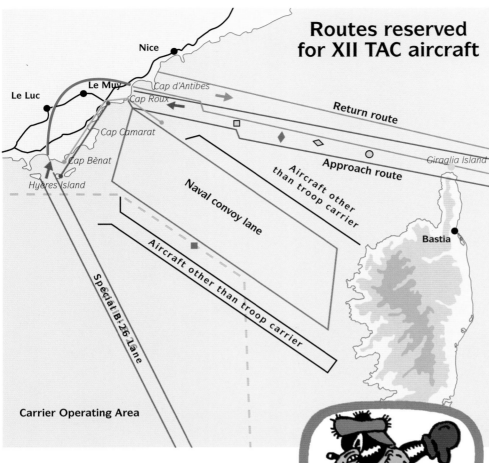

Routes reserved for XII TAC aircraft

Carrier Operating Area

zone were under the control of the Air Task Force Commander on the *Catoctin* [25]. It was here that the reports sent by the reconnaissance aircraft were collated, as well as intelligence debriefings of the carrier planes and fighter-bombers. But routine orders were decentralized to avoid the problems encountered in Salerno and Anzio where the flagship had been saturated by radio reports. The network interferences that had appeared during the two training exercises that had taken place in the bay of Naples just before the first convoy weighed had

slightly: they were flown over and beyond the beaches. All day long Lightnings and Thunderbolts criss-crossed the sky attacking artillery positions and patrolling above the beaches [22], while the fighter-bombers took on the defenses and road bridges between Hyères and Nice [23]. Some went as far as the Durance River [24] on armed reconnaissance flights, while the medium bombers aimed their strikes at roads and railroads beyond the assault area. The heavy bombers that were not participating in Operation Yokum bombed the Fréjus defenses and the bridges over the Rhône.

General control of operations was carried out by MATAF, but support planes operating in the assault

also been corrected.

The *Catoctin* thus coordinated aerial alert and sea rescue missions in liaison with HMS *Antwerp*, specially equipped as an air-sea rescue ship. Outside the assault area coordination was relayed to the 63rd Fighter Wing. It monitored the missions - pursuit, attack and reconnaissance - for maximum effectiveness, by adapting the targets minute-by-minute to the changing situation, and strove to avoid mistakenly bombing friendly troops. FDT-13 [26] took charge of air defense. It could be replaced if necessary by an LSF, HMS *Ulster Queen*, playing the role of fighter director ship. She was accompanied by three LSTs equipped with GCIs providing round-the-clock radar watch. On the evening of August 15, another LSF, HMS *Stuart Prince*, was located to the south of the convoy route, half way between Corsica and the French coast. This ship insured forward radar control for the Ajaccio sector, thus acting as relay between the LST-GCIs in the assault zone and the ground radars in Corsica. The planes flying from the island toward the assault area were controlled by the 87th Fighter Wing in Furiani.

August 15 was thus the day with the heaviest participation of air forces in the Mediterranean, with more than four thousand sorties [27].

Insignia of American P-47 Thunderbolt squadrons:
• 66th Fighter Squadron (57th Group).
• 65th Fighter Squadron (57th Group).
(Computer graphics by Yann Robert)

Top right.
August 16, 1944. Major Franklin L. Robinson, CO of the 48th Fighter Squadron, 14th Fighter Group, who attacked vehicles west of Toulon. He was hit by heavy Flak from the port and crashed at the entrance to the little town of Reynier.
(Private collection)

Captain Thomas E. Maloney of the 27th Fighter Squadron, 1st Fighter Group, photographed in his P-38 on the Salsola airfield in March 1944.
(Private collection)

22. From 0755 to 1940.
23. From 0815 to 2000.
24. From 1230 to 1545.
25. Manned by Navy and 2nd Air Combat Control Squadron (Amphibious) personnel.
26. Fighter Director Tender No 13, one of the three LST (2)s transformed by the Royal Navy and brought back from Normandy. When she arrived in the Mediterranean around August 3, 1944, her antenna system was modified by the XII TAC to be compatible with the MAAF frequencies. On board was Brigadier General Glenn O. Barcus, commander of the 64th Fighter Wing, with USAAF air controllers for defensive missions and RAF controllers for night pursuit.

North American P-51D Mustang from the 2nd Squadron, 52nd Fighter Group.

525th Fighter Squadron, 96th Group insignia.
(Computer graphics by Yann Robert)

Republic P-47D Thunderbolt from the 527th Squadron, 86th Fighter Group.

Republic P-47D Thunderbolt of French Groupe de Chasse I/4 'Navarre'

A Squadron 111 Royal Air Force Supermarine Spitfire Mk IX.

Supermarine Spitfire Mk IX of French Groupe de Chasse I/3 'Corse'

Computer graphics by André Jouineau

Rear Admiral Calvin T. Durgin, commander of Task Group 88.2, talking with the VOF-1 pilots in the Ready Room of USS *Tulagi* (CVE-72).
(US Navy)

Background photo.
August 13, at 12.30. Task Group 88.1 aircraft carriers pass convoy TM-1 from Taranto carrying equipment for the French divisions.
(IWM - A25270)

Below.
VF-74 pilots in front of the F6F-5 Hellcat flight line on the deck of the USS *Kasaan Bay* (CVE-69). Their leader, Lieutenant Commander H.B. Bass, was killed on August 20, 1944 at Saint Bonnet-le-Froid, east of Annonay, while he was attacking a convoy of vehicles with five other planes.
(Private collection)

On August 20, Lieutenant David Stanley Crockett, USNR, a VOF-1 pilot, was hit by Flak over the port of Toulon as he was observing enemy fire.
He bailed out, was captured and taken to the Arsenal. He was liberated with other aviators three days later.
(IWM - NYP 41 922)

August 7, 1944. Fleet Air Arm Squadron 881 and HMS *Pursuer* are training near Malta.
A Martlet is being brought onto the flight deck where a reinforced crew takes charge of it.
(IWM - A 25 188)

Below.
On the *Pursuer*, armorers are loadings bombs under a Martlet's wings.
(IWM - A 25 274)

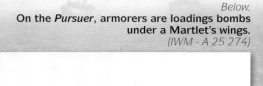

HMS *Emperor*, a Bogue-class escort carrier, was transferred to Britain by the United States as a result of the Lend-Lease Act.
(IWM - A 21 920)

Deck crew are moving out of the way a Martlet that aborted on take-off at the last moment.
(IWM - A 25 277)

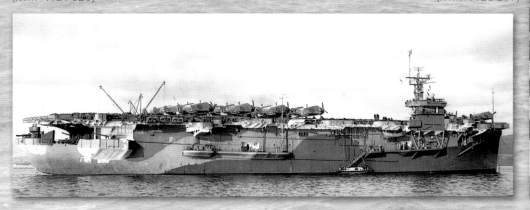

A Fleet Air Arm Squadron 800 Grumman Hellcat Mk I on HMS *Emperor*.

A Grumman Hellcat F6F-5 of VOF 1, the CVE-72 *Tulagi*'s Squadron One.

Fleet Air Arm Squadron 807 Supermarine Seafire LIIC on HMS *Hunter*.

Fleet Air Arm Squadron 898 Grumman Martlet Mk V aboard HMS *Searcher*.

HMS *Delhi*, a light anti-aircraft cruiser providing protection for the TG 88.1 carriers.
(IWM - A 23 717)

(Computer graphics by André Jouineau)

Right and below, right.
Along with Hessian matting, Aviation Engineers used two other systems for covering airstrips: pierced-steel planking (PSP) and Sommerfeld (square-mesh) matting.
(USAAF)

The Fifteenth Air Force had supported Overlord by bombing the railroad yards in the south of France in May and June, but the Eighth Air Force, on alert, only had to intervene once in support of Dragoon [28]. The Luftwaffe undertook only sixty sorties [29], and ten more the next day. The only Luftwaffe reinforcements - thirty Me 109s - arrived from Italy:

"The German fighter force still was utterly incapable of interfering with the Allies or protecting its own troops or bases. By week's end the German bomber force had to move back to the Lyons area. German bombing operations were attempted at dusk on the 15th through the 19th by small forces of Ju 88s against both sea and ground targets, with inconspicuous results, although German reconnaissance undoubtedly had been successful in spotting the invasion convoys in Ajaccio harbor on the morning of the 12th." [30]

D + 1 TO D + 2

The following days XII TAC concentrated on railways and roads further and further to the north and west. At first, this was to keep reinforcements from reaching the beach head, but then, as the Allies progressed rapidly, it served to slow or stop the enemy retreat, particularly in the Montélimar bottle-neck. The fighter-bombers also kept up their action against coastal traffic toward Nice and Monaco, and the Marauders began operations against the Toulon defenses on the 17th.

But the primary objective was of course to pro-

27. *4,249 including 3,880 tons dropped and 46 planes lost compared to 9 enemy planes destroyed.*
28. *On August 14, 1944 against airfields in the vicinity of Dijon.*
29. *On August 15, 1944, only 4 FW 190s were spotted, and of the 17 enemy Me 109s engaged in dogfights by the XII TAC, three were shot down.*
30. *MAAF Report on Operation Dragoon. On August 12, 1944, a report from Armeegruppe G mentioned the presence of two convoys composed of 75 to 100 warships and landing craft.*

AIRFIELD CONSTRUCTION PROGRAM
AAF Engineer Command (MTO)

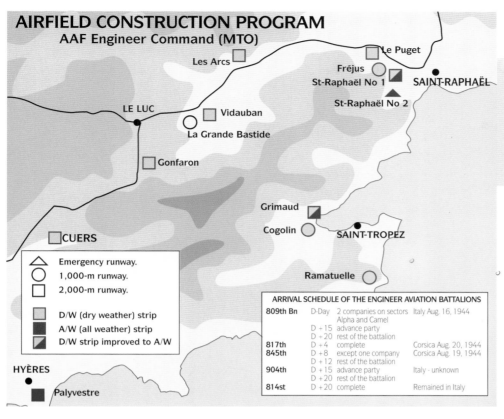

Emergency runway.
1,000-m runway.
2,000-m runway.

D/W (dry weather) strip
A/W (all weather) strip
D/W strip improved to A/W

HYÈRES
Palyvestre

ARRIVAL SCHEDULE OF THE ENGINEER AVIATION BATTALIONS

809th Bn	D-Day	2 companies on sectors Alpha and Camel	Italy Aug. 16, 1944
	D + 15	advance party	
	D + 20	rest of the battalion	
817th	D + 4	complete	Corsica Aug. 20, 1944
845th	D + 8	except one company	Corsica Aug. 19, 1944
	D + 12	rest of the battalion	
904th	D + 15	advance party	Italy - unknown
	D + 20	rest of the battalion	
814st	D + 20	complete	Remained in Italy

	LENGTH	PLANES	FLYABLE	COMPLETED	UNITS
St-Raphaël 2	1 000 m	Crash	D + 1	D + 2	
Ramatuelle	1 000 m	Fighters	D + 3	D + 6	324 Wing (RAF) 225 Sqn (RAF)
Frejus	1 000 m	Fighters	D + 4	D + 6	322 Wing (RAF)
Grimaud	2 000 m	Ftr. Bomb. A/W	D + 7	D + 8 D + 35	GR 2/33 (FAF) 111th T/R Sq 23rd PRU
St-Raphaël 1	2 000 m	Night Ftr. A/W	D + 8	D + 11 D + 45	324th Ftr Gp
Le Puget	2 000 m	Ftr. Bomb.	D + 12	D + 13	27th Ftr Gp
Les Arcs	2 000 m	Ftr. Bomb.	D + 13	D + 15	79th Ftr Gp
Vidauban*	2 000 m	Ftr. Bomb.		D + 17	57th Ftr Gp
Cogolin	1 000 m	Fighters	D + 12	D + 17	251 Wing (RAF)
Gonfaron	2 000 m	Ftr. Bomb.	D + 18	D + 20	4th EC (FAF)
Cuers	2 000 m	Ftr. Bomb.	D + 20	D + 22	86th Ftr Gp
Hyères	2 000 m		D + 50		

* Also called Le Luc

An armorer loads ammunition for the eight cal .50 MGs in the nose of a B-25J Mitchell.
(USAAF)

Left.
A Twelfth Air Force Beaufighter night fighter plane.
(USAAF)

French squadron GR I/33 'Belfort' insignia.
(Private collection)

Previous page, bottom.
August 15, 1944. B-26s taking off rom a fog-covered base in Sardinia.
(IWM - EA 33 705)

A brand-new Marauder has just been delivered to the French Air Forces. An airman is covering the American marking with the French tricolor roundel.
(DR)

tect the invasion fleet along the coast were the Kampfgruppen 26 and 100 bombers tried to attack several times. The Ju 88s and Do 217s were stopped by heavy antiaircraft fire, and then attacked time and again at their bases in Valence and Toulouse.

Once the sky had become quieter, the first planes from Corsica could land on the airstrips that had been built by the Aviation Engineers. Planning for these airfields had started in February 1944. At that time information had been collected about favorable terrain, their geological characteristics, local resources and weather… It was apparent right from the beginning that the coming battle, considered a slow, difficult one, would entail a maximum amount of close air support that could not be provided for long by the planes based in Corsica or on carriers. The autumn rains could start any time, so it was indispensable to build numerous all-weather air-strips that could handle as many planes as possible. At first four engineer battalions were assigned to this task. But since it was not expected that Marseilles - where the better terrains were located - would be taken before D + 40 to 60 at the earliest, two more battalions were added to speed up construction before the bad weather set in. The final plan includ-

ed five battalions from Corsica or Italy during the first three weeks. And the very ambitious program called for building an emergency runway within the beachhead, then nine airstrips before D + 25, followed by three all-weather strips between D + 35 and D + 50.

So Squadron 72 Spitfires were able to land at Ramatuelle on August 18, and they were joined two days later by the 2nd flight of the French GR II/33.

GERONIMO!

"*Geronimo!*" was the Test Platoon's war cry when they jumped out of the plane door, and it became the American paratroopers' slogan.
Thus the 503rd, which became the 509th, inscribed the words on its unofficial pocket badge. The badge was adopted when the battalion was performing guard duty for the Fifth Army HQ in Italy. It represents a jumper positioned in the doorway of a C-47, nicknamed the 'gingerbread man' because of his shape.
(Private collection)

Since November 1942, every Allied amphibious operation in the western Mediterranean had usually been accompanied by paratroops dropped to isolate the beachhead and keep enemy reinforcements from reaching the beach head.

This type of action had often proved disappointing, but in Provence it was to be a brilliant success. In this, as in everything else, the American 'Greenhorns' had soon become professionals, surpassing their Allies thanks to their powerful war machine and their incomparable technology. They had come a long way since the half-failure of Operation Torch when the 2nd Battalion, 509th Parachute Infantry Regiment [1] had been in charge of seizing the airfields south of Oran [2]. For 'Dragoon,' the First Airborne Task Force would be part of the largest air and naval armada ever assembled in the Mediterranean.

Paratrooper from the 517th Parachute Infantry Regiment.
(Reconstruction Provence 1944)

Paratroopers from the 82nd Airborne Division check their equipment before boarding the plane for a test jump in North Africa. *(US Army)*

Paratroopers ready to land under their canopies during a training jump in North Africa. *(US Army)*

Loading a Waco glider with a 75-mm Pack Howitzer during an exercise in North Africa. *(US Army)*

FROM HUSKY TO ANZIO

After Torch, during the following invasion, Operation Husky in Sicily, it was planned that the two parachute regiments of the American 82nd Division would be committed piecemeal because of the lack of planes. The first wave had thus taken off from Tunisia in the evening on July 9, 1943. But navigation was tough, due to the dark sky, the strong wind and the tortuous route which the planes had to take, skimming the waves to avoid flying over the fleet and the enemy radars. The pilots missed the first turn, then failed to recognize the shoreline which they had only seen in photos. Even though only about one eighth of the paratroopers landed on the assigned jumping zone, the mission was nevertheless completed.

Two nights later the rest of the paratroops arrived to reinforce the beachhead. The first unit jumped without mishap, but the others became targets for trigger-happy land- or ship-based antiaircraft crews. Several planes turned back, and those that managed to reach to the coast dropped paratroopers all over the countryside. Once on the ground some men even fell to friendly fire [3].

Even though the scattered drop created havoc in the enemy lines, the Allies concluded to a failure due to a variety of causes: insufficient training of the Troop carrier crews and airborne troops, hasty preparations and reconnaissance, poor use of the paratroops… Instead of being dropped on the beaches, they could have been landed grouped, with very little risk, on the central plateau from where they could have attacked the enemy rears.

During the ensuing discussions, it was decided to use pathfinders to guide the planes, and to provide the lightly-armed paratroopers with more bazookas and anti-tank grenades. Likewise the gliders would carry anti-tank guns. Rallying troops on the ground - the moment when the paratroopers are the most vulnerable - was speeded up by special training and making the men carry as much as possible instead of dropping equipment in so many separate containers and cases.

After Sicily, the 82nd Division retired to Kairouan and prepared a jump at Capua, over the Volturno, then another in Rome, none of which did come off, and ended up reinforcing the beachhead in Salerno by air. The 2/509 was dropped over Avellino to harass

Above.
**The equipment of a paratrooper rifleman in the Mediterranean during the summer of 1943.
The M1 rifle has been dismantled in two main parts for the jump. It would be carried insigne a special padded case. Also note the pocket compass, trench knife, the four 'rigger-made box-shaped ammunition carriers, K-ration and first aid packet.**
(National Archives)

Above.
The 82d A/B Division shoulder patch. After heavy fighting in Sicily and Italy, the division left for England, leaving some of its units the Mediterranean.
(Le Poilu)

Right.
A Douglas C-47 plane taking-off from a North African airfield with a CG-4A Waco glider in tow.
(National Archives)

Left.
504th PIR paratroopers firing the 60-mm M2 mortar near Venafro, in the Abruzzi mountains of Italy.
(National Archives)

the enemy rears. The operation, hastily prepared and without secure intelligence information, was a fiasco: navigational errors, inoperative pathfinder beacons, night drops at a height of seven hundred meters, resulting in scattering, no radio contact with the Fifth Army HQ, presence of important enemy forces… The paratroopers of the 'Lost Battalion of Avellino' nevertheless formed small groups and did the best they could to accomplish their mission, until the survivors [4] final-

ly joined up with the Allied troops marching on Naples.

After a short stay in that city with a mission of maintaining law and order, the 82nd Division moved to Northern Ireland, leaving the 504th Regimental Combat Team in Italy at the request of the Fifth Army, in need of infantry troops. The 504th and 509th were engaged in mountain warfare and sustained heavy losses. As a result, the

1. Activated on November 1, 1942 by changing the name of the 2nd Bn, 503rd PIR, which had itself been activated on February 24, 1942 with the 504th Bn, formed on October 5, 1941 at Fort Benning, Georgia.
2. Dropped after a 2,400-km night flight from England, the battalion hardly took part in the fighting.
3. Casualties in dead, wounded and missing were 81-132-16 for the 504th PIR and 7-30-53 for the 52nd Troop Carrier Wing, which also lost 23 planes shot down and 36 damaged.
4. 532 out of the 641 that had jumped on September 14, 1943.

509th Parachute Infantry Battalion [5] had to be withdrawn from the front and assigned to guard 5th Army HQ.

After the two units had had a chance to recuperate, they landed in Anzio on January 23, 1944. Then the 504th left the beachhead to rejoin its division in England, and the 509th, with two batteries from the 463rd Field Artillery Battalion [6], moved to Salerno on April 5 to prepare for Anvil [7].

THE AIRBORNE TASK FORCE AND PROVISIONAL TROOP CARRIER AIR DIVISION

From the beginning in Algiers, AFHQ and Force 163 planners - without really knowing what they could count on - requested that the amphibious assault be assisted by paratroopers dropped before H-Hour. The mission was originally tailored for a regiment, then assigned to a group equal to four battalions.

But in May it became clear that at least a division would be needed to capture the key roads and railway hubs behind the beaches. At Bouzareah, the planners were convinced that they would be able to pull a division out of a hat somewhere!

But sufficient troops and planes are the *sine qua non* of any airborne operation. And so the War Dept.'s suggestion that an airborne division be committed, followed by three infantry divisions landed by plane on D + 10 near Avignon, was refused for lack of means. Later, the idea of the French 1er Régiment de chas-

Below.
Surrounded by reporters, General Clark, Fifth Army commander, studies the map on the Rome city line with the II Corps commander, Major General Keyes, and Brigadier General Frederick, commander of the 1st SSF at the time. *(National Archives)*

Combined exercise taking place at Fort Bragg, North Carolina, with the participation of paratroopers and troops landed directly by C-47s.
(National Archives)

Even though it was not official, the Airborne Troop Carrier shoulder patch was authorized locally for troop carrier crews.
(Private coll.)

Top left.
Garrison cap badge worn at the First Airborne Task Force HQ. Its red and white colors were probably inspired by the 1st SSF badge.
(Le Poilu)

seurs parachutistes jumping onto Elba was given up for the same reason. And as far as Operation Caïman was concerned, this operation, imagined by General De Gaulle in support of the maquis in the Massif Central, could not be launched, according to the Allies, until the beachhead was secure, and means of transportation became available.

Since the Americans wanted priority given to Anvil, available units in the United States were assigned to General Patch, to make up his airborne division. Thus at the end of May and during the month of June two battalions arrived at the Airborne Training Center in Sicily. The 550th Airborne Infantry Bn (Glider) and the 1st Bn, 551st Parachute Infantry Regiment (Separate) had been activated in the Panama Canal Zone [8]. As for the 517th Regimental Combat Team [9] which had arrived in Italy at the end of May, it was immediately committed north of Rome to gain combat experience. Next, in answer to a special order from the War Department, thirty-six staff officers [10] joined them in mid-July.

At Salerno, the 509th, joined in May by the British 2nd Independent Parachute Brigade [11], came under the control of the Seventh Army, along with the two battalions of the French 1er RCP [12]. At the same time, a howitzer battalion [13] was transformed into a glider unit, and two 8.2 in. -mortar companies and an antitank company [14] undertook training in glider landings. NATOUSA in Algiers was also providing special-

---

5. *The 2/509 became the 509th PIB on December 10, 1943 in Venafro.*
6. *A 75-pack howitzer Bn. activated on February 22, 1944 in Nettuno.*
7. *After 73 days on the front, the battalion had 125 men left out of a theoretical strength of 640.*
8. *Respectively on July 1, 1941 and November 26, 1942.*
9. *Including the 517th PIR and 460th Prcht FA Bn activated on March 15, 1943 in Georgia and assigned to the 17th Airborne Division until March 10,1944.*
10. *Coming from the 13th Airborne Division activated on August 13, 1943 at Fort Bragg, North Carolina, and now stationed at Camp Mackall, and from the Airborne Command created on March 23, 1942 at Fort Benning, Georgia, to organize and train airborne formations.*
11. *Activated in August 1942. The Br. 2nd Brigade had participated in operations in the south with the 1st Airborne Division. When the division returned to England in November 1943, the brigade was the only British parachute unit in the Mediterranean.*
12. *They had been training in Trapani since April 7, 1944.*
13. *602nd Field Artillery Bn (75 Pk How) activated on July 20, 1942 in Colorado and sent to Italy on January 3, 1944 via Alaska and French North Africa.*
14. *Belonging to the 442nd Infantry Regt (Nisei) (Separate) which had arrived in Italy on May 28, 1944, made up of Japanese-Americans. The M1 antitank guns were exchanged for British 6-pounder variant that could be loaded into gliders.*

Unofficial Fifth Airborne Training Center pocket patch. FABTC was based successively in Oujda, Kairouan, Trapani and Rome. *(Private collection)*

C-47 from the 79th Troop Carrier Squadron (436th TCG).
(Computer graphics by André Jouineau)

PREPARATIONS IN THE VICINITY OF ROME

When General Frederick took command in Lido di Roma [17], he knew he could count on qualified pilots, four hundred airplanes and five hundred gliders. Many of the latter were still in their shipping crates [18]. In order not to arouse the suspicion of the Germans, none was sent from England. And the C-47s arrived discretely at night via Gibraltar or Marrakesh.

The British or American paratroopers were generally well trained, with combat experience and used to fend on their own. But there was not enough time to allow them to train with the aviators as hoped.

Most of the effort was actually brought to bear on the technical and tactical instruction of the newly-assigned units. The AB Training Center played a vital role in this respect for the paratroops, in Sicily, and then on Ciampino (Rome) airfield for the glider formations. Personnel from the 550th Battalion set up a school where the various units attended between July 20 and August 5: artillery, chemical mortars, engineers, signal, medics, ordnance. This center also furnished the ABTF with four hundred experienced para-

British paratroopers from Company C 4th Para Bn. photographed in Italy.
(Musée de la Libération '15 août 1944' - Le Muy)

ized training for engineer, signal and medical detachments.

All of these troops finally made up a division-size formation, which, on July 12, received the title of Seventh Army Airborne Division (Provisional), changed a week later to First Airborne Task Force (ABTF), commanded by Major General Robert T. Frederick, former leader of the Special Service Force. Now the problem was to find the means to airlift this 'division.'

The only planes available in the Mediterranean at the time were two groups of C-47s from the 51st Wing of the Twelfth Air Force [15], and one hundred and sixty gliders. SHAEF made up the difference by lending pathfinders, the 52nd and 53rd Wings and 375 glider pilots from the IX Troop Carrier Command belonging to the Ninth Air Force. These units arrived from England between July 12 and 20, and were joined at the beginning of August by 350 pilots [16], and gliders sent from the United States. These units were then called the Provisional Troop Carrier Air Division, led by Major General Paul L. Williams, commander of the IX TCC, who had just participated in Overlord. His job was to gather the gliders, complete training and plan the operation with the ABTF in the few days left before D-Day.

Right. **A 4.2-inch mortar gunner from a Chemical mortar battalion in Italy. It was known for its rapid rate of fire, precision and mobility, the ideal weapon for infantry close support.**
(National Archives)

Below.
British pathfinder from the 1st Independent Parachute Platoon equipped with a chest harness 'adapted' for carrying heavier loads. *(IWM - NA 18 609)*

15. They had participated in 'Husky' and had just come back to Italy after operating from April to June with the Chindits in Burma.
16. So that each glider could have two pilots.
17. Today Lido di Ostia.
18. They were all put together by August 5, 1944.

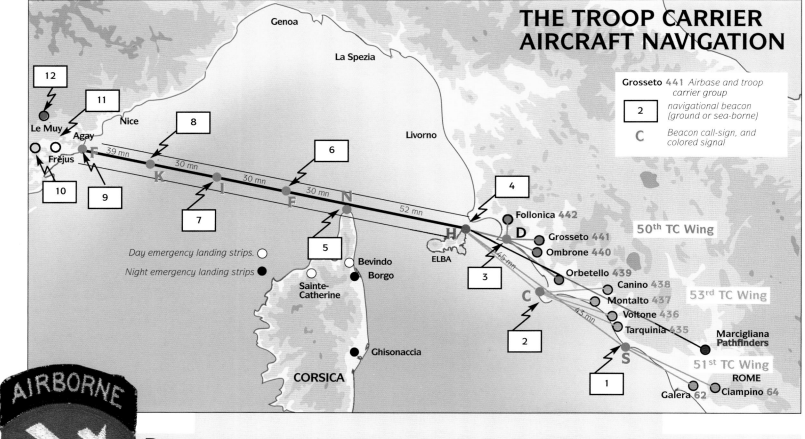

THE TROOP CARRIER AIRCRAFT NAVIGATION

Grosseto 441 *Airbase and troop carrier group*

2 *navigational beacon (ground or sea-borne)*

C *Beacon call-sign, and colored signal*

Genoa

La Spezia

Nice

Le Muy

Agay

Fréjus

39 mn — F — 30 mn — K — I — 30 mn — F — 30 mn — N — H — 52 mn

Livorno

ELBA

Follonica 442

Grosseto 441

Ombrone 440

Orbetello 439

Canino 438

Montalto 437

Voltone 436

Tarquinia 435

Marcigliana Pathfinders

ROME

Galera 62 — Ciampino 64

50th TC Wing

53rd TC Wing

51st TC Wing

D

C

S

Day emergency landing strips.

Night emergency landing strips.

Bevindo

Borgo

Sainte-Catherine

Ghisonaccia

CORSICA

AIRBORNE

ROUTES, NAVIGATIONAL AIDS AND PROTECTION OF THE TROOP CARRIER FLEET

The Airborne Command was activated on March 23, 1942 in Fort Benning, Georgia, for organizing and training the new airborne formations. Its shoulder patch was approved on March 22, 1943.

(Le Poilu)

● MISSION ALBATROSS
D at dawn. 396 C-47s
Time over DZ 76 minutes. Arrival on DZ 0423
Indirect protection
● Western diversion force at 0400
● Fighters from the DAF on patrol around Genoa from dawn to 0630
● MACAF Beaufighter night fighters: 2 in Calvi, 2 in Ajaccio, 2 north of corridor
Direct protection
● 4 DAF A-20 Intruders 4 miles from coast, ready to destroy any projectors
● Escort of 36 Spitfires from the XII TAC on return flight

● MISSION BLUEBIRD
D morning. 71 C-47s with gliders
Time over DZ 13 minutes. Arrival on LZ 0614
Indirect protection
● 12 DAF fighter-bombers on patrol
● Fighters from the DAF on patrol around Genoa from 0730 to 0900
Direct protection
● Escort furnished by MASAF: 48 P-51s from the 31st Ftr Gp from Elba to the DZ and back

● MISSION CANARY
D afternoon. 42 C-47s
Time over DZ 1 minute. Arrival on DZ 1810
Indirect protection
● 12 DAF fighter-bombers for Flak interdiction beween Bomb Line and DZ
● Fighters from the DAF on patrol around Genoa from 1700 to 2000
Direct protection
● Escort furnished by MASAF: 48 P-51s from the 31st Ftr Gp and 48 P-38s from the 82nd Ftr Gp from Elba to the DZ and back

● MISSION DOVE
D afternoon. 332 C-47s with gliders
Time over DZ 53 minutes. Arrival on LZ 1819
Indirect protection
● 12 DAF fighter-bombers for Flak protection beween Bomb Line and DZ
● Fighters from the DAF on patrol around Genoa from 1700 to 2000
Direct protection
● Escort furnished by MASAF: 48 P-51s from the 31st Ftr Gp and 48 P-38s from the 82nd Ftr Gp from Elba to the DZ and back

● MISSION EAGLE
D + 1 morning 100 C-47s
Time over DZ 6 minutes Arrival on DZ 0813
Indirect protection
● 12 DAF fighter-bombers for Flak protection beween Bomb Line and DZ
● Fighters from the DAF on patrol around Genoa from 0700 to 0830
Direct protection
● Escort furnished by MASAF: 48 P-38s from the 82nd Ftr Gp from Elba to the DZ and back

Caption to map, position of beacons

1 - ATLANTA. 51st TCW D/P Cape Linaro.
2 - BURBANK. 53rd TCW D/P Lividonia Point.
3 - CLEVELAND. 50th TCW D/P Ala Point.
4 - DENVER. IX TCC D/P Cap de Vita.
5 - ELKO. Waypoint Giraglia Island.
6 - FRESNO. Waypoint HMS *Ulster Queen*.
7 - GALLUP. Waypoint HMS *Antwerp*.
8 - HOBOKEN. Waypoint PT 209.
9 - ITHACA. Reference point for the drop: Le Trayas.
10 - DZ 'A' Marked by 517 Pathfinders. Yellow light and panels
11 - DZ 'C' Marked by by 509 Pathfinders. White light
12 - DZ 'O' Marked by by 2nd Bde Pathfinders. Red light and panels
D/P: Departure Point

Briefing of Troop Carrier group leaders on 6 Aug 1400, PTAD CP at Lido di Roma

50th TC WING			
Follonica	Serial 4	**509th BCT** *Time at 'Denver'*	0258
	Serial 17	**550th Gliders**	1640
Grosseto	Serial 5	**509th BCT**	0303
	Serial 18	**Gliders**	1648
	Serial 19	**Gliders**	1656
Ombrone	Serial 6	**517th RCT**	0308
Orbetello	Serial 7	**517th RCT**	0313
	Serial 20	**Gliders**	1704
53rd TC WING			
Montalto	Serial 8	**517th RCT** *Time at 'Denver'*	0318
	Serial 16	**551st PIB**	1643
Canino	Serial 9	**517th RCT**	0323
	Serial 21	**Gliders**	1712
Tarquinia	Serial 14	**Gliders 2 Bde**	0635
Voltone	Serial 15	**Gliders 2 Bde**	0643
51st TC WING			
Galera	Serial 10	**2 Bde** *Time at 'Denver'*	0328
	Serial 11	**6 Para**	0333
	Serial 22	**ABTF Gliders**	1720
Ciampino	Serial 12	**4 Para**	0338
	Serial 13	**5 Para**	0343
	Serial 23	**ABTF Gliders**	1728

The 13th Airborne Division shoulder patch. Activated at Fort Bragg in Aug. 1942. The division was not fully committed, some of its units were shipped to the Mediterranean for the Dragoon drops.

(Le Poilu)

troopers and took charge of the parachutes necessary for getting supplies through by air [19].

Frederick would have liked a dress rehearsal before the operation. But the exercise dubbed 'Preface', scheduled after August 6 in the gulf of Salerno and involving the different sequences of the airborne operation, could not be executed, for the gliders and cargo parachutes had not been delivered on time. Moreover, the number of personnel parachutes was insufficient and there was also a lack of parachute packers. But at least the nine teams of pathfinders were well prepared [20]. And all the Carrier planes formation leaders undertook training flights with three planes, based on the same characteristics as those of the operation, and with markers placed in the same positions.

Nobody had forgotten Sicily, so Frederick had groups of 36 planes fly in daylight over a part of the planned route, to show the sailors the sort of plane formation they could expect. Tactical flights escorted by fighters were also part of the training, to test the pilots and dispatchers in ground support. The glider troops had a chance to practice at least one landing.

One last disadvantage was the lack of maps and adequate photographs. The only maps available were at a scale of 100,000 whereas large scale military maps were needed, and the vertical photos of the DZs and LZs, even though excellent, were larger than the requested scale of 10,000. The oblique photos were of no interest to the pilots, but showed wooden stakes stuck into the ground as obstacles for gliders.

Preparations ended on August 12, after a rehearsal without planes or gliders in the vicinity of Rome. Even though the ABTF was an imperfect melding of diverse formations, it had nevertheless become "*a powerful force with a great advantage over the other large airborne units: the division commander was also the troop carrier commander. The effectiveness of this system was proved time and again during Operation Dragoon.*" [21]

Gunners from the 320th Glider FA Battalion, 82nd Division, participate in a demonstration firing of their brand new 105 M3 howitzers. Unfortunately none of the airborne units in the Mediterranean had received this weapon. *(DR)*

Above.
The 17th Airborne Division shoulder patch. Activated at Camp Mackall in April 1943. After lending some units to the Airborne Task Force, it was not committed as a whole before the Rhine crossings in 1945.
(Le Poilu)

Left.
Diagram showing the formation for C-47 tugs and gliders (intervals in meters).

Right.
Formation diagram for troop carrier planes.

19. They had only been requisitioned on July 10 and weighed a total of 300 tons. They arrived from French North Africa by air and sea before August 10.
20. Their training was supervised by a lieutenant from the 82nd Division who had jumped in Normandy with the 505th PIR team.
21. John R. Galvin, Air Assault: the development of airmobile warfare, *Hawthorn Books*, New York, 1969. Total strength was 9,732 men.

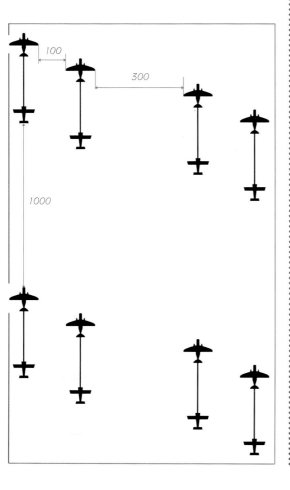

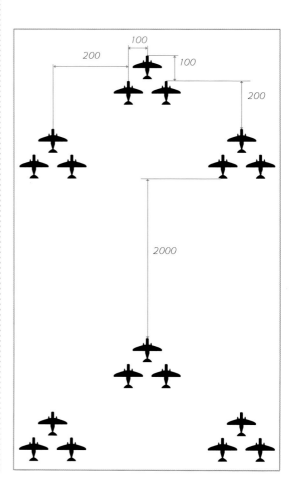

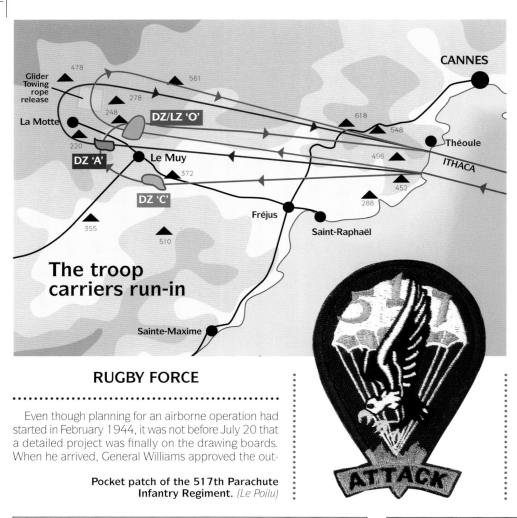

The troop carriers run-in

RUGBY FORCE

Even though planning for an airborne operation had started in February 1944, it was not before July 20 that a detailed project was finally on the drawing boards. When he arrived, General Williams approved the out-

Pocket patch of the 517th Parachute Infantry Regiment. *(Le Poilu)*

line plan and the choice of the Rome area for basing the transport groups. His staff settled in at Lido di Roma and started studying the technical aspects of the operation: schedules, corridors, rendez-vous points, traffic diagrams, etc. They left to the commanders of the airborne and carrier units the choice of their dropping zone and the loading of men and supplies.

The crews were experienced and the technical progress of the pathfinders meant that the first wave could be dropped early in the morning. In choosing the itinerary, the possibility of a stop-over in Corsica was considered, but it was dropped because of cramped space on the airfields along the east coast, and the fact that the planes would then have to take a detour to avoid the mountains. There were three criteria involved in the choice of a corridor for the fleet of transport aircraft: the possibilities of air control and guidance, the height between the planes and surface vessels so as to avoid catching flak from 'friendly' ships, and a minimum number of mountain peaks to fly over.

The salient points of the plan were decided on July 25 and orders sent out on August 5, but changes nevertheless took place right up to the last minute. For example, Mission 'Flamingo, a parachute drop of the two battalions from the 1[er] RCP behind the enemy lines on D + 4 at the earliest and on 48 hours' notice, was canceled [22].

The idea of flying supplies in on the first evening was also given up. G-2 expected weak enemy resistance and considered that an air operation would not be necessary. The ABTF jumped with a minimum of supplies, and the quartermasters prepared for an operation on D + 1 involving 112 C-47s loaded with two days worth of rations and ammunition. Another seven days worth were stocked on bases in Italy and could be delivered to any isolated ABTF or Seventh

---

2nd (Br) INDEPENDENT PARACHUTE BRIGADE GROUP
Brigadier C.H.V. Pritchard (flies from Galera)

- 4 Para Bn - Lt Col H.B. Coxen
- 5 (Scottish) Para Bn - Lt Col D. Hunter
- 6 (Royal Welch) Bn - Lt Col V.W. Barlow
- 64 Field Bty, RA
- 2 Para Bde, REME
- 2 Para Sqn, RE
- 2 Para Bde Gp Provost Section
- 2nd Indep Para Platoon
- 23 Indep Prcht Platoon, AAC
- 1st Indep Glider Pilot Sqn
- 127 Para Fd Ambulance
- 751 Para Bde Coy, RASC
- 2 Para Bde Gp Signals Coy
- 2 Para Bde Gp Comp Coy, RASC
+ Co A, 2nd Chemical unit, RAF

Assignments:
— **Secure area 5** for subsequent glider landings (**4 Bn** - Le Muy, **5 Bn** - Le Mitan, **6 Bn** - La Motte)
— **Prevent movement** of enemy forces within assigned sector
— **Clear Le Muy** of enemy forces prior to nightfall on D-Day
— **Assist advance** of seaborne forces by neutralizing enemy strongpoints to the East, within range of weapons.
— **Be prepared to attack** to the East or North on ABTF orders.

- **Pathfinders**
— **Serial 3**: 3 Pathfinder C-47s (from Marcigliano). Passage over point 'Burbank' 0155, drop over DZ 'O' at 0334
- **Mission Albatross**
— **Serial 10:** CP 2nd Brigade in 36 C-47s from the 62nd TCG (Galera). Passage over 'Atlanta' 0248, drop over DZ 'O' 0454
— **Serial 11:** 6 Para and 5 Para (-) Bns 27 C-47s from the 62nd TCG (Galera). Passage over 'Atlanta' 0253, drop over DZ 'O' 0459
— **Serial 12:** 4 Para Bn 36 C-47s from the 64th TCG (Ciampino). Passage over 'Atlanta' 0258, drop over DZ 'O' 0504
— **Serial 13:** 5 Para Bn (-) 27 C-47s from the 64th TCG (Ciampino). Passage over 'Atlanta' 0303, drop over DZ 'O' 0509
- **Mission Bluebird**
— **Serial 14:** 64 Lt Arty Bn (-) and 300 AT Btry 35 C-47s from the 435th TCG and 35 Horsas (Tarquinia). Passage over 'Burbank' 0612, release over LZ 'O' 0814
— **Serial 15:** 64 Lt Arty Bn (-) and 516 Co, Hqs 36 C-47s from the 436th TCG and 36 Wacos (Voltone). Passage over 'Burbank' 0620, release over LZ 'O' 0822

509th BATTALION COMBAT TEAM

- 509th Prcht Inf Bn, Lt Col William Yarborough (Lido di Roma)
- 463rd Prcht FA Bn (75-mm Pk How) Lt Col John Cooper (Frascati) + 1st Platoon, 596th Prcht Engr Co.
Assignments:
— **Occupy zone No 4**.
— **Prevent enemy movement** within designated zone.
— **Give fire support** to the (Br.) 2nd Brigade.
— **Support the advance** of sea-borne forces by neutralizing enemy positions to the east, within the range of weapons.

— **Be prepared to attack** to the east or south on orders from ABTF

- **Pathfinders**
— **Serial 1** (3 Pathfinder C-47 from Marcigliana) Passage over 'Denver' 0145, drop over DZ 'C' 0323
- **Mission Albatross**
— **Serial 4** (45 C-47s of 442nd TCG from Follonica), passage over 'Denver' 0251, drop over DZ 'C' 0423
— **Serial 5:** (45 C-47s of 441st TCG from Grosseto), passage over 'Denver' 0256, drop over DZ 'C' 0423

517th REGIMENTAL COMBAT TEAM

- 517th RCT, Lt Col Rupert D. Graves (flies from Ciampino)
- 1st Bn - Major William J. Boyle
- 2nd Bn - Lt Col Richard J. Seitz
- 3rd Bn - Lt Col Melvin Zais
- 460th Prcht FA Bn - Lt Col Raymond L. Cato (Frascati)
+ 596th Prcht Engr Co (-)
+ Co D, 83rd Chemical Bn (gliders)
+ 3rd Platoon, 596th Prcht Engr Co
+ Det. 696th Medical Collecting Co
Assignments
— **Secure areas 1, 2 and 3**
— **Prevent enemy movement** within sector of responsability
— **Neutralize** enemy resistance in La Motte
— **Secure LZ 'A'** for subsequent glider landings
— **Be ready to attack to** the west or

northwest on orders from ABTF
- **Pathfinders: Serial 2** - 3 Pathfinder C–47 s from Marcigliana, passage over 'Burbank' at 0150, drop over DZ 'A' 0330
- **Mission Albatross**
— **Serial 6:** 2/517 + Platoon 596th Eng. Co., 45 C-47s of 440th TCG at Ombrone, passage over 'Cleveland' at 0301, drop over DZ 'A' 0435
— **Serial 7:** 3/517 + Platoon 596th Eng Co 45 C-47s from the 439th TCG at Orbetello, passage over 'Cleveland' at 0306, drop over DZ 'A' 0440
— **Serial 8:** 460th FA Bn (-) 45 C-47s from the 437th TCG at Montalto, passage over 'Burbank' 0259, drop over DZ 'A' 0445
— **Serial 9:** 1/517 and Btry B, 460th FA Bn, 45 C-47s of 438th TCG at Canino, flies over 'Burbank' 0304, drop over DZ 'A' 0440

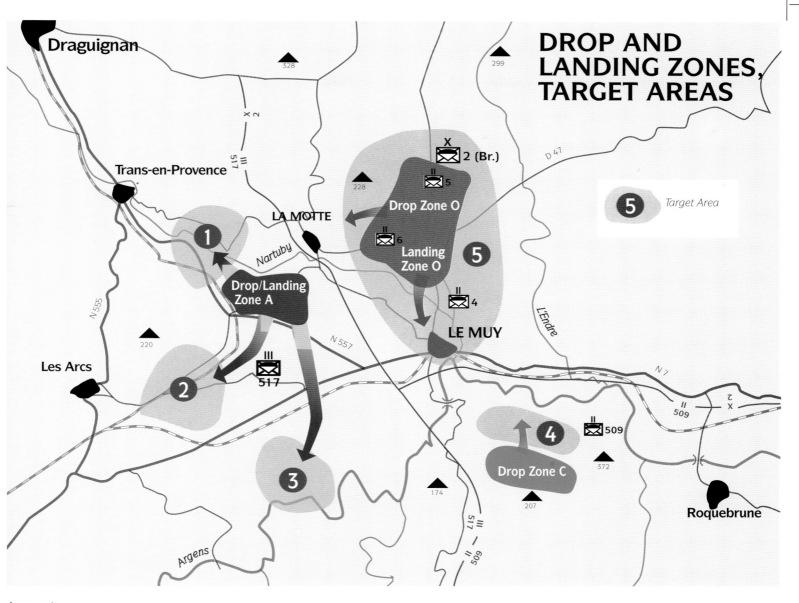

DROP AND LANDING ZONES, TARGET AREAS

Drop Zone O

Landing Zone O

Drop/Landing Zone A

Drop Zone C

Draguignan

Trans-en-Provence

LA MOTTE

Nartuby

Les Arcs

LE MUY

Roquebrune

Argens

5 Target Area

Army unit.

For parachute drops, twenty-three 'serials' were organized. The first three carried the scouts. Then the first wave included the ten serials of Mission Albatross [23] and the two glider series comprising Mission Bluebird. Eight more series were scheduled at the end of the afternoon: one of paratroopers (Canary) and seven of gliders (Dove) [24]. Three zones were chosen around Le Muy. They were closer to each other - as Frederick and Williams had requested - than those defined in the Naples plan. And the second wave was delayed in order to allow the paratroopers to remove all of 'Rommel's asparagus' sticking up on the glider landing zones.

The ABTF or Rugby Force was under the direct control of the Seventh Army until contact was made with the troops that had landed on the coast. Its mission was to keep the enemy from moving from the Argens River valley [25] toward the beaches. The paratroops had to prepare for and cover the arrival of the gliders by securing objectives around Le Muy.

The night of August 15 was clear and warm, but the weathermen had forecasted that visibility would be reduced once the planes were beyond Corsica [26]. The pathfinders took off as planned at 0100 from Marsigliana for a flight of more than eight hundred kilometers. They were followed an hour later by the other serials, all heading for Elba, with their lights on and amber-colored recognition lights turned seaward. For the pilots, orders were simple: "*In event crews fail to locate designated DZs or LZs on first pass, all pilots must drop paratroops and release gliders in the assault area in France as near DZs and LZs as possible* [27].". No paratrooper nor glider was to be brought back to Italy!

GO!

The fourth serial had just passed the last waypoint when the deception operation started further to the East. While the Navy faked an invasion at

La Ciotat, five hundred dummies were dropped by parachute west of Signes, and nine thousand windows scattered from planes simulated a major airborne operation [28].

Near Le Muy, the nine pathfinder crews should have been busy marking the jumping zones. Actually, once beyond the coastline, the pilots found themselves lost in thick fog, and had to fly by instrument. The only crews to manage to reach the correct spot were those of the British 2nd Brigade. The others could not carry out their mission: either they landed too far east of Le Muy, or they were closer but unable to find their directions in the dark.

The poor guidance and continuing lack of visibility hindered the fleet following them, spread out over more than one hundred sixty kilometers.

The pilots had not received any signals, so those of the first two serials decided to rely on their instruments, and turned on the green light over a large cottony cloud. Half of the 509th BCT landed on DZ 'C,' but the other half jumped south of Saint-Tropez. Sixteen Five-O-Niners, who had jumped

22. *Officially the 1er RCP was not selected because of linguistic problems and training that was considered insufficient. General de Gaulle's desire to keep this regiment in reserve for maintaining law and order certainly had a bearing on the decision.*
23. *396 C-47s, 5,607 infantry troops, gunners and engineers.*
24. *348 C-47s and gliders, 2,250 men.*
25. *In Operations Order No 1 dated July 30, 1944, VI Corps added that they were to support the progression of the 36th Division by taking the German defenses northwest of Fréjus from the rear.*
26. *The high-pressure system centered around the North Sea covered all of Western Europe with haze that limited visibility to less than 800 meters at the time.*
27. *PTCAD Field Order No 1 for Operation Dragoon, August 8, 1944.*
28. *The operation took place from 0400 to 0420 using five Dakotas from RAF Squadron 216 and 30 planes from the 334th Quartermaster Company, Air Resupply from Galera via Ajaccio. Neither the German command nor the radar operators were duped by this deception.*

too early with their captain, disappeared in the water.

The arrival of the 517th RCT paratroopers at dawn was a complete muddle; none of them landed on their DZ. The 1st Battalion was spread out over Trans, Lorgues and Les Arcs. The 3rd was scattered over ten kilometers around Fayence and a battery from the 460th fell near Fréjus. Part of the 2nd landed in La Motte and the remaining third on the hills north-east of Le Muy.

The 2nd Brigade, with two teams on its DZ, was luckier. But actually only about two-thirds of the men [29] were correctly dropped and able to assemble rapidly. At 0615 La Motte was occupied by the 6th Para Battalion. The Brigade CP was installed at Le Mitan, and radio contact was made with the 36th Division which was still at sea. By that time two-thirds of the first wave had gathered around Le Muy.

Bluebird, the following mission scheduled for 0815, was made up of British Horsa and American Waco gliders transporting the 2nd Brigade howitzers and antitank guns. But as the leader of serial 14 passed point Elko, he received a radio message from General Williams telling him to return to Italy, because the landing zone was covered with fog. The PTCAD commander, remembering Normandy, did not want the

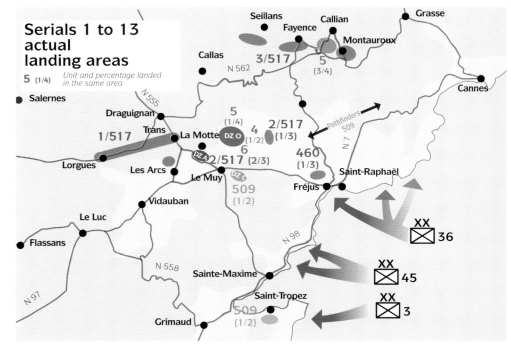

Serials 1 to 13 actual landing areas

5 (1/4) *Unit and percentage landed in the same area*

Left.
On the Marcigliana airfield, Captain Peter G. Baker, commander of the 1st Independent Parachute Platoon, demonstrates the use of the S-Phone to guide in the planes.
(IWM - NA 18 605)

The American pathfinder sleeve badge. *(Private coll.)*

Left.
The Eureka beacon, presented here by two men from the 1st Independent Parachute Platoon, sends back the signal from a plane - at a maximum distance of fifty kilometers - allowing the pilot to home in.
(IWM - NA 19 610)

Right.
Paratroopers from the 1/551st PIR on board a C-47 flying toward the assault zone on the afternoon of August 15. The men appear relaxed and some are even smoking, something which surprised the few French liaison paratroopers, for whom smoking was forbidden so as not to damage the parachutes.
(IWM - EA 33 703)

---

29. Including half of the 4 Para, a company from the 5th and 70% of the 6th.
30. 33 gliders out of the 37 landed on the LZ without injury, but 8 pilots were wounded when they landed in nearby vineyards.

Opposite page. Background:
Dropping the 517th PIR on the afternoon of August 15.
(IWM - EA 33 702)
1. **Photo taken from the cockpit of a C-47, showing parachute canopies on DZ 'A.'**
(IWM - EA 33 701)
2. **Paratroopers from the 517th PIR in La Motte.** *(Seventh Army)*
3. **On the afternoon of August 15, the planes transporting the 1/551st PIR fly over the Esterel massif before approaching their DZ.**
(US Navy).
4. **Brigadier Pritchard, OC British 2nd Brigade, riding through Le Muy in a French jeep.**
(DR)
5. **Two German officers and an NCO are being led toward a POW cage by two paratroopers from the 509th PIB. One is armed with an M3 Tommy gun.**
(IWM - IA 34 490)

heavily loaded Horsas to sustain major losses on landing. However he allowed the Wacos to continue. The leader of serial 15 arrived over Le Muy at 0820 and saw that LZ 'O' was covered in a grayish haze, so decided to circle above until he was able to see the ground. At 0926 the first plane thus let its glider cable go and the glider plunged down through a light mist. Now that the zone was visible, the landings could take place under optimal conditions [32] and guns and jeeps soon

Top to bottom.

The British airborne troops formation sign: Pegasus on a maroon background, the same color as the beret worn since November 1942 by the Parachute Regiment, and which inspired the nickname 'Red Devils' given to them by the Germans.
(Private collection)

Pocket patch of the 463rd Parachute FA Battalion attached to the 509th PIB.
(Private collection)

Breast patch worn by the 596th Airborne Combat Engineer Company.
(Le Poilu)

Horsa British glider.
(Computer graphics by André Jouineau)

379337

Pocket patch of the 460th Glider FA Battalion.
(Le Poilu)

Waco CG-4A *Hadrian* glider.
(Computer graphics by André Jouineau)

Horsa and Waco gliders crashed around Le Mitan. One of them hit a house, another ended up with a missing wing, clipped by one of 'Rommel's asparagus.'
(US Army)

The nose of a Waco glider that terminated its flight in a vineyard.
(US Army)

Above, left. **Loading a jeep into a Horsa glider (this scene takes place during preparations for Overlord).**
(CH 12 829)

Left.
Signalmen from the 512nd Airborne Signal Company pose in front of the Waco glider that will fly them to France.
(DR)

landed safely.

By this time the 2nd Brigade had secured its perimeter and the 509th had occupied the high points above the Argens River and its bridge. Elements of the 1/517th were fighting around Les Arcs and the 2/517th was in contact with the British at La Motte. The 517th CP and the first aid station were installed at the Sainte-Roseline castle, where stragglers soon started to converge.

THE GLIDER STREAM

Meanwhile serial 14 had landed in Tarquinia and taken off again with their tanks full at 1500. Near Cap Corse, the stream [31] was joined by one of the two Horsas whose tugs had landed on the island with engine trouble, then by a Waco from serial 15 that had turned back from France by error. At 17.45 the serial flew over the coastline and approached LZ 'O,' visible from eight kilometers away in spite of the battle smoke. The gliders were let go at a height of four hundred meters and landed - sometimes three at a time - on the wide open zone.

Behind them came Mission Canary transporting the 551st PIB [32]. The C-47s arrived over DZ 'C' and dropped their paratroopers, who landed nicely grouped. But they hardly had time to get out of the way before the drone of more engines could be heard to the east. It was Mission Dove. The serials were supposed to cross the shoreline at intervals of ten minutes - according to General Williams' methodical plan.

With the exception of a serial 19 glider which made an emergency landing in Ombrone, everything went

---

31. 35 Horsas with 233 men, 35 jeeps, 30 guns and 14 t. of ammunition
32. 47 officers and 796 enlisted men.

551st PARACHUTE INFANTRY BATTALION

● Lt Col Wood G. Joerg (Lido di Roma)
● + 1 Platoon 887th Engr Co
Assignment: relieve elements of the 517th RCT in Area 1 and assume the missions of the relieved units.
● **MISSION CANARY** Serial 16 - 42 C-47s from the 437th TCG (based at Montalto), flyover at 'Burbank' 1624, drop over DZ 'A' at 1810

Above.
Aerial photo of the gliders landing area.
(DR)

well at first. But past point 'Cleveland,' the C-47s of the first serial - then those of the following four - had to slow down to avoid the Mission Canary planes that were intersecting their route. Then, near Elko, the lead pilot announced that his glider was vibrating and that he would make a forced landing in the water. But instead of letting his cable go, the pilot of the C-47 turned to the right toward Corsica where the glider could land on dry ground. But he forgot to radio the other planes! So all the other pilots - disciplined and believing that the mission had been called off - followed. The leader realized his error, and once he had released his Waco tried to reinsert himself into the line of planes, where he finally ended up in second place.

These maneuvers resulted in quite a mix-up in the perfect organization of the mission. Some planes slowed up so as not to pass those in front of them; others gunned their engines, thus putting their Wacos, which could not take a speed of over 240 km/h, at risk. During these confused maneuvers, four Serial 18 gliders fell into the water [33].

Intervals were no longer respected, and the first two

INSTRUCTIONS FOR GLIDER PILOTS

SAFETY PRECAUTIONS

— Inasmuch as possible, no personnel should board a glider loaded with equipment. Jeeps, guns and trailers are to be tied down at the rear during take-off.
— After release of the glider and during final approach, the co-pilot releases the equipment. In the event of an emergency landing, the nose of the glider must be raised high enough so that the load slides underneath the crew as it is thrown forward. Particular care must be taken with bulldozers, which are authorized for airlifting by glider even though they weigh 4 tons.

LANDING ZONE EQUIPMENT.

The following aids are to be set on the LZ:
— **A Tee** in the center of each zone and a beacon in the best position 800 meters away;
— **A smoke bomb** at the base of each Tee to indicate the wind direction. To allow pilots to get their bearings, each zone is normally divided into four sectors designated by Roman numerals.
The T and the numerals are formed with fluorescent panels 4 x 1 m, separated by the length of one panel. On LZ 'O' the smoke bombs are green and the panels red. On LZ 'A' they are respectively yellow and blue.
The minimum length required for a Waco landing is 400 meters.

EVACUATION PROCEDURE

All glider pilots must report to the Division CP. After assembling, they are directed to a beach from where they will be taken back to Calvi or Ajaccio. From there, they must report to nearest airfield where they will be flown back to their unit.

Unofficial bullion embroidered pocket patch of the 551st Airborne Infantry Battalion.
(Le Poilu)

MISSION DOVE

● 550th Airborne Inf Bn. Lt Col Edward C. Sachs (Lido di Roma)
● 1 Platoon 887th Engr Co
● 602nd FA Bn (based at Ciampino)
Assignment: land in the northeast part of the LZ;
– be prepared to reinforce 517th RCT and 2nd Brigade;
– or for any attack or counter-attack mission,
– or to collect and issue air-dropped supplies.
● 887th Airborne Engineer Company: division reserve, assembly area and mission to be assigned on landing.

— **Serial 17** 550th PIB (-) 48 C-47s from the 442nd TCG and 48 Wacos, flyover at 'Cleveland' 1631, release over LZ 'O' 1819

— **Serial 18** 1 Co. from 550th PIB and 602nd FA Bn (-) 48 C-47s from the 441st TCG and 48 Wacos, flyover at 'Cleveland' 1639, release over LZ 'O' at 1827

— **Serial 19** 602nd FA Bn (-) and 2 platoons 442nd AT Co 48 C-47s from the 440th TCG and 48 Wacos, flyover at 'Cleveland' 1647, release over LZ 'O' at 1835

— **Serial 20** 442nd AT Co (-), 512th Signal Co and Co A, 2nd Cml Bn, 47 C-47s from the 439th TCG and 47 Wacos, flyover at 'Cleveland' 1655, release over LZ 'O' at 1843

— **Serial 21** 512th Signal Co (-), 696th Med Coll Co and Ordnance Det (-), 47 C-47s from the 62nd TCG and 47 Wacos, flyover at 'Burbank' 1649, release over LZ 'O' at 1851

— **Serial 22** ABTF HQ and 887th Engr Co (-) 47 C-47s from the 62nd TCG and 47 Wacos, flyover at 'Atlanta' 1633, release over LZ 'O' at 1859

— **Serial 23** MP Platoon and Ord Det (-) 47 C-47s from the 64th TCG and 47 Wacos, flyover at 'Atlanta' 1641, release over LZ 'O' at 1908.

serials reached LZ 'O'at the same time. The others arrived in order but not according to schedule [34].

Thus it was chaos over the Argens river valley: four serials one on top of the other from two hundred to one thousand meters up, released 180 Wacos at the same time!

With all these gliders swooping down from every direction, the main job of the pilots was to avoid collisions, then choose a suitable landing spot that might have already been selected by another harried pilot. First come first serve - the first gliders picked the best spots and the latecomers had to be content with 'bumpy' fields. Often the decision was made at the last minute and the landing took place too fast and in a field surrounded by trees. On the ground the 'Rommelspargeln' could not stop the gliders, but slowed them down [35] and often tore off their wings.

Even though as usual the jeeps and guns were difficult to unload from the gliders, they were in working order. But losses were considerable: seventeen killed, one hundred fifty-eight wounded [36] and only fifty salvageable gliders.

Once on the ground, the pilots headed for the closest CP where they were put in charge of its security as well as guarding POWs until their evacuation.

LE MUY, LES ARCS AND DRAGUIGNAN

In the early evening on August 15, the roads in the Argens valley leading toward the beaches had been cut. Beyond, near Fayence and Lorgues, the paratroopers, often guided by resistance fighters, multiplied their attacks on convoys or isolated trucks while continuing their trip toward Le Muy through the woods or in makeshift vehicles. To the south, along the road leading to Sainte-Maxime, contact had been made at 2030 with a reconnaissance patrol from the 45th Division. And with the assistance of the local guerillas, the paratroops lost in Saint-Tropez were able to liberate the city [37], where they were soon met by the 3rd Division.

Sporadic fighting had occurred as the units moved toward their assembly areas or targets. But generally speaking, there had been hardly any serious resistance, except at Les Arcs and Le Muy which were still held by the Germans. When Frederick [38] asked Brigadier Pritchard why the Le Muy junction had not been taken, he explained that the available strength of 5 Para was insufficient for the mission and that the antitank guns had been delayed. Frederick was furious about this [39] and

Above.
**A glider on the ground is guarded
by British paratroopers, while
another Waco prepares to land.**
(US Army)

**Shoulder patch of the
2nd Chemical Mortar Battalion,
showing a dragon spitting fire on a
blue and gold background.
Company A landed by
glider and contributed to the
capture of Le Muy.**
(Le Poilu)

**As was the case with the 2nd Bn,
the shoulder patch of the 83rd
Chemical Mortar Battalion was
only authorized locally. For
Dragoon, Company D was also
glider-borne.**
(Le Poilu)

hurried off to his CP which had been installed at 1800 in a farm in Le Mitan. However, he knew that Le Muy was well defended, so he contacted the commander of the 550th AIB and ordered him to attack the next morning.

At dawn on the 16th the men from the 'Five-and-a-half' tried in vain to take the village. Then the attack

---

33. Only twelve men were saved by the rescue boats.
34. Scheduled at 1827, 1840, 1848, 1849, 1854 and 1905.
35. The stakes, 4 m high and 15 cm wide, were planted superficially and spaced far apart by conscripted Frenchmen. These obstacles were thought to be connected to mines by wires.
36. 11 dead and 32 injured among the pilots, 6 dead and 126 injured among the passengers.
37. They took 240 prisoners as well as the gunners from an antiaircraft battery and two coastal artillery batteries.
38. He jumped with the 11th series.
39. What he did not know was that Pritchard had received orders from SACMED to save his men for missions more in line with British strategy.

began again at 1140, along with elements of the 509th and the 6 Para. And at 1500, after some house-to-house fighting, Le Muy and seven hundred Germans [40] were finally captured.

In the meantime, from 1000 on, 116 C-47s from Mission Eagle [41] dropped seventeen thousand containers on LZ 'O.' But they were dropped from seven hundred meters while a strong wind was blowing, so were scattered everywhere in the confusion [42].

To the west, two 517 battalions were trying to liberate Les Arcs and meeting stiff resistance. At 1800 the 3/517 — after arriving at Sainte-Roseline, forty kilometers from the spot where they had unfortunately been dropped two hours before — came to help them out with heavy mortars and howitzers. Then, at 1935, contact was made at the railroad crossing with the infantrymen from the 45th Division from Vidauban.

It was actually north of Le Muy that the most important and unexpected events took place. On the morning of the 16th, the ABTF CP was informed that the FFI had taken control of Draguignan. Frederick decided to send over a company from the 551st. After a few skirmishes they were able to enter the city and, at 2300, obtain the

The **442nd Regimental Combat Team** shoulder patch, approved in December 1943. It represents Liberty brandishing her torch with the national colors in the background. Its antitank company landed by glider with the ABTF.

Left.
At Le Mitan, discussion between Allied paratroopers and local resistance fighters.
(Musée de la Libération '15 août 1944'- Le Muy)

Right.
Two paratroopers from Company B, 509th PIB, misdropped near Saint-Tropez, try to reach their battalion, assembling in Le Muy.
(National Archives)

Below.
On August 18, at the Seventh Army CP in Saint-Tropez, Generals Patch and Frederick interrogate Generalmajor Ludwig Bieringer, commander of the FK 800, captured at Draguignan.
(National Archives)

The **676th Medical Company** set up two first aid stations: one at Sainte-Roseline with the 517th PIR, the other - pictured here - near the farm at Le Mitan where the ABTF CP was based.
(National Archives)

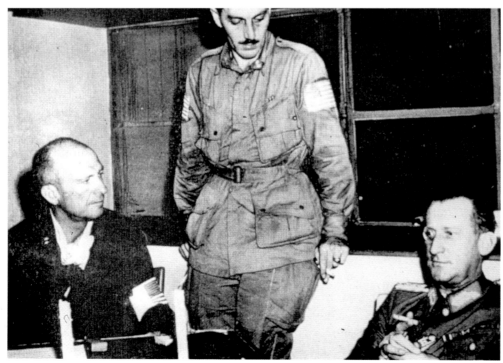

surrender of the Feldkommandantur 800 strongpoint and then, the next day, the headquarters of the LXII.AK.

The airborne operation thus ended successfully for the Rugby Force. Even though the troops had been dispersed as they jumped, this had not had any real effect on their action, since they had already practically accomplished their mission on the evening of the 15th. On the contrary, the sticks spread out over the area created diversions that complicated the task of the German command, who had to react to both sea and air landings.

40. Mostly from the Flak and GR 932.
41. Scheduled according to plans at 0813 and 0818 in two series of 50 C-47s.
42. Because British and Americans did not use the same equipment. During the night, drops of signal and medical supplies were successfully carried out without assistance from the pathfinders.

THE ALPHA SECTOR LANDINGS

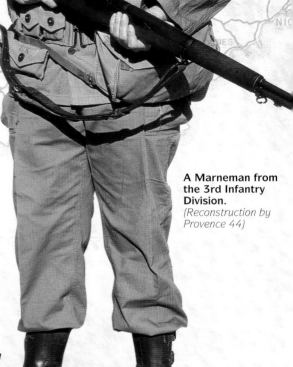

The assault on the coastline between Cavalaire and Saint-Tropez was assigned to the 3rd Infantry Division, commanded since February 17, 1944 by Major General John W. O'Daniel [1]. The 3rd div. was the most battle-wise and experienced of the three assault divisions, having already participated in three invasions: Morocco, Sicily and Anzio.

The mission assigned by VI Corps was as follows:
— Land on beaches 259 (Red Beach, Cavalaire) and 261 (Yellow Beach, Pampelonne) and neutralize any resistance;
— Take Saint-Tropez and clean out the peninsula;
— Assist the 45th Division in capturing the La Foux beach;
— Progress rapidly in order to make contact with Romeo Force [2] and advance to the Blue Line, destroying any enemy forces along the way;
— Cross the Blue Line on orders from the corps.

On June 13, the division moved to Castel Porziano, near Lido di Roma, before returning to Naples:

"For all hands, this move meant only one thing: more amphibious training, what else? For this is what it had always done after being withdrawn from the line! And grizzled veterans of Casablanca, Sicily, and Southern Italy summarized the prevalent feeling in a few words: 'Where the hell's it going to be this time?' " [3]

A Marneman from the 3rd Infantry Division.
(Reconstruction by Provence 44)

View of the western part of Cavalaire Bay, with the cape cliffs in the foreground, then the wharf, the beach and the Grand Hotel, the Arbouses farm surrounded by cultivated fields.
(US Army)

Concrete tetrahedrons on the western end of Cavalaire beach. On the left is the narrow-gage track used for construction, and in the background the Pradels hilltops.
(US Army)

center [8]. A combined arms maneuver was mounted at the end of July in the gulf of Gaeta, the only part of the near shoreline resembling that of Provence. As usual, the 10th Engineer Battalion was tasked with sweeping the beaches and the surrounding hills, a job that involved losses [9]. At the end of the exercise, the equipment remained on the boats [10] which headed for their docks: LCTs to Baia, LCIs to Pozzuoli, LSTs to Nisida, freighters and transport ships to Naples.

On August 7, a final briefing brought together admirals, generals and unit commanders down to battalion level. General Truscott first gave the men general reminders about amphibious operations [11], and then each division commander presented the main points of its plan. The next day the 3rd Division soldiers began loading: "*As yet*, naively noted a division historian, "*only a few of the troops knew their final destination.*" [12]

Actually the operation was a poorly-kept secret:

Previous page, top letft
The 3rd Division shoulder patch, adopted on October 24, 1918. Blue is the infantry color, and the three white bands symbolize the three campaigns of 1917-18, including the Marne.

Determined men can land anyway [4]

....

On June 19 movement south began by road, with the heavy elements [5] following later from Civitavecchia in LSTs. And five days later, all units had assembled near Pozzuoli. A planning team was immediately organized to prepare the operation, in liaison with the VI Corps staff in Naples, and a training center was established in Pozzuoli with the help of the 1st Naval Beach Battalion from Salerno. The instruction at the center was familiar to the veterans: embarking and disembarking from landing boats, attacking pillboxes, crossing barbed wire and mine fields, combat in combination with tanks...

Several technical rehearsals took place on the Mondragone beaches, once the mines and booby traps had been cleared by the division engineers. There were nevertheless important differences. For example, it was no longer a single battalion per regiment that was trained in beach assault, but all its rifle component. Likewise, the four divisional 'patrols' [6] were assigned to the two first-wave regiments, to destroy enemy guns flanking the two beaches. And since the division did not go to Salerno, special displays of new weapons and equipment were organized at Pozzuoli for them.

To prepare the assault, which was to last from H-90 to H+15, Rear Admiral Franck J. Lowry's [7] Task Force 84, in charge of landing the troops, had at its disposal a battleship, six light cruisers and five destroyers. Any firing opportunities would be observed by planes or the nine Shore Fire Control Parties in contact with their support ships, and with the Navy liaison officer assigned to the division artillery, which thus had a true naval fire direction

Above.
August 8, 1944 at 1300. The loading of the 3rd Infantry Division in Nisida is just about completed. The LSTs with the pontoons have already left, but four others from TG 84.1 are still at dock. No 178 in the foreground is carrying five LCVPs for the assault and gunners from the 9th and 634th Bns. No 74 served as mother ship for the landing craft.
(National Archives)

Top right.
Distinctive insignia of the 9th Field Artillery Bn.
(Le Poilu Collection)

Right.
Campaign streamers in the colors of the European-African-Middle Eastern Campaign Medal for the Marne division battles before invading Provence: Algeria-French Mo rocco (November 8-11, 1942), Tunisia (November 17, 1942-May 13, 1943), Sicily (July 9-August 17, 1943), Naples-Foggia (September 9, 1943-January 21, 1944), Anzio (January 22-May 24, 1944), Rome-Arno (May 25-June 12, 1944).
(Le Poilu Collection)

---

1. 'Iron Mike' had been Truscott's deputy in the division since December 1, 1943, until Truscott became deputy then commander of VI Corps.
2. Once their liaison mission terminated, the Commandos d'Afrique would come under division control and assemble at La Mole as soon as conditions permitted.
3. History of the Third Infantry Division in World War II, Donald G. Taggart, Infantry Journal, Washington, 1947.
4. Conclusion of General Truscott's speech during the August 7, 1944 briefing.
5. 96 tracked vehicles from the 756th Tank Bn and 66 DUKWs from the 52nd QM Bn.
6. The special battle patrols were provisional units, 5 officers and 150 men strong.
7. Commander of the 8th Amphibious Force. He had already led the assault on Anzio.
8. An SCR-610 team also accompanied the Commandos d'Afrique.
9. 18 killed and 43 wounded.
10. After lengthy studies, the loading capacity was increased to 4,500 vehicles instead of the 3,337 planned.
11. He had created the Rangers, and it was under his command that O'Daniel had organized the FAITC at Arzew.

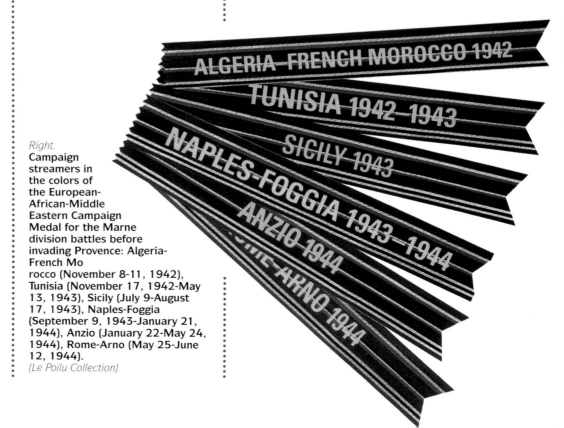

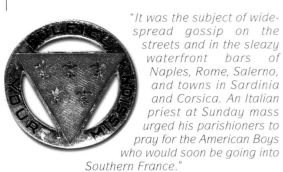

"*It was the subject of wide-spread gossip on the streets and in the sleazy waterfront bars of Naples, Rome, Salerno, and towns in Sardinia and Corsica. An Italian priest at Sunday mass urged his parishioners to pray for the American Boys who would soon be going into Southern France.*"

A store in Pozzuoli broke out with a new show-window display a large stack of maps of the French Riviera. A juvenile hustler in a Naples bordello bid farewell to her longtime patron, a member of the 45th Infantry Division: "*Guess you won't be visiting again since you're going into Southern France.*" The startled GI paid up and left. [13]

Even 'Axis Sally,' the Radio Berlin broadcaster, spoke about it: "*You parachute boys won't have to worry about bailing out over southern France. We'll have a reception committee waiting for you, and the flak will be so thick you can simply walk down on it.*" [14]

The Allies remained nevertheless confident. At the end of the last general briefing, James V. Forrestal, Secretary of the Navy, was invited by Admiral Hewitt to say a few words. He expressed his faith in the success of the coming operation!

An operation so well organised...

The invasion fleet was placed under Admiral Hewitt's orders at least twenty-four hours before setting sail, and assembled in seven ports:
- Naples and Salerno: equipment transport

The Piper Cub L-4H belonging to the air observation section of the 3rd Infantry Division Artillery CP.
(Drawing: André Jouineau)

Above. **Marnemen boarding an LST to participate in the dress rehearsal in the gulf of Gaëte. Notice LSTs 603, 74 and 141, part of Task Unit 84.1.3. N° 603 should be carrying 23 officers, 465 men and 61 vehicles from six different units. N° 141 participated directly in the attack and became the target of an 88-mm cannon and the enemy machine-guns.** *(US Army)*

Top left. **Divisionary Artillery insignia inherited from the 3rd FA Brigade, deactivated in 1939. The DivArty was made up of three 105 HM2 howitzer battalions (10th, 39th, 41st), and one 155 HM1 battalion (9th).**
(Le Poilu Collection)

Rear Admiral Frank J. Lowry, CTF 84, and Major General John W. O'Daniel on the bridge of the USCGC *Duane*. The 3rd Infantry Division commander is wearing the badge of his division and the Distinguished Service Medal received for " *exceptional services in an important function.* **"** *(US Coast Guard)*

Left.
LST(P) (Flight Deck) 906 from Task Unit 84.1.1 loading the nine artillery planes to participate in Exercise Shamrock on July 31 in Gaete. For Provence, she left from *Castellamare* and carried ten L-4s plus 481 soldiers and 38,000 liters of drinking water. *(US Army)*

ships, landing boats, freighters and Sitka Force [15].
- Taranto and Brindisi: freighters, troop transports, Delta Force support ships.
- Palermo: Camel Force support ships.
- Malta: aircraft carriers and Alpha Force support group.
- Oran: freighters and troop transports.

But because of their different characteristics, notably speeds, the three assault forces could not navigate as a team. So the support ships

12. *History of the Third Infantry Division, op. cit.*
13. *Operation Dragoon, The Allied Invasion of the South of France, William B. Breuer, Presidio Press, Novato, 1986.*
14. *Operation Dragoon, op. cit.*
15. *307 landing craft, 75 freighters or transport ships, 165 escort ships.*

sailed alone and the other boats formed three homogenous convoys, organized in three sections corresponding in the navigation orders to the three sectors, *Camel*, *Delta* and *Alpha*. Once the convoys had reached Capu Rossu on the west coast of Corsica, each section was to turn west and now under the orders of its own Task Force commander head for the meeting point where the attack force was to form. After the attack the empty boats were to assemble off Cap Camarat under the control of destroyer *Jouett*. The LSTs

The LCT sailors took advantage of the stopover in Ajaccio from 0830 on the 12th to 2000 on the 13th to take a swim in the gulf. LCT 203 from Task Unit 84.1.4 carried 200 tons of ammunition that it took six hours to unload in Cavalaire because no one wanted it.

August 10. It is raining and the LCTs in convoy SS-1B are heading for Ajaccio *(Private collection.)*

August 9 at 0930. A half-hour later the first and slowest of the assault convoys under the orders of the commander of Task Force 84 set sail from Naples heading for Corsica. Because of the length of the crossing, the lack of commodities on board and the need to take on fuel and water, it had to stop in Ajaccio, where everything was ready for refilling fuel and water tanks, and to give the soldiers and crews a few hours rest.

On the 10th two convoys carrying French troops left from Taranto-Brindisi and Oran. Then the next day, from Salerno, Oran and Taranto, three convoys weighed anchor for Propriano, with *Sitka Force*, French Combat Command No 1, and the Delta support group [17].

On the 12th the aircraft carriers left Malta, and at the same time rapid convoy SF-2 and the *Sitka support group* took to sea from Ajaccio and Propriano. Likewise convoy SM-1 set sail from Naples in the evening, moving toward the assault zone. The soldiers from the 3rd Division hanging over the railing saw a small point on the sea heading toward them full speed ahead. It turned out to be a destroyer approaching the convoy, with a man standing on the bridge.

"*It's Churchill*," yelled someone.

and the craft heading back to Ajaccio and Naples would be grouped to the east, those heading for Oran and the troop landing craft to the southeast. Two LSTs were also assigned to shuttle between Calvi and the assault zone.

Orders to execute the plan [16] were given on

The 41st Field Artillery Bn. distinctive insignia, adopted in March 1942. *(Le Poilu Collection.)*

Above. On the *Duane*, last minute check of the SCR 609-610 radios to be used for liaisons between the ship and the Shore Fire Control Parties on the ground. *(US Coast Guard)*

Below. For the Provence invasion, HMS *Orion* hoisted the flag of Rear Admiral J.M. Mansfield, Commander Task Group 84.7. After artillery preparation, she was in charge of covering the Cavalaire beach off La Croix. *(IWM - A 18 771)*

16. *Western Naval Task Force Plan 4-44 or Dragoon Attack Plan dated July 29, 1944, and comprising 18 annexes.*
17. *It was met at sea by the French 10th light cruiser division sailing from Bizerte.*

The cry echoed through the LSTs and soldiers and sailors crowded the deck to get a look at the great man, who answered the cheers of the American troops with his famous victory sign: "*Prime Minister Winston Churchill, in Italy to confer with Italian Minister Bonomi, had been unable to resist seeing off the invasion convoy, and to wish Godspeed and a quick, successful victory to the United States troops. It was a favorable omen.*" [18]

On the 13th two convoys loaded with equipment set sail from Naples and TF-1 left Taranto with elements of Armée B. The Camel and Alpha support groups also sailed and the *Ramillies* left Algiers. During the afternoon SF-2 entered the gulf of Ajaccio and met SS-1 which had arrived the previous morning and was preparing to leave

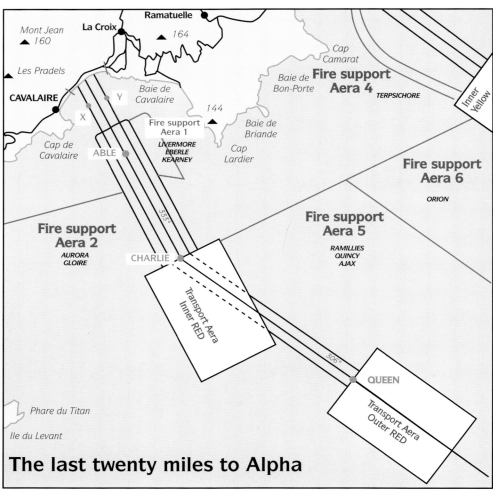

The last twenty miles to Alpha

that evening for the assault zone.

On the 14th convoy SY-1 left Propriano and was met along the way by the Sitka support group. Then the Camel and Delta support groups caught up with convoy SF-1. To Admiral Cunningham, who observed the convoys crossing the straits of Bonifacio, the operation appeared to be off to a favorable start. Thus at 1818 he sent the signal: "*Carry out Operation Dragoon!*." Then he added for Admiral Hewitt: "*All convoys have passed at the planned moment. An operation so well organized must succeed.*"

Nothing eventful happened during the crossing. The boats stuck to their schedule, with the exception of three slowpokes who nevertheless arrived in the assault zone on time.

Approaching Cavalaire

After studying its sector, the 3rd Division staff reached a number of conclusions. First of all, the beaches and their approaches were perfectly visible from the hills along the coast. It was therefore necessary, before attempting anything, to seize Les Pradels and hill 325 above and to the west of Ramatuelle. Next it was clear that the narrow La Mole valley, difficult for tanks, and highways 98 and 559 would have to carry most of the heavy traffic. There was no major highway

18. *History of the Third Infantry Division, op. cit.*
19. *Reinforcements included Co A 756th Tank Bn, Co A 601st TD Bn, Co A 3rd Chemical Bn, Co A 3rd Medical Bn, Co A 10th Engineer Bn and 10th FA Bn (at first), six Naval Shore Fire Control Parties, Det 66617th Mine Clearing Co (Gap Team), Det 3rd Signal Co, Prisoner of War Interrogation Team.*

Above left.
LST 906 anchored at Castellamare di Stabia, in the gulf of Naples. On the deck, on either side of the runway, 66 m long by 5 m wide, can be seen planes from the 9th, 39th, 41st and 59th FA Bn.
(US Army)

Below.
LCTs from Task Unit 84.1.5 beached on the Porticcio beach. LCT 222, visible in the photo, carried 28 vehicles including 25 jeeps.
(Private collection)

through the Maures hills. The roads from Grimaud to Collobrières or from Sylvabelle to Saint-Tropez via Ramatuelle were in poor shape and of limited use.

The Cavalaire beach, 3,500 meters long and between 20 to 50 meters wide, was moderately well defended. The Navy considered it acceptable because on the northwest side they would be able to beach all the landing craft and ships. And anchoring in the bay would be easy. The infantrymen agreed: the beach was suitable for infantry troops, bulldozers and, after a little preparation, trucks.

Three kilometers to the east Sylvabelle beach called Cavalaire Bay (East) or Beach 260 (Green Beach) was one thousand meters long and thirty wide. It was a sandy beach and could be used

under the same conditions as the west beach. The 7th Infantry Regiment [19] with two battalions in the first wave, would land on Red Beach to capture the heights of Les Pradels and La Croix. Once this village had been taken, they were to head along Route 559 to Gassin to cover the advance of the 30th Infantry Regiment [20]. This regiment would land next and was in charge of holding the La Foux crossroads and clearing out Cogolin as they were going through.

Above.
The Cavalaire port and bay today.
(Private collection)

Below. **August 15, 0600 to 0730. Bombing Cavalaire Cap and beach. The B-26s from the 17th Bombardment Group dropped 94 130-kg fragmentary bombs, while the 319th and 320th used a total of 3,762 ordinary 50-kg bombs.** *(MATAF)*

And during the night a violent storm came up, with wind, rain and lightning that hit several barrage balloons. Around nine o'clock the next day, as the convoy was going through the Bonifacio straits, the weather started to improve. And in the morning of the 12th the boats anchored in the gulf of Ajaccio.

The men took advantage of the stopover to disembark at Porticcio, get minor repairs done and fill the fuel and water tanks either at dock [23] or with the help of LST 32. In the middle of the afternoon on the 13th the soldiers came back on board, and at 1900 authorisation to set sail was delivered by CincMed on HMS *Largs*. The *Duane* took up its position at the head of the convoy again and moved out of the gulf at 2240. The night was lovely and the sea calm.

On the 14th at 0925, HMS *Kimberley* carrying CincMed reported enemy patrol boats off the assault zone. At 1040 section SS-1 came under the control of CTF 80 and the *Duane* moved to section SS-1B which she took over guiding at 1235. At noon, Commander Harold C. Moore, commander of the *Duane*, took to the loud-speaker to explain the mission assigned to the Task Force and to wish the members of the division on board a successful operation.

At 1535, when the coast of France appeared on radar screens, SS-1B was at full strength with LCT 237 along behind. The sea was still calm and the weather perfect. At 1935 LST 32 [24] reported that it was taking over radar watch: everything was going as planned.

On the 15th at 0200, the elements bound for Yellow Beach moved away from the convoy. On the radar screen, the transport ships and then the LCTs could be seen arriving in the Yellow zone, while the Alpha support group moved along on the port side.

At 0300 the guides were anchored at the waypoints; there was not much wind so they had no trouble staying put.

At 0450 the destroyer *Somers* reported that she had fired on an enemy ship. One minute later the *Duane* entered the assault zone and turned off her engines. Then the first LSTs and LCTs arrived in the marshaling zone: they were scattered because of the various currents that they had encountered during the night, and the dif-

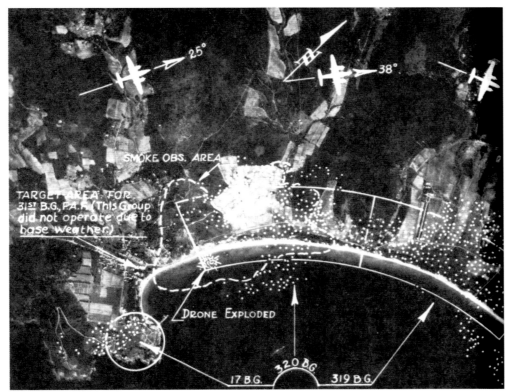

General O'Daniel and his staff boarded USCGC *Duane* [21] on August 9th at 1,300 in Naples harbor [22]. This was Admiral Lowry's flagship, as commander of the LCT convoy during the crossing. The LCTs left Baia and formed their convoy which was soon joined by HMS *Stuart Prince*. At 1645 the *Duane* placed itself at the head of the SS-1 section to pilot the convoy. Two hours later, four LCT(R)s with a patrol boat were sent to La Maddalena to load rockets and meet them in Ajaccio.

At dawn on the 10th the patrol boat sent out to check along the convoy reported that everything was ready. But during the day several craft either broke down or had trouble keeping up. Just before nightfall, HMS *Zetland* reported that two LCTs were being towed and that the convoy was stretched out over twenty-five kilometers.

7th Infantry Regiment insignia, adopted in 1925, with a bale of cotton and bayonets recalling the War of 1812. Their motto:
" Willing and able ".
(Le Poilu Collection)

20. Reinforcements included Co C Cml Bn, Co C 3rd Med Bn, Det 3rd Signal Co, Prisoner of War Interrogation Team.
21. 2000 t ship, part of the Treasury Secretaries series, belonging to the Coast Guard and transformed to become the flagship of the amphibious fleet.
22. Reginald Ingraham, reporter for Time and Life magazines, was already on board.
23. The Duane filled hers at the St Joseph wharf.
24. An LST from TF 84 equipped with a GCI.

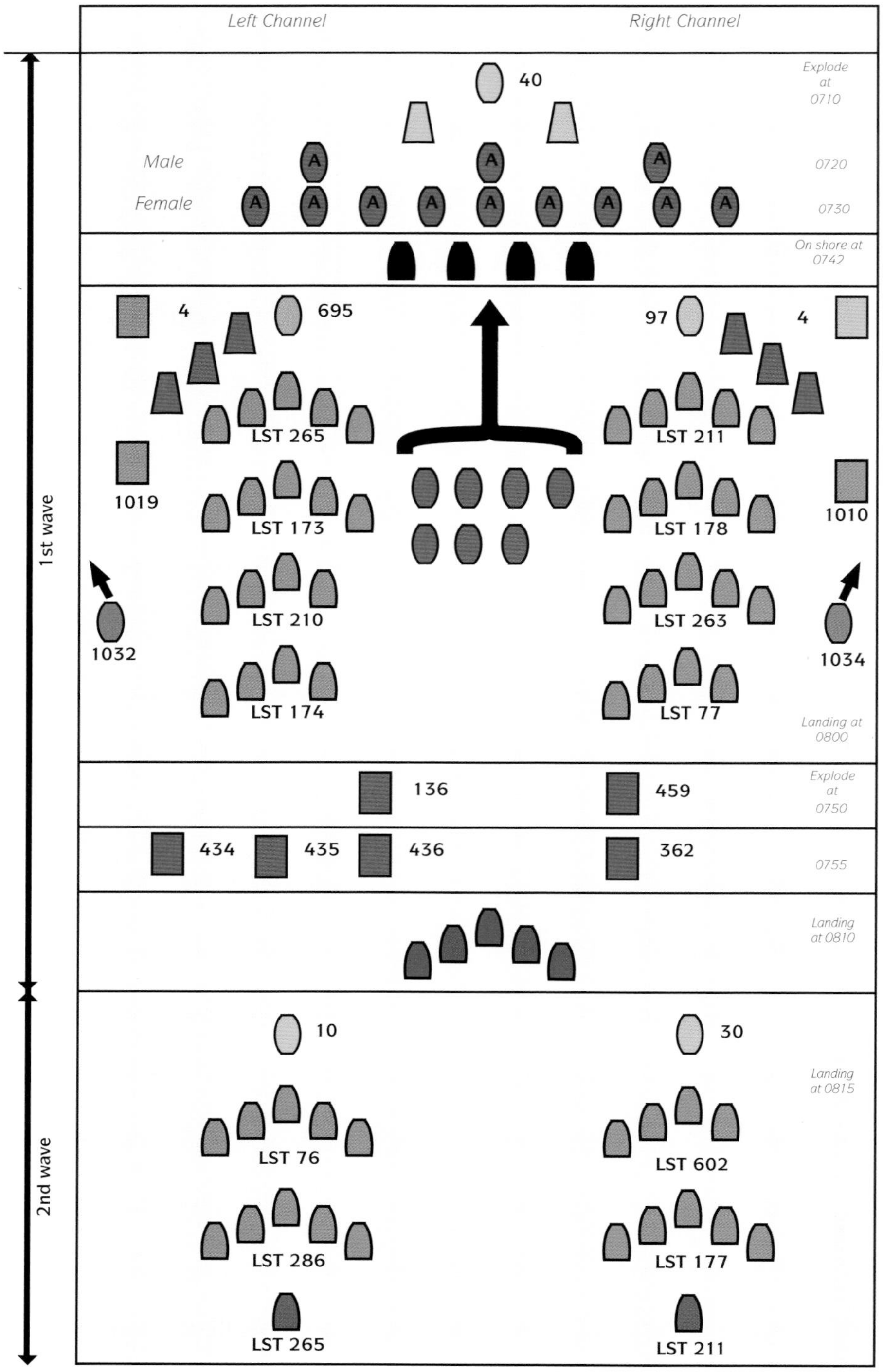
Left Channel
Right Channel
40
Explode at 0710
Male
Female
A
0720
0730
On shore at 0742
4
695
97
4
LST 265
LST 211
1019
1010
LST 173
LST 178
LST 210
LST 263
1032
1034
LST 174
LST 77
Landing at 0800
1st wave
136
459
Explode at 0750
434
435
436
362
0755
Landing at 0810
10
30
Landing at 0815
LST 76
LST 602
2nd wave
LST 286
LST 177
LST 265
LST 211

ferent boats they had in tow. Far away to the west the destroyers continued their battle.

The first wave on Red Beach

The boats in the order of their arrival first assembled southeast of Cap Lardier in the Outer Transport Area [25]. Then from the ten-nautical-mile reference point 'Queen' where the *Duane* was anchored, they were to move to the Inner Transport Area. There they would take the channel that had been opened by the mine-sweepers. The entrance to the channel was controlled by PC 1227 stationed at point *Charlie*, the five-mile point.

Besides the identification and piloting craft and the assault vessels, the Red Beach Assault Group, or TG 84.1, had five task units for support: LCT(R), demolitions, shallow water assistance, smoke screens and beach team [26].

CTU 84.8 took charge of the mine sweeping, which began at 0440 and was finished by 0630. By that time the zones where the transport and support ships would be anchored, and the channel leading to within one thousand meters of the beach, had been cleared. At 0545, even though visibility was reduced by a morning mist, four BMSs [27], two LCSs carrying the Scouts [28], and an LCC left for the beach. Behind them the LSTs, LCTs, transport ships and support craft had arrived at 0500. The LCIs were scheduled to land at 0640. The battleships and cruisers had already been firing on the coastal batteries for the last twenty minutes. After that, three destroyers and the cruisers *Gloire* and *Aurora* neutralized the beach defenses until 0750. On board these ships the SFCP prepared to go ashore [29].

THE FIRST TWO WAVES AT ALPHA

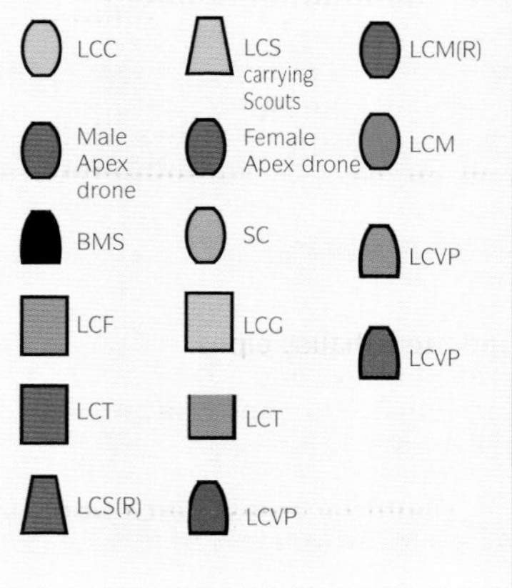
LCC
LCS carrying Scouts
LCM(R)
Male Apex drone
Female Apex drone
LCM
BMS
SC
LCVP
LCF
LCG
LCVP
LCT
LCT
LCS(R)
LCVP

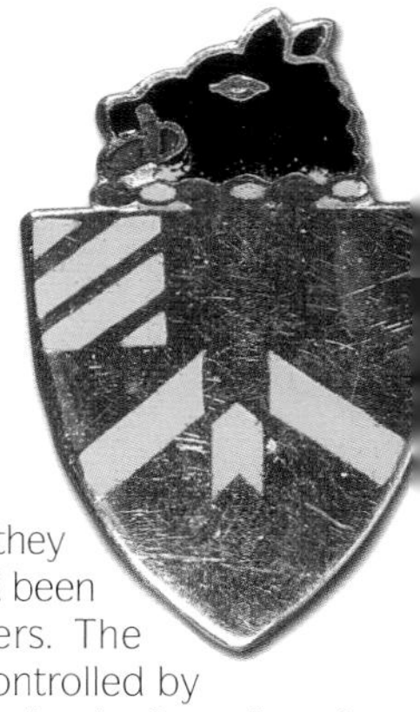

30th Infantry Regiment insignia adopted in 1923. The regiment had already received the DUC for its action in Sicily and at Monte Rotondo. *(Le Poilu Collection)*

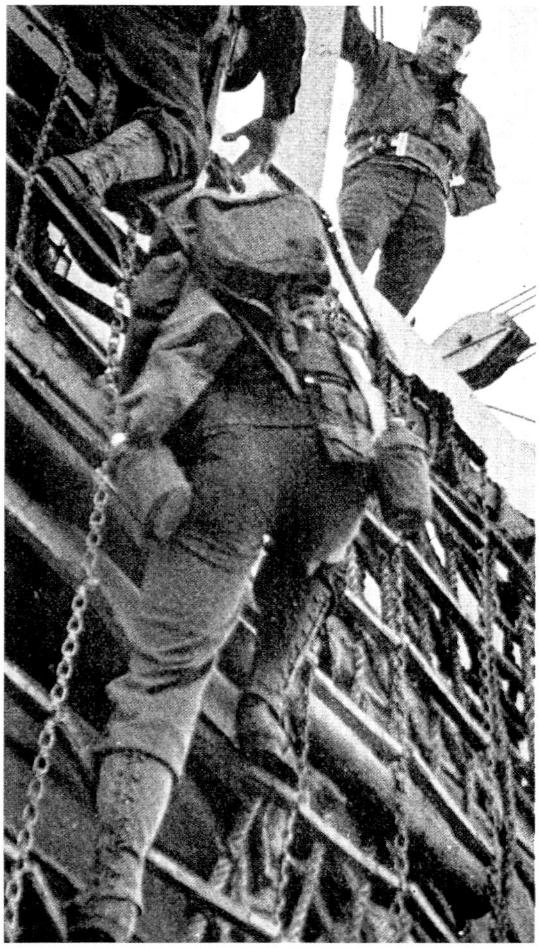

Below. **For the infantry troops, the assault begins by climbing down the net between the deck of the transport ship and the LCVP that will carry them to the beach.** *(US Army)*

25. Divided into three sectors, from left to right: LCIs, LCTs and LSTs or transport ships.
26. Co A, 1st Beach Bn Lt P.A. Beardsley USNR, Beachmaster, attached to the 3rd Bn, 36th Engr Regt in the beach group.
27. Boat minesweepers whose job it was to clear shallow waters and smoke generating.
28. Amphibious Scout Section 1A in charge of beach hydrographic reconnaissance.
29. At H + 15 : No 2 (Ajax) and No 9 (Eberle) for the 2/7 Inf Regt, No 4 (Aurora) and No 5 (Livermore) for the 3/7 Inf Regt. At H + 60 : No 8 (Orion) for the 3/30 Inf Regt.

But when the LSTs arrived in the Outer Transport Area, they took too much time launching the first Apex boats [30]. These remote-control boats passed point 'Queen' twenty minutes late. The drones were able to make up for lost time and finally arrived at point Able where LCC 40 was anchored, right on schedule. Each male boat passed three times to pick up the crews of the female drones [31]. Some of the boats hit tetrahedrons as they went by and belw them up, others came to rest on the beach and hit mines. They all exploded correctly but were too bunched up on the left side of the beach. After the explosions, as the coastal minesweepers navigated the shallow water behind LCC 40, the Scouts marked the channel with beacons and posi-

The Grand Hotel in Cavalaire-sur-Mer sustained a direct hit by two shells that tore through the front of the building. The pines in front have been cut, perhaps to clear the field of fire or to be used as buttresses in the trenches. *(US Army)*

Below.
Panoramic sketch of Red Beach as represented on the map distributed by AFHQ, drawn from information furnished by the 8th Fleet and printed thanks to the 19th Field Survey Coy in July 1944. *(US Navy)*

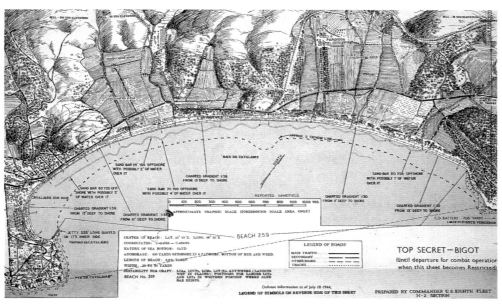

tioned themselves to serve as guides for the first wave.

The first-wave landing boats had been circling around 'Queen' since 0600. They left eighteen minutes later and were followed at more or less regular intervals by the next four waves. Then the *Duane*, travelling at five knots, headed for 'Charlie', with the landing craft trailing behind. She was in position at 0732. A few minutes later a Thunderbolt fighter suddenly hit the water; its pilot [32] had bailed out and was rescued by PC 1169.

At 0750, as wave No 4 had just passed 'Charlie' ten minutes ahead of schedule, the six LCT(R)s from the Royal Navy 22nd Fleet opened fire. Soon the LCM(R)s and the LCS(R)s followed suit. Until H-hour, as the LCF and LCG 4 flailed the coastline with their gun's fire, rockets continued to fall on the shore [33]. That short-range support, coupled with the guns from the fleet and the aerial bombings, created a devastating effect. The seashore was hidden behind a curtain of fog, smoke and dust. Two landing craft ran into each other, and rockets from LCT(R) 167 fell short into the water. . .

Then a German machine gun rattled on Cap Cavalaire and an 88-mm gun took direct aim at the LCF. A screen of smoke soon stretched along the west side of the approach channels.

The rest of wave No 1 was following: two LCTs, each one carrying two DD tanks [34], the two LCM(Smoker)s, two formations of four groups of LCVPs piloted by an SC [35] or an LCC, five CVPs carrying the demolitions units [36] who would clear the beaches and approach lanes of any remaining obstructions [37].

The assault on Red Beach

Operations were directed from LCI(L)(C) 954 by Captain O.F. Gregor, CTG 84.1, with the help of Colonel Wiley H. O'Mohundra, commander of the 7th Regiment. He had a deputy assigned to each sector of the beach. Lieutenant Commander Holmshaw, for example, after leading the first wave ashore, was in charge of sector 1. "*This organization worked perfectly, because the experienced officers were immediately able to appreciate the situation, act promptly, and keep the appropriate personnel informed.*" [38]

The LCVPs of the first two waves were grouped together in fours or fives so that a company with three rifle platoons landed first in the center and on each flank, the heavy weapons platoons following a minute later to the right and left.

The first wave thus arrived right on time at H-hour: the 3rd Battalion, 7th Infantry Regiment was on the left and the 2nd on the right. Concerning the con-

30. Remote-controlled LCVPs stuffed with explosives.
31. There were three successive series of three female Apexes between H-50 and H-30.
32. Lt. J.H. Sturmer, USAAF, whose plane collided with another P-47.
33. The firing sequence was originally planned as follows: H-10, two LCT(R)s; H-5, four LCT(R)s; H-4, eight LCS(5)s; H-2, eight LCM(R)s.
34. Sherman Duplex-Drive tanks from the 756th Bn with a " skirt " designed to permit them to float in the water.
35. Wooden submarine chaser.
36. Naval Combat Demolitions Units N° 9, 10, 53 and S-2.
37. As compared to the plan, only one LCT(R) and one LCVP were missing.
38. Report of Amphibious Operations conducted against the enemy by units of the Alpha Red Assault Groups, in Southern France during the period of 9 August 1944 to 25 August 1944, by CTG 84.1 and dated October 1, 1944. TG 84.1 was made up of 25 LSTs, 43 LCI(L)s including one British boat, 34 LCTs of which 16 were British, 5 PCs, 3 SCs and 5 LCCs.

Above.
756th Tank Bn DD (Duplex-Drive) tank on the beach in Cavalaire. Notice the raised "skirt", the two screws at the rear and the exhaust pipes. In the background a DUKW carrying a 105-mm howitzer. *(US Army)*

Unofficial breast patch worn by the crews of the 756th Tank Bn. *(Le Poilu Collection)*

dition of the beach on landing, opinions differed. For some "*the naval rocket barrage which had immediately preceded the assault had apparently had good effect, as a dense, even, pattern of bursts was observed inshore, and the first prisoners taken were well shaken up.*" [39] For others "*rocket craft were supposed to have drenched the beach to set off land mines, but rockets are difficult to aim and there were a number of misfires, so that the eastern half of Cavalaire beach was still thick with mines when the troops came ashore. Naval combat demolitions teams, arriving at 0810, went to work on shoal-water obstacles. These were so generously spaced and so clearly visible in the water that landing craft had little difficulty skirting them.*" [40] Whatever the truth may be, a tank hit a mine and sank. Then the same thing happened to two LCVPs, resulting in the loss of sixty men from the 2nd Battalion. The landing craft in the next three waves continued to hit obstacles or mines. Others were hit by fire coming from the ground defenses with consequent damages or loss. [41]

But by 0825, when the bravest Germans moved out of their dugouts to open fire with their machine guns and mortars, there were enough DD tanks on the beach to discourage them. While the 36th Engineers cleared pathways across the mined beach, and the sailors blew up the obstacles in the water, patrols were already advancing beyond the surfline. A radio message was sent to the *Duane* at that time saying that operations were progressing normally. Then purple smoke from the beach at 0850 signaled that all defenses had been neutralized and that the

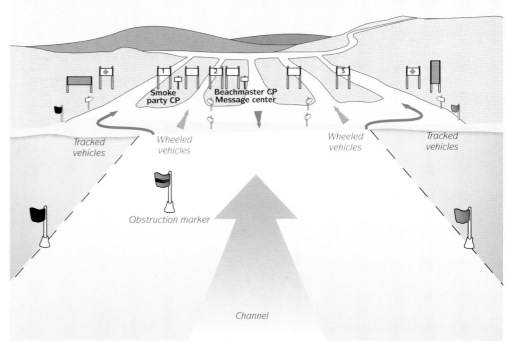

Planned organization for a Red Beach section

Smoke party CP

Beachmaster CP Message center

Tracked vehicles

Wheeled vehicles

Wheeled vehicles

Tracked vehicles

Obstruction marker

Channel

Left.
On Cavalaire beach, 3rd Infantry Division engineers are exploding a mine placed on the surface of the water.
(US Army)

Top left.
Insignia of the 10th Combat Engineer Bn. (*Le Poilu Collection*)

Right
The mines and obstacles remaining after the passage of the first waves were destroyed by the Beach Group engineers.
(US Army)

Above.
Insignia of the 601st Tank Destroyer Bn which received the Distinguished Unit Citation for having stopped the German tanks at the Kasserine pass in Tunisia.
(Coll. Le Poilu)

elements of the 30th Regiment could land. At 0925 the 7th Regiment CP left LCI(L) 954 for a site on dry land.

Everything went as scheduled until the seventh wave. But the first elements of the reserve regiment which had left at 0920 were twenty minutes late. And just as the DUKWs guided by a PC [42] were about to be released at one thousand meters from the beach, the Beachmaster and the engineers closed the beach at 0950 because of the mines and obstacles [43]. Three LCVPs and four LCIs had been damaged by Teller mines as they were beaching on the right-hand side of the zone were none of the Apex

39. *History of the Third Infantry Division*, op. cit.
40. *Samuel Eliot Morison, The Invasion of France and Germany 1944-1945, Oxford University Press, London 1957.*
41. *In all, TG 84.1 lost 6 LCVPs with 19 craft damaged; human losses were 10 dead and 58 wounded.*

Top.
At 1115, the 8A wave left LCC 40 and headed directly for Red Beach. LCT 1144 tried to beach twice, but was stopped by concrete obstacles both times. At 1145 she finally reached the beach even though one of her rudders was damaged. First out were the armored cars of Troop C/117th Reconnaissance Squadron, then the M15 half-tracks of the 441st Antiaircraft Automatic Weapons Bn, armed with a 37-mm gun and two .50 caliber machine guns.
(National Archives)

Above.
General O'Daniel on the Cavalaire beach talking with the 36th Engineers CO.
(National Archives)

Right.
The Alpha Red US Navy Beachmasters are equipped with binoculars and a handie-talkie. Note also the SP (Shore patrol) armband worn by most Navy personnel assigned on the beach.
(National Archives)

The 3rd Medical Battalion distinctive insignia.
(*Le Poilu Collection*)

drones had detonated.

Then activity started again and wave No 8 headed for the shore. Visibility along the coast was considerably impaired by the smoke, so at 1044, General O'Daniel and part of his operations staff left the *Duane* aboard LCVPs from LSTs 914 and 210. After noon the Beachmaster confirmed the landing count: 8,000 men, 70 vehicles, 44 DUK-Ws.

At 1355, as the three LSTs carrying the pontoon causeways were being sent ashore where the Seabees were waiting to put them together, the other ships approached the coast to be unloaded by the LCTs. Five minutes later, the French liaison team [44] on LCI(L) 954 had landed. Then at 1500 the rest of the staff left the *Duane* for the new division CP installed at La Croix.

Two Czech prisoners, interrogated before being

transferred to another ship, swore that there was no major German unit between Saint-Tropez and Toulon: only and handful of few German officers and Armenian 'volunteers.' At that time the heat was still bearable, except inside the boats. On land the cicadas had started their clamorous singing which they briefly interrupted when a rocket fell close by.

At 1621, LCI(L) 192 approached Red Beach and dropped its hind anchor in water 40 fathoms deep. A minute later the ramps were lowered and the soldiers headed for the beach. At 1628 the ramps were raised and the LCI moved away. *(US Army)*

Left.
GIs astride their GMC abandoned by a landing craft and surrounded by water, wait for some one on the beach to get them out of their mess. In the foreground, beside a trench covered with cane fencing, two dead soldiers lie on a stretcher. In the distance a DUKW has just come off an LST with its door ajar. *(US Coast Guard)*

Battle Patrols and Infantry Battalions

The 7th Infantry Battle Patrol had landed on the left flank with the first wave. Its mission was to head for Cavalaire, two kilometers to the west, and to reach the cape from which the enemy had a view and firing capability over the beach. The patrol was delayed by mines and harassed by snipers, but finally reached its objective [45]. The 3/7 which followed managed to clean out the village and then the peninsula, in spite of stiff resistance lasting until 1030. Then, accompanied by tanks and TDs, the battalion continued along the coast road, met up with the 'Commandos d'Afrique,' and went on with them until nightfall when they were stopped by a road-

---

42. Steel submarine chaser.
43. At that time, 92 LCVPs, 4 LCTs and 31 LCI(L)s and already beached and then left the zone.
44. A naval lieutenant and two sailors.

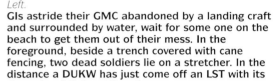

Previous page.
Explosion of an underwater mine in front of Red Beach.
(National Archives)

Right
Alpha Red Beachmaster's CP, put up by Company A, 1st Naval Beach Battalion. The two Navy officers in their beige uniforms are talking with two French officers from the liaison team.
(National Archives)

The six LCI(L)s of the sixth wave stop off Red Beach. The soldiers took only seven minutes to leave No 668, but the landing craft wasted 20 minutes untangling its anchor, entwined with a cable from another LCI. No592 on the left had run onto a mine and can only lower one ramp. The next boat, No 593, touched a concrete obstacle that pierced a hole in one of its tanks. The 30th Infantry soldiers nevertheless disembarked and at 0926 the craft withdrew. *(US Army)*

Bottom right.
The first prisoners, including many "Russians" who declared they were victims of forced conscription, were gathered near the beach to be evacuated to Italy. *(US Army)*

Inset.
Insignia of the 15th Infantry Regiment adopted in 1925 and bearing a dragon, symbol of the Regiment's long stay in China.
(Le Poilu)

block at Pointe de Layet.

On the right flank, the troopers of the 3rd Reconnaissance Patrol were luckier. First they ran into a group of twenty Germans who could hardly wait to be captured. Further on they bagged one hundred fifteen more. They reached Sylvabelle at 1030, and having accomplished their mission, returned to their unit.

The 2/7 arrived on the right and encountered many obstacles: tetrahedrons, mines and barbed wire over the first five hundred meters, but resistance was light and they soon reached La Croix in spite of sporadic mortar and small arms fire. By 1045 they had passed the village and were marching toward their objective, the hilltop west of Gassin. They reached it at 1430 and made contact with the 30th Infantry.

The leading elements of this regiment had landed after the 7th Infantry at 0920 and progressed rapidly in order to relieve the 2/7. Company K from 3/30 entered the village of Cogolin at 1415. The 1/30 had crossed town and was followed by the 3/30. At 1500 Company G met elements from the 15th Infantry. Then at 1640 the battle patrols from the two regiments met on the peninsula between the beaches of Cavalaire and Pampelonne.

The 15th Infantry Regiment [46] had been

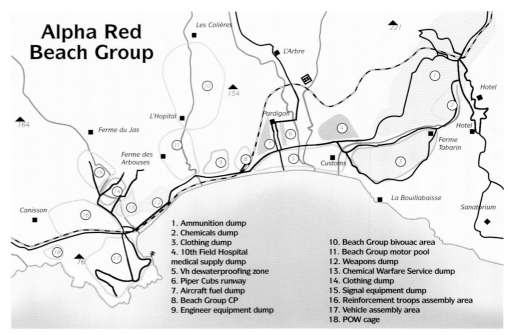

beached at Pampelonne by Commodore C.D. Edgar's TG 84.3 in conditions just about the same as those at Cavalaire. The LCVPs were launched by the assault transport ships *Samuel Chase* and *Henrico*, and the first wave of eleven hundred men touched shore at exactly 0800. The second followed at 0811, four minutes early. Soon after, the officer commanding the first wave from the *Henrico* reported that they had met no resistance.

Just as on the west side, a few rockets fell short, and the under-water obstructions were easily avoided. The beach was also obscured by smoke and enemy resistance amounted to nothing more than a few machine-gun spurts. The only serious incident took place at 0630

Alpha Red Beach Group

1. Ammunition dump
2. Chemicals dump
3. Clothing dump
4. 10th Field Hospital medical supply dump
5. Vh dewaterproofing zone
6. Piper Cubs runway
7. Aircraft fuel dump
8. Beach Group CP
9. Engineer equipment dump
10. Beach Group bivouac area
11. Beach Group motor pool
12. Weapons dump
13. Chemical Warfare Service dump
14. Clothing dump
15. Signal equipment dump
16. Reinforcement troops assembly area
17. Vehicle assembly area
18. POW cage

Top left.
36th Engineer Combat Regiment shoulder patch.
(*Le Poilu Collection*)

Left.
DUKWs from the 52nd Quartermaster Bn (Mobile) shuttle between the beach and the boats anchored in the Cavalaire Bay.
(US Navy)

Below.
The Camel Red Beach Group first aid station, installed in an abandoned blockhaus.
(US Navy)

reached the outskirts of town at 1500 the infantrymen found themselves face to face with the paratroopers. Together they quickly silenced the last resistance and by 1945 had taken about one hundred prisoners.

In the afternoon the eastern part of Red Beach had to be closed again for mine sweeping. Consequenly Green Beach was opened at 1800 even though its exits were heavily sown with mines. At that time the unloading capacity at Cavalaire was two LSTs by pontoon causeway, eight LCTs and three LCIs.

All troops comprising the first echelon had landed, and the assault phase in Alpha sector could

45. *After replacing his platoon leader who had been killed by a mine on the beach, Sergeant James P. Connor, with only 11 sound men out of 36, was able to kill 7 Germans, take prisoner 40 others, and capture 3 machine-guns. He was decorated with the Medal of Honor for this action.*
46. *Reinforced by Co B 756th Tk Bn, Co B 601st TD Bn, Co B 3rd Cml Bn, Co B 3rd Med Bn, Co B 10th Engr Bn and 39th FA Bn (at first), three Navy SFCPs, Det 6617th Mine Clr Co (Gapping Team), Det 3rd Sig Co, PW Interrogation Team.*

when the British mine sweepers found themselves under a volley of machine-gun fire coming from two little boats anchored near Cap Camarat. The flotilla immediately took aim with all its cannon and machine-guns. At 0648 the boats were sunk and the crews abandoned ship and headed for the coast in lifeboats.

By 0955 Yellow Beach had been completely cleared and four Tank Destroyers had just landed. At 1020 the transport ships started to unload, and then the LSTs ten minutes later. Their vehicles were ferried to the beach in LCTs. The beach was shallow, therefore pontoon causeways were constructed so that the vehicles would be able to unload directly from the LSTs. At 1400 all of the boats had been unloaded, but, in spite of the efforts of the engineers and sailors of Company C, 1st Beach Battalion, the beach soon became congested because the exits were too narrow.

The two lead battalions, 3/15 to the right, 1/15 to the left, took less than forty minutes to annihilate the beach defenses, and arrived around noon on the hilltops four kilometers from the shore. Then the 2/15 overtook them and the 3/15 headed north toward Saint-Tropez. As they

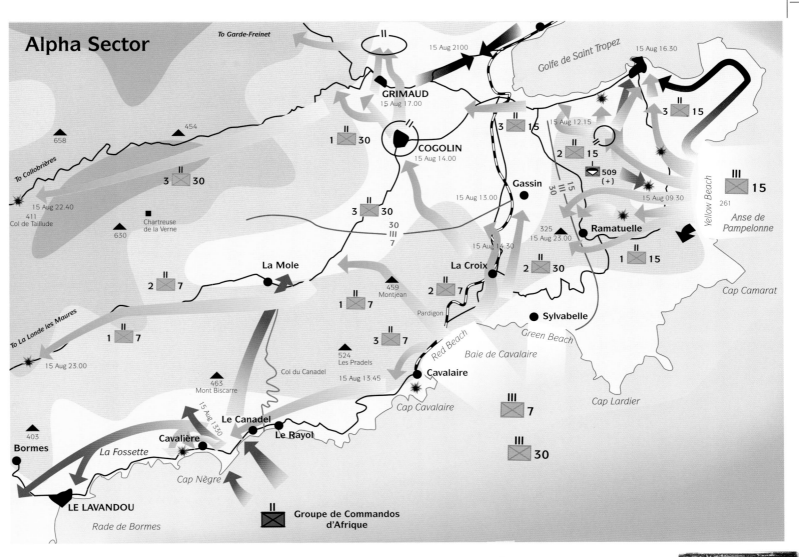

Alpha Sector

To Garde-Freinet

Golfe de Saint Tropez

15 Aug 2100

15 Aug 16.30

GRIMAUD
15 Aug 17.00

15 Aug 12.15

454

658

To Collobrières

1 | 30

COGOLIN
15 Aug 14.00

3 | 15

2 | 15

509
(+)

3 | 15

15

III
30

15 Aug 09.30

III | 15
261

Gassin

15 Aug 22.40
411
Col de Taillude

3 | 30

3 | 30

15 Aug 13.00

Yellow Beach

Anse de Pampelonne

630

Chartreuse
de la Verne

30
III
7

325
15 Aug 23.00

Ramatuelle

La Mole

La Croix

15 Aug 14.30

2 | 30

1 | 15

Cap Camarat

2 | 7

2 | 7

1 | 7

459
Montjean

Pardigon

Sylvabelle

Green Beach

1 | 7

630

524
Les Pradels

3 | 7

Red Beach

Baie de Cavalaire

15 Aug 23.00

Col du Canadel

15 Aug 13.45

Cavalaire

III | 7

Cap Lardier

463
Mont Biscarre

Cap Cavalaire

403

15 Aug 1330

Le Canadel

Le Rayol

III | 30

Bormes

Cavalière

La Fossette

Cap Nègre

LE LAVANDOU

Rade de Bormes

Groupe de Commandos
d'Afrique

---

be considered terminated.

Way beyond the targets

The support ships did not get much of a chance to intervene after H-hour. The ground troops made rapid progress and had little need to call on naval fire: either there were no targets or the FSCPs were soon out of range. So the Gunfire Support Group moved west to take on targets between

Cap Nègre and Cap Bénat. The LCCs, with the plane from the cruiser *Quincy*, and sometimes the 3rd Division artillery Cubs [47], took charge of air and sea observation.

At 1710, once the snipers had been taken care of, the 1/30 entered Grimaud. They were soon joined by the 3/7 on their tanks. They continued along toward Collobrières but were stopped at the Taillude gap. During the night they overcame all resistance and were able to enter the village at 3:00 AM. To the north, the 1/30 went through La Garde-Freinet around 0435 and headed for Les Mayons where they captured about twenty prisoners. On the south side, elements from the 7th Infantry were progressing beyond La Mole at nightfall, when they were stopped by an enemy strongpoint of six or eight machine guns and four antitank guns. It took them until noon of the next day to silence the enemy guns.

At sea, the reorganization plan had been activated at 1656, so that the naval forces could carry out the missions involved with maintaining the fleet along the coast and assisting the troops inland [48]. The LCT(R)s had arrived in the Camel sector that morning to participate in the invasion of the Frejus beach. And PT boats had been sent as reinforcements to patrol along the western flank of the assault zone.

At nightfall the Saint-Tropez peninsula had been

Insignia of the 10th Field Artillery Battalion adopted in 1923 by the regiment, which fought in WWI with the division.
(Le Poilu Collection)

Top.
Around 0830 on Yellow Beach. The soldiers are pouring out of the LCVPs from APA 26 Samuel Chase and AKA 15 Andromeda, part of wave No 3, and assembling to the right. The smoke pots placed by the first wave are still burning.
(National Archives)

Above.
An LCVP from the assault freighter *Oberon* carries a wrecker to Yellow Beach. AKA 14, part of Task Unit 84.3.1 unloaded men and material between 1524 and 1825.
(National Archives)

Above.
At 0853, LCI(L) 674 stopped eight meters from the shore, one hundred meters to the right of the left-hand side of Yellow Beach. The first soldiers from the 2/36th Engineeers are on the beach while medics behind them carry stretchers.
(National Archives)

Below.
The Pampelonne beach today, seen from the bends in the road between Gassin and Ramatuelle.
(Private collection)

Right.
A 3rd Signal Company jeep has run into trouble on Yellow Beach and is being pushed by the sailors and soldiers of the Beach Group.
(National Archives)

completely cleared, all the mines removed from Cavalaire beach, and the Liberty ships that had arrived in the afternoon were being unloaded, with the cargo placed in trucks carried by LCMs [49]. Losses were light and a large number of prisoners had been taken [50].

From August 16 on, the convoys arrived more and more rapidly [51]. Yellow Beach, where the exit passages were unfavorable, was closed the next day [52]. On the other hand, Cavalaire remained a major unloading point for the next three weeks.

49. During the day 16,000 men, 2,150 vehicles and 225 tons of supplies were unloaded. On the 17th these numbers were respectively 48,200, 6,438, and 1,060.
50. Losses were 264 for the 3rd Division, reinforced, 36 for the Navy; 1,600 prisoners were taken.
51. That day, for example, 81 ships left the zone and 76 arrived, including three US Army hospital ships and a PT boat shuttling back and forth to Ajaccio for the blood bank.
52. An air strip was nevertheless prepared there.

Left.
Pampelonne beach seen from the south. The 1/15 had landed on the left and progressed toward Ramatuelle. They had taken the high ground in the background. The other two battalions landed on the right-hand side and marched north to occupy the hills on the right, with the town of Saint-Tropez hiding behind them.
(National Archives)

Insignia of the 39th Field Artillery Battalion adopted in 1940.

(Le Poilu Collection)

Right.
Yellow Beach on the morning of August 16. Around a Piper Cub which had to make a forced landing, prisoners are talking with their guards. Off the beach, LST 140 continues to unload its equipment. The ship is actually the Task Force 85 LST(GCI).
(National Archives)

DELTA SECTOR

The 45th Infantry Division had been commanded since December 1943 by Major General William W. Eagles [1]. It had participated in the invasions of Sicily and Salerno, then fought in the Abruzzi where it had earned a French citation. It was next committed in Anzio before being withdrawn on June 5 and assembled near Rome two days later.

Traveling by sea or by land, the men arrived on June 26 around Battipaglia, near Salerno, where the division was attached to the Army Service Forces for supplies, and to the Seventh Army for administration, training and plans. It was finally assigned to the central section of the VI Corps sector, the area between the gulf of Saint-Tropez and Saint-Aygulf. Its mission was:

- On assault beaches 263 A (Red and Green Beaches, La Nartelle South), B (Yellow Beach, La Nartelle North) and C (Blue Beach, Garonette Plage): destroy enemy resistance; take Sainte-Maxime and clear beaches 262 (Grimaud Beach), 262 A (Sainte-Maxime South) and 263 (Sainte-Maxime);
- take the high ground on the South side of the Argens River overlooking Beach 264A, capture Villepey and assist the 36th Division in clearing the beach;
- advance rapidly to make contact with Rugby Force and reach the Blue Line, destroying any enemy elements along the way;
- land the reserve regiment and employ it only with corps authorization;
- then cross the Blue Line on orders from corps.

August 14. One of the three SOC-3 Seagulls from VOS-2 on CL 41 *Philadelphia*. The biplanes were launched on the 15th between 0559 and 0627: two observing for CTF 86 in the Sitka sector, one for the *Philadelphia* herself.
(National Archives)

A 45th Division GI.
(Reconstruction by 'Provence 44')

Top left.
The 45th Infantry Division shoulder patch. The four sides represent the four states where it was first levied: Colorado, Oklahoma, New Mexico and Arizona. But when it was activated in September 1940, its men came from the National Guard of the first three states only. The thunderbird is an Indian symbol for infinite happiness.
(Private collection)

AT THE INVASION TRAINING CENTER IN SALERNO

● ●

From June 24 on, the division worked at the amphibious training center. The ITC was under the command of Brigadier General Henry C. Wolfe and had left Port-aux-Poules for Salerno during the spring, then, on June 10, came under the control of the Seventh Army with the job of supervising training for the formations assigned to Anvil.

At first it was decided that each division would come independently, one after the other, to train [2]. But the program was changed. The 45th and 36th Divisions thus arrived together at Salerno and participated simultaneously in the training programs between July 1 and 17. The 3rd Division remained around Pozzuoli.

Memories of September 1943 were still vivid, as described by a 171st Battalion artilleryman:

"The same beaches, the same hills, the same dust and sand; but conditions have altered the situation and, though we almost expected the whine of shells and the roar of German planes, we found a refreshing, reassuring stillness, serene and peaceful [3]."

Right.
August 7. During Thunderbird, the final training exercise, a DUKW transporting a 105 HM2 Howitzer arrives on the Salerno beach.
(US Army)

Right
A 105 self-propelled M7 howitzer of the 69th Armored Field Artillery Bn photographed during waterproofing training at the Salerno FAITC.
(US Army)

Below.
As before on the beaches of Arzew and Port-aux-Poules (Algeria), the dress rehearsals in Salerno took place in conditions as close as possible to reality.
(US Army)

ed on the DUKWs, then practice continued with the tanks coming off the LSTs. Orders were clear: do not approach the beach unless the pathes through the shallow-water obstacles had been cleared and marked.

However it was impossible to find a firing range to test the new Sherman 105-mm gun, so the crews had to embark without ever having fired a single round at a target.

---

1. He was the same age as most of the American generals, between 48 and 50, but he was the only West Pointer. Like the others with the exception of O'Daniel he had not fought in World War I. He was a friend of Truscott's and had been his 3rd Division deputy until November 23, 1943.
2. 45th Div from June 24 to July 1, 3rd Div from June 28 to July 14, 36th Div from July 6 to July 30.
3. As quoted in the US Seventh Army Report of Operations, op. cit.
4. On July 27, 1944 19 lieutenants and 144 gunners were attached to the Seventh Army.

The proximity of the sea permitted them to use landing boats for training and then take a swim for relaxation. The surrounding hills were ideal for maintaining physical fitness, 25 miles or compass march, tactical exercises, firing... And while the troops were training their equipment was being refurbished.

The gunners learned to fire from the DUKWs. And eighteen SFCPs were organized in Arzew, then trained in Salerno with personnel taken from a replacement depot [4]. Twelve others were furnished by the division artilleries so that each division would have eight teams to accompany the assault battalions.

The tank crews went through a three-week training program learning how to adapt their machines to amphibious operations. The Shermans were furnished with a skirt and propelers churned by their engines, allowing them to float and move in water. To evacuate the tanks in case of immersion each man received a special apparatus used by submarine sailors, and they were taught how to use them in a huge industrial basin in Battipaglia which had been adapted by the 40th Engineer Regiment. Learning to drive the machines through water start-

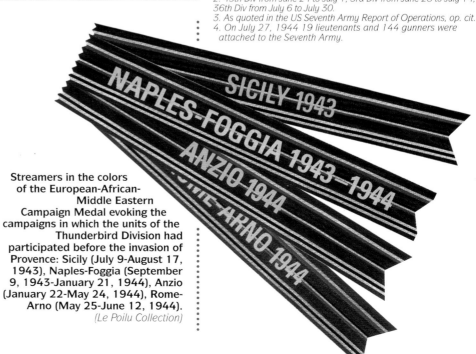

Streamers in the colors of the European-African-Middle Eastern Campaign Medal evoking the campaigns in which the units of the Thunderbird Division had participated before the invasion of Provence: Sicily (July 9-August 17, 1943), Naples-Foggia (September 9, 1943-January 21, 1944), Anzio (January 22-May 24, 1944), Rome-Arno (May 25-June 12, 1944).
(Le Poilu Collection)

As for the Beach Groups, the study that took place at Bouzareah in March 1944[5], concerning the unloading of freighters and transiting of troops and supplies, made it possible to define the organization and function of these units. They were considered to be miniature bases organized around a regiment of engineers reinforced by elements from the Services and the Navy, and were under the control of the VI Corps during the assault phase.

The Beach Battalion was to be landed with a Regimental Combat Team to help crossing the obstacles, unload the troops on the right beach and then organize the necessary supply dumps. At Salerno the training was of course organized around the first part of the mission, and the engineers drove tank dozers, used explosives and Bengalores, laid Sommerfeld matting...

Most of the engineers had already participated in preceding amphibious operations, so their instruction, for lack of time, was limited to presenting new methods and familiarizing the men with new material. And they were also used for the instruction of the infantry, tank and artillery units about destructions, mine warfare and crossing obstacle. The services had also participated in campaigns with the divisions to which they were attached, so more effort was put into organization than into training.

On August 7 the two divisions executed maneuvers Cowpuncher at the mouth of the Garigliano for the 36th and Thunderbird in Salerno for the

Above,
The three beaches of Delta sector, between Cap Sardinaux and Arpillon point. In the foreground can be seen the hamlet of La Nartelle, then the winding coastal road and, in the background, the white shape of the Hotel Résidence in La Garonnette-Val d'Esquières. *(US Army)*

In the middle of the afternoon on August 12, the LSTs left the Nisida, Torre Annunziata and Castellamare berthings and formed the convoy heading directly for the assault zone. The convoy was composed of sections SM-1, SM-1A and SM-1B, placed under Commander Task Force 85, and included the *Biscayne*, Admiral Bertram J. Rodgers[6] flagship. As they pulled out of Naples along the cleared channel, they passed Churchill, waving and wishing good luck to the soldiers and sailors. It was an impressive moment for the Americans.

Arriving near the straits of Bonifacio, section SM-1B had a moment of hesitation. In order to respect the prescribed distances, its guide had to stop so as not to overtake the preceding convoy which seemed to have a hard time entering the straits. Actually sections SM-1A and B finally approached the cleared channel from the south after crossing more than a mile of water that sup-

45th in conditions as close as possible to reality: combat ammo, obstacles similar to those which had been reported in Provence, use of the complete range of weapons and explosives... The Navy, for example, used the Apex boat towing two drones loaded with ten tons of explosives and guided by remote-control toward the obstacles, the Reddy Fox, the Navy version of the Bengalore, Woofus, or rockets shot from the landing craft, and demolition teams specializing in destruction of underwater obstacles with the help of portable explosives.

At the end of the maneuver, the troops headed for their staging areas to load the invasion ships.

APPROACHING THE BEACHES

Above.
Panoramic sketch of beach 263A (La Nartelle South) as represented on the map distributed by AFHQ, drawn from information furnished by the 8th Fleet and printed thanks to the 19th Field Survey Coy in July 1944.
(US Navy)

Top left.
The 45th 'Divarty' distinctive insignia, representing the various divisional symbols on the artillery red background.
(Le Poilu Collection)

5. *By a work group including in particular Captain Robert A.J. English, Admiral Hewitt's deputy for Force 163, and Colonel Edwin C. Eller from the Seventh Army Engineers.*
6. *After serving in the Pacific, he joined Admiral Mountbatten's staff at the end of 1943, then took charge of 8th fleet amphibious operations when Anvil was momentarily canceled.*

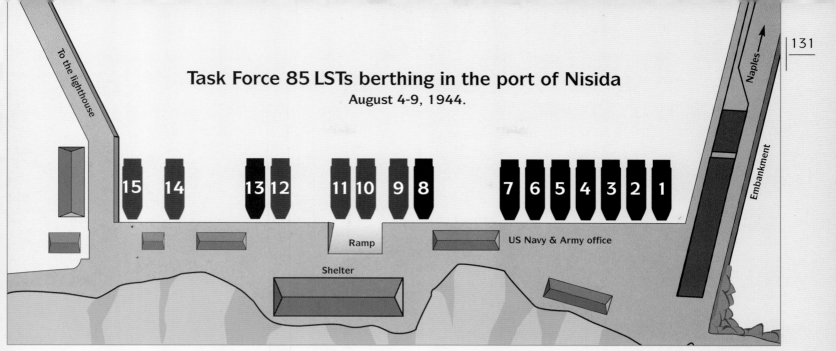

Task Force 85 LSTs berthing in the port of Nisida
August 4-9, 1944.

Berth	No 2	LST 690	TU 85.5.2	LST 495	TU 84.5.2
Berth	No 3	LST 664	-	LST 548	-
Berth	No 4	LST 655	-	LST 656	TU 85.5.2
Berth	No 5	LST 505	TU 85.4.1	LST 494	TU85.4.2
Berth	No 6	LST 692	-	LST 561	-
Berth	No 7	LST 550	-		
Berth	No 9	LST 995-P	TU 85.7.3	LST 665	TU 85.5.2
Berth	No10	LST 996-P	TU 85.6.3	LST 228	TU 85.4.2
Berth	No11	LST 997-P	-	LST 691	-
Berth	No12	LST 53	-	LST 1021-P	TU 85.9.1
Berth	No14	LST 1019-P	TU 85.8.3	LST 526-P	-
Berth	No15	LST 1020-P	-	LST 140-P	-

The ships loaded personnel and equipment in two shifts:
— first series starting on the 5th at 0900 and the 9th at 0600, the second series following behind.
— LST 526 FD (flight deck) loaded her planes on wharf H of the port of Naples on the 8th.
— LST 140 GCI was the fighter control ship.
— LST 53 was a mother ship (flotilla base ship).
— letter P indicates that the ship transported pontoons.

TU 85.4.2	LST Unit, *Red Beach Assault Group.*
TU 85.5.2	LST Unit, *Green Beach Assault Group.*
TU 85.6.3	LST Unit, *Yellow Beach Assault Group.*
TU 85.7.2	LST Unit, *Blue Beach Assault Group.*
TU 85.8.3	LST Unit, *Division Reserve Assault Group*
TU 85.9.1	LST Unit, *Corps and Division Group.*

lighter, until we could see the hills and the buildings that dotted the coast[7]."

At 0500 the LSTs and the assault transport ships assembled in their respective zones. Since 0449 the *Biscayne* had stopped in the bay of Bougnon, across from the beaches. Visibility was good and the sea calm.

The three beaches were situated north of well-defended Cape Sardinaux. Some of them were poorly adapted for the LSTs because of reefs or sand banks. They were narrow[8] and bordered by a road and a railroad track, which represented obstacles for the invading forces. Behind them the cultivated slopes rolled up rapidly into the Maures forest.

As in the case of Alpha, the sector was defended by an infantry battalion and a coastal battery. But this one was German[9] and supported by only one artillery group instead of two. The numerous blockhouses, some camouflaged as residences, and

7. The Fighting Forty-Fifth, the Combat Report of an Infantry Division, *Army and Navy Publishing Company, Baton Rouge, 1946.*
8. *About 500 m wide.*
9. *IV/GR 765 at Alpha, 1/GR 765 at Delta.*

posedly contained mines. No other incident occurred during the rest of the trip.

On the 15th at 0300, the British 19th fleet and two American mine-sweepers started to sweep the zone, but no mines were found. At 0440 the convoy of LCTs arrived in the interior zone, followed soon after by the support group. On board the soldiers waited anxiously:

"At that hour it was too dark to see anything. For a while we listened to the noises of the crew and watched the dim shadows of the other ships go by. As the light broke in the sky behind us, we could see the destroyers close to shore, firing point-blank into the enemy's known defenses. The coast itself, as far as we could see, was quiet. No answering gun flashes, only one or two fires... Slowly the picture unfolded as the sky became

Above.
In the port of Nisida, elements from the 189th Field Artillery Bn board the LSTs with their 155 M1 howitzers.
(US Navy)

Right.
Plane observer at watch on board the *Philadelphia*. Around 2100 on the 15th, as the cruiser was leaving shore, a Ju 88 flying over the fleet came under fire for about three minutes, but then disappeared into the clouds without having been touched. *(US Navy)*

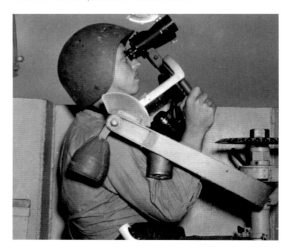

the various guns, especially the 220[10] positioned at Les Issambres, would have to be dealt with. And all the more because the coastal defense guns were installed in such a way as to cover a wide sector. Consequently, the number of enemy weapons able to intervene simultaneously on each beach was estimated at:

	75 mm	88 mm	105 mm	150 mm	220 mm
263A	21	4	28	18	4
263B	21	8	28	18	4
263C	21	8	32	14	4

The 45th Division G-2 nevertheless considered that "*a simultaneous landing on all beaches will reduce the number of guns firing on any one beach at least 75% from the figures given in the Beach Reports. With our naval support there is no doubt that the effect of enemy fire will be of minor importance[11].*"

About the defending soldiers the G-2 wrote: "*807 Ost Bn[12]. Strength 600 to 1,000 men. One company in division zone of action near Sainte-Maxime. This unit contains Russian troops (Volunteer PWs) trained and equipped to fight as infantry. Their equipment consists mainly of captured Russian weapons. These units are usually under strict German supervision.*

1 Bn 765 Regt 242 Inf Div. This regiment is responsible for the coastal sector, beach 263 incl to beach 264, excl. This is a regular German Infantry Bn. Estimated strength, 500 men."

The conclusion was that "*the enemy will defend at the beaches with the garrison now in position, delay our columns with demolitions, mines, and small delaying forces, and attempt to defend the high ground near Vidauban and Le Luc.*"

THE 157th RCT ON THE LEFT

As the 45th Division had requested, and because of its position in the center of the invading forces,

Left.
Locally manufactured insignia of the Colorado National Guard 157th Infantry Regiment, adopted in 1926. The Spanish colors, the fort, the sea lion symbolize Manilla, and the wigwams are a reminder of the Indian frontier where the regiment served. The unit received the DUC for its action at Anzio. *(Coll. Le Poilu)*

Bottom left.
August 16. In front of a Beachmaster's tent, Rear Admiral Bertram J. Rodgers, CTF 87, listens to a report of unloading operations on the beach. The soldier on the left is wearing the Seventh Army badge, the US armband as well as that of the Shore Parties which was reserved for members of the Navy. *(US Navy)*

Below.
Panoramic sketch of beach 263C (La Garonnette) as represented on the map distributed by AFHQ, drawn from information furnished by the Eighth Fleet. *(US Navy)*

the task force was made up of five assault groups and one group of division and army corps reserve elements, with boats divided up as follows:

To the above can be added twelve assault transports or freighters with five destroyers, about twenty mine-sweepers, plus the warships[13] and support craft[14] commanded by Rear Admiral C.F. Bryant, CTG 85.12, on board *Texas*.

The aerial bombardment was observed after 0550,

	Red	Green	Yellow	Blue	Div	Reserve
SC	2	2	1	-	-	-
PC	-	-	-	1	-	-
LCC	2	1	1	1	-	-
LST	105	2	1	5	2	3
LCI	7	6	2	1	19	3
LCT	7	7	3	14	4	14
LCG	1	-	-	1	-	-
LCF	1	-	-	1	-	-
LCT(R)	-	2	1	2	-	-
LCM(R)	2	2	2	2	-	-
LCS	4	4	4	4	-	-
LCM	1	1	1	1	-	-
LCVP	1	1	26	26	-	-
Total	38	31	43	55	25	20

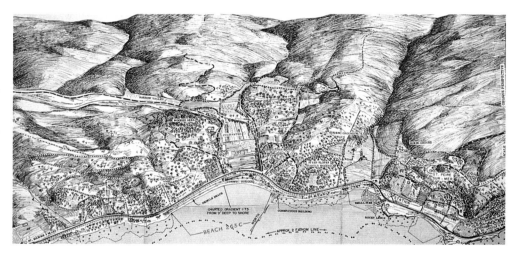

Above.
The first LCVPs, transporting 180th Infantry soldiers, approaching Blue Beach. *(National Archives)*

10. Made for the French by Bethlehem Steel Corporation in 1918.
11. Field Order No 1, Annex 1, Appendix 2, Enemy Order of Battle, dated August 3, 1944.
12. Actually the aserbeidschan.Infanterie-Btl 807 activated in Poland, transferred to the Western front in November 1943. It became IV/GR 765 on April 19, 1944.

MAXIME

M.E.I.U. M.36. 3

SEMAPHORE SARDINEAUX P^t GARONNE P^t

the counter-battery guns intervened at 0640 and continued until 0815, with the ships approaching to within three thousand meters of the coast. Then the scouts reported the absence of underwater obstacles, so Admiral Rodgers decided not to use the Apexes. The support craft opened fire at 0749 and fired more than six thousand rockets at the beaches over ten minutes until the first wave touched dry ground. The intense bombing by the fleet and aviation had a devastating effect: all the big guns were silenced, with their gunners either killed on the spot or having fled. No enemy shot reached the transport zones. About sixty mortar shells and a few shots from a 75 fell in the access channels, without doing

Above.
Oblique snapshot of the rubber sponge model made in the United States. The space between the Preconil valley and Arpillon point, also known as Pointe Garonne, is visible. Notice the interior road skirting the hills with the semaphore. The first tanks of the French 2^e Cuirassiers took this road after landing at La Nartelle.
(US Navy)

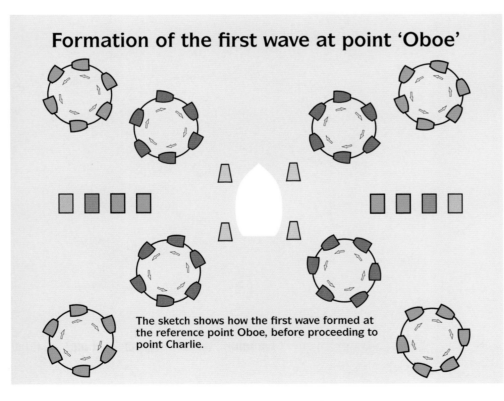

Formation of the first wave at point 'Oboe'

The sketch shows how the first wave formed at the reference point Oboe, before proceeding to point Charlie.

any damage.

The infantry troops aboard the LCI(L)s noted:

"*We headed for Red Beach on Cap Sardinaux. As we approached the shoreline we could see smoke from brush fires, blackened places, sites of bomb bursts, and some buildings slightly damaged. Then, as the details of the scene came into view, we could see the breaches in the seawall where the demolition crews had made openings for the assault platoons. In the water off Green Beach, we could see a tank with only the turret showing. One damaged*

Above right.
Major General William W. Eagles, commander of the 45th Infantry Division.
(US Army)

landing craft was the only injured ship we could see. How different from Sicily, Salerno! [15]"

The 157th Regimental Combat Team[16] was to land on Beach 263A with two battalions in the lead 3rd Bn to the left on Red Beach, 1st Bn to the right on Green Beach and the third in reserve. All the assault craft first assembled in transport zone No 2, which they left through the swept channel to reach point Oboe, seven nautical miles out, marked by PC 545. Maintaining their course at 53°, they passed point Charlie at four-and-a-half nautical miles where PC 1593 was located, and continued to Able, a mile and a half from the shoreline. From there, the waves fanned out and headed for their beach, with the LCCs and SCs alternately guiding from the various reference points.

Visibility was difficult because of the smoke and dust from the bombings.

At 0746 the LCT(R)s started firing over the first waves heading for the shore. At 0756 the Woofuses took over. Two minutes before, the LCMs had used

13. The battleships Texas *and* Nevada, *light cruisers* Philadelphia, Georges Leygues, Montcalm, Le Fantasque, Le Terrible *and* Le Malin, *8 destroyers.*
14. *2 LCGs, 2 LCFs, 6 LCT(R)s, 8 LCM(R)s, 16 LCSes.*
15. *The Fighting Forty-Fifth,* op. cit.
16. *157th Inf Regt reinforced by the 158th and 160th FA Bn, Co A 120th Engr Bn, Co A 120th Med Bn, Det 6617th Engr Mine Clearing co, Naval SFCP, Co A 83rd Cml Bn, Det 45th Signal Co, Co B 191st Tank Bn, Co C 645th TD Bn, Btry A and C 106th AAA AW Bn, CIC, PW Interrogators.*

their machine guns on the left flank in support of them.

The first wave from the 3/157 touched ground at 0802 on the far right of Red Beach. Since destroyers and LCMs were still firing at the Sardinaux point, Captain Harold E. Parker, CTG 85.5 on board LCI(L)(C) 520, anchored four hundred meters from the beach, decided not to use smoke screens so as not to hinder the shooting.

By then the second wave had arrived on Green

Above.
August 16. Wounded men are being evacuated aboard a PT boat. *(US Navy)*

Below.
After landing its first load for the Task Unit 85.9.2 reserve group, Royal Navy LCT(3) 344 shuttled between the Liberty ships and the beach. Here she is landing material for an engineering unit. *(US Navy)*

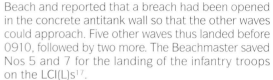

Insignia of the 158th Field Artillery Bn.
(Le Poilu)

Top.
August 15. The ballet of the landing craft that soldiers and sailors called the 'treadmill' between the beaches and the ships, as seen from the *Catoctin.* **In the distance can be seen the smoke from the bombs exploding on the Frejus beach around noon time.**
(US Navy)

Right.
There were no obstacles present off the Nartelle beach. Close defense was provided by an antitank wall which has been breached here to let the trucks through, flanked by three machine guns on Tobruk mounts and a mine field stretched up to and including Sardinaux point. *(DR)*

Gun casemate built by the Germans on the side of Cap Sardinaux across from San Peire.
(DR)

Beach and reported that a breach had been opened in the concrete antitank wall so that the other waves could approach. Five other waves thus landed before 0910, followed by two more. The Beachmaster saved Nos 5 and 7 for the landing of the infantry troops on the LCI(L)s[17].

Lieutenant Colonel Walter P. O'Brien and his staff left LCI(L) 952 at 0844 and took an LCVP to Red Beach.

At 0955, after having tried unsuccessfully to get through to the LSTs by radio to transmit the Beach-

master's order requesting them to move to within three thousand meters of the beach, the CTG 85.4 left for the transport zone and sent signals to the LSTs ordering them to move in. Then at 1104 the Beachmaster ordered the DUKWs to unload the howitzers they were carrying on the beach.

At 1303 Captain Parker and his operations officer came to Red Beach to confer with the Beachmaster. Tracks had been opened, and through the exits thus created the vehicles and personnel were able to leave the beach rapidly and methodically. Neither the Beachmaster nor the engineers had any complaints or suggestions. A half hour later a first pontoon causeway had been constructed, and at 1500 four LSTs could be unloaded simultaneously. Meanwhile, from 1420 on, the LCI(L)s of Task Group 85.8 beached with vary-

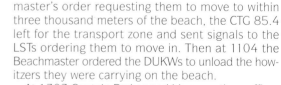

---

17. This took place between 0950 and 1100.

ing degrees of success some ran into sand banks and unloaded the men of the 1st Battalion.

At 1552 CTG 85.4 went aboard the *Biscayne* to talk with CTF 85. Eight minutes later the reorganization plan came into effect. Parker, henceforth the CTG 85.18 in charge of controlling the convoys leaving the assault area, moved aboard LCI 952 to a position fifteen miles out to sea.

THE 180th RCT ON THE RIGHT

In the center of the sector, the landing of Colonel Robert L. Dulaney's 180th Combat Team[18] went like clockwork. The first wave of the 2nd Bn approached Delta Yellow at 0758 without finding any mines or obstacles to block their path to the beach. Just a few shells fell here and there around them. At 0801, in thirty centimeters of water, the four Sherman DDs roared out of LCT 558 and immediately fired on four German pillboxes, completely destroying them. But one of the tanks hit a mine and exploded. The other LCTs didn't even bother to drop anchor: the beach was secure and there were no sand banks. Then they headed back out to sea to off-load the LSTs and the freighters which were beginning to arrive in the zone.

At 0833, LCI(L)(C) 196, with Commander W.O.

Above.
Photo showing Val d'Esquières with the huge Hotel Residence on the banks of the Garonnette. This snapshot appears in Volume 5 of the ISIS Report on France, Mediterranean France, published in May 1943. *(Private collection)*

Top left.
Insignia of the 180th Infantry Regiment of the Oklahoma National Guard, adopted in 1927. The symbols are a reminder of their Indian heritage. The Choctaw motto means: "*Ready in wartime as in peacetime.*" *(Le Poilu)*

Floyd, CTG 85.6, on board, positioned itself five hundred meters from the shore, between Yellow and Blue Beaches. The 1st Bn disembarking on the latter. They met little resistance and suffered few losses The only problem was on board LCT 604, behind the first six LCVPs. Just after point Able, the shock of a falling shell caused the engine to stall. The crew was able to get her going again, and she headed for the beach. But the smoke from the rockets was so thick that visibility was reduced to less than twenty-five meters. The LCT ran into a wharf on the right flank of the beach and got stuck. Unable to move, the boat unloaded its four tanks at 0805. With the Shermans gone, the craft was able to withdraw. But the land mines had not been destroyed and all the

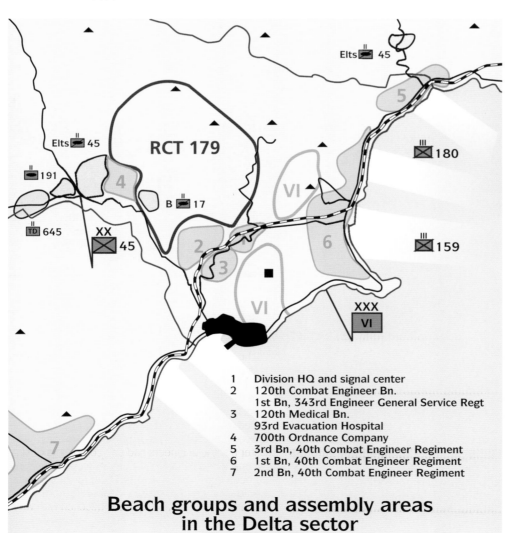

Beach groups and assembly areas in the Delta sector

1 Division HQ and signal center
2 120th Combat Engineer Bn.
　1st Bn, 343rd Engineer General Service Regt
3 120th Medical Bn.
　93rd Evacuation Hospital
4 700th Ordnance Company
5 3rd Bn, 40th Combat Engineer Regiment
6 1st Bn, 40th Combat Engineer Regiment
7 2nd Bn, 40th Combat Engineer Regiment

The gunners manning one of the Philadelphia's 'pom-pom' watch an LSM go by. *(US Navy)*

tanks exploded.

As soon as the beaches had been cleared, the battalions spread out in opposite directions, according to plans. 1/157 skirted Sainte-Maxime and reached Plan de la Tour at nightfall. 2/157, which had followed it onto the beach, spent the night nearby, then headed for Vidauban in the morning of the 16th. After they had cleaned out Sardinaux point, and following information from civilians saying that the five hundred Germans in Sainte-Maxime had left, 3/157 marched directly on the city. But when the first elements reached the outskirts, they were stopped by a blockhaus and several barricades. Maneuvering to the north, I Company first ran into machine gun fire, then waged a furious street fight-

18. *180th Inf Regt reinforced by the 171st and 189th FA Bn, 59th Armored FA Bn, co C 120th Engr Bn, Co C 120th Med Bn, Naval SFCP, Co B 83rd Cml Bn, Det 45th Signal Co, Co C 191st Tank Bn, Co A 645th TD Bn, Btry B and D 106th AAA AW Bn, PW Interrogators, CIC.*

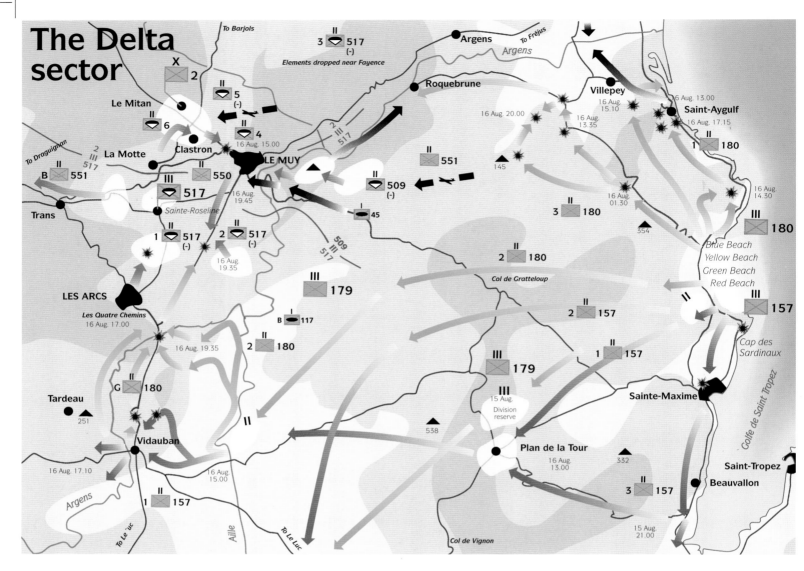

The Delta sector

ing. Once the stiffest resistance had been silenced, a platoon was sent to the waterfront where two strongpoints were still holding out: one at the Hotel du Nord, the other near the port. K Company intervened then, and the fighting finished with numerous enemy dead and sixty prisoners taken. The battalion then continued along the coastal road and made contact with advance elements of the 3rd Division. The men headed for Plan de la Tour where they spent the night with the 1/157.

On the right, 1/180 headed for the high ground above St Aygulf. But the men advancing along the coast met stiff resistance, and tanks and TDs had to be engaged to neutralize it. It was dark before the battalion arrived at the first houses of the village, so they waited until the next day to take action. Covered by C Company to the north, B Company with the help of tanks attacked on the south side. Resistance was strong and the SFCP requested help from the destroyers. As a result St Aygulf was finally occupied.

2/180 simply moved up the hills overlooking the beach. From there the men received orders in the afternoon to progress toward Vidauban. As for 3/180 landed at 0900 behind the 1st Bn, they climbed up to high ground and met heavy resistance at the Bougnon gap.

General Eagles came ashore at 1100 and installed his CP near Sainte-Maxime[19]. General Truscott came to see him there in the afternoon. The 179th RCT[20] landed at 1145 and assembled behind Delta Green. The day ended[21] with the announcement that a platoon from the 45th Reconnaissance Troop heading toward Le Muy had liaison with the paratroopers.

Right.
Headquarters platoon of a 1st battalion company from the 180th Infantry passes Shermans from the 191st Tank stopped on the road to St Aygulf. *(US Army)*

The insignia of the 191st Tank Battalion was authorized in 1942. The wildcat was inspired by the first insignia of the Tank Corps worn in 1917. The battalion was formed with tank companies from the National Guard of several states: New York, Massachusetts, Virginia, Connecticut. *(Le Poilu)*

The 40th Engineer, working in association with the 4th Naval Battalion, did not run into any major difficulties, contrary to the 36th Engineers at Alpha. On 263A, where the 1st battalion started operating, obstacles were rapidly eliminated, the concertina barriers and one-meter-thick wall were breached. Thanks to the pontoons and the motorized cranes, the LCTs and LCMs were unloaded at a rapid pace, while the DUKWs shuttled back and forth between the ships and the supply dumps created in back of the road. The 3rd battalion arrived with the 180th Infantry, and the slant of the beach was such

The Bougnon Bay beaches today, seen from the top of the Issambres water tower. Sardinaux point is clearly visible. The city of Ste-Maxime is partly hidden by the semaphore hill, and St Tropez and the peninsula are covered with mist.
(Private Coll.)

Top, inset.
Insignia of the 179th Infantry Regiment, Oklahoma National Guard, adopted in 1927. *(Le Poilu Coll)*

Below.
On the Nartelle beach, German prisoners waiting to be evacuated by craft. *(US Army)*

Above.
Beaches are now secured, even if shells fall sometimes, combining explosions smoke with pine forest fires. A LCT, with vehicles of a supply unit aboard, approaches *Yellow Beach.* *(IWM - IA 33 990)*

that unloading could be done on dry ground. However Blue Beach, where exiting proved difficult, was closed on the 16th, once beach 263 had been opened.

The 2nd Bn had landed at Pampelonne at 1900, later than planned. They started by helping the 36th Engineers to neutralize mines and booby-traps. Then they left for St Tropez and cleared the port so that seven LCTs could dock there from then on. They also cleared several corridors through the mine field covering beach 262, and equipped a new site called Red Beach 2 which rapidly became the most important in the sector[22].

In the Delta sector, because of the complex nature of the invasion on four different beaches but close to each other, a large number of ships and landing craft had to assemble in a narrow space about ten miles offshore. And the support ships — as in the channels — were also numerous. The first seven waves landed exactly on schedule and sometimes even a few minutes early.

"The seventh wave was all ashore by 0910. Without enemy opposition, it was a dream landing [23].*"*

19. Precisely at the intersection of the roads to Le Muy and Plan de la Tour. The VI Corps CP was being installed to the west of Sardinaux point at the time.
20. 179th Inf Regt reinforced by Co B 120th Engr Bn, Co B 120th Med Bn, Naval SFCP, Co C 83rd Cml Bn, Det 45th Signal Co, PW Interrogators, CIC.
21. Results: two officers and 107 men killed or wounded, 205 prisoners, 33,000 men and 3,000 vehicles landed.
22. It could handle simultaneously 6 LCMs, 19 LCIs, 5 LCTs, had a passage for DUKWs and numerous supply dumps.
23. Samuel E. Morison, The Invasion of France and Germany, Oxford University Press, London, 1957.

CAMEL
SECTOR

According to the Force 163 plan, the 3rd Division was scheduled to land on the east or right side of 'Camel' and the 36th Division on the west or left in LCIs, LCTs, and LSTs. The 45th Division was to travel on the transport ships and be taken ashore by the smaller landing craft and amphibious trucks, invading through several small beaches on either side of Saint-Tropez. When General Truscott heard of this plan, he requested that the attribution of sectors and the assignment of boats be modified. Admiral Hewitt and General Patch accepted the idea, so Truscott chose the 3rd Division, one of the most experienced, for the left flank, so that they could start their march on Toulon as soon as possible. The 36th would disembark on the right and play a mainly defensive role. The ships were equally divided among the divisions so that each had a sufficient number of LSTs and landing craft to simultaneously land two regimental combat teams.

BEACH 264 (B)

An infantry officer from the 36th Division.
(Reconstruction by 'Provence 44')

Top left.
Originally the 36th Infantry Division was made up of soldiers from Texas and Oklahoma. These states were symbolized on its patch (approved on November 12, 1918) with a T for Texas and an arrowhead suggesting the Indian Territory, the early name of Oklahoma. Then the division became part of the Texas National Guard.

Left.
The Drammont coastal battery photographed on July 11, 1944 at 1100 by a Lightning from the 3rd Photographic Group flying at 30 meters. One can clearly see the two uncamouflaged casemates, the road and the railway tracks, the hillock overlooking the beach. *(SHM)*

A DEFENSIVE MISSION

The 36th Division had a reputation for bad luck. It was engaged for the first time at Salerno and suffered heavy losses at San Pietro in December 1943[1]. The same thing happened during the attempt to cross the Rapido the following month[2]. Major General John E. Dahlquist was the commander since its withdrawal from the front in June 1944, but he was not part of Truscott's team.

According to the new plan, the division was to insure protection of the VI Corps right flank as far as La Napoule, and liaison with the paratroopers in the Argens River Valley. In the order of operations[3], the mission was thus stated:

Right, top the bottom.
The Flak battery on Camp Long point whose three 88-mm guns completed the bay of Agay defenses but also protected the Drammont radar station. *(DR)*

One of the casemates for 150-mm of the Drammont battery, also called 'Pierre Blave point battery,' that were flattened under 220 t of bombs on August 11 and 13, then shelled by ten ships on the morning of the 15th. *(DR)*

Gun casemate built on the beach airfield, at the entrance to the Naval Airbase. *(DR)*

Left.
Distinctive insignia of the 45th Division Headquarters.
(Le Poilu)

- assault beaches 264B (Green Beach, Cap Drammont west) and 265A (Blue Beach, Anthéor), and clear them of all resistance;
- capture Agay and clear beach 265 (Yellow Beach);
- assault beach 264A (Red Beach, Saint-Raphaël north) at H + 6, capture Fréjus and continue advance rapidly to gain contact with Rugby Force and Rosie Force[4], which would be attached to the Division once contact was established, and assembled around Fréjus;
- seize and hold the Blue Line zone and destroy all enemy therein;
- maintain contact with the 45th Division;
- then advance from the Blue Line on Corps orders.

Possession of the sector around Fréjus was vital for the 36th Division which needed a vast beach near a railway line to bring in battle supplies. The port of Saint-Raphaël and the possibilities of constructing airfields interested the VI Corps, but Truscott was thinking especially about the Argens valley, which was a natural access inland, through which could pass the tanks of the French Combat Command No 1 which was at his disposal.

Of course the Germans were also aware of the strategic value of the Gulf of Fréjus, and they improved their defenses by placing mines and obstacles, as indicat-

Above.
Aerial view of the Romains cove battery which commanded access to the gulf of Fréjus and covered the whole beach toward the north, from its position on Saint-Aygulf point. Its three 75-mm guns were sheltered in pillboxes still visible today, built underneath the houses touching the coast line.
(DR)

Right.
Streamers in the colors of the European-African-Middle Eastern Campaign Medal for the campaigns in which the Thunderbird Division participated before invading Provence: Naples-Foggia (September 9, 1943 to January 21, 1944), Anzio (January 22 to May 24, 1944), Rome-Arno (May 25 to June 12, 1944).
(Le Poilu)

ed on the photographs brought back by the Allied reconnaissance planes.

According to the 36th Division G-2, two battalions from Grenadier-Regiment 765[5] and one of volunteers from the Eastern front[6], three artillery groups[7]

1. 1,200 men: 150 killed, 800 wounded, 250 missing.
2. 1,681 men: 143 killed, 663 wounded, 875 missing.
3. 36th Infantry Division Field Order No 53 dated August 1, 1944.
4. Demolition party constituted by the Corsica Naval Assault Group and landed near Le Trayas to undertake destructions to block the Corniche road and Route 7.

NAPLES-FOGGIA 1943–1944
ANZIO 1944
ROME-ARNO 1944

and various other units[8] held the sector. And from the neighboring division could come a battalion or a regiment for counter-attack reinforcements. But all of these formations were static and had no tanks to support them. In conclusion, "*it is certain that the enemy will defend the beaches to the full extent of his ability. This defense will be very effective due to the preparation of positions and previous rehearsals of defensive plans. Local counterattacks will be employed probably very early after our landing*[9]."

In the analysis and discussion of enemy possibilities, the G-2 added:

"*The effect of resistance groups also had not been considered because the coastal area has largely been evacuated of civilians and it is highly doubtful that they will make their presence felt in the early stages of the operation*[10]."

PREPARATION

To the south of Saint-Raphaël, Camel Red stretched out over almost three kilometers in front of the naval air base. It was the only beach in the sector that could be used for installing supply dumps and landing supplies on a large scale. But it was strongly defended and caught under the cross fire from the cannons positioned at the two ends. Moreover, the number of obstacles and mines placed in the water and sand had increased significantly since the month of May[11].

Green Beach was more than eight hundred meters long. Its approach was difficult because of the Ile d'Or, and exit passages for trucks were uncertain. Leaving the sand, one first met round pebbles, then piles of large rocks with the road above them, the railway line and stone quarries overlooked by a wooded hillside where a battery was hiding out on the slopes. Yellow Beach was better, but the net or cable stretched across the roadstead exit made it impossible to be used by the first waves. So it was finally Blue Beach that

Left.
Distinctive Insignia of the 36th Infantry Division Artillery, representing the coat of arms of the state of Texas on the artillery scarlet background.
(Le Poilu)

Right.
Captain Don P. Moon was originally intended to be commander of an amphibious group in the Mediterranean. He was promoted Vice Admiral in January 1944 to head the landing at Utah Beach. He was then named to command the Camel Force, but took his own life on August 5, 1944.
(National Archives)

Opposite page.
August 10. 36th Division GIs boarding LCI(L)s in Pozzuoli harbor.
(National Archives)

Opposite page, far right.
Distinctive Insignia of the 111th Engineer Combat Battalion.
(Le Poilu)

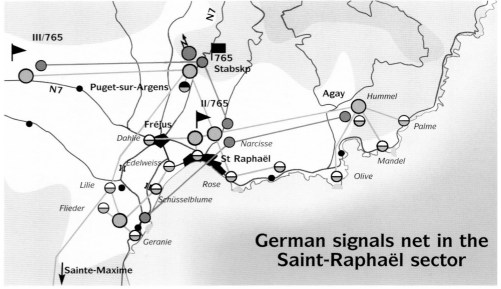

German signals net in the Saint-Raphaël sector

Symbol	Description
⚡	Radio station in the division net
●	Radio station in the command or coast defense net
●	Telephone exchange
⊖	Telephone station
◐	Telephone station connected directly to Sainte Maxime
◖	Searchlight

Opposite page.
A platoon from the 36th Division off-loading from an LCVP during a live ammunition exercise at the ITC in Salerno.
(National Archives)

Opposite page, bottom left.
August 11 in Pozzuoli. First Lieutenant Sam Jackson of the 36th Reconnaissance Troop distributes Invasion French notes to his men.
(National Archives)

5. *II/765 between St Aygulf and Agay, III/765 on reserve near Puget.*
6. *Ost-Btl. (Russ.) 661 organized on the Eastern front from an Estonian security battalion and then transferred to France.*
7. *242nd anti-tank and 1048th Assault guns, with a total of 38 75-mm guns in Le Muy, 1192nd Field Artillery in Fréjus.*
8. *4th company of the 63rd Luftwaffe Training Regiment in Fréjus, two fortress engineering companies in Saint-Raphaël.*
9. *Certain identifications were erroneous. Thus the 242nd Anti-tank battalion was actually a company in Toulon, and the other was the 1038th and not the 1048th. As for the Eastern battalion, it was effectively holding the coast north of Anthéor, but was part of the 148th Division.*
10. *36th Infantry Division Field Order No 53, Annex No 2, G-2 Estimate, dated August 1, 1944.*
11. *A mine field stretching across the gulf, one or two rows of concrete tetrahedrons topped with mines along the shore, two rows of barbed wire on the beach and then an anti-tank ditch four-meters deep in front of a 2-m high wall 1-m thick, mines on the beach, on the roads leading to the beach and the surroundings, blockhouses, etc.*

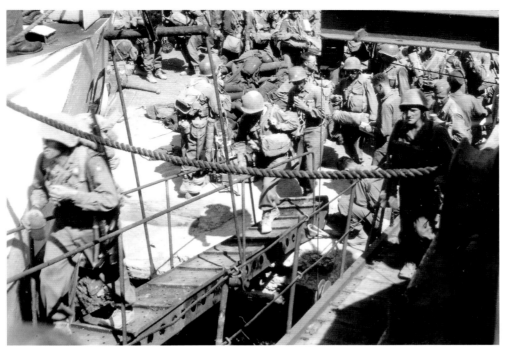

was chosen, even though it could only be used by small craft and infantry soldiers on foot. All of the beaches opened onto Route 98, which necessarily passed through either Saint-Raphaël or Fréjus, meaning that both of these cities had to be captured rapidly.

In the end, the beaches east of Saint-Raphaël were chosen for the assault, and the landing to the south was delayed timewise to allow the Navy to dredge the mines and destroy the defensive positions.

In charge of landing operations and support for the Texas Division, "*Task Force 87 was assembled and prepared for Operation Dragoon in a minimum of time. It was formed from units from three separate Theaters, those already in the Mediterranean waters, those which had just participated in Operation Neptune[12], and recent arrivals from the United States[13]. Commander Task Force 87 and his planning staff,*

Distinctive insignia of the 36th Reconnaissance Troop: the Texas coat of arms on the yellow cavalry background. *(L e Poilu)*

having just completed Operation Neptune, arrived from the United Kingdom in Naples on 1 July, setting up headquarters in the same building with the other two Assault Force Commanders, all three Assault Division Staffs, and the Sixth Corps Headquarters. This concentration led in a cooperative and harmonious relationship without which the preparation of plans for Dragoon would have been extremely difficult.[14]"

Rear Admiral Don P. Moon who had commanded the landing on Utah Beach, was the last task force commander to arrive in the Mediterranean. He

---

12. 3 warships, 5 cruisers including the Montcalm and the Georges Leygues, 23 destroyers, 9 high-water mine-sweepers, 12 assault transport ships, 22 LSTs. Neptune was the naval part of Overlord.
13. Including 43 LSTs out of the 71 participating in Dragoon.

judged that the Task Force 87 plans were imperfect and that the preparation of his ships was insufficient, and requested on August 4 that Dragoon be delayed. Admiral Hewitt was not opposed to the idea. How-

A GI from the 36th Division climbing on board a troop transport ship. *(Provence 44)*

ever before making a final decision, he wanted to see the general rehearsal scheduled for the 7th. But Moon, mentally and physically exhausted, committed suicide the next day. Hewitt replaced him at the last minute by his chief of staff, Rear Admiral Spencer S. Lewis, who had participated in the elaboration of the plans.

On August 13 at 1530, the Bayfield, floating the flag of Admiral Lewis, moved out of the bay of Naples and placed itself at the head of the convoy that had left its moorings in Castellamare three hours earlier. The ten transport ships and assault freighters crossed the straits of Bonifacio the following morning. Then progressively the different elements passed under the control of CTF 85[15]. At 2009, the *Bayfield* changed directions and headed toward the beaches.

AT ESQUILLON POINT

The attack in the Camel Sector began with the engagement of the French naval assault group[16] in

Top left.
Pennant of the light cruiser *Emile Bertin*. *(SHM)*

Below.
Distinctive Insignia of the 142nd Infantry Regiment, part of the Texas National Guard since 1917. It was adopted in 1929 and its design was inspired by the battle of the Aisne and the Saint-Etienne church.
(Le Poilu)

General view looking west of the development on Miramar hill, not yet covered with trees and houses. Note the Corniche road and Esquillon point, partially hiding the cove below the cliff where the GNAC sailors landed.
(Private Collection)

Gun crews from the *Emile Bertin* gaze at the coast of Provence. *(IWM - A 25 292)*

charge of blocking the roads to Cannes. Commander Seriot assembled his officers on August 10 to create the teams and distribute the missions. Blocking the coastal road fell to Lieutenant Letonturier and destruction of the bridge on Route 7 to Lieutenant Commander Marche. This was the most difficult job, because the bridge was situated in the middle of a forest and could only be reached after a difficult march of fifteen kilometers through the undergrowth.

On the 14th the men boarded a French submarine chaser No 52 at Calvi and took off immediately for Bastia. There, five minutes before leaving, Seri-

ot gathered his troops and announced that the landing would take place in France.

Soon four PTs left the diversionary group and sped off at a speed of thirty-five knots. The sea was calm,

14. *Commander Task Force Eighty Seven Action Report, Assault on the beaches of Southern France, dated September 7, 1944.*
15. *LCTs at 1100, LSTs at 1700, support group at 1800, LCIs at 2300.*
16. *66 sailors and First Sergeant Azzalier, an explosives expert from the 71st Colonial Engineer Battalion.*

there was no wind, and the night was clear with a slight mist. The men slept on deck, rolled in blankets loaned by the Americans.

At 0115 rubberboats were launched at eighteen hundred meters from the coast. Then Seriot left in a trawler with the Scout and Raiders team and at 0150 reached the landing point: a beach of pebbles fifteen meters wide at the back of a cove. To attract the boats toward him, he had to use a flashing red light, because the radio was jammed and inaudible. At 0200 automatic fire was heard from the road, followed by a red, then a white flare. Seriot then guided Marche's four boats into the cove. Before returning to his motor boat[17], he also guided Letonturier, whose three rubber boats had landed on the rocks where Marche's men were crowded together[18].

They started off toward the road. Suddenly, half way between the sea and the clifftop, a tremendous blast was heard: Ensign Auboyneau and three other sailors had just hit a mine. It was 0250. Marche decided to continue on.

But below them, Lieutenant Servel and two sailors were killed as they went through the barbed wire barrier. Then five others were wounded when they tried to come to the aid of their comrades. Around 0400 Letonturier was also hit by a mine fifty meters

Left.
Insigna of the 132nd Field Artillery Battalion, approved in 1928. Its design xas inspired by the origin and battle honors of this Texas Regiment since 1879: yellow Cavalry-colored Rio Grande, Spanish-American palm tree. *(Le Poilu)*

Right.
Before boarding ship, 36th Division GIs were issued a K-ration, a D-ration, water purification tablets, salt tablets and two packs of cigarettes.
(National Archives)

Below.
Panoramic sketch of beach 264A (Saint-Raphaël North) as represented on the map distributed by AFHQ, drawn from information furnished by the Eighth Fleet and printed thanks to the 19th Field Survey Coy in July 1944.
(Private collection)

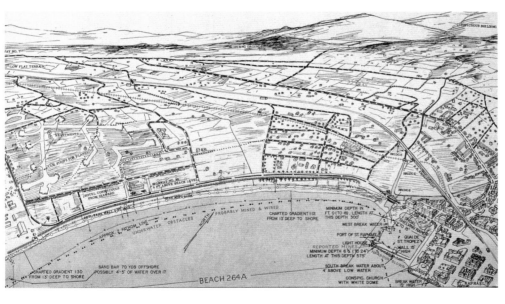

BEACH 264A

from the road. A half-hour later more explosions went off, followed by flares that lit up the team heading forward toward the road. Lieutenant Commander Marche was killed and his men did their best to destroy the documents he was carrying with him.

The detachment had lost nine dead and seventeen wounded. The survivors were pinned down, without a doctor[19]. They were no longer able to execute their mission.

At 0500 some men appeared on the road: they were Germans. Engineer Officer Chaffiotte, the only remaining uninjured officer, started a dialogue using a Petty Officer as interpreter. The Germans thought they would come in by sea and indicate an unmined path to evacuate the wounded. But at 0830, the French decided to change plans. Following information furnished by a soldier, Letonturier got up to reconnoiter a different passage through the mine field. As he had almost reached his goal, he hit another mine, resulting in a broken leg.

So Chaffiotte took command and decided to head

---

17. He was back on board at 0245, 25 minutes later that the authorized hour.
18. Each man was carrying about 45 kg, 30 kg of TNT and 100 Thompson rounds.
19. He had gone back out to sea with five sailors, was rescued by a destroyer and taken aboard the Duguay-Trouin at 1545.

Oblique photo taken on July 11, 1944 at 1100 by a plane of the 5th Photographic Group, showing the city, port and beach of Saint-Raphaël. The arrows show the blockhaus.
(SHM)

BEACH 264 (A)

and *Champlin*, preceding the *Bayfield*, had taken up radar positions in the transport zone. And at 0400 convoy SF-1 joined them, guided by their light signals. As they arrived the landing boats formed groups: one per beach and two for support composed.

A battleship and a heavy cruiser that had taken part in the Normandy invasion, six light cruisers including two French, and nine destroyers formed Task Group 87.7, under Rear Admiral Morton L. Deyo[22]. The *Tuscaloosa*, the admiral's flagship which had left from Belfast, had taken part in a firing campaign near Oran as it went by.

For spotting, the group had the two planes on the *Brooklyn*, nine Shore Fire Control Parties and three BD teams[23], plus, in certain cases, Cubs and advance artillery observers. Since the SFCPs followed the battalion ashore, it was decided that a BD team[24] on each beach would momentarily take over during the landing.

The support ships got into position and the *Tuscaloosa* radar spotted the transport planes approaching the coast along the prescribed route. The sailors were happy to observe that the enemy flak had not reacted in the same way that it had two months earlier in Normandy. Only a few red and white flares could be seen heading skyward. At 0340, as the *Parker* was arriving at its station, four Allied C-47s zoomed by overhead[25].

At 0635 the fourteen ships in charge of support for the landings on the beaches of Le Drammont and Anthéor[26] were in position. As the sun came up, visibility decreased little by little, to the point that the planes flying over the zone soon reported that it was

back toward the sea. He ordered his men to follow in his tracks, and headed down toward the rocks: he was now able to see the trip wires on the ground. The sound men and those only slightly wounded followed. However the slope was too steep to carry the invalids: they would have to be picked up later on top of the cliffs. After carefully crossing two hundred fifty meters, twelve men reached two rubber boats, in which they were able to reach the spot indicated by the Germans as being free of mines, near Deux Frères point.

Suddenly two twin-engine planes appeared out of nowhere, dived over the boats and opened fire.

"*Machine gun bullets ricocheted everywhere. Everybody jumped into the water, in an unspeakable confusion. We took cover in a cave. And then the Germans on the land, furious, opened fire.*[20]"

Once the planes had left the Germans stopped firing. But then the men had to climb back up onto the cliff, be frisked… It was starting to get hot. The wounded were thirsty and the water canteens were empty. Fortunately two healthy men were authorized to go get the wounded, who were transported to a nearby house by Russian soldiers[21]. At 1630 there were only dead bodies left in the mine field.

THE BOMBARDMENT GROUP

Further to the south, at 0230, the destroyers *Boyle*

	RED BEACH	GREEN BEACH	BLUE BEACH	SCREEN	RESCUE
SC	3	3	2	2	-
PC	2	2	1	1	-
LCC	3	3	-	-	-
LST	3	14	5	1	-
LCI	6	23	1	-	3
LCT	15	15	-	1	1
LCG	1	1	-	-	-
LCF	1	1	-	-	-
LCT(R)	6	6	2	-	-
LCM(R)	-	-	-	-	-
LCS	9	7	3	-	-
LCM	2	2	-	2	7
LCVP	20	7	-	-	-
Total	**81**	**84**	**14**	**7**	**11**

Top left.
Bombing of Red Beach on the morning of August 15. Notice on the left the French Naval Air Base pier and the taxiways leading to the airplane shelters and on the right the port and city of Saint-Raphaël.
(National Archives)

Above left.
The insignia of the French light cruiser *Duguay-Trouin*.
(SHM)

impossible for them to observe. Nevertheless the *Arkansas* and HMS *Argonaut* opened fire at 0650: the first on the German casemates at Le Drammont, without kindling any enemy reaction[27]; the second on four 155s in position north of Cannes. And the *Tuscaloosa* silenced the two batteries north of Saint-Raphaël. The destroyers attacked their targets with several rounds of barrage salvoes, followed by airburst shells to kill the gunners. While the fleet was pounding the shore, planes had made four passes over the beaches to drop their bombs[30]. The result was such a cloud of dust that the CTG 87.7 had to order a cease fire at 0750 and wait until the coast was visible again. Likewise, the planned use of smoke shells was delayed.

Firing observed by plane started again at 0829 when the Nields took on a battery that had just opened

20. Personal notes of IM Chaffiotte.
21. From the IV./GR 239 whose CP was in Le Trayas.
22. He had directed the support group at Utah Beach.
23. The teams had Beedex equipment, well-adapted to beaches.
24. BD 11 Blue Beach; BD 12 Green Beach; BD 13 Red Beach.
25. Undoubtedly the lost C-47s that dropped their sticks over St. Tropez.

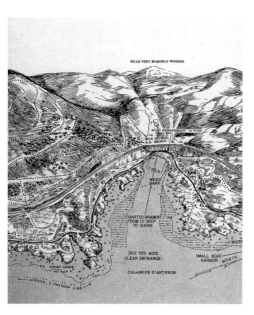

pushed on through the Esterel hills to reach Route 7, thus effectively covering the right flank of the VI Corps.

The first LSTs from the Green Beach assault group arrived in the transport zone where the landing craft[30] would be launched at 0445. Then, at 0600, the LCVPs were lowered along the sides and filled with soldiers before organizing themselves into waves.

At 0630, six coast minesweepers, guided by SC 522, left Baker, the ten thousand meter point where PC 546 was located. LCI(L) 19, carrying Robert Morris, CTG 87.4, followed them to Easy, the four thousand five hundred meter point, marked by SC 1043. Then, since the landmarks on the shore were completely hidden by the smoke and the dust from the bombings, the boat continued on to How, one thousand meters further, to make sure that the BMSes were taking the right direction. Once back at Easy, it took charge of the first wave, and accompanied the craft to within two thousand meters of the beach.

At Blue Beach it was Commander L.R. Herring, CTG 87.5, on LCI(L) 951, who directed operations. His LSTs were an hour early, and the sweeping of the channel had not been finished, so his boats had to zigzag among the minesweepers to reach the launching zone. They arrived on time and the first wave was ready right on schedule.

"*Shallow-draft minesweepers swept lanes to within 500 yards of Camel Green and Blue Beaches, and small boats acting as markers took up positions along these cleared lanes. Assault troops crouched low in their landing craft as boat serials formed and headed for the shore. Ahead of the first wave were rocket ships mounting tiers of rocket launchers. As these drew within firing range of the*

fire. At 0850 the Parker was able to enter into contact with the SFCPs. Then ten minutes later, the visibility improved and the men were able to distinguish the landmarks on the coast.

Enemy reaction was generally sporadic and imprecise. But north of Anthéor, the Argonaut came under fire for an hour without the crew being able to locate the firing pieces. So the cruiser entered the gulf of La Napoule and then moved south of the Lérins Islands, firing on any and every known enemy position around Cannes. But as she came back into the gulf at 1100, she had to admit that the German artillery was still not neutralized.

GREEN AND YELLOW BEACHES

It was the 141st Regimental Combat Team[29] that had the job of landing first, to clear the Agay beach which had been designated to receive the supplies. Afterwards, one of the battalions was to cut across towards Théoule, while the rest of the regiment

Above.
The plane from the cruiser *Brooklyn* is flying over the Camp Long antiaircraft battery which has just been pounded by the Bombardment Group.
(National Archives)

Top.
Panoramic sketches of beaches 264B (Drammont West) and 265A (Anthéor) as represented on the maps distributed by AFHQ, drawn from information furnished by the 8th Fleet and printed thanks to the 19th Field Survey Coy. in July 1944.

Right.
The shore around Saint-Raphaël seen from the bridge of a Royal Navy minesweeper. In the foreground notice the reefs of the Lion de Mer and in the distance the white houses topped by the Byzantine dome of Notre-Dame de la Victoire.
(IWM - A 25 222)

26. The fire power assigned to Blue Beach can be explained by its situation at the far right-hand side of the assault area and the presence of enemy batteries on the north and east sides.
27. According to CTG 87.7, "we learned that the cannons had been withdrawn from their casemates and loaded into wagons a day or two before the assault". The battery had been bombed on August 11 and 14, 1944, then again at dawn on the 15th. It had received a total of 225 tons of bombs, to which should be added the 66 armor-piercing and 48 explosive shells from the Arkansas.
28. Part of the air bombing raids had to be called off because the ceiling was too low.
29. 141st Inf Regt reinforced by the 131st FA Bn, Co A 111th Engr Bn, Co A 111th Med Bn, Co D 2nd Cml Bn, Co A 753rd Tank Bn, Co B 636th TD Bn.
30. The LCIs did not arrive until after 0700.

GREEN BEACH

Insignia adopted in 1942 by the 753rd Tank Battalion, activated at Fort Benning, Georgia on June 1, 1941.
(Le Poilu)

beach, they discharged their rockets in the defenses.[31]"

Assault and support craft arrived at the departure line at 0730. Then they moved forward, with the LCT(R)s discharging their rockets at 0750 on either side of the beach, followed five minutes later by the LCS(S)es aiming at the center.

"*Advancing at full speed, the assault craft approached the beaches in the immediate wake of*

The two six-inch (152/47) stern turrets of the *Brooklyn* open fire. In the distance is the *Duguay-Trouin*.
(National Archives)

the rocket ships. At H-Hour the 2nd and 3rd Battalions, 141st Infantry, grounded their landing craft on the rocky shale of Camel Green Beach: the troops rushed forward in the face of slight machine gun, small arms, and antiaircraft fire. At almost the same time the 1st Battalion struck Camel Blue Beach under heavy concentrated enemy fire. The Germans directed the fire of their antitank gun upon the assault boats and made several direct hits, causing casualties.[32]"

At Le Drammont, two LCTs landed their DD tanks just after the first wave. Nearing the shore, one of them had its 'skirt' torn off by a shell, and the engine compartment flooded, but it nevertheless made it to

Waves		Composition		Mother ships
① H		G/141 I/141 E/141		LST 491, 48, 230
② H + 5		753 Tk Bn		LCT 1017, 682
③ H + 10		KG/141 3/141 HQ, 2/141		LST 47, 49, 50
④ H + 12		540 Engineers		LST 491
⑤ H + 20		HQ 2/141 L/141		LST 282, 283
⑥ H + 30		F/141 HQ 3/141		LST 281, 501
⑦ H + 40		625 607 594 563 753 Tk Bn. + 636 TD Bn.		7 Shermans 7 TDs 9 tank Dozers
⑧ H + 60		347 339 93 FA Bn.		
⑧A H + 65		258 76 540 Eng. HQ 141 Inf		
⑨ H + 80		131 FA Bn		LST 501
⑩ H + 85		1018 540 Eng. 1019 364 Vehicles HQ 540		
⑪ H + 100		Co 2nd Com Bn		LST 491
⑫ H + 105		297 259 274 290 294 GA GB GC GD GH		1Bn 143 Inf
⑬ H + 120		284 264 274 280 292 GE GF GG GH HQ		2Bn 143 Inf

On August 17 at 1455, as the *Tuscaloosa* seen here from the *Brooklyn* positioned herself off Cannes, four batteries situated on the shore front opened fire on the cruiser and got her in their sights several times.
(National Archives)

the beach. Once on dry land, the Shermans advanced behind the infantry soldiers and, since there was no opposition, the teams took off the floating equipment. Then the 540th Combat Engineer Regiment beach group, in association with the 8th Naval Beach Battalion, got themselves organized and the 143rd RCT[33] started to land.

The beach proved to be far better than had been thought, even though the enemy reacted, once they had overcome their surprise. Thus when several British LCTs arrived at 0840, No 625 got her engine and principal dynamo ripped out by several 20-mm shells.

31. Seventh Army Report of Operations, op. cit
32. Ibid.

After being set afire by a flying bomb, LST 282 ran aground on the Pierre Blave rocks. *(National Archives)*

Above.
General view of Green Beach, originally considered suitable for landing one reinforced regiment. It was covered by a 75-mm gun on Ile d'Or, and was only a narrow strip of pebbles beside an abrupt slope. On the right is the little port of Pousseï, with a road connecting it to Route 7, but with no access to the beach. *(National Archives)*

Inset, above.
The insignia of the 141st Infantry Regiment is a reminder of its Texas origins and its participation in fighting in Cuba and in France. It received the DUC for its action in Salerno, and was decorated again with the distinction 'Riviera'. *(Le Poilu Coll.)*

Left.
Infantrymen and medics aboard LCVPs approach Green Beach. On the ground, other soldiers are heading for the assembly point. *(National Archives)*

LCT(R) 450, part of the Red Support Craft Unit (TU 87.3.10) off the gulf of Fréjus, awaiting orders to fire. *(National Archives)*

The enemy artillery deployment were impressive: a 75-mm and a 105-mm battery on the south bank of the Argens, another 105 on the slopes north of St Raphaël, two 100s on the high ground northwest of the port. But, most important, the Artillerie-Pak-Abteilung 1038 had eight or ten late-model 88-mm guns[35] aimed at the beach. They could be moved at will, and were thus able to escape the bombardments.

From 1205 to 1220, ninety Liberators dropped almost two hundred tons of bombs on the beach. But when the minesweepers came back at 1235, they again found themselves under a hail of shells. The Apex boats that followed them twenty-five minutes later got the same reception and only three drones worked correctly: the nine others wandered off course and even threatened the other friendly boats before being destroyed.

At 1310 the cloud of dust and smoke that had followed the bombing had dissipated enough so that the *Tuscaloosa*, the *Arkansas*, the *Emile Bertin* and four destroyers could range their barrage fire. During this time, the LCVP waves had been formed and they were advancing toward the shore in back of the rocket craft. Then at 1345 they suddenly stopped and remained glued to the spot for forty-five minutes even though there were no shells falling around them. But when the first wave had taken off again and was within three thousand meters of the shore, the enemy artillery opened fire. Consequently Captain Leo B. Schulten[36] aboard LCI(L) 195, took the initiative of deciding to postpone the landing for a half-hour. At the same time he requested instructions from CTF 87.

Admiral Lewis was of no mind to cancel the invasion, but to send the 142nd RCT onto Red Beach as planned appeared to him to be a big mistake. Visibly, the barrage bombing had not had the intended effect, the mine-sweeping was not finished, the drones had not worked and the LCT(R)s from the other sectors had not arrived. Moreover, the stop decided on by Schulten would certainly have allowed the Germans to reoccupy their positions. There was no longer any hope of surprise, so that an assault launched under these conditions could only result in heavy losses among the soldiers and the sailors.

At first he tried to reach Dahlquist to get his opinion. The two men had prepared an alternative plan, a landing of the 142nd RCT in Le Drammont, and he knew that it would be possible to order the change without too much confusion. According to reports received, Camel Red could be easily skirted on the land side, and Camel Green was a completely acceptable alternative. But it was possible that Dahlquist also needed the 142nd on the Fréjus beach for tactical purposes.

Lewis tried in vain to get through to the 36th Division CP whose radio communications were not yet working. At 1415 he could wait no longer, and ordered Schulten to cancel the invasion of Red Beach and to send the 142nd RCT to Green Beach.

"*The initiative of the subordinate commanders and the excellent training of the minor craft were very evident in the celerity of reorganization, shifting to the new area and effecting the landing at a new H-Hour, only one hour fifteen minutes later. They are entitled*

Her commander, Lieutenant T.R. Evans of the Royal Navy Volunteer Reserve, was killed. Beside her the ramp of No 607 was hit, but the boat was able to go on. Twenty minutes later another British LCT, No 339, was hit by a shell from an 88, killing two soldiers. At Blue Beach, two LCVPs from LST 51 were sunk around 0830, and fifteen minutes later, LCI 951 was hit by a dozen shots that damaged her hull and wounded the gunners. Nevertheless the landing at Anthéor was finished at 1100.

At 1000, when General Dahlquist left the Bayfield to install his HQ ashore, he received confirmation that the invasion of the 142nd RCT[34] on Red Beach would begin at 1400.

RED BEACH

At 1100, when the first mine-sweepers ventured in to within one thousand seven hundred meters of Red Beach, they were caught under a violent artillery barrage. They nevertheless moved in to within five hundred meters, but had to withdraw, since the destroyers were unable to silence the active enemy batteries.

Above, top to bottom.
While the *Brooklyn's* plane observes the coastline, the first wave of LCVPs leaves Anthéor cove and the second moves in. Notice the viaduct with one arch destroyed, and on the far right the emplacement of the neutralized antiaircraft battery.
(National Archives)

A 636th Battalion tank destroyer has just left LST(6) 49 and is making its way among the blocks of stone encumbering part of Green Beach.
(National Archives)

After the soldiers landed, Green Beach was used for landing vehicles. In the foreground a DUKW has stopped on a pile of stones as it was getting ready to enter an LST. At the end of the beach, note the column of trucks, and the two barrage balloons that have been lowered closer to the ground. In the background, the letters mark the Cape Drammont semaphore (A), the Würzburg radar antenna (B) and the exit passage for the vehicles (C).
(National Archives)

35. 143rd Inf Regt reinforced by the 133rd FA Bn, Co C 111th Engr Bn, Co C 111th Med Bn, Co B et C 2nd Cml Bn, Co C 753rd Tank Bn, Co C 636th TD Bn.
36. 142nd Inf Regt reinforced by 132nd FA Bn, Co B 111th Engr Bn, Co B 111th Med Bn, Co B 753rd Tank Bn, Co A 636th TD Bn.
37. The group was created in June 1944 in Pomerania.
38. He himself was CTU 87.3.1, deputy to Captain W.O. Bailey, CTG 87.3 and commander of the 3rd transport division on APA 28, the Charles Carroll.

1. Aviation Engineers built three air strips in the assault area: one behind Pampelonne beach and two with an emergency strip on the left bank of the Argens River
(IWM - CL 955)

2. In Ramatuelle, a team of RAF mechanics works on one of the Squadron 43 Spitfires.
(IWM - CL 998)

3. Carpenter erect a control tower right in the middle of a vineyard.
(IWM - CL 954)

4. After landing his Spitfire on the Ramatuelle airstrip, Flying Officer R. Fischer, a New Zealand pilot serving in Squadron 93, takes his pack out of the plane.
(IWM - CL 1056)

5. Flight Lieutenant P. Mitchell, the first RAF pilot to arrive in Provence by sea, talking with two American NCOs acting as flight controllers from a radio car.
(IWM - CL 974)

6. Lieutenant Colonel Evans, from the Aviation Engineers, talking with RAF officers: Group Captain W.G. Duncan-Smith, DSO, DFC & Bar, Squadron Leader Le Petit, 324 Wing administrative officer, Flight Lieutenant E. Galitzine from Squadron 72.
(IWM - CL 958)

IWM - CL 955.

where Dahlquist explained to him that he had not been consulted and that the Navy alone had made the decision. Now Truscott head to look for another beach to land the CC No 1.

At 2043 four Dornier 217s were reported approaching the sector. They appeared and dropped their bombs on the *Bayfield*. The antiaircraft guns on the ships opened fire and soon the area was covered with smoke. From one of the planes over the land came a flying bomb which made a direct strike on LST 282. The ship burst into flames and had to be abandoned after about forty men, mostly soldiers, had been killed or wounded.

to the highest praise for this smooth and effective accomplishment.[37]"

The first waves of the 142nd arrived in Le Drammont around 1515, and at 1600 its lead elements had already overtaken the last soldiers of the 143rd, marching along the coast toward Saint-Raphaël. It was intended that the regiment turn west to be ready to attack Fréjus at 2000. However the difficult terrain, and some skirmishes, slowed down their progression, so that at nightfall the regiment was still four kilometers from the city.

When the decision was made to change beaches, General Truscott was aboard the *Catoctin* off the gulf of Fréjus:

"But suddenly, the whole flottilla of landing craft halt just a few thousand yards from the beach. What was wrong? Were they waiting for the Maverick drone to settle? Admiral Hewitt endeavored to communicate with Admiral Lewis. Then, while we watched, helplessly, to our profound astonishment the whole flottilla turned about and headed to sea again. Hewitt, Patch, and I were furious. The Admiral promised an investigation. But an intercepted message from Admiral Lewis, reported that, owing to beach opposition, they were landing RCT 142 over the Agay beaches in accordance with the alternate landing plan.[38]"

So Truscott left by LCVP for the Drammont beach

Above.
Late in the morning on August 15, at the foot of the Drammont semaphore, elements from the 3rd Bn, 143rd Infantry off-loading from LCI(L)122 belonging to Task Unit 87.4.3. The R4 bulldozer is decorated with symbols of both Company A, 540th Engineers, and the 8th Naval Beach Bn. The two units were associated to build the Camel beach groups.
(National Archives)

Below.
Insignia of the 143rd Infantry Regiment of the Texas National Guard, adopted in 1929. *(Le Poilu)*

Early the next morning, the 142nd Infantry entered Fréjus. Then the 141st routed a motorized column that had ventured onto Route 7 from Cannes with the intention of launching a counteattack. Fréjus was finally occupied at 1330. Meanwhile the 143rd had cleaned out Saint-Raphaël at 0930, but met strong resistance as they approached the beaches.

Red Beach was finally opened on August 17 at 1900.

37. *Action Report of Invasion of Southern France, Commander Transport Division Three (CTG 87.3) dated September 1, 1944.*
38. *Command Missions, op. cit.*

Right.
August 17. Sappers from the 540th Combat Engineers placing explosives to breach the seawall along the Fréjus beach. A series of mines found on the beach were also added to give more wham to the explosion.
(National Archives)

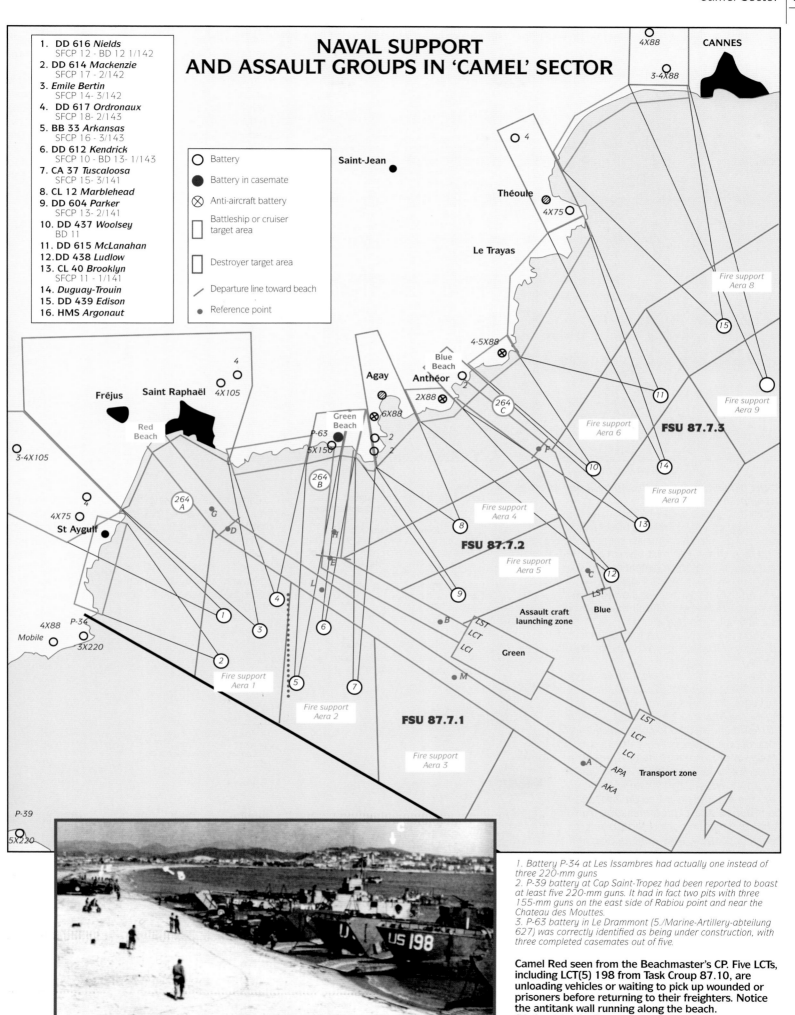

NAVAL SUPPORT AND ASSAULT GROUPS IN 'CAMEL' SECTOR

1. DD 616 *Nields*
   SFCP 12 - BD 12 1/142
2. DD 614 *Mackenzie*
   SFCP 17 - 2/142
3. *Emile Bertin*
   SFCP 14- 3/142
4. DD 617 *Ordronaux*
   SFCP 18- 2/143
5. BB 33 *Arkansas*
   SFCP 16 - 3/143
6. DD 612 *Kendrick*
   SFCP 10 - BD 13- 1/143
7. CA 37 *Tuscaloosa*
   SFCP 15- 3/141
8. CL 12 *Marblehead*
9. DD 604 *Parker*
   SFCP 13- 2/141
10. DD 437 *Woolsey*
    BD 11
11. DD 615 *McLanahan*
12. DD 438 *Ludlow*
13. CL 40 *Brooklyn*
    SFCP 11 - 1/141
14. *Duguay-Trouin*
15. DD 439 *Edison*
16. HMS *Argonaut*

○ Battery
● Battery in casemate
⊗ Anti-aircraft battery
▭ Battleship or cruiser target area
▭ Destroyer target area
／ Departure line toward beach
• Reference point

1. Battery P-34 at Les Issambres had actually one instead of three 220-mm guns
2. P-39 battery at Cap Saint-Tropez had been reported to boast at least five 220-mm guns. It had in fact two pits with three 155-mm guns on the east side of Rabiou point and near the Chateau des Mouttes.
3. P-63 battery in Le Drammont (5./Marine-Artillery-abteilung 627) was correctly identified as being under construction, with three completed casemates out of five.

Camel Red seen from the Beachmaster's CP. Five LCTs, including LCT(5) 198 from Task Croup 87.10, are unloading vehicles or waiting to pick up wounded or prisoners before returning to their freighters. Notice the antitank wall running along the beach.
(National Archives)

HERE COME THE FRENCH ...

The soldiers from the Free French Division or the Algerian Infantry Division who landed on the evening of August 16 in Cavalaire bay or near Saint-Tropez, were not the first. They had been preceded by Special Forces who jumped over occupied France to assist the maquis, organize guerilla warfare, prevent the Germans from blowing up the port installations and prepare for the arrival of the Allied forces.

Then eleven French Air Force squadrons had flown many missions over the occupied Riviera, twice as many units as had participated in Overlord. Next the French sailors came, on thirty ships, from battleships to tankers, in other words almost the entire French fleet of the time. We have already noted that the 'Groupe de Commandos d'Afrique' and the sailors from the 'Groupe d'assaut naval de Corse' landed early morning on August 15 at Cap Nègre and Esquillon point.

Then finally, a bit later, French paratroopers jumped with the ABTF at Le Muy to serve as guides and interpreters.

Above.
Women volunteers landed with the French troops: secretaries, transmitters, ambulance drivers, nurses...
(Reconstruction by Provence 44)

Inset, top left.
insignia of the *Commandant Dominé*, ex-*La Rieuse*, a French sloop moored in England in June 1940, that joined up with the FNFL. In Provence. She was part of TG 80.6, the Antisubmarine and Convoy control group.
(SHM)

Left.
On the forecastle of a sloop participating in the SM-1 convoy escort, the commander is announcing to the crew that the invasion will take place the next day on the coasts of Provence.
(National Archives)

THE SPECIAL FORCES

In the Draguignan sector was located Lieutenant Commander Allain, from the 'naval air commando,' which had been formed in September 1943. At that time about twenty sailors from the French Naval Aviation, were assembled by Lieutenant Commander Jacquelin de la Porte des Vaux, a member of the Free French Naval Forces. His idea was to be parachuted into the maquis within the invasion area to organize beach teams. But he tried in vain to find planes to carry him and his men over France.

Then the DGSS, the French 'Special Service' Command, took control of this picturesque group which moved to the Club des Pins in Zéralda, near Algiers. The sailors were trained there by British commandos — parachute jumping, commando actions, security, study of the sabotage methods used by the Germans, etc — corresponding to the new mission assigned to this 'counter-sabotage group[1],' a mission devised by the French and accepted by the Allied services: protection of the ports of Sete, Toulon and Marseilles from destructions that the Germans might want to undertake before their withdrawal. They would be assisted by the FFI, who would previously have been equipped with weapons dropped by parachute.

'Sampan,' the first team, was assigned to Toulon. The men were dropped in advance during the night of June 13 to 14, on a spare drop zone near Cucuron, north of Pertuis, because the intended DZ had just been occupied by the Germans. They were followed on July 18 by Team 'Caïque' for Marseilles. Then

Above.
During an exercise in February 1944 near Staoueli, members of the Bataillon de Choc are placing explosives on a railway track.
(AFHQ)

The maquis went wild. Ammunition was distributed and the leaders hurried back to their CPs. The men donned their equipment and hurried off to their assigned targets, to which Allain, at the last minute, added another: the 'radar' above Fayence. It was destroyed in the evening by the Mons FTP with the help of the Fayence AS and members of the SAP[2].

came 'Lougre' and 'Gédéon,' parachuted during the night of August 11 to 12 for Toulon.

Lougre jumped east of the city, near Draguignan. Allain, the commander, convoked the FFI leaders on August 14 at 1500. They were all present — except the one from Le Muy — and were briefed on the measures to be taken: preparing airstrips to receive the gliders, guide liaison teams with the paratroops as soon as they arrived...

"*At 2014,*" wrote Allain later, "*while we were eating dinner together in a clearing used as a mess hall, we were thrilled to hear the sentences announcing the invasion for within three days, then within twenty-four hours!*"

Above, left.
During training near Zeralda, a student is learning how to jump from an airplane on a model representing the door of a *Dakota* and the trap door of a *Halifax*.
(ECPAD)

Above right.
The student is about to jump, hanging from a cable that simulate true landing conditions.
(ECPAD)

Then Lougre, during the night, with headlights out and traveling very slowly, headed for Le Muy.

"*At 0510 as we were arriving in the little village of La Motte,*" Allain went on, "*we heard a sound that I easily recognized, the purr of the Douglas C-47, our training plane at the parachute school. The murmur became louder and soon filled the air. There must have been a lot of them! Then white sails filled the sky, tens, hundreds, thousands of them, as we were able to see*

1. I.e. Counterscorch group.
2. FTP: Communist-led 'Franc-Tireurs Partisans;' AS: Armée secrète; SAP: 'Section atterrissage et parachutage,' i.e. reception parties when Allied agents or supplies were dropped over occupied France.

Left.
Once they have placed their dynamite on the tracks, the Shock soldiers hastily withdraw.
(ECPAD)

Right.
A student suspended from a rope harness learns the gestures for opening his parachute and floating down underneath it.
(ECPAD)

Above.
Insignia of the 1er régiment de chasseurs parachutistes, who lent a few troopers to the ABTF as guides and interpreters.
(Private collection)

once the sun had risen, when we noticed a multitude of small white spots strewed about in the pastures, hanging from trees, high-tension wires and on housetops. My gendarmes could not believe their eyes."

They made contact easily and the guides were assigned to the parachute companies. In the afternoon Allain managed to find General Frederick, the commander of the First Airborne Task Force, who requested him to remain with him until they were able to join the troops that had landed on the beaches. Shortly afterwards he found in Le Muy his radioman and liaison agent who had been dropped near Brignoles and had crossed the enemy lines safely.

Team Gédéon jumped in uniform. Their mission was to "*assemble the Var maquis groups, organize them, participate in the taking of Toulon with as many men as possible, then join up with mission Sampan.*" They operated north of Toulon and then in the western suburbs, but, with 'Sampan,' they were unable to prevent destructions in the port. At least they were

Below.
During an exercise jump, a paratrooper has just landed and prepares to deflate and gather the shroud.
(ECPAD)

able to participate in the liberation of the city, along with the FFI and the Bataillon de choc [3].

In Marseilles 'Caïque' had no better luck: the port installations were destroyed and the naval firefighters, patriots who had not received any weapons by parachute, could only stay in their barracks.

Within the assault zone three French Jedburgh officers also arrived on August 14. They were part of liaison teams Cinnamon and Sceptre. The later was dropped in the Alpes-Maritimes and the men had joined up with some of the lost elements of the 517th Parachute Regiment. Near La Motte was also Capitaine Fournier, a member of Interallied Mmission Michel, who had come with his British colleague to greet the paratroopers from the ABTF [4] as they landed.

3. *Lieutenant j.g. Ayral was killed by error in the western suburbs of the city.*
4. *See Paul Gaujac,* Special Forces in the Invasion of France, *Histoire & Collections, Paris 1999.*

THE 'CHOC' AND THE PARAS

With the Allied paratroopers jumped French soldiers who had assembled at Lido di Roma eight days before. They were thirty, of which half came from the 1er régiment de chasseurs parachutistes [5] and the other half from the Bataillon de Choc in Corsica. Some members of the latter, with Adjudant Lombard, were originally assigned to the British 2nd Brigade and the 6 Para, others were with the 551st Parachute Bn.

Captain Boffy from the 1er RCP jumped on the Le Mitan DZ with the ABTF HQ. At noon he settled in La Motte "*after designating the former mayor as provisional city mayor, and saluting the flag that he had just hoisted on the balcony of the city hall, amidst the cheers of the population [6].*" He then tried to phone Draguignan, using the direct line that a leader of the 'Chantiers de Jeunesse[7]' had mentioned. However no one answered.

Then he went out to watch the arrival of the gliders during the afternoon:

"*The gliders landed under excellent conditions, in the vineyards. I believe that I remember more of them arriving on the 16th, so that they were everywhere, with their equipment scattered over the ground, on the roads, etc. The equipment disappeared very rapidly with the help of the civilian population (undoubtedly after the war the inhabitants of the region will be able to open shops or rubber boat rentals.[8]*"

At 0700 the next morning, a young boy arrived panting on a bike and asked to speak to Boffy. He had been sent by his father, a guard in an electric plant a kilometer away, who had received a phone call from a 'Capitaine Fontes, FFI district leader.' This captain said that the city was under the control of the gendarmes, the police and the FFI, but they did not have enough heavy weapons to hold out against a German counter-attack. They requested immediate help from the American troops.

Boffy tried in vain to get through to Fontes, who

Below.
American issue duffle bag belonging to Captain Borie, General De Lattre's aide-de-camp, bearing the colored bars Transport Quartermaster (TQM) baggage markings of the Armée B headquarters.
(SHAT)

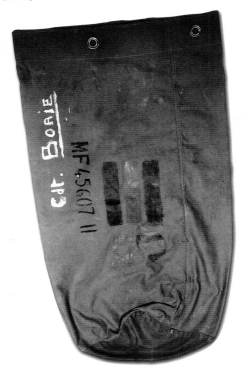

Above.
August 15, 1944. Aboard a LCI(L), the Armée B G-4 advance party, under Major Meltz, shown here on the left in the lower photo arriving off the coast of Provence, across from Cavalaire Bay.
(SHAT)

he did not know. He feared a trap, and suggested to General Frederick that he go to Draguignan with a few men, using the best car that the 'Chantiers' could spare. But Frederick refused and at 1255 ordered the 551st PIB to head for the city: "*The FFI are presently fighting in Draguignan.*

5. The 1[er] RCP left Sicily for the vicinity of Rome at the beginning of July 1944.
6. Report on Operation Dragoon, by Captain Boffy.
7. A compulsory form of national service organization.
8. Report on Operation Dragoon, by Captain Boffy.

They will hold out until your arrival."

Taking as assembly point a washhouse one kilometer from La Motte, the battalion column set out, with Companies A and B in the lead, followed by Lieutenant Colonel Wood Joerg's CP. A civilian calling himself a Swiss citizen had reported "*a pocket of resistance composed of SS members and student NCOs numbering about one hundred, in a farm near the road*," so they requested fire support by radio:

"*Unfortunately the guners, instead of bombing the farm and the intersection as had been requested, shelled the eastern edge of Draguignan. There were a few houses destroyed and civilians wounded.*[9]"

Actually the resistance was rapidly overcome and the column took up its march again, with the companies progressing along both sides of the road, through the vineyards and terraced olive orchards.

"*Members of the FFI and the FTPF from the surrounding villages and from Draguignan had joined us and became our guides. After an interminable wait on a wooded hilltop overlooking the village*

about eight hundred meters away, the Colonel decided during the night to make his entrance into Draguignan. He placed himself at the head of the column, behind him came his Headquarters Company, then the rest of the regiment. He had already asked about the best hotel in the city. The Hotel Marguerite[10] had been suggested, since the Hotel Bertin[11] was mined. So he decided to install his CP at Hotel Marguerite.

By 3: 00 AM we had taken Draguignan almost without firing a shot, except for a rather amusing gunshot fired by a drunk FTPF near the Hotel Semerilla, under the following conditions. The Colonel, marching in front, had seen two headlights: it was an Opel traveling at FFI speed. He immediately gave signs, using himself as an example, to his men to flatten themselves against the walls of the houses and hide in the shadows. I admired the rapidity with which the paratroopers responded. The car came closer, and as it passed by the Colonel rushed toward it, brandishing his

Above.
A Sherman tank from one of the 1ʳᵉ division blindée Heavy Ordnance units stopped on the coastal road between La Nartelle and Sainte-Maxime. In the background on the right, notice the wooded Sardinaux cape.
(Private collection)

Top left.
Insignia of the 15ᵉ Bataillon medical, of the 1ʳᵉ division blindée.

Left.
In the Sainte-Maxime dewater-proofing zone, a nurse from the 15ᵉ Bataillon medical checks her truck's engine.
(National Archives)

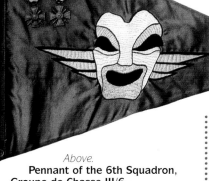

Above.
Pennant of the 6th Squadron, Groupe de Chasse III/6 "Roussillon," whose P-39 Airacobras provided convoy protection under North African Coastal Command.
(Service historique de l'armée de l'air)

Right.
'Mass on board' by Jouanneau-Irriera. General De Monsabert, his staff and the 2/3ᵉ RTA, had embarked on the LSI *Circassia*.

Colt, firing into the air and shouting a sentence in English. The car stopped. The whole HQ company surrounded it, shouting, and then they noticed that it was the Colonel's deputy, who had left in search of information an hour before, and was bringing back a German negotiator to discuss the surrender of the German forces holding one side of Draguignan. Seeing this German officer, the hot-blooded FTPF let go a shot from his old Lebel. He missed...

A little later, I took over administration (for a period of about five days) of the civilian life of the city. The American paratroops pushed on to Fayence, Figanières, etc. The only fighting done in Draguignan afterwards were manhunts involving rooftop snipers[12]."

COMBAT COMMAND No 1

9. Captain Boffy's report, op. cit.
10. Located at No 27, rue Nationale (today rue Georges Cisson), 17 rooms.
11. Located at No 15-17, Boulevard Marechal-Foch, 40 rooms.
12. Captain Boffy's report, op. cit.

On the beaches, other French soldiers belonging to Combat Command No1 attached to the VI Corps had begun landing in the Bougnon Bay.

As soon as the first outline plan had been known, General Sudre, the CC I commander, had spoken with General Truscott on July 5 about the role of his unit. They had rapidly agreed to land at Fréjus and progress along the Argens River valley toward the north or northwest. The CC would also be able to move west and participate in clearing the southern bank of the Durance River while the battles of Toulon and Marseilles were being fought.

Above.
Landing at Sylvabelle.
(Marc Kosloff Coll.)

Top right.
August 18 at noon. 'Dupleix', a half-track of 4/7ᵉ Chasseurs d'Afrique, is being lowered into the LCM that will carry it to La Foux beach.
(Private collection)

long, stuffy affair, typically French in the number of courses and order of serving. American rations were supplemented by fish and fruit obtained locally, and accompanied by an ordinary local Italian wine[13]."

After the meal, during coffee, de Lattre, in a long speech in French, accused Truscott of not respecting military and diplomatic protocol by coming to inspect one of his units without his permission and in his absence: it was an insult to him personally and to the honor of France. Truscott answered that it was not so much an inspection as it was an attempt at coming to an agreement with a formation that would be under his orders, and that in any case, the invitation came from the commander of the 1st DB. De Lattre then suggested that the plan be studied privately, thus effectively leaving the group of French officers speechless.

The problem was actually how to use the CC 1. He explained that General de Gaulle and himself had accepted that the unit be placed under American command, on condition that it return under French command by D + 3 at the latest, that is by August 18. For Truscott, it was an army problem, involving General Patch, to whom he reported. Patch was furious that De Lattre had not spoken to him before about it.

Anyway, the CC 1 elements who had spent the last two months lolling around in the areas of Assi ben Okba, boarded eight ships[14] at Oran and Mers El-Kébir. After an uneventful passage the convoy arrived as scheduled on the 15th at 1700 in the Camel sector:

"The silhouette of Saint-Raphaël could be made out through the mist. With its flag flying, the Emile Bertin lay at anchor facing Le Drammont. Beside us a tanker was carrying sections of a metal bridge. To port, an American Memphis-class cruiser[15]; to starboard, a number of Benson-type destroyers. Explosions in the distance. Smoke unraveling itself along the beach[16]."

At Drammont the freighter *Tarleton Brown* had only

On the 14th, an officer brought Truscott Sudre's project, along with an invitation from General Touzet du Vigier, commander of the French 1st Armored Division, to visit CC 1. The VI Corps commander thus took a plane in Naples and arrived in Oran with his staff officers as well as those of the 3rd and 36th Divisions with whom the Combat Command would undoubtedly be working. And the details of the plan were worked out in perfect agreement.

Six days later, Truscott was invited to lunch by General de Lattre de Tassigny who had just returned to Naples. Surrounded by twenty Division commanders and staff officers, the Army B commander gave him a cool reception. It was followed by the lunch, "*a*

Above.
The period caption says: 'These Goumiers from North Africa, among the toughest fighters in the world, are traveling along the coastal road toward the front. The spectators on the left in the photo are part of the senegalese troops that participated in the invasion.' This scene probably took place at La Nartelle.
(National Archives)

13. Command Missions, *op. cit.*
14. *LSI(L)* Winchester Castle, *British LST(1)s* Bruiser *and* Thruster, *Greek LST(2)s* Samos *and* Lemnos, *Liberty ships* John C. Breckenridge *and* John S. Pillsbury.
15. *Probably the CL 12* Marblehead.
16. *Diary written by Lieutenant Deloupy, chief medical officer of the 2ᵉ Cuirassiers.*

been able to unload ten tanks for the 3[e] Chasseurs d'Afrique[17] when it received orders to cease operations. Truscott had decided to land the CC 1 in the Delta sector and thus to reroute the convoy to Bougnon Bay where it could land in complete security.

"With their bows toward the shore, our ships stopped in one-and-a-half meters of water. It was 2210. We were forty meters from the beach in the Nartelle bay. A projector threw a furtive ray of light over the area for a few seconds, then darkness again. And the men worked feverishly in the dark removing the vehicles from their chains while the English struggled with their pontoons. It took them two hours to complete the causeway in front of us[18]."

The vehicles crossed the beach, occasionally getting stuck in the sand, guided by tiny lights marking

the cleared path, then pushed through the breach in the antitank wall and dewaterproofed three kilometers further on. At 0700 tanks continued to arrive, and taking the coastal road or the one inland skirting the hill around the semaphore, they crossed Sainte-Maxime and assembled further on, in the woods on the road to Plan de la Tour. But unloading the Liberty ships, which was usually quite long, delayed their assembling [19].

Above.
August 16. Armée B headquarters Merlinettes (female radio operators) on the La Foux beach, near exit No 1. These women are veterans who already served in Italy.
(National Archives)

Left.
August 17 in Saint-Tropez gulf. Tank destroyers of the 2/7e régiment de chasseurs d'Afrique (RCA), are being unloaded from a freighter into LCMs.
(National Archives)

Right.
Pennant of the appropriately-named Groupe de Chasse I/7 'Provence,' whose Spitfires based in Calvi provided protection for the beach zone. *(SHAA)*

Below.
August 17. Soldiers from the 3e Tirailleurs algériens cross the 'Chemin de fer de Provence' railway track. They have landed at Grimaud beach and head for the assembly area near Cogolin.
(National Archives)

By the 16th, at noon, most of the CC 1 units were ready to fight. The mission they had received from the VI Corps was to exploit the advance of the 45th Infantry Division along the road from La Garde-Freinet to Gonfaron, trying to reach Brignoles and eventually Saint-Maximin.

At 1500 the Shermans of the 2[e] Cuirassiers began rolling toward the Col de Vignon. They crossed La Garde-Freinet and Les Mayons. Then, at 1630 a platoon from the 4th squadron entered Gonfaron, surrounded by the joyous cries of the population. A pocket of resistance which appeared three kilometers to the north was rapidly silenced.

Three days later, on the 19th at 1300, the CC1 which had just occupied Saint-Maximin received orders from the VI Corps to place itself under the Army B command. Truscott, a connoisseur of military etiquette[20], thanked Sudre:

"It has been such a distinct honor and pleasure having you serve this command that your leaving

---

17. *The CO and his detachment rallied his squadron the next day in Gonfaron after skirting Fréjus.*
18. *Dr. Deloupy's journal. Even though the crew was Greek, the naval personnel assembling the pontoons was British.*
19. *The boom of the freighter* John Breckenridge *broke, which meant that the six Jeeps of the traffic control unit were stuck. They finally reached the unit on the 20th, in Méounes.*
20. *Truscott and Patch were cavalry officers, as was initially De Lattre, but he opted for the infantry during WWI.*

August 17 on La Foux beach. A landing craft manned by a Royal Navy crew unloads Dodge weapons carriers.
(National Archives)

Below.
United Nation bulletin No 41 dated August 16, 1944 'brought to the French people by the Allied aviation' announcing the invasion in Provence.
(Private Coll.)

us is a compounded loss... The officers of this headquarters join me in wishing you good luck, good hunting, and continued success[21]."

THE FRENCH DIVISIONS LAND

At that time, D +5, not only were the first two French infantry divisions arriving at Hyéres from the east and surrounding Toulon from the west, but also the elements of the third were fighting directly to the northeast.

Because of the rapid conquest of the beachhead and the ease with which the US Army and Navy logistics experts adapted to the evolving situation, the French 9th Colonial Division was actually two days ahead of schedule. Thus the battle of Toulon could begin sooner than had been thought.

21. Letter dated August 20, 1944.

LANDING SCHEDULE OF 'ARMEE B' UNITS
(D + 1 to D + 45)

	1ʳᵉ DMI	3ᵉ DIA	1ʳᵉ DB	9ᵉ DIC	2ᵉ DIM	4ᵉ DMM	5ᵉ DB
16/08	■	■	■				
18/08	●	●	■	■			
20/08				■			
21/08				●			
24/08				●			
25/08	▲	▲			■		
28/08				▲	●		
30/08					●		
04/09	◆	◆					
05/09				◆		■	
09/09			●			■	
14/09			▲				■
19/09			◆		●	●	■
24/09						▲	●
29/09							

The divisions were scheduled in two to four echelons as shown in the table at left.
In comparison with the planned schedule, the divisions which came after the first wave were able to land several days early:
● **two** days early for the 1st echelon of the 1ʳᵉ DB and the 9ᵉ DIC, and the 2nd echelon of the 2ᵉ DIM;
● **three** days early for the 2nd echelon of the 9ᵉ DIC;
● **five** days early for the 1st echelon of the 4ᵉ DMM and the 5ᵉ DB.

■ 1st echelon (actual)   ■ 1st echelon (scheduled)
● 2nd echelon (actual)   ● 2nd echelon (scheduled)
▲ 3rd echelon   ◆ 4th echelon

Abbreviations
DB: division blindée (armored div.)
DMI: division de marche d'infanterie (aka. Division française libre)
DIA: division d'infanterie algérienne
DIM: division d'infanterie marocaine
DMM: division marocaine de montagne
RACL: régiment d'artillerie coloniale du Levant
HE: hôpital d'évacuation
HC: hôpital complémentaire
RCCC: régiment colonial de chasseurs de chars

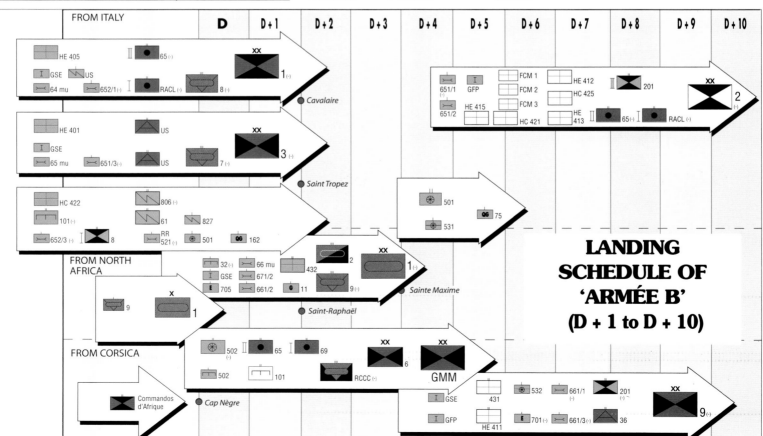

LANDING SCHEDULE OF 'ARMÉE B' (D + 1 to D + 10)

T O U L O N
F I R S T ...

While the first French troops were landing and assembling to attack Toulon, two of the three divisions of the American VI Corps were advancing inland, covering the landing of the 2nd Corps, while the third one was protecting the right flank of the bridgehead.

The successive positions of their CPs were as follows:

	3rd Inf Div	45th Inf Div	36th Inf Div
August 15	La Croix	Sainte-Maxime	Saint-Raphaël
August 16	Grimaud	-	Fréjus
	Collobrières	-	-
August 17	-	Vidauban	Le Muy
August 18	Gonfaron	Salernes	-
August 19	Brignoles	Fox Amphoux	-
August 20	Trets	Esparron	-

Above.
Rifleman from the 3e division d'infanterie algérienne
(Reconstruction Provence 44)

Top left.
The French Bataillon de choc beret badge.
(Militaria Magazine)

Left.
August 22, 1944. Elements from the 1re DMI were approaching La Garde and Le Pradet. A column from the 1er bataillon du génie is going through Hyères, guided by a soldier from the divisional traffic direction platoon.
(National Archives)

242.J.D.
Schwerpunktkarte
Verteidigungsbereich Toulon
Stand: 25.7.44.

from Vidauban to Barjols, and the 36th Division relieved the ABTF around Le Muy-Les Arcs while at the same time leaving a regiment on the coast to protect the right flank of the VI Corps.

At 0630 the 3e Commando d'Afrique reached Le Lavandou, deserted by the Germans. As they continued along toward Cap Bénat they were able to capture along the way numerous soldiers only too happy to surrender. At the cape, the battery was empty and the guns had been destroyed. Lieutenant Colonel Bouvet installed his CP at the intersection of the Bormes road, and Captain Ducournau with the 1er Commando continued along to La Londe, ten kilometers away. At 1350 the 2nd Battalion, who were heading the 7th Infantry progression along Route 98,

1. Captain Thorel, commander of the 2nd Commando, was killed, along with his liaison agent, Mohamed Ben M'Bark.

THE ATTACK POSITION

In the 3rd Division sector, Company G, 30th Infantry, with tanks in support, reached Carnoules on August 16 at 0530. Then Gonfaron, attacked by the 2nd Battalion, fell at 1400. Finally, in spite of a few German self-propelled guns, Company K captured Pierrefeu at 1819. Further south, along the coast, the African commandos progressed, led by the 1st Commando, along the ridge line where a few forest fires were burning. At 1800 the 2nd Commando took the La Fossette battery after a violent bombardment from the fleet and an hour of fierce fighting[1]. And in the evening they reached Saint-Clair.

The next day, August 17, the 3rd Division elements on the left flank were sent to the Real Martin and Gapeau Rivers with orders to hold the banks until the arrival of the French 2nd CA, scheduled for around the 20th. The others assembled in the area around Le Luc, with the goal of attacking along Route 7 toward Brignoles and then on to Saint-Maximin with the help of CC 1. Likewise the 45th Division sent a regiment

Top.
Map indicating the enemy defense positions in the Toulon defense sector, updated by the 242.ID headquarters on July 25, 1944. *(BA-MA)*

Above.
General de Lattre de Tassigny, Armée B commander, photographed on the *Batory* flanked by Colonel Olié, and Captain Borie, his aide-de-camp. *(Private collection)*

Right.
General de Larminat, commander of the 2nd Corps, is still wearing the shoulder patch of the 1re DFL. *(Pierre Ichac)*

April 16. The inhabitants of Cogolin watch as the soldiers hurry by, coming from the La Foux beach and heading toward their assembly area.
(Pierre Ichac)

August 16. Soldiers from the 2e Corps HQ go through Cogolin, guided by the Traffic Control Group No 521, identified by their white helmets.
(Pierre Ichac)

Right.
Captain Ducournau, leader of the 1er Commando d'Afrique, comments the capture of Mauvanne battery on August 18 for war correspondents.
(Musée de l'Armée, Paris)

the tank, spotted the closest machine gun and headed toward it, covered by his squad. He killed the gunners in spite of the bullets whistling around him[2]. The rest of the company was inspired by Bender's courage. They rousted out and charged forward with a whooping war cry. Thirty-seven Germans were killed and twenty-six captured, along with two antitank guns.

The fighting continued all through the night, and on the morning of the 18th, the reconnaissance patrols around La Londe-Les Maures reported that the enemy had abandoned the village.

Below.
The Mauvanne battery in the background, seen from the road leading to the back side of the Galoupet hill.
(National Archives)

was stopped just after Saint- Honoré, but a few gun shots, then machine-gun rounds followed by shells. At the last turn before the bridge over the Maravenne, a French civilian warned the first infantrymen of a roadblock two hundred meters on. The Company E soldiers on four tank destroyers and three Shermans immediately dismounted and scattered on both sides of the road to surprise the Germans. But a well-camouflaged machine-gun, firing from the southern slopes, hit several GIs. Then an antitank gun destroyed one of their tanks. The others moved into firing position to neutralize it, but in vain. Then Staff Sergeant Stanley Bender suddenly climbed up onto the wreck of

The 1er Commando arrived about this time, as the road beside the La Pascalette château was being shelled. Further on some American tanks were stopped on the side of the road: their crews were waiting in the shade of the plane-trees to be relieved. One thousand five hundred meters further on, on Galoupet hill, rounds from the fleet guns were raining down on the woods where, according to the Americans, a German battery was hidden. With Bouvet's authorization, Ducournau reconnoitered the position and found it bristling with blockhouses and pillboxes.

August 17. German soldiers captured by the commandos d'Afrique are handed over to FFI guards.
(Musée de l'Armée, Paris)

2. For his heroic action, Sergent Bender later received the highest American award: the Medal of Honor.

Left
General Diego Brosset, commander of the 1st infantry Free French Division.
(DR)

He took the initiative of deciding to attack the position by surprise, from the rear. The commandos stole through the maquis, cut their way through the barbed wire and cleaned out the blockhouses one by one.

Above.
Insignia of the 5e Régiment de chasseurs d'Afrique.
(Militaria Magazine)

Left.
La Londe-les-Maures first aid station.
(Marc Kosloff collection)

Below.
August 17. The light tank squadron of the 5e chasseurs d'Afrique, which had landed at La Nartelle moves along the coastal road to their assembly area in Grimaud.
(ECPAD)

And thus, with the Mauvanne battery[3] silenced, the ships of the fleet could move into the roadstead of Hyères.

At 1405 on the 19th, the 7th Infantry 3rd Battalion was relieved by the French and returned to St Honore to take trucks to Brignoles. At noon on the following day, near Pierrefeu, the 1st and 2nd Battalions likewise moved north. Truscott was in a hurry to recover his 3rd Division and send it toward the Durance and the Rhône.

MANEUVERING AROUND TOULON

That was also General De Lattre's intention. From his CP in Cogolin he wired General De Gaulle in the evening of the 18th:

"General Patch is impatient for me to relieve the US 3rd ID so that he can send it toward Aix on Route 7. Consequently, considering the landing delays, particularly concerning the 3e DIA, I have given the following orders:

1. This evening, the 18th, and tomorrow, the 19th, the 1re DFL will relieve all elements of the US 3rd ID up to Solliès and will take command of the Bouvet commando, which has been ordered to take Le Coudon and, if possible, Le Faron.

All of the 1re DFL will be ready for action on the 20th. From now on they will seize any chance to move north of Hyères and take Les Maurettes.

2. On the 19th, the 3e DIA will send five companies to the Cuers-Pierrefeu area. General de Monsabert will establish his CP north of Pierrefeu. Every effort will be made to accelerate the landing of the 3e DIA which has been delayed.

3. The CC 2 of the 1re DB and the 2e RSAR, delayed, will assemble on the 20th in the region of Carnoules. I intend to send them toward La Roquebrussane-St Zacharie."

This decision, involving preparations for engaging the two French divisions at Hyères and Toulon, had just been taken, when two events caused the plans de be reconsidered. First of all, Lieutenant j.g. Sanguinetti, part of Mission 'Sampan,' arrived from Toulon to inform the Allies that there were no German troops north of the city. Then the Seventh Army announced that the LSTs which had participated in the assault had been sent back to Corsica, meaning that not only the 9e DIC but also the Bataillon de choc and the Moroccan Goums[4] would be able to land forty-eight hours ahead of schedule. Moreover, the units, being transported with their equipment, could be directed immediately toward the assembly areas. At the end of the day the LSTs beached between Cavalaire and Sainte-Maxime, wherever they could find an available beach, and began to unload.

De Lattre then decided to try to take Toulon by surprise and as soon as possible, by engaging the enemy at Solliès-Pont, where the German defenses were weakest, with a group from the 9e DIC reinforced by an armored detachment, with orders to undertake a raid into the center of town and on the port. The 3e DIA would in that case no longer be needed to cover the attack of the 1re DMI, and could be launched further west, in the area supposed to be weakly defended.

---

3. *Four 15 cm sKc/28 guns from the 3rd battery of the Marine Artillerie Abteilung 627, plus infantry soldiers from GR 917 retreating before the American advance.*
4. *The 1st, 2nd and 3rd groups of Moroccan tabors, seconded by the 1st Battalion from the 69th Mountain Artillery Regiment. These were the only Moroccan formations participating in the battle of Provence, initially intended to be used in the mountains north of Toulon. However certain Moroccans were serving individually in the 22nd North-African Battalion of the 1st DMI, and in the 2nd African commando.*

Left, top to bottom.

The Golf Hotel commanding the Gapeau River crossing was reduced to smithereens after the naval and field bombardments and the BIMP assault.

The 101st Engineer Regiment sappers clearing the bridge over the Gapeau after its destruction.

A bulldozer clears fallen beams off the deck of the bridge.

The by-pass created in the dry bed of the river was not easy to use; the banks were steep and two wreckers were needed to raise some heavy vehicles, including a 1er RFM Sherman.
(Private collection)

Below.
A sketch of the German prisoners.
(Marc Koslof collection)

above.
A tank destroyer of the 8ᵉ RCA was hit by an antitank gun on the outskirts of Hyères.
(National Archives)

Above.
August 21. A group of BM 21 Senegalese soldiers in Hyères.
(Private collection)

On the morning of the 19th, he visited the Seventh Army HQ installed at Hotel Latitude 43 in Saint-Tropez, to explain the changes in the original plan. Patch accepted them and agreed to take back the CC 1 and the Commandos d'Afrique under his orders. It was then decided that the VI Corps would be relieved between Les Salins d'Hyères and La Roquebrussane before noon on the 20th at the latest. The CC 1 would join at Meounes on the 19th at 2100.

Armée B thus had to quickly take Toulon, and then Marseilles. General de Larminat, commander of the 2ᵉ Corps, was in charge of coordinating the actions of the 1ʳᵉ DMI and the 9ᵉ DIC, the later being reinforced by the four available battalions of heavy artillery, and by the Groupe de commandos that had Le Coudon as their objective. To Monsabert he attributed the CC 1 to help strengthen his effort at sur-

THE FRENCH 1re DIVISION DE MARCHE D'INFANTERIE

The 1re DMI evolved from the 1re Division Française Libre (DFL, Free French division) which had fought in the Western desert and in Tunisia with the British VIIIth Army. The division, which had kept the British terminology and steel helmet, was activated on August 24, 1943. It was first a 'motorized infantry' formation, then became 'division de marche' (provisional) on April 27, 1944. This name was more appropriate to its status as a partially motorized division of the expeditionary corps. In spite of the name changes, the division was always referred to as 'DFL'[1], by those who served in it. It had been equipped with British materiel, which it traded for the American standard in order to participate in the Italian campaign during the May offensive and continue until the pursuit beyond Rome[2]. It was commanded by General Brosset[3], and made up of the 1er Régiment de fusiliers-marins (Reconnaissance) and three brigades of three battalions who, in association with a 105 howitzer battalion and a combat engineer company, constituted three RCTs.

The first echelon embarked at Taranto on five ships in convoy TF-1 — the Polish LSI *Sobieski*, the British transport ships *Durban Castle* and *Staffordshire*, the British freighter *Empire Pride*, and the Dutch *Volendam*. This first echelon comprised most of the division:

- HQ and Compagnie de QG n° 50 (HQ Co.)
- 1er régiment de fusiliers marins - capitaine de corvette de Morsier [4]
- 1re brigade (RCT 1) colonel Delange[5] - 1er & 2e bataillons de légion étrangère[6], 22e bataillon nord-africain, 1st arty Bn. (105)
- 2e brigade (RCT 2) colonel Garbay[7] - Bataillons de marche n° 4, 5 & 11, 2d arty Bn. (105)
- 4e brigade (RCT 3) colonel Raynal - BM n° 21 et 24, Bataillon d'infanterie de marine et du Pacifique, 3d arty Bn. (105)
  - 4th arty Bn. (155)
  - 21e groupe antillais de DCA (AA artillery)
- 1er bataillon du génie (engineers)
- Bataillon de transmissions n° 1 (signals)
- 1er détachement de circulation routière (traffic control)
- Ambulance chirurgicale légère - médecin-commandant Vignes [8], Ambulance Hadfield-Spears - médecin-colonel Vernier[9], 1er bataillon médical, section d'évacuation féminine de la Marine (medical, collecting and light surgical units)
- 9e compagnie de réparation divisionnaire (Ordnance)
- 1er groupe d'exploitation de l'intendance. (QM)

Lieutenant-Colonel Simon's 8e régiment de chasseurs d'Afrique was also attached to the division. Its three tank destroyers squadrons had supported the division since its arrival in Italy.

The division also had five Forward Observer Bombardment Parties (British equivalents of the American SFCPs) composed of a Royal Artillery officer and several Royal Navy radio operators to carry out liaisons and adjust naval fire.

The 101st, 102nd, 103rd transport companies were part of the second echelon and arrived later. The 21e GDCA (AA Arty), heavily motorized, took care of transportation once they had set up their batteries.

During the fighting the division CP was successively at Gassin (August 17), La Cheylanne northeast of La Londe (August 19), and at the western limits of Hyères (August 22 to 26).

---

1. In the message sent on August 18, 1944 to the head of government, the Armée B commander used this name on purpose.
2. See Paul Gaujac, Le corps expéditionnaire français en Italie, Histoire & Collections, 2003.
3. Honored as 'Compagnon de la Libération' on November 20, 1944 as commander of the 1re DFL.
4. Honored as 'Compagnon de la Libération' on November 17, 1945 as commander of the 1er RFM.
5. Honored as 'Compagnon de la Libération' on February 2, 1941 as commander of the Tchad Bataillon de tirailleurs sénégalais.
6. The 2e BLE (Bataillon de la Légion Entrangère landed late and did not participate in the battle of Hyères.
7. Honored as 'Compagnon de la Libération' on June 25, 1941 as commander of the BM No 3.
8. Honored as 'Compagnon de la Libération' on December 27, 1945 as divisional surgeon.
9. Honored as 'Compagnon de la Libération' on March 7, 1945 as the Spears ambulance senior medical officer.

Arm badge of the 1re division de marche d'infanterie.
(Militaria Magazine)

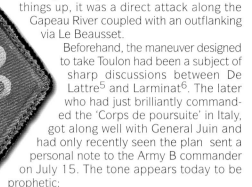

Below.
August 21.
A German officer captured near Sollies is being taken to a CP to be interrogated.
(National Archives)

Above.
"*Two members of the Forces Françaises de l'Intérieur guarding the Var FFI headquarters in Toulon, after participating in the liberation of the port. August 29, 1944.*"
(IWM IA 36 110)

rounding the city on the west side. To sum things up, it was a direct attack along the Gapeau River coupled with an outflanking via Le Beausset.

Beforehand, the maneuver designed to take Toulon had been a subject of sharp discussions between De Lattre[5] and Larminat[6]. The later who had just brilliantly commanded the 'Corps de poursuite' in Italy, got along well with General Juin and had only recently seen the plan sent a personal note to the Army B commander on July 15. The tone appears today to be prophetic:

"Toulon will be defended by guns... The defense is fearsomely effective... The enemy is expecting an attack from the east... Armée B is attacking in the direction where the enemy is strongest... We will sacrifice a division for nothing."

His suggestion was, on the contrary, to "*clean out Toulon after conquering and consolidating the Army objective (Avignon), by asphyxiation and concentric actions; this will be more economical and probably faster than a direct action. Actually, the solution I propose means that we will be successively attacking, with the major part of our resources, the two major enemy forces, the stronghold of general and regional reserves and then the Toulon stronghold, instead of taking them both on at the same time.*"

If that solution could not be adopted, Larminat thought that Toulon should be attacked from the north, between Solliès-Pont and Evenos, with two divisions, extended to the west by the Moroccan goums, and covered on the east down to the seacoast by a third division.

De Lattre, who arrived in Naples the next day, signed a note to Larminat reminding him that the main objective was Toulon and that all available means should be used there. But the proposed maneuver was not rejected: it would simply be studied along with other hypotheses under consideration by the Armée B staff.

---

5. Honored as 'Compagnon de la Libération' on November 20, 1944 for his role as commander of the French First Army.
6. Honored as 'Compagnon de la Libération' on August 1, 1941 as a member of the 'Conseil de défense de l'Empire'.

Above.
Colonel Garbay, 2nd Brigade commander, discussing the progression of the RCT 2 elements with French navy Lieutenant Commander de Morsier leader of the 1er Régiment de Fusiliers Marins, the Free French division reconnaissance unit.

HYERES AND THE EASTERN SUBURBS OF TOULON

After landing on the beaches of Cavalaire, Sylvabelle and La Foux, the French had to wait for their equipment to be unloaded from the cargo ships. The 1re DMI waited in the assembly area between La Croix and Gassin, the 3^e DIA grouped southwest of Grimaud. But since time was running short, the two division commanders — Brosset for the Free French Division (1re DMI), Monsabert for the Algerian Division — decided on the 17th to send without further ado their infantry west and to assemble their troops for moving out immediately as soon as they landed.

Early in the morning of the 18th, the three battalions of the 2nd Brigade thus left their bivouac and headed along Route 98 toward La Verrerie. Bataillon de Marche (BM) 11, leading, reached the hamlet at noon, while BM 4 in the rear, was still at the Gratteloup path. A dozen GMCs of the French West Indian AA Battalion were to follow two hours later with their baggage. Then

Above.
Panoramic view - taken from the Croix Faron road - of the city and the port of Toulon from the Saint-Mandrier peninsula to Cap Brun. The city, the commercial port, the Mourillon arsenal and the eastern suburbs are visible, with Fort Faron in the foreground.
(National Archives)

Above.
Insignia of the Bataillon de Marche No 21, formed in 1943 from a Djibouti unit that had joined the Free French forces.
(Militaria Magazine)

Left and above, right.
August 24. Surrender of Fort Sainte-Marguerite:
1. Colonel Raynal with capitaine Fournier, Bataillon de Marche No 21 commander.
2. Colonel Raynal, 4th Brigade commander, speaking with Korvettenkapitän Dr Frantz, commander of Marine-Flak-Abteilung 819. A Navy officer from the 1er RFM is translating.
3. The prisoners are assembled: twenty officers, 571 enlisted men, including only 150 from the Kriegsmarine.
(Private collection)

when the road was clear, the 1st Brigade battalion that had just landed would move out.

It was terribly hot. The men had trouble marching: the night that they had spent on the land could not compensate for the week they had spent cooped up on board the ships. Not all of them had been able to land without getting wet, and now their twill field dress were stiff with the dried salt from the sea water.

The 4th Brigade took Route 559 along the coast. At Le Lavandou, the first battalion received a hero's welcome before stopping just beyond the village. In spite of their fatigue and the suffocating heat, no soldier wanted to be the last. On the 19th the French began relieving the US 7th Infantry Regiment: the 3rd Battalion in the Réal Martin valley was relieved by the French 2nd Brigade, the 2nd Battalion near Saint-Nicolas, by the 4th Brigade.

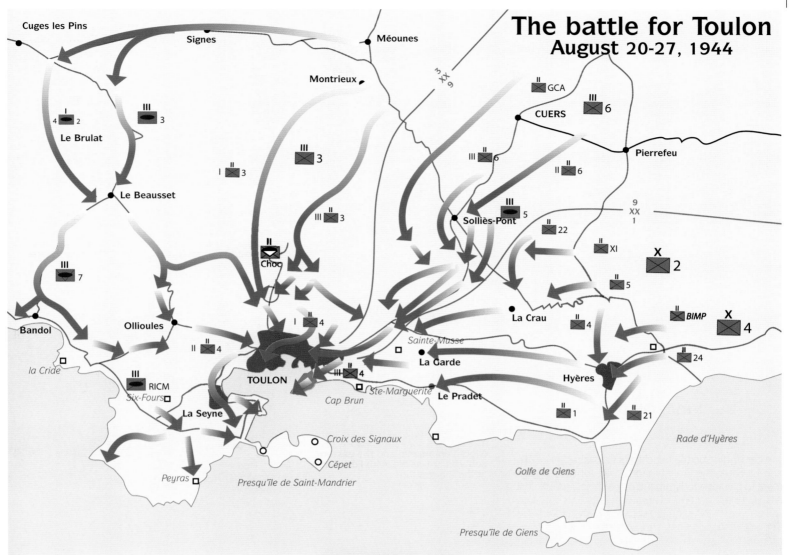

The battle for Toulon
August 20-27, 1944

The division's mission for the next day was to take the outer defenses of Toulon: Mont Redon, the Fenouillet hills and the city of Hyères. For this they would act in liaison with an RCT from the 9th DIC that had arrived on the right near Pierrefeu.

The action of the 2nd Brigade took place to the north. BM 11 started out at dawn and crossed the Gapeau at the Marseillaise ford. Then the soldiers occupied the Pousselous hills, but were unable to take the pillboxes on the south side where enemy resistance was concentrated. They were counter-attacked and had to give up some ground, but were able to hold the Maubelle convent. The 22e BMNA from the 1st Brigade was engaged for support on their right flank. On the left, BM 5 was able to take Mont Redon after hard fighting, and managed to keep it in spite of the counter-attacks. The situation which had been confused was stabilized around 1730.

The 4th Brigade crossed the Gapeau during the night and reached the Maurettes slopes at dawn. But a violent counter-attack pushed them back to their departure point. They struck out again at 1700 with the help of all the naval and field artillery. At the end of the day, the BIMP took the Oratoire, and held out in spite of several counter-attacks. But to the left, BM 24, once across the river, could not advance. The men were pinned down by fire coming from the Golf Hotel, which the enemy had transformed into a fortress. Further south, BM 21, originally the reserve unit, advanced along the Chemin de Fer de Provence railway line and reached the outskirts

Insignia of the 7e régiment de chasseurs d'Afrique, a tank destroyer formation that had inherited the traditions of the Chantiers de la Jeunesse. Attached to the 3e DIA, the regiment helped them encircle Toulon by occupying Bandol.
(Militaria Magazine)

Right.
August 21. 'Men from the 7e régiment de chasseurs d'Afrique reaching the Bandol viaduct,' a sketch by Lieutenant Jouanneau Iriera. The Sherman instead of a Tank destroyer is a figment of the artist's imagination.
(Musée de l'Armée, Paris)

of Hyères south of the Lazarine barracks[7]. Fighting continued on the 21st at dawn along the entire front held by the division. BM 11, with the help of the artillery, pushed through the defenses and entered La Crau at nightfall. BM 4 relieved BM 5, and from the Maurettes

---

7. Losses on August 20 were 25 killed including 2 officers, and 124 wounded including 6 officers.

protecting the advance of the Beaufort Task Force[11] toward La Valette.

The commandos left for Le Coudon at 0745. At the same time two Senegalese battalions were striking out from southeast of Cuers toward Solliès-Pont, where they arrived at 1445. But enemy resistance was stiff and a TD squadron was put at the disposal of the 6e RTS as the arrival of the 1st Battalion was announced.

On the 21st, in spite of the fog, the commandos reached the heights of Le Coudon at 0800 and by 1315, after a short fight[12], had occupied the fort. In the plain Task Force Salan occupied Solliès-Pont at 0900, then Solliès-Ville three hours later. But the ene-

hill was able to cover the BIMP as they undertook the assault of the Golf Hotel[8], while the two other battalions of the 4th Brigade finished clearing out the city of Hyères. The outer defenses of Toulon were practically broken up[9], when Armée B sent out word that ammunition was running short and should be used sparingly.

On the 22nd, the division approached the Toulon inner defense line, including the Touar hills and the towns of La Garde and Pradet. BM 11 entered the hilly forests, among flaming pine trees, and was able to repulse a counter-attack with the support of the 1er RFM light tanks. On the left flank, BM 24 reached La Garde, but was pushed back by a counter-attack. Finally the BIMP launched an assault at 2100 and was able to clean out the town in spite of heavy losses. On the south side, BM 21, with the help of the artillery, silenced resistance in Le Pradet. And in the rear, RCT 1 surrounded the Mont des Oiseaux and covered the division across from the Giens peninsula, still in the hands of the enemy.

During the next two days, in liaison with the 9e DIC attacking at La Valette, the last pockets of resistance fell one by one: Mont des Oiseaux, San Salvadour, Carqueiranne, Sainte-Marguerite, Cap Brun, Sainte-Musse. At the end of the day the entire sector east of Toulon was controlled by the 'Division Française Libre.' But the division received orders not to enter Toulon, whose mopping up was assigned to the 9e DIC. So the DFL consolidated the positions it held.[10]

TOULON

On the 20th at 0140, the Groupe de commandos d'Afrique, which had just been attached to the 9e DIC three hours earlier, received orders to cross the Gapeau between Solliès-Pont and Solliès-Toucas, and take the Coudon hill, then support the action of the Salan RCT in the plain. That later RCT was activated a few minutes later with a mission of reaching La Farlède and

Above.
August 22. Marching behind a light tank from the 3e régiment de spahis algériens de Reconnaissance, a platoon from the Bataillon de choc advances toward the center of Toulon.
(National Archives)

Right.
After skirmishing with the Germans on the western outskirts of Toulon, the Bataillon de Choc troopers 'chew the rag' with the FFI patriots and an American sailor from a photo team.
(National Archives)

8. *In answer to a request by the FOB, the* Georges Leygues *fired 77 rounds at the target.*
9. *Losses on August 21 were 61 killed including 2 officers, and 165 wounded including 6 officers.*
10. *1re DMI losses for the period between August 19 and 24, 1944 were 229 killed including 14 officers, 692 wounded including 33 officers, for 3,000 Germans taken prisoner during combat and 4,000 more that had surrendered.*
11. *2nd (medium tank) squadron and a light tanks platoon from the 5e RCA, with the special platoon from the 3e RCA.*

Right.
August 25. At the foot of Mont Faron, the Artigues Fort, which had resisted repeated onslaughts of the 6e régiment de tirailleurs sénégalais, is being bombarded by the warships
(National Archives)

Left.
August 26 at Saint-Jean du Var. A German prisoner is being pushed and shoved to the assembly point by a 1ʳᵉ DMI jeep and an irate Frenchwoman.
(National Archives)

Above.
Insignia of the 9ᵉ division d'infanterie coloniale (DIC).
(Militaria Magazine)

Left.
August 26 in Saint-Jean du Var. Under the watchful eyes of the onlookers, German prisoners are heading for the 'cage' in the La Valette stadium, escorted by a 9ᵉ DIC NCO.
(National Archives)

THE FRENCH 9ᵉ DIVISION D'INFANTERIE COLONIALE

The 9ᵉ DIC was activated on July 16, 1943 at Mostaganem, with elements of the disbanded 1ʳᵉ DIC coming from Northern and Western Africa. Commanded by General Magnan since January 30, 1944, it was shipped to Corsica in April to participate in the conquest and then the occupation of the island of Elba in June and July.

The convoy carrying the first echelon of the division — Colonel Salan's 6ᵉ régiment de tirailleurs sénégalais, 3ᵉ Bataillon of the 'Régiment d'artillerie coloniale du Maroc,' Compagnie de génie No 71/3, 3rd Collecting Company from the 25ᵉ Bataillon médical — left Ajaccio on August 17 at 2100 and the first elements were ashore at Sylvabelle at 1615 on the 18th.

The second echelon landed three days later:
- 4ᵉ RTS (Lieutenant-Colonel Bourgund)
- 13ᵉ RTS (Colonel Voillemin)
- 1ᵉʳ bataillon du RACM
- 1st Collecting Company from the 25ᵉ Bat. Medical,
- Engineer Company No 71/2
- parts of the 21st Ordnance company and the 25th Quartermaster Group.

Various general reserve units were also attached to the division: Colonel Rousseau's Régiment colonial de chasseurs de chars (RCCC) with three tank destroyers squadrons, Lieutenant-Colonel Salbat's[1] 18ᵉ RTS, the 1st Battalion of the 101ᵉ Régiment du génie. Four FOB parties were attached.

During the battle it was also supported by:
– on the 20th, the US 6th Field Artillery Group, comprising the 36th FA Bn (155 HM1) and 634th FA Bn (155 Gun), plus the 62nd AAA Gun Bn (90 AA);
– on the 22nd, the 2ᵉ (155 HM1) Bataillon from the 'Régiment d'artillerie coloniale d'AOF.

The division CP was successively installed at La Mole (August 18), Pierrefeu (August 19), Cuers (August 20), Solliès-Pont chateau (August 23), the Sainte-Anne barrack in Toulon (August 25), Beaulieu (August 16 to September 6).

1. Who, with his 2nd battalion, was finally in charge of occupying the islands off Hyères and the Giens peninsula.

Above.
August 26, at Fort Malbousquet, inside the Navy shipyards. Senegalese soldiers from the 4ᵉ RTS and the ambulances from the 25ᵉ Bataillon Médical are waiting for the surrender of the German garrison.
(Dr Heckenroth Collection)

my artillery was violent and defense was stubborn. The Shermans from the 5e Chasseurs d'Afrique managed to get to the opposite bank of the Gapeau and reach the attack position south of La Farlède, but paid a heavy price: nine tanks out of seventeen were destroyed and three platoon leaders out of four injured.

At 1800 Armée B announced that Group L had been disbanded. General de Larminat, who had been in charge of coordinating the action of the 1ʳᵉ DMI and the 9ᵉ DIC since 1700 on the 19th, had asked to be relieved of this command. So he left La Verrerie, near Bormes, and installed his CP at the Le Camp crossroads, north of Toulon, waiting for the job of coordinating the action of the 3ᵉ DIA and the 1ʳᵉ DMI when the later would be engaged against Marseilles[13]. Patent disagreements between De Lattre and Larminat during the planning in Italy had become worse now that the headquarters and staffs of Armée B and the 2ᵉ Corps were side-by-side. General Magnan was so informed that he was to take charge of the sur-

rounding and capture of the Toulon sector, where he would take over as military commander.

On the 22nd at 0800 the Salan group broke out from La Farlède and one hour later the tanks entered

12. See Paul Gaujac, La bataille et la libération de Toulon, Nouvelles Editions Latines, Paris, 1994.
13. He later left the 2ᵉ Corps command on De Lattre's request, in circumstances still unclear today.

General view of the port and city of Toulon after the Liberation.
(National Archives)

the 3e régiment de tirailleurs algériens (RTA), guided by members of the FFI, left the region of Cuers-Pierrefeu, crossed the Morières forest and reached Revest-les-Eaux and the Croupatier hills the next day. At the same time the spahis, after a short fight, occupied the Le Camp intersection, then Cuges and Le Beausset, thus effectively cutting off the retreat of any Germans who wanted to leave Toulon by Ollioules.

Reinforced by the Bataillon de choc that was maneuvering around Le Faron, the Linarès group sneaked into the outskirts of the city on the 21st. To the west, the Spahis and the Chasseurs d'Afrique tank destroyers liberated Bandol, thus isolating Toulon off from the outside. Street fighting continued on the 22nd and 23rd. The Saint-Pierre powder plant finally gave up, and the Spahis Algériens arriving from Bandol liberated Sanary and negotiated the surrender of the La Crite battery and the fort at Six-Fours. Then on the 24th, the elements who had been relieved by the 9e DIC assembled and left for Marseilles, followed on the 25th by the last battalion of the 3e RTA.

Finally, around 1600, the Six-Fours commander accepted a surrender including the forts around him, to take place at noon the next day. But the two regiments — 3e Spahis Algériens and 7e Chasseurs d'Afrique — were relieved of their mission in Toulon and assembled in Beaus-

La Valette. But the Senegalese riflemen were unable to follow and the Chasseurs d'Afrique tanks found themselves isolated without any infantry. The 'raid' on Toulon had ended almost before it began.

On the 23rd the tanks were finally freed, and an RICM squadron sent in as reinforcements reached Saint-Jean du Var. The next day, the 6^e RTS on the east, and the 4^e RTS to the west and northwest, entered the city of Toulon. On the 25th and 26th, the forts of Sainte-Catherine, Artigues, Lamalgue and Malbousquet were neutralized one after the other.

On the west side, where the rest of the RICM and the 13^e RTS were now engaged in the footsteps of the elements from the Algerian Division, Six-Fours and Peyras also surrendered. The 3^e DIA had engaged its troops toward Toulon from August 19 on. Two battalions from

Right
US Navy officers inspecting one of the Cepet battery 340 turrets.
(National Archives).

Below.
August 26 in Toulon. Passing a column of jeeps that has stopped on the Boulevard de Strasbourg, an M8 SPG leaves the square in front of the Palais de Justice, followed by the scout cars of an RICM reconnaissance squadron.
(National Archives)

set, so it was the Colonial soldiers who accepted the surrender resulting from the negotiations.

At 1030 on the 27th, the 9ᵉ DIC officially entered the city. And at 0800 on the 28th, the German garrison at Saint-Mandrier, both soldiers and sailors, laid down their weapons. Toulon and the region were completely liberated[14].

SAINT-MANDRIER

This positive result was partly due to the Naval and Air Forces that, during the whole battle, had supported the progression of ground troops and neutralized part of the formidable artillery of the enemy fortresses. Starting on August 19th, the heavy cruiser *Augusta* and the battleships *Lorraine* and *Nevada* had bombarded the Saint-Mandrier peninsula and port to test their defenses. And the Marauders had been pounding the Cepet 340 battery.

On the 20th the coast batteries were systematically attacked from 0730 to 1820 by the cruisers *Quincy* and *Georges Leygues* which had moved in to assist the *Nevada* and *Lorraine*. The firing was generally observed by plane, although the *Leygues* and the destroyers approached the coast sufficiently to be able to do their own observing. The guns of the cruiser *Aurora* were adjusted by a forward observer, but it had to withdraw quickly behind a protective

smoke screen from the light cruiser *Le Malin* so as not to get hit by enemy shells. That same day the B-26s came back, and with a new approach technique, were able to get some hits in spite of the intense Flak.

A commando action was under consideration at the time to destroy the Saint-Mandrier batteries[15]. But the plan would have needed strong air power, and the medium bombers were busy supporting the advance of the land troops to the north. So the project was abandoned. After a day's respite, the bombings started again on the 22nd, when the Support Force was joined by the *Montcalm*. The same thing happened on the 23rd from 0945 to 1745, and now the *Gloire* was also on the scene.

To force the garrison on the peninsula to surrender, it was decided to attack it with a large number of ships. And since Admiral Davidson, CTF 86, was off Marseilles at the time and was worried about the minesweeping around the port, and since moreover he considered the problem to be a typically English-French one, he assigned command of the Saint-Mandrier action to Captain G. Barnard, CBE, DSO, skip-

Top right.
August 27 in Toulon. M. Diethelm, French Defense secretary, with General de Lattre, followed by General Magnan, who has kept the British helmet he wore when he commanded the Corps Franc d'Afrique in Tunisia.
(National Archives)

Above.
The heavy cruiser *Quincy*, participating in the bombardment of the Saint-Mandrier peninsula, under fire from a German battery.
(National Archives)

Above, inset.
The pennant of the battleship *Lorraine*, launched in 1913 and whose 340-mm guns did wonders in Provence.
(SHM)

per of HMS *Aurora*. Barnard was thus placed in an uncomfortable position: he was the junior captain and found himself commanding Vice Admiral Jaujard, leader of the 4th Cruiser Division of which the *Montcalm* and the *Georges Leygues* were part. However he did a satisfactory job, because, according to the British Admiralty, he "*was as efficient as he was tactful in fulfilling his mission.*"

The *Aurora* and the *Lorraine*, protected by two destroyers, took up positions south of Porquerolles at 0700, and were soon joined by the *Montcalm* and the *Fantasque*. *Gloire* and *Georges Leygues* were in the Hyères roadstead. But contact with the army was difficult to obtain, and they had insufficient knowledge about the friendly troops positions. Firing finally began at 0928, with the *Gloire* adjusted by an FOB. Then the *Lorraine* opened fire on Cepet at 1422, and, according to the observation plane, successfully hit her targets. The *Aurora* also started firing, and at 1540 HMS *Ramillies*, just arriving from Propriano, joined in. Then at 1555 HMS *Sirius* entered the zone and added support. A final pounding took place at 1800 and, since no sign of activity appeared on the peninsula, a cease-fire was ordered at 1900. At that moment barged in the destroyer *Simoun*, floating the flag of Vice Admiral Lemonnier, French Navy Chief of Staff. The destroyer ignored the signal and opened fire[16]...

Barnard thought at the time that the whole peninsula could be rapidly occupied if all of the Marines from the ships' detachments were sent ashore. Nevertheless the bombardment continued, and another ship, the cruiser *Omaha*, added her guns[17].

Finally on the 28th, Konter-Admiral Ruhfus, *Seekommandant französiche Riviera* and *Festung Toulon* commander, finally agreed to surrender.

---

14. 9ᵉ DIC losses for the period between August 20 and 27, 1944 were 215 killed including 14 officers, 876 wounded including 34 officers, for 6,000 Germans taken prisoner during combat and 3,000 more that had surrendered.
15. This might have been assigned to Groupe naval d'assaut de Corse, which had stayed on the island.
16. Apparently HMS Aurora had some trouble convincing the Simoun to give up her 'private bombardment.'
17. Between August 13 and 20, 1944, the peninsula was hit with 785 tons of bombs, almost all of them targeting the Cepet battery. And from August 19 to 27, the Allied ships fired 8,698 90- or 340-mm shells.

and MARSEILLES

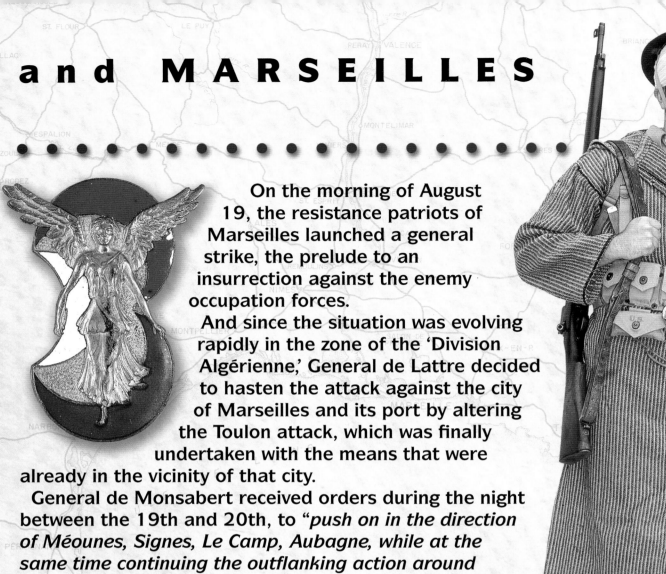

On the morning of August 19, the resistance patriots of Marseilles launched a general strike, the prelude to an insurrection against the enemy occupation forces.

And since the situation was evolving rapidly in the zone of the 'Division Algérienne,' General de Lattre decided to hasten the attack against the city of Marseilles and its port by altering the Toulon attack, which was finally undertaken with the means that were already in the vicinity of that city.

General de Monsabert received orders during the night between the 19th and 20th, to "*push on in the direction of Méounes, Signes, Le Camp, Aubagne, while at the same time continuing the outflanking action around Toulon via Mont Caumes and Le Croupatier.*" So he had to divide his men — plus the CC 1 assigned to the Aubagne mission — so as to undertake the movement toward Marseilles while at the same time pursuing the outflanking on the north and northwest sides of Toulon.

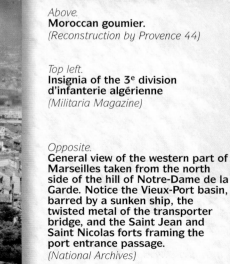

Above.
Moroccan goumier.
(Reconstruction by Provence 44)

Top left.
Insignia of the 3e division d'infanterie algérienne
(Militaria Magazine)

Opposite.
General view of the western part of Marseilles taken from the north side of the hill of Notre-Dame de la Garde. Notice the Vieux-Port basin, barred by a sunken ship, the twisted metal of the transporter bridge, and the Saint Jean and Saint Nicolas forts framing the port entrance passage.
(National Archives)

The CC I had arrived in Méounes in the evening of the 19th and relieved Task Force Bonjour at Le Camp so that they could participate in the blockade of Toulon by the west. Then, followed by the 3/7ᵉ RTA, it headed for the Ange pass and overcame the enemy resistance at the Coulin crossroads. By evening it had occupied Gemenos, Pont-de-l'Etoile and the outskirts of Aubagne. But Aubagne appeared to be solidly held by the enemy.

Behind them, Task Force Chappuis[1] was assembling at Signes and the goumiers, still on foot, headed for Gareoult from where they would spread out over the Sainte-Baume hills. The Marseilles battle thus depended on the battle for Toulon, and obliged the commander of the 3ᵉ DIA to wage a double war in two different cities sixty kilometers from each other.

WITH THE III/7ᵉ RTA

This battalion was the only one at full strength and with a certain number of vehicles. The men left first their bivouac at the Isle mill, west of Cogolin, on the afternoon of the 19th. They crossed Collobrières, then Pierrefeu,

Above.
Insignia of the 7ᵉ Régiment de tirailleurs algériens
(Private collection)

Below.
Map indicating the enemy defense positions in the Marseilles defense zone, established by the 244.ID staff on March 25, 1944.
(BA-MA)

Cuers, Puget-Ville, Gareoult, Méounes behind the light tanks of the Spahis.

"Suffocating heat in the vehicles, roasted and roasted again by a pitiless sun, white dust clouding the rosemary bushes, maquis, odors of aromatic cooking, numbing speed. What did we look like? Here were villagers that had tumbled out into the streets to greet us, frenetic cheering; elsewhere were half-dead villages, trying hard to hold the little breath they had left after so many trials.

We drove blindly through the dazzling countryside, without knowing whether, around the next bend, the thick air would suddenly be dancing with bullets, if the unforeseeable skirmish was not suddenly going to fill the uncanny calm with its anger.

We didn't know where the enemy was; he was retreating; on the roads he left nothing but strong-

Above, right.
Some of Marseilles' defenses:
1. The single 240-mm gun located at the Ratonneau battery.
2. The Pharo battery with four 65-mm guns near the old fort.
3. One of the three 75-mm gun casemates of the Corbière battery.
4. One of the three 90-mm gun casemates of the Niolon battery.
(Private collection)

points.[2]*"*

Beyond Cuges they reached the Ange gap and then blocked the road to Aubagne. But pillboxes and an anti-tank barrage stopped their advance. Lacking artillery, they had to wait for the Shermans following behind to burst through the barrier and roll down into the plain.

At 0400 on the 21st, the battalion column lined up again and, through the burned-out forest where the hot coals were still smoking, arrived after dawn in Coulin, then Gémenos, St Pierre and reached l'Etoile at 0900. There the men received new orders.

---

1. 7ᵉ RTA, 2nd Squadron of the 3ᵉ RSAR, 1st battalion of the 67ᵉ RAA (African artillery), one Co. from the 83ᵉ bataillon du génie, one collecting co. from the 3ᵉ Bataillon médical.
2. Le 7ᵉ tirailleurs algeriens dans la bataille, Imprimerie Nationale, Trier, 1948.

Below.
'The insurrection in Marseilles,'
photo by Julie Picotte.
(Musée de l'Armée Paris)

THE 3ᵉ DIVISION D'INFANTERIE ALGÉRIENNE

The 3ᵉ DIA evolved from 'Division de Constantine' which fought in Tunisia from November 1942 to April 1943. It was officially activated on May 1 as its first equipment from America was arriving in Algiers, but was not actually completely formed, under General de Goislard de Monsabert[1], until the end of July when it moved in the vicinity of Algiers. In September, the men moved to the area of Oran in order to train at the Invasion Training Center established between Arzew and Mostaganem.

In December some of its units embarked in Oran or Bizerte for Naples. On January 9, 1944, they occupied the Venafro sector after relieving the 45th Infantry Division. Then they fought first in the Abruzzi until March, next in the battle of Garigliano where the division breached the Gustav line at Castelforte, and finally participated in the march on Rome and Sienna in June.

For Provence, the first echelon embarked at Taranto on five ships of convoy TF-1 the Polish LSI *Circassia*, the British transport ships *Cameronian* and *Worcestershire*, the Polish transport ship *Batory*, the British freighter *Eastern Prince*.
This echelon was composed of:
- EM & compagnie de QG n° 83 (HQ & HQ Co.)
- 3ᵉ régiment de spahis algériens de reconnaissance - colonel Bonjour
- 3ᵉ régiment de tirailleurs algériens - colonel Gonzales de Linarès
- 7ᵉ régiment de tirailleurs algériens - colonel Chappuis
- 1ᵉʳ & 2ᵉ groupes of the 67ᵉ régiment d'artillerie d'Afrique (105-mm)
- Battery A of 37ᵉ groupe de FTA (AA Artillery)
- 83ᵉ bataillon du génie (engineers)
- compagnie mixte de transmissions 83/84 (signals)
- détachement de circulation routière, 183ᵉ et 283ᵉ compagnies de transport (traffic control, truck Cos)
- 3ᵉ bataillon médical
- 3ᵉ compagnie de réparation divisionnaire (Ordnance)
- 3ᵉ groupe d'exploitation de l'intendance (QM).

In addition, Lieutenant-Colonel Van Hecke's 7ᵉ Régiment de chasseurs d'Afrique was attached. With its three squadrons of tank destroyers, it had provided support for the division since its arrival in Italy.

Four FOB parties were also attached to the Algerian Division. The elements that arrived with the other echelons were:
- The 4ᵉ Régiment de tirailleurs tunisiens
- The 3rd and 4th groups of the 67ᵉ RAA
- The rest of the 37ᵉ GFTA.

On the 18th the division was reinforced by the 3rd (155 HM1) battalion from the 65ᵉ RAA, the 2nd Battalion of the 101ᵉ Régiment du génie, and General Guillaume's 'Groupe de Tabors marocains.' Then the next day it was reinforced the landed elements of the 4th Squadron, 2ᵉ RSAR.

During the fighting, the division CP was successively at Cogolin (August 16), Portonfus (August 17), Amirauté farm near Grimaud (August 18), Les Videaux near Pierrefeu (August 19), near Puget-Ville then Signes (August 20), Chibron Camp (August 22).

On August 23, when the battle was raging in both Toulon and Marseilles, the CP was divided in:
– forward CP in Marseilles — at the Collège Michelet rue Foch, then Palais de Longchamp and finally XV Corps Hotel;
– rear CP at Le Revest near Toulon, then at Château de Magny south of Gémenos.

1. Honored as 'Compagnon de la Libération' on November 20, 1944 as commander of the 2ᵉ Corps d'armée.

Monsabert had just decided to surround Marseilles without waiting for Toulon to fall or for the 1ʳᵉ DMI to arrive for reinforcement. While occupying the enemy by simultaneous operations around the city fringes on the south, east and north, outside the major communications routes, he launched his two available infantry battalions through the steep stark hills of l'Etoile:
- II/7ᵉ RTA via Roquevaire, Le Pilon du Roi and La Gavotte,
- III/7ᵉ RTA via Allauch.
That action was completed by the CC 1 pushing directly along the Huveaune valley from Aubagne and

Above.
'French soldiers near Allauch, August 1944,' by Pierre Jouanneau-Iriera.
They are of course Algerian soldiers from the 3/7ᵉ tirailleurs algériens.
(Musée de l'Armée Paris)

two maneuvers on the flanks:
- to the North, the 1ᵉʳ GTM ('Groupe de tabors marocains') along the Cadolive, Simiane, Estaque range;
- to the South, the 2ᵉ GTM into the Saint-Cyr range and the 3ᵉ GTM along the coast, via Cassis and the La Gineste pass.

From Pont de l'Etoile the III/7 column — guided by three FFIs who offered their services to lead them up to the Garlaban, six hundred meters above — took the Lascours trail and, after winding back and forth up the hill under a blazing sky, finally reached the crossroads five hundred meters from

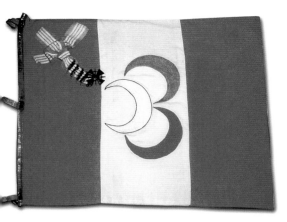

the village. There they made a necessary halt before undertaking the steep slopes of the Plan de l'Aigle.

At 1130 the column started out again. Major Finat-Duclos was leading, with Captain Toulouse, the CP and the guides. Even though they were carrying the strict minimum, they were nevertheless heavily loaded: weapons, ammunition, rations. The land was rocky with a few tufts of wild heather. The pebbles rolled away under their feet. No one spoke.

After another halt at 1330, they continued along up the Garlaban ravine. They passed the spring and then crossed the gap near the Baume Sourne cave, refreshingly cool. It was 1600.

Then they began descending toward Allauch along paths cut out amongst the trees, vines and shrubs. Near Cante Perdrix they noticed some suspicious movements and the 9th Company took the lead. Actually the movements came from guerilla fighters from the 'Attila camp', dressed as policemen, gendarmes or sailors, in overalls or shorts, who greeted the soldiers:

"*We embraced each other, some men were crying, it was ten minutes of deep emotion. Then Major Finat-Duclos' voice brought us back to order.* [3]"

The 9th Company was sent on to Allauch with some FFI groups. At 1700 the soldiers entered the village to the sound of bells ringing. The Germans, who had taken refuge in a workers' housing estate on the outskirts of the town, where expelled by the 10th Company. At dusk the battalion received orders by radio to defend the village and not to move until the morning of the 22nd.

THE CUIRASSIERS AND THE ZOUAVES AT SAINT-JULIEN

So on the 22nd at 0600 the battalion left for Les Olives, with the 10th Company leading, followed by the CP. They reached the village at 0830. Across the way could be seen Germans going about their work. A maneuver was undertaken and the 10th got the Germans in their sights. But the enemy reacted promptly and counter-attacked with the help

Top left.
Pennant for the commanding general of the 3ᵉ division d'infanterie algérienne.
(Musée de l'Infanterie, Montpellier)

Above.
Early in the morning on August 23, the Zouave half-tracks lead the Cuirassiers tanks through Saint-Julien, escorted by the Tirailleurs.
(Private collection)

Left.
A Tobruk fashioned from the turret of a German Mark II tank on a concrete base, built at the foot of Fort Saint-Nicolas to cover the entrance to the Vieux-Port in Marseilles.
(National Archives)

of the La Rose and Merlan batteries. Their aim was to maintain the integrity of the inner defensive belt around Marseilles, of which one of the keys was the La Rose crossroads.

"*Shells were whistling around, landing in gardens, squares, breaking through roofs, cutting off telegraph poles, destroying the easy grace of these suburban country homes. Everybody hunkered down, waiting for the end of the storm that had burst over the deserted, silent streets. The battalion commander walked up and down with his map-holder in his hand, appearing both curious and absorbed. The first aid station and a 10th Company shelter were hit. The doctor looked after the wounded.*

Toward 17.00 the enemy artillery was silenced. The commander went back up to the CP. Some young boys went to pick bunches of the first grapes on the treillises and gave them to the thirsty soldiers.

News came that the Aubagne blockade had been breached and that the tanks were coming. [4]"

Yes, around 1900 a column of tanks and half-tracks was seen at Trois Lucs and Saint-Julien. Preceded by FFI mem-

3. *Ibid.*
4. *Ibid.*

Above.
'Fabert' was one of the five Shermans of the 2nd platoon, 2nd Squadron of the 2ᵉ Cuirassiers attached to the Tirailleurs Bataillon Martel.
(OFIC)

Below.
Insignia of the 2ᵉ Régiment de Cuirassiers.
(Private collection)

Below.
August 25.
The tirailleurs mop up in Marseilles.
(National Archives)

Bottom.
August 30. In the deserted streets of Marseilles after the fighting, a French Navy firefighter is examining a 7.5-cm Pak 97/38 gun, the antitank version of the French 75-mm field piece.
(National Archives)

THE 1ʳᵉ DIVISION BLINDEE

The 1ʳᵉ DB originated as two formations commanded successively by Colonel Touzet du Vigier:
● the 'Centre d'organisation des unités blindées' (Armored center) in Algeria, created in Oran in the fall of 1942,
● the 'Brigade légère mécanique' which participated in the Tunisian campaign in January and February 1943.
It was thus natural that Du Vigier, who had been promoted to Brigadier General on December 25, 1942, be named as commander of the new division under formation on January 28, 1943.
The 1ʳᵉ DB was officially activated on May 1 at Mascara and assigned at first to 1ᵉʳ corps blindé. But the later was disbanded on August 15 and it then constituted the 1st 'Invasion Corps' with the 2ᵉ, 3ᵉ and 4ᵉ 'divisions nord-africaines.' Thirteen days later, Du Vigier received his third star.

Then the 4ᵉ DMM left for Corsica and the 2ᵉ DIM and 3ᵉ DIA were committed in Italy. But the 1ʳᵉ DB remained in Algeria, where the men continued training. The division gave some of its equipment to the 'Division Leclerc' (2ᵉ DB) which was sent to England in May 1944. At that time, the 1ʳᵉ DB was organized into three Combat Commands, and two were involved in the battle of Provence.

The first element, which began landing in the evening of August 15, was made up of the units from CC 1 under General Sudre:
● état-major de la brigade de chars (Brigade HQ)
● 5ᵉ escadron de reconnaissance du 3ᵉ régiment de chasseurs d'Afrique (Recce squadron)
● 2ᵉ régiment de cuirassiers (medium tanks)
● 3ᵉ bataillon de zouaves portés (armored infantry)
● 2ᵉ escadron de TD du 9ᵉ régiment de chasseurs d'Afrique (Tank destroyers)
● 1ᵉʳ groupe du 68ᵉ régiment d'artillerie d'Afrique (M7 105-mm HMC)
● Compagnie du génie 88/2 (engineers)
● 1ʳᵉ compagnie du XVᵉ bataillon médical
● 1ᵉʳ escadron du 11ᵉ groupe de réparation (Ordnance)
With them arrived a radio half-track from the Compagnie des transmissions 91/84, the traffic control platoon from the base, one platoon of the 191ᵉ Cie de transport, maintenance vehicles belonging to Compagnie du matériel 661/2, and fractions of diverse units: CIC, Ordnance, Compagnie de réparation d'engins blindés (tank repair co.) 671/2, 66ᵉ Compagnie de munitions, 705ᵉ Compagnie de ravitaillement en essence (POL supply).

These elements were initially committed with the VI Corps, then returned to Armée B for the battle of Marseilles.

The second element also embarked at Oran and started going ashore at the same time of the first. But since the troops were on board six Liberty ships, unloading took longer and continued until August 23. It was made up of the CC 2 units of Colonel Kientz:
● état-major de la brigade de soutien (Reserve brigade HQ)
● 1ᵉʳ escadron de reconnaissance et peloton spécial du 3ᵉ régiment de chasseurs d'Afrique (tank destroyers)
● 5ᵉ régiment de chasseurs d'Afrique (medium tanks)
● 1ᵉʳ bataillon de zouaves portés (armored infantry)
● 3ᵉ escadron de TD du 9ᵉ régiment de chasseurs d'Afrique
● 3ᵉ groupe du 68ᵉ régiment d'artillerie d'Afrique (M7 105-mm HMC)
● compagnie du génie 88/1 and elements of Compagnie 88/16 (engineers)
● 2ᵉ compagnie du XVᵉ bataillon médical
● 2ᵉ escadron du 11ᵉ groupe de réparation (ordnance)

They were accompanied by part of the Division staff, the 91ᵉ Cie de QG (HQ Co.) with its traffic control platoon, Cie des transmissions 91/84, the Division Artillery and Engineer staffs, the 191ᵉ Cie de transport minus one platoon, maintenance vehicles from Cie du matériel 661/2 and a fraction of the armored vehicles of the Compagnie de réparation d'engins blindés 671/2, the 66ᵉ Cie de munitions and 705ᵉ Cie de ravitaillement en essence.

The division was also accompanied by General reserve units: 2ᵉ régiment de spahis algériens de reconnaissance (2ᵉ corps d'armée), 432ᵉ bataillon médical, 32ᵉ Cie géographique (Survey), 2nd Squadron of the 11ᵉ Groupe de la Garde. CC2 was engaged partly in Toulon, partly north of Marseilles. Once reassembled it made up, with CC 1, Task Force Du Vigier sent to Avignon and then to cross the Rhône River.

The division CP was set up in Grimaud on August 17 and then transferred to Saint-Zacharie (August 21), Cabriès (August 23), Grans (August 24), the Avignon agricultural school (August 26) and Champfleury (August 27-28).

bers on bicycles, it had left Aubagne, now cleared by the Goumiers, at 1300 and taken the route going through Camoins and La Valentine. The column was followed by the 1/7e RTA infantry which had been in reserve until that moment and which Colonel Chappuis had decided to launch into the battle. During the night, a delegation of Marseilles Resistance had come to announce that the population had taken to the streets, but that the FFI were too few and not well enough armed to control the situation. Montsabert answered their request by deciding to send the cuirassiers and the zouaves toward Marseilles by a secondary road that appeared to be neither blocked nor mined nor congested.

At Les Olives the situation was now under control and the III/7e RTA was able to turn west and toward Saint-Jérôme safely. The men received rations and ammunition during the night.

On the north side, the 2e Tabor was blocking the road to Aix-en-Provence, but the 3e and 12e Tabors were in trouble in Cadolive and Peypin.

On the left flank of the 1er GTM, the II/7e RTA had arrived by truck in Gréasque and during the night of August 21 to 22 had occupied the lower slopes of the Etoile hills. Then, with their heavy weapons and their ammunition on their backs, under the scorching sun, they climbed to the top of the jumble of rock known as the Pilon du Roi, and came down the other side to the rocky slopes of La Mure. They had no liaisons with the regiment CP and the battalion commander could not report their position east of Gavotte, less than two kilometers from the northern suburbs of Marseilles.

On the south side the two groups of tabors had finished isolating Marseilles by occupying the Chateau de la Gelade and the crossroads south of La Bedoule. The only way out of Marseilles for the Germans was the road to Martigues. But the Seventh Army [5] knew that Generalleutnant Schaeffer, commander of the 244. Infanteriedivision, had been assigned by the Führer to command the Festung Marseille and that he would remain in the city, even after the port installations were destroyed, which took place on the 22nd.

In the morning, Truscott and De Lattre had been informed, by a 'secret source' [6] that the 11. Panzerdivision was west of Aix. Each general reacted accordingly, De Lattre by placing the two combat commands of the Task Force Du Vigier south of the Durance River to cover the left flank of the Americans and protect Marseilles. The progression of the 3e DIA into the outskirts of Marseilles was therefore not to his liking, because it involved part of the tanks on which he had counted to combat the German armored division. He was all the more furious because General de Larminat, present, had approved Monsabert's decision to penetrate into the center of Marseilles.

From the information he was receiving from the center of the city, it appeared that it was premature to attempt an entry. The troops risked being drowned among the crowds of people in the streets and obliged to fight house-to-house combats, whereas a progressive encircling with all available means — including the 1re DMI which was scheduled to arrive as soon as it had reached the eastern suburbs of Toulon — might lead to a battle outside the city center.

THE JARRET, A MODERN RUBICON

He therefore convoked Monsabert to the CC 1 CP in Gémenos and, in the presence of Generals de Larminat and Guillaume, gave orders not to enter Marseilles, but allowed him to choose himself the line where his troops would stop.

Inset, above.
Badge for the 2e bataillon de zouaves portés.
(Private collection)

Top right.
The 7e RTA reaching the slopes of the hill of Notre-Dame de la Garde on August 25. The tirailleur at right is ready to fire an antitank grenade.
(National Archives)

Above.
"The inhabitants of Marseilles seeing a Liberation Army 35-ton tank for the first time." The 'Sainte-Odile' (3rd Squadron, 2e Cuirassiers, has stopped in front of the Palais de Longchamp.
(OFIC)

Then, so that there would be no misunderstanding, he confirmed his orders in writing to the 3e DIA at 2100:

"General De Monsabert, with the following means at his disposal 7e RTA, 1er, 2e and 3e GTM, CC1 less the light elements detached to protect the Roquefavour aqueduct will continue his maneuver of encircling Marseilles. Without the authorization of the General commanding the Army, he will in no case pass the line running: stream 4 km east of the Saint-Barthélemy coast

5. Thanks to their access to 'Ultra' (deciphered German radio messages service) Devers, Patch and Truscott (since he had commanded the Anzio beachhead), knew since August 18 — at the same time as the Nineteenth Army command — that the Fuehrer had ordered the fortresses of Toulon and Marseilles to be defended to the last man.
6. Probably Ultra, as had been the case on August 17. The division was supposed to counter-atttack at Brignoles.

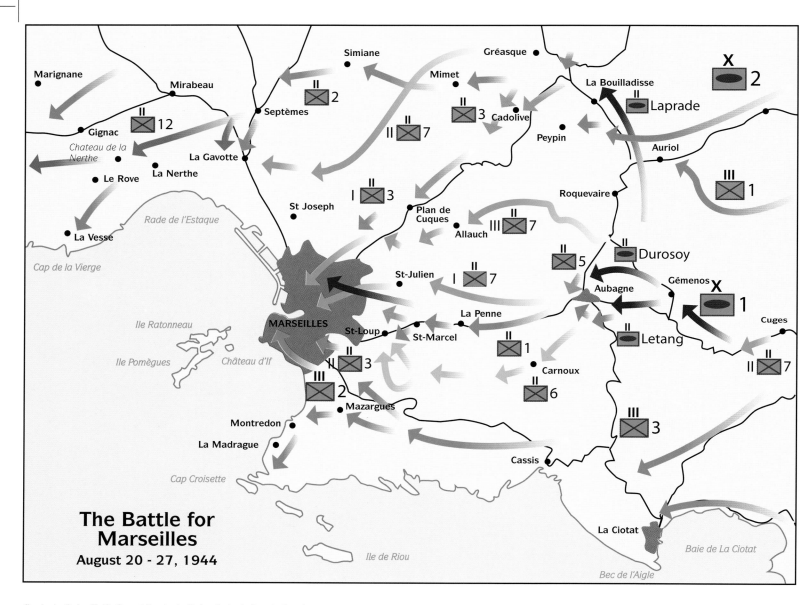

The Battle for Marseilles
August 20 - 27, 1944

(included) Le Petit Canet (included) La Calade (excluded). It is intended that the rest of the 3e DIA, and if possible the 1st DFL, be sent to Marseilles as soon as the evolution of the situation in Toulon permits."

The stream chosen on purpose by Monsabert was the Jarret, an underground waterway that a soldier would certainly have trouble locating on the terrain because there is no trace of it on the surface. He thus satisfied Chappuis who was waiting for him after the meeting and whose units were well aware that the news of the arrival of the French troops has spread like wildfire and that hundreds of men and women were skirting the German roadblocks to meet the 'tirailleurs,' zouaves and cuirassiers. He could not figure out how he could fail to respond to the public enthusiasm and order his soldiers to lay down their weapons until the 3e RTA and the 3e RSAR arrived from Toulon.

Thus at dawn on the 23rd, the I/7e RTA left Saint-Julien, cheered along the way by the inhabitants of Marseilles. A tank sqaudron also started out and had soon overtaken the column. Then, arriving down the Boulevard de la Blancarde, Tirailleurs and Cuirassiers reached the La Madeleine intersection at 0800, surrounded by a delirious crowd. On orders from Chappuis, the battalion headed for the Vieux-Port and the Prefecture, and a motorcyclist was sent to the Division to report on the movement.

At 0900, as the tirailleurs were parading down the Canebière, the German artillery raised a ruckus. And at 1000, the Shermans received orders to retreat to their departure point. Monsabert did not want to let one of his battalions get isolated, and he agreed with Gener-

al Du Vigier to keep the entire CC 1 for the time being. Then he hurried off to the Collège Michelet and ordered General Sudre to engage his troops in the center of Marseilles in support of the infantry. A truce was agreed on at 1500, but negotiations were not finalized and the hostilities started again at 1915.

From that moment on, two battles were being waged

"*The review and the parade in front of the government officials and General de Lattre de Tassigny, in which participated the Marseilles and Provence FFI, were much more than simple military ceremonies, the crowning moment for battles won.*

Something else was vibrating, singing along the Quai des Belges. Under the rays of the sparkling sun, it was the heart of an immense crowd, the fervor of overwhelming emotion. Fleeting instants filled with too much meaning for them to be described, but which leave their mark permanently on the soul of each of us."

And then, more prosaic, the narrator continued:
"*For a week the Regiment remained in the great city that honored it.* [7]"

But victory in Toulon and Marseilles had been costly for Armée B. The reasons were numerous: the enthusiastic spirit and wild temerity on the part of the troops, the fact that the artillery had been forbidden to fire near houses to avoir civilian casualties, stiff defense by the German forces who were not keen on falling into the hands

simultaneously: one on the outskirts to finish surrounding the city and capturing the last pockets of resistance still holding out; the other within the city limits to silence one by one the enemy strongholds.

The first battle was being fought by the three groups of tabors and the II/7ᵉ RTA. The second, carried on by the 7ᵉ RTA and the CC 1 tanks, reinforced on the 25th by the two battalions of the 3ᵉ RTA from Toulon, involved bringing assistance to the II/7ᵉ RTA isolated at the Château des Tours by violent counter-attacks, and fighting around the Racati, La Nerthe and Le Canet batteries, where the commander of the III/7ᵉ RTA was killed with his artillery liaison officer at his side. But the most spectacular action was the taking of Notre Dame de la Garde on the 25th, involving Shermans, tirailleurs, goumiers, sappers and FFI fighters.

On the 27th: "*It was Sunday. If we hadn't known what day it was the dresses of the Marseilles women would have told us. Pious ladies were heading for church. At 0800 I took the chaplain to the 4th Squadron with their tanks lined up along the Prado: his mass provided competition for the parish churches as many local Catholics joined the soldiers to pray and take communion. A lot of onlookers also. It looked something like the crowd at a racetrack.*

- What about you, aren't you going to defend France? a girl asked her brown-haired sweetheart.

- Forget it he answered, pointing to the tanks. Look: France can defend herself quite well!

When mass was over, our soldiers started singing the Marseillaise."

At 2000 there were only a few pockets still resisting and the Germans asked for a cease-fire so that negotiations could begin.

THE PRICE OF VICTORY

On the 28th at 0900, General Schaeffer came to the Military Governor Hotel. His conditions were accepted and surrender was scheduled for the 28th at 1300. Unending columns of prisoners were then led to the camp at Sainte-Marthe and at 1900 the bells of all the churches of Marseilles rang out the liberation. It had come at a price: one thousand four hundred killed or wounded, of which half were from among the goumiers.

Thirty-six hours after Toulon had been captured by the two colonial divisions, Marseilles was taken by the two Algerian divisions and the Moroccan goums.

The 29th was dedicated to celebrating the victory:

Top left.
A Tobruk made out of the turret of a French tank near the Place de la Major in front of the cathedral. It was part of the close protection system of La Joliette harbor.
(National Archives)

Top, right.
Insignia of the 2ᵉ groupe de tabors marocains led by Colonel Boyer de Latour. They sailed from Corsica and with the help of the tanks were able to 'burst the Aubagne bulwark' and infiltrate the southern sections of Marseilles through the Saint-Cyr hills.
(Private collection)

Above and right.
August 27. Colonel Chappuis, the 7ᵉ RTA CO, receives the German delegation coming to negotiate the surrender of the German garrison in Marseilles.
(Pierre Ichac)

of the FFI or the colonial soldiers...
Even though the number of Germans captured between August 15 and 28 is known — about 35,000 — the number of French losses is more difficult to ascertain. Armée B announced 1,513 killed including 96 officers, 5,396 wounded including 141 officers. But in August 1946, a report concerning all of the campaigns in France and Germany mentioned 933 dead, 3,732 wounded and 19 missing.

Considering the average number of men participating during the fourteen days of fighting, it is possible to calculate average daily losses per one thousand men and compare them to losses during other periods (see table below).

It is evident that, considering total losses — three times as many as at Belfort or Colmar, with the hardest days being August 23 and 24 — the battle of Provence was the most costly, and thus the most difficult, that Army B, which later became the French First Army, had to wage.

Period	Strength	Duration	Killed	Wounded	Missing	Total
Provence	50,000	14	1,30	5,30	0,03	6,63
Pursuit	77,000	27	0,33	1,60	-	1,93
Vosges	123,000	49	0,34	1,42	0,03	1,79
Belfort-Mulhouse	237,000	15	0,68	1,88	0,06	2,61
Stabilization	248,000	52	0,23	0,88	0,10	1,21
Colmar	265,000	20	0,39	1,73	0,06	2,18
Watch on the Rhine	262,000	33	0,05	0,16	-	0,21
Siegfried Line	250,000	15	0,09	0,29	-	0,38
Germany	252,000	40	0,29	0,66	0,02	0,97

Top, left.
Badge of the 3ᵉ Régiment de spahis algériens de reconnaissance, a corps reserve unit.
(Private collection)

Top right.
The imposing structures of Fort Saint-Jean and the metal remains of the transporter bridge guard over the entrance to the Vieux-Port, where the American soldiers are arriving to get the port installations back into running order.
(National Archives)

Above.
The Jarret was crossed and victory is certain: Generals de Lattre and Monsabert have forgotten their quarrels.
(ECPAD)

Below.
August 29. The 2/7ᵉ régiment de chasseurs d'Afrique crews here those of half-track 'Bigorneur II' ('Basher') and tank destroyer 'Batailleur' - wait for the parade to begin.
(ECPAD)

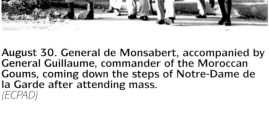

August 29. The Colors of the 3ᵉ régiment de tirailleurs algériens parading on the Quai des Belges, carried by Second Lieutenant Laurie.
(ECPAD)

August 30. General de Monsabert, accompanied by General Guillaume, commander of the Moroccan Goums, coming down the steps of Notre-Dame de la Garde after attending mass.
(ECPAD)

7. Le 7ᵉ tirailleurs algériens dans la bataille, *op. cit. See Paul Gaujac,* La guerre en Provence 1944-1945, une bataille méconnue, *Presses Universitaires de Lyon, 1998.*
8. Including Colonel Rousset, divarty commander, killed during a reconnaissance in Marseilles on August 28, 1944.

The August 29 parade on the Quai des Belges.
1. Civilian and military authorities salute from a command car as the crowd sings 'La Marseillaise.'
2. The Colors of the 3e RSAR flying on an M8 HMC.
3. The tank destroyers of the 2/7e Chasseurs d'Afrique pass in front of the assembled brass.
4. The M7 HMCs of the 1/68e régiment d'artillerie d'Afrique, roll towards the Vieux port and pass by FFI groups preparing for the parade.

5. "FFI members parading in Marseilles," photo by Julie Picotte. *(Musée de l'Armée Paris)*
6. The Communist-inspired Francs-Tireurs Partisans (FTP) march behind a red banner and are saluted with clenched fists by the crowd.
(All pictures ECPAD except otherwise mentioned)

THE PURSUIT

As French troops were relieving the elements of the 3rd Infantry Division, General Patch could be satisfied. His first objective — conquering a beachhead — had been met. The capture of the ports of Toulon and Marseilles was now the objective of the French units. These harbors would insure a logistics base for the Allies that would be necessary for their northward advance to meet the troops that had landed in Normandy, the 7th Army's third objective. But until the ports fell into the Allies hands, supplying the American divisions in fuel and ammunition would be such that it would limit the size of operations. Patch was in agreement with Truscott to take advantage of the rapid German retreat and to keep the 19. Armee from escaping or from counter-attacking the VI Corps further north in the Rhône valley. It was for this reason that Truscott had organized 'Task Force Butler.'

Above.
An FFI Patriot.
(Reconstruction by 'Provence 44')

Top, left.
Insignia of the French 1re Division blindée.
(Private collection)

Left.
Afternoon of September 2. Coming from Planfoy where they left the rest of the regiment waiting for gas, the Reconnaissance Troop of the 5e Chasseurs d'Afrique, enters Saint-Etienne to the applause of the locals.
(OFIC)

TASK FORCE BUTLER

Truscott had based an important part of his maneuver on an armored unit to be engaged in Frējus with a mission of joining up with the paratroops and crossing the Blue Line to exploit the Allied advantage. To be prepared for any eventuality, and in case the bridges over the rivers had been destroyed and the banks heavily defended, his staff had even placed among the first waves Engineer bridging troops to get the tanks across the Argens River.

That explains why he was so angry when the landing on the Frējus beach was canceled. This was the attack position that he had wanted for his tanks. He also thought that the construction of airstrips would be delayed, which meant that his troops risked being deprived of close air support[1].

As far as General Sudre's CC 1 was concerned, Truscott concluded from his first contacts with General de Lattre de Tassigny, and from the evasive answers given by Patch to his questions about the French combat command, that the later would be withdrawn from his command at D + 3, perhaps even before. Therefore he decided on August 1 to organize a light mechanized group[2] which he assigned to his deputy, Brigadier Frederick B. Butler. The initial plan was that Task Force Butler would assemble around Le Muy on D + 2 at the earliest and prepare to attack toward the west or northwest.

Actually, since June General Wilson had been considering the possibility that Armeegruppe G, unable to contain the Seventh Army beachhead and hold the city of Toulon, would concentrate all its defensive power on Marseilles and the approach roads to the Rhône River. In that case, the area east of the city and the valley of the Rhône itself would be only lightly defended. According to information received, the division engaged on that flank had been practically neutralized by the resistance fighters.

On August 11, therefore, SACMED suggested "*two new courses of action. First, he suggested that the Seventh Army could strike northwest directly from the beachhead to the Rhône north of Avignon, leaving only minimum forces in the Marseilles area to secure the left flank and to contain German units in the Rhône delta[3]. A second possibility was to strike generally north from the beachhead through the Provence Alps toward the Grenoble area, over one hundred miles north of Toulon.[4]*" In the later action he apparently saw nothing more than

Above.
Coming from the right bank of the Rhône, a Pz Kw V Panther from Panzer-Regiment 15 of the 11.Panzerdivision approaches the Guillotière bridge amid the indifference of the inhabitants of Lyon. It was thanks to this division, placed as rear guard, that the German troops and service personnel in the south of France were able to escape the Rhône River valley.
(DR)

Right.
Combat badge of the German armored formations.
(Militaria Magazine)

Below.
Coming from the right bank of the Rhône and heading for Bourg en Bresse, vehicles belonging to a Flak company from an infantry division Antitank battalion cross the Lafayette bridge.
(DR)

a way of protecting the Seventh Army right flank and stimulating FFI activity east of the Rhône River.

Patch and especially Truscott found in Wilson's suggestions an opportunity to exploit any little weakness in the German forces between the Rhône

1. CC 1 actually arrived more rapidly than scheduled at the Argens River and even above Le Muy. Concerning the airfields, Sisteron, not included in the plans, was opened on August 23, 1944, Le Luc on the 25th (a week earlier than scheduled) and Cuers on the 27th (ten days ahead of time).
2. Including elements of the 36th Division (2nd Bn from the 143rd Infantry Regt, collecting company from the 111th Medical Bn) and the 117th Cavalry Reconnaissance Squadron (Mechanized), 753rd Tank Bn with two companies of medium tanks, Company C from the 636th TD Bn, 59th Armored FA Bn (self-propelled 105s), Company F from the 344th Engineer General Service Regt, 3426th Quartermaster Truck Company, detachment from the 87th Ordnance Company (Heavy Maintenance), about 3,000 men and a thousand vehicles.
3. This proved to be more or less – but at Army level - the plan proposed by General de Larminat to de Lattre.
4. Jeffrey J. Clarke and Robert Ross Smith, Riviera to the Rhine, *US Army Center of Military History, Washington, DC, 1993.*

The Allied divisions' command posts in Southern France

	1re DB	1re DMI	3e DIA	3rd Inf Div	45th Inf Div	36th Inf Div
08.18	Grimaux	Gassin	Grimaux	Gonfaron	Salernes	-
08.19	-	La Londe	Pierrefeux	Brignoles	Fox Amphoux	-
08.20	-	-	Puget-Ville	Trets	Esparron	-
08.21	Ste Zacharie	-	Signes	Aix	Mirabeau	Sisteron
08.22	-	Hyères	Chibron	-	-	Aspres
08.23	Cabries	-	Marseilles	-	Aspres	Marsanne
08.24	Grans	-	-	-	-	Crest
08.25	-	-	-	Cadenet	-	--
08.26	Avignon	-	-	Le Barroux	-	-
08.27	-	St Rémi	-	Crillon	-	-
08.28	-	-	-	La Bégude	Vif	-
08.29	Bagnols s/C	Est Nîmes	-	-	Voiron	-
08.30	-	-	Gardanne	-	-	Chabeuil
08.31	Vals	-	-	Voiron	Lancin	-
09.01	Montfaucon	Montfaucon	Pont de Claix	Crémieu	Lagneux	Villette s/Paize
09.02	Civrieux	-	Challes	Lagnieu	Vieux	-
09.03	-	-	-	Poncin	Meyat	Satolas
09.04	Tournus	Tassin	Chatillon	Le Fied	Bourg	St Trivier
09.05	-	-	St Laurent du Jura	Pagnez	Lons-le-S.	Louhans
09.06	Chalon	-	Doubs	Besançon	Ornans	Arbois

and the Italian border. The VI Corps commander had at his disposal TF Butler whose missions, even though they were minor ones in the main plan, could easily be enlarged if justified by the situation. Consequently he established plans to send the task force towards the Durance River as soon as it was assembled ashore. At that point it would be able either to cross the Durance and strike toward the Rhône near Avignon or progress toward the north striking toward the Rhône further upstream or continuing to Grenoble and Lyon. The VI Corps would then be able to outflank the German defenses in the lower Rhône Valley and block the retreat of Armeegruppe G.

All of that of course depended on how fast the Seventh Army could reach the Blue Line, how much of a fight the Germans would put up in the beach area, and on their reaction to the invasion. Patch's and Truscott's project was nevertheless corroborated by Colonel Henri Zeller's report on August 6 in Naples.

Below.
August 19. A jeep from Task Force Butler's 117th Cavalry Squadron leaves the village of Cruis heading for Sisteron.
(Private collection)

Zeller had arrived from France where he was commander of the FFI on the east side of the Rhône. He considered that the FFI practically controlled the Alps and that consequently the Allies, once they had conquered a strip of coast twenty kilometers deep, should "*take a chance' and launch light columns, with a few tanks and guns, along all the south-north routes.*" After reaching the line Aix-en-Provence-Brignoles-Draguignan they "*should be in Grenoble within forty-eight hours, and from there turn back to the Rhône River Valley to cut off the German retreat around Valence, or better, if possible, at Lyon.[5]*"

On August 11[6], as already mentioned, SACMED exposed his two possible maneuvers and added a concise paragraph which went something like this:

"*Be ready to strike with light forces along the Durance valley toward the north and Sisteron, planning to contact and motivate the Vaucluse maquis groups. This will also present the advantage of furnishing important protection for your right flank.[7]*"

LYON IS LIBERATED

As the troops on the east flank of the beachhead passed the Blue Line, it became evident, from the reconnaissance patrols carried out by the 36th Cavalry Reconnaissance Troop and the information received from Ultra sources, that the Germans would not be any threat on TF Butler's right side. So the TF left Le Muy early in the morning on August 19, following in the footsteps of the elements of the 45th Division along the road to Barjols, then turned north. At noon the column had reached the Verdon River. The bridge had been destroyed and, in spite of help from local civilians and FFI members, it was 1600 before they managed to cross. Butler had only five hours of fuel left, so decided to stay at that spot until he

5. Henri Zeller, Rapports sur mes missions à Alger et à Naples.
6. That is, five days after discussions between Patch and Zeller, whose pseudonym was 'Faisceau' (Cluster). When Patch shook hands with Zeller after the success of the invasion, the French considered the engagement of TF Butler as the result of the 'Plan Faisceau,' even though the conception of the project was much older: it resulted from 'Rankin' and was Wilson's idea.
7. Quoted by Arthur Layton Funk, in Hidden Ally, Greenwood Press, New York 1992.

1. August 16. 45th Division soldiers progressing north of Sainte-Maxime pass a civilian bus on the Toulon line that has been hit by machine gun fire from the Allied fighter bombers.

2. A tank destroyer from the 601st Battalion attached to the 3rd Division advances toward Route 7.

3. August 20. Without waiting for a bridge to be built, the 645th TD Bn tank destroyers cross the Durance heading for Mirabeau where the FFI forces are waiting for them.

4. August 20. While the 157th Infantry Regiment soldiers cross the footbridge over the breach in the Saint-Paul bridge that had been destroyed by the Germans, the sappers from the 120th Engineer Combat Bn are busy preparing a passageway for vehicles. For fear of a tank attack, ammunition is being transported to Mirabeau in civilian trucks driven by FFI fighters.

5. August 16. The 45th Division soldiers cross the Blue Line and begin the long pursuit that will lead them as far as Bourg-en-Bresse.

6. On August 21 at 0600, the 30th Infantry Regiment, 3rd Division attacked Aix-en-Provence. Covered by the other two battalions, the 3rd Bn entered the city and had finished clearing it out at 1000.

7. August 22. Soldiers of a mortar platoon of the 143rd Infantry, 36th Division, enters Grenoble.
(National Archives)

received supplies scheduled to arrive during the night.

During this time, Troop C, after following a slightly different route, met up with the part of the LXII. Korps staff that had escaped the paratroopers, and captured General Neuling.

The next day the column crossed the Durance River, while Troops A and B remained on the banks, and entered the city at 1800. The column, delayed by untimely strafing by Allied fighter-bombers, joined up later. The only meeting with the Germans took place at Digne, where an armored patrol, with the help of an FFI battalion, obtained the surrender of the garrison.

From that moment on, the rhythm of the pursuit increased rapidly, since the Seventh Army and the VI Corps had been warned by Ultra sources, as we have seen, that Hitler had ordered Armeegruppe G and the 19. Armee to evacuate the city.

But such rapid progression created problems, for radio communication was difficult if possible at all because of the long distances and the mountainous terrain. For lack of liaisons, there was hesitation between the VI Corps, the 36th Division and TF Butler as the battle of Montélimar was about to start. It lasted until August 29. As a result, the divisions of the 19. Armee, even though they lost one fifth of their men, were able to escape north.

On the 30th TF Butler was therefore disbanded. This marked the end of the pursuit from the Provence beachhead. The objective of the VI Corps was now Lyon and the 36th Division was advancing rapidly toward the city. On the opposite bank of the Rhône, the 1st DB and 1st DMI, having crossed the river on emergency bridges, assembled northwest of Avignon to strike out toward the north. On September 1, they came under the orders of the 2nd Corps, reactivated under General Monsabert, who had given up the 3rd DIA to General Guillaume coming from the Tabors.

On September 2, the 36th Division arrived on the outskirts of Lyon and stopped, in order to let the French make their entrance into the '*city of the Gauls*'

Above.
An LSD is launching landing craft that will travel up the Rhône and assist the French troops in crossing onto the right bank of the river and then in keeping them supplied.
(National Archives)

Below.
The pursuit.
(Marc Kosloff Collection)

first. Patrols had reported that the Germans had left. The next day the first elements of the 1st DMI entered the city. So the Dragoon troops had accomplished their mission. The Seventh Army had routed the Germans and reached its goal more than two months ahead of schedule.

Toulon was occupied seven days ahead, Marseilles twenty-eight and Lyon eighty-one. The comparison between the areas planned by the Germans to delay their opponents, the plans of the Allies and the reality of their progression, shows how fast the landing forces were able to advance and how profoundly the plans were disrupted (see table below):

Agenda	Date	German goals	Planned objectives	Objectives reached
D	15.8			
D + 3	18.8			*Blue Line*
D + 8	23.8	Avignon		
D + 9	24.8		*Blue Line*	
D + 10	25.8			Avignon
D + 12	27.8			**Marseilles**
D + 13	28.8			**Toulon**
D + 15	30.8			Montélimar
D + 19	3.9			**Lyon**
D + 20	4.9		Toulon	
D + 21	5.9	Lyons		
D + 27	11.9			Dijon
D + 31	15.9	Gateway to Bourgogne		Belfort Gap
D + 40	24.9		Marseille	
D + 90	15.11	Belfort Gap	Lyon Mâcon	Drive to the Rhine

LOGISTICS HAVE TROUBLE KEEPING UP

The wild pursuit did bring with it problems, for an army exploiting its advantage is a huge consumer of fuel. And in the case of the Seventh Army, the logistics experts had predicted that, as during other amphibious operations in the Mediterranean, the fighting would be violent and would necessitate large quantities of ammunition. Moreover, the lengthening distances between the beaches and the front made things worse: the operational situation and the logistics plans were more and more out of phase. On September 14, that is D + 30, the troops had passed Dijon and Vesoul, cities that should have been reached on D + 90 according to the plans.

At first the arrival of supplies depended on the availability of beaches. Operations on Alpha Red (Cavalaire) were maintained in spite of difficulties caused by mines. On Alpha Yellow (Pampelonne) they were moved because of sand banks and then abandoned because of the distance to be covered before reaching the major highways. In Delta sector, the beaches in the Bougnon bay were fortunately replaced on the evening of August 16 by Beauvallon-Grimaud-La Foux beaches at the back of the gulf. The army had also intended to use the ports of St Tropez and Ste Maxime. But actually only the freighters carrying medical equipment anchored there, since the Navy and the Air Forces had taken them as their bases.

In the eastern sector, the fact that

Above.
Insignia of the 344th Engineer General Service Regiment activated in Louisiana and attached to the VI Corps.
(Le Poilu)

Left.
A season's greetings card for 1945 printed by the French First Army and decorated with a map showing the island of Elba and the cities liberated in 1944.
(Private collection)

it had been impossible to take Camel Red (Fréjus) had delayed for thirty-six hours the arrival of certain supplies. On Camel Green (Le Drammont) operations were completely improvised, due to the fact that the beach took charge of Camel Red traffic until the evening of the 17th, and then replaced the Agay beach when that one was closed on the 19th. The beach groups were soon overwhelmed and the supply dumps on the coast saturated, for lack of workers and specialized equipment. On D + 30 (September 14) the problem had not yet been solved, because it was difficult to modify the composition of the convoys and

the loading of the ships. Part of those designated to transport the service units from Africa, Italy or Corsica had been diverted to allow the Army B second echelon to land more rapidly. And recruiting of French civilians[8] and the use of Italian formations[9] did not solve the problem.

But later the bases in the ports finally took over. The one in Toulon was opened on September 5 and the base was completely operational fifteen days later. In Marseilles it took longer to get the port back in shape, because the destructions had been more massive. Nevertheless the first Liberty ship was unloaded in the harbor on September 15, and by the end of the month fifteen cargo ships could unload at the docks. And Port-de-Bouc had been protected by the FFI, so its refineries were rapidly put back into service and, on September 10, a pipeline was under construction toward Lyon.

Along with the 325,000 men that landed in September should be added the supplies for the armies and for the civilian population, the vehicles and fuel unloaded on the beaches and in the ports:

	BEACHES	TOULON	MARSEILLES	PORT-DE-BOUC
SUPPLIES	343 800 t	3 500 t	115 300 t	37 400 t
CIVIL AFFAIRS	6 000 t	19 300 t	-	-
VEHICLES	12 570	23 630	32 800	
FUEL	1 600 b	80 000 b	10 000 b	240 000 b

But in spite of the tonnage landed in September, logistics problems limited air and land operations, and the lack of vehicles and fuel was felt everywhere. Under these conditions, using the vehicles of the combat support and support units, and taping the German supply depots were only expedients.

It was during the month of September that the liaison between the forces invading through Normandy and those coming from Provence took place, between the 10th and the 12th. Consequently the 6th Army Group became operational on the 15th at 0001 and passed from AFHQ control to that of SHAEF, from Wilson to Eisenhower. At that time it had at its disposal the American Seventh Army and the French Army B which became the '*Première Armée*' four days later. The great adventure of Anvil-Dragoon thus ended northwest of Dijon, within range of the borders of the Reich.

8. *1,000 on August 20, 1944, 7,000 on September 15, 1944.*
9. *3 companies on August 21.1944, 7,000 men on September 30.1944.*

Below.
Anchored in the gulf of Saint-Tropez, Liberty ships are waiting for landing craft to come and unload their cargo. It will be ferried to the beach and then stocked in dumps before being hauled to the troops advancing beyond Lyon.
(National Archives)

EPILOGUE

On November 15, 1944 the French First Army launched its second offensive toward the Rhine, reaching it four days later. Even though it had advanced more than seven hundred kilometers in three weeks, it took then two and a half months to cover the last hundred kilometers to the river.

The stiffening German defense as they approached the Reich, the lack of fuel and then of ammunition to continue the offensive, the need to reassemble and resupply the forces after the pursuit undertaken back in Provence, can explain this delay. However, another influencing element were certainly the successive changes made in the Allied deployment.

Actually on August 28, General Patch asked the VI Corps to continue north to Dijon to assist General Patton's divisions arriving from the northwest. While Army B would have to concentrate its forces on the Belfort gap and the Rhine valley. Then on Septem-

Top.
The Rhône American Cemetery in Draguignan where soldiers, sailors and aviators who fell in Provence between 1942 and 1945 were laid to rest.
(Musée de l'Artillerie photograph, with the authorization of the ABMC, Mediterranean Region)

Above, left.
The gulf and village of Saint-Tropez during the commemoration ceremonies in August 1945.
(ECPAD)

Above, right.
First anniversary celebration of the Liberation in front of the Cannes War Memorial.
(ECPAD)

Top.
The Boulouris cemetery, close to the Drammont beach, where most of the French and Colonial soldiers that fell in Provence are buried.
(Private collection)

Left.
The colors of the 1er groupement de bataillons de choc parading on the boulevard de Strasbourg in Toulon during ceremonies in August 1945.
(SHM)

Above.
General de Lattre de Tassigny, Army Inspector General, and Lieutenant General Goislard de Monsabert, commander of the French occupation troops in Germany, arriving in Cavalaire to preside over the ceremonies of the first anniversary of the invasion of Provence.
(SHM)

(SHM)

Free French soldiers gaze at FFI and officers of the old French Army nicknamed 'Naphtalinés' because their uniforms had been taken out mothballs.
(Watercolor by Marc Kosloff)

Above.
On July 11, 1945, Admiral Henry Kent Hewitt was made 'Grand Officier de la Legion d'Honneur' and decorated with the Croix de Guerre and palm by Vice Admiral Fenard, chief of the French Navy Mission in Washington.
(*National Archives*)

Right.
First pamphlet about the Battle of Provence published in 1945 by the Office Français d'Edition.
(*Private collection*)

ber 2, considering that this plan was already outdated because of the rapid evolution of the situation, General Truscott suggested that the VI Corps — whose three divisions were already assembled east of Lyon — take over the Armée B mission. And because Armée B had lost time gathering its forces around Bourg-en-Bresse before marching on Belfort. Truscott added that a direct attack toward the northeast would give the Seventh Army a final chance to block the German 19. Armee between Dijon and the Vosges mountains.

But all of this was decided behind General de Lattre's back. And he was all the more furious at not having been consulted, in that he was commanding seven divisions and the VI Corps only three. And so, all at once on the 3rd, he suddenly announced the creation of two French army corps: 1er CA on the right of the VI Corps, and 2e CA on the west side of the Rhône and Saône rivers.

Patch tried to smooth things over by agreeing to this plan, and divided the Belfort gap between the VI Corps in the north and the 2nd CA in the south. But the Germans had had time to recover and the rapid advance was now a thing of the past.

Finally, and in accordance with General Eisenhower's wishes, Patch solved the problem. The Americans proceeded to the north, but toward Strasbourg, and the French, assembled east of the Saône River, had Mulhouse as their objective. The Seventh Army reached Saint-Dié, but the 2e CA was beaten in the Vosges and sustained heavy losses.

At the same time, the replacement of black African soldiers by volunteers from the Maquis

considerably disorganized the two French colonial divisions.

Thus it was mid-November before the offensive on the Rhine was finally launched. The VI Corps attacked in the Vosges on the 12th, followed the next day by the XV Corps striking toward the Saverne gap. Then on the 14th, the 1er CA attacked Belfort. On the south side, the 1re DB entered Mulhouse on the 22nd, and to the north the 2e DB irrupted in Strasbourg on the 23rd and continued on to Sélestat. But the 5e DB was not engaged to meet up with the 2e as it should have been, and consequently a pocket of German troops remained on the left bank

of the Rhine
around Colmar, and was not taken until February 9, 1945.

It was therefore in Colmar on the Champ de Mars that, eleven days later, General De Lattre pinned the Croix de Guerre Fourragere on the 'Marne Division' colors for having "*fought continually for 169 days, from the beaches of the Mediterranean to the banks of the Rhine.* [1]"

Thus ended the Franco-American adventure that had begun in August 1944 on the shores of Provence. The French soldiers had come home victorious and chased the Germans to the Rhine.

The GIs would never forget the trip that took them from the sunny beaches of the Mediterranean to the cold, dark forests of the Vosges. One of them, back at home fifty years later, expressed the feelings of many when he said: "*I wouldn't exchange that experience for a million dollars. But I wouldn't give five cents to do it over again.* [2]"

---

1. *Decision No 588, March 15, 1945.*
2. Quoted in *Southern France, 15 August - 14 September 1944, op. cit.*

ACRONYMS AND ABBREVIATIONS

AA	Anti-Aircraft
AAA	Anti-Aircraft Artillery
ABTC	Airborne Training Center
ABTF	Airborne Task Force
AFHQ	Allied Force Headquarters
AFN	Afrique Française du Nord
AGC	Amphibious Force Flagship
AK	Armee Korps
AKA	Attack Freighter
AOF	Afrique Occidentale Française
APA	Attack Transport
APD	High Speed Transport
ARB	Air-Sea Rescue Boat
ARL	Auxiliary Repair Ship, Landing Craft
ARST	Salvage Craft Tender
ARV	Auxiliary Repair Ship, Aircraft
AS	Armée Secrète
ASRC	Air Sea Rescue Craft
BCS	British Chiefs of Staff
BCT	Battalion Combat Team
BG	Bataillon du génie (engineers)
BIM	Bataillon d'infanterie de marine
BIMP	Bataillon d'infanterie de marine et du Pacifique
BM	Bataillon de marche
BM	bataillon médical
BMS	British Minesweeper
Bn	battalion
CA	Corps d'armée
CB	Construction Battalion (Navy seabees)
CBE	Commander in the Order of the British Empire
CC	Combat command
CCS	Combined Chiefs of Staff
CEF	Corps expéditionnaire français
CEFI	Corps expéditionnaire français d'Italie
CFA	Corps franc d'Afrique
CFLN	Comité français de la libération nationale
CincMed	Commander in Chief, Mediterranean
CNWTF	Commander Naval Western Task Force
CruDiv	Cruiser Division
CTF	Commander Task Force
CTG	Commander Task Group
CTU	Commander Task Unit
D	Day
DB	Division blindée (armored div.)
DCA	Défense contre avions (AA arty)
DD	Destroyer
DD	Duplex Drive
DFL	Division française libre (Free French div.)
DI	Division d'infanterie
DIA	Division d'infanterie algérienne
DIC	Division d'infanterie coloniale
DIM	Division d'infanterie marocaine
Div Arty	Division Artillery
DMI	Division de marche d'infanterie (aka DFL)
DMM	Division marocaine de montagne
DSO	Distinguished Service Order
EM	Etat-major (HQ)
FA	Field Artillery
FAA	Fleet Air Arm
FAF	Forces aériennes françaises

FAITC	Fifth Army Invasion Training Center
FDT	Fighter Director Tender
FFI	Forces Françaises de l'Intérieur
FOB	Forward Observer
FTA	Forces terrestres antiaériennes (AA arty)
FTPF	Francs-tireurs et partisans français (Communist partisans)
G-1	Personnel staff section
G-2	Intelligence staff section
G-3	Operations and training
G-4	Supplies
G-5	Civil affairs
GADCA	Groupe antillais de DCA
GCI	Ground controlled interception
GI	Government Issue
GPRF	Gouvernement provisoire de la République française
GR	Grenadier-Regiment
GTM	Groupe de tabors marocains (Goums)
HMS	His Majesty's Ship
HMCS	His Majesty's Canadian Ship
ID	Infantry Division
ID	Infanterie-Division (Ger.)
ISTDC	Inter-Service Training and Development Center
JCS	Joint Chiefs of Staff
JMO	Journal des marches et opérations (War diary)
LCA	Landing Craft Assault
LCA(HR)	Landing Craft, Assault (Hedgerow)
LCC	Landing Craft, Control
LCF	Landing Craft, Flak
LC(FF)	Landing Craft (Flottilla Flagship)
LCG(L)	Landing Craft, Gun (Large)
LCH	Landing Craft, Headquarters
LCI(G)	Landing Craft, Infantry (Gunboat)
LCI(R)	Landing Craft, Infantry (Rocket)
LCI(L)	Landing Craft, Infantry (Large)
LCI(C)	Landing Craft, Infantry Command)
LCI(M)	Landing Craft, Infantry (Mortars)
LCM	Landing Craft, Mechanized
LCM(R)	Landing Craft, Mechanized, Rocket
LCP(L)	Landing Craft, Personnel (Large)
LCQ	Landing Craft, Headquarters
LCS(L)	Landing Craft, Support (Large)
LCS(M)	Landing Craft, Support (Medium)
LCS(R)	Landing Craft, Support (Rocket)
LCT	Landing Craft, Tank
LCT(R)	Landing Craft, Tank (Rocket)
LCV	Landing Craft, Vehicle
LCVP	Landing Craft, Vehicle and Personnel
LSD	Landing Ship, Dock
LSE	Landing Ship, Emergency Repairs
LSF	Landing Ship, Flak
LSG	Landing Ship, Gantry
LSG	Landing Ship, Gun
LSI(L)	Landing Ship, Infantry (Large)
LSI(M)	Landing Ship, Infantry (Medium)
LSI(S)	Landing Ship, Infantry (Small)
LSP	Landing Ship, Personnel
LST	Landing Ship, Tank
LZ	Landing Zone
MAAF	Mediterranean Allied Air Forces

MACAF	Mediterranean Allied Coastal Air Force
MASAF	Mediterranean Allied Strategic Air Force
MATAF	Mediterranean Allied Tactical Air Force
MinDiv	Minesweeping Division
MLC	Motor Landing Craft
NATOUSA	North African Theater of Operations, US Army
OB	Oberbefehlshaber
OKH	Oberkommando des Heeres
OKW	Oberkommando der Wehrmacht
OT	Organisation Todt
PC	Patrol Craft
PC	Poste de commandement (CP)
PIB	Parachute Infantry Battalion
PIR	Parachute Infantry Regiment
POL	Petroleum, Oil and Lubricants
PTCAD	Provisional Troop Carrier Air Division
QG	quartier général (HQ)
RAA	Régiment d'artillerie d'Afrique
RACM	Régiment d'artillerie coloniale du Maroc
RAF	Royal Air Force
RCA	Régiment de chasseurs d'Afrique
RCP	Régiment de chasseurs parachutistes
RCT	Regimental Combat Team
RD	Reserve-Division
Regt	Regiment
RICM	Régiment d'infanterie coloniale du Maroc
RN	Royal Navy
RNVR	Royal Navy Volunteer Reserve
RSAR	Régiment de spahis de reconnaissance
RTA	Régiment de tirailleurs algériens
RTS	Régiment de tirailleurs sénégalais
SACMED	Supreme Allied Commander, Mediterranean
SAP	Section d'atterrissage et de parachutage
SD	Sicherheitsdienst
SFCP	Shore Fire Control Party
SC	Submarine Chaser
SHAEF	Supreme Headquarters, Allied Expeditionary Force
SOS	Services of Supply
SR	Service de renseignement (intelligence)
SSF	Special Service Force
TAC	Tactical Air Command
TCC	Troop Carrier Command
TCG	Troop Carrier Group
TCS	Troop Carrier Squadron
TF	Task Force
TG	Task Group
TQM	Transport Quartermaster
USAAF	United States Army Air Forces
USCGC	United States Coast Guard Cutter
USN	United States Navy
USNR	United States Navy Reserve
USS	United States Ship
WNTF	Western Naval Task Force

With competence and energy, the 'Association du musée franco-américain du débarquement de Provence' keeps alive the fervent memory of the Liberation of France.
(Provence 44)

ACKNOWLEDGMENTS

The author wishes to thank the following for their assistance in the preparation of this book:
- *General Bernard Devaux*, director of the Musée de l'Armée, Paris, and his collaborators
- *General Jean-Jacques Senant*, head of the French Army Historical service (SHAT) at Vincennes, as well as Madame *Sandrine Einhornheiser* and *Jean-Marie Linsolas*
- *Contre-Amiral Alain Bellot*, head of the French Navy Historical service (SHM) in Vincennes, and his collaborators.
- *General Roland Le Bourdonnec*, head of French Air Force Historical service (SHAA) in Vincennes, and his collaborators
- Mademoiselle *Geneviève Etienne*, director of the Archives départementales du Var in Draguignan, and her collaborators.
- *Dr Manfred Kehrig*, director of the German military archives in Freiburg im Breisgau, and his collaborators.
- *Lieutenant-colonels Pierre Saint Pôl* and *Gilles Aubagnac*, director and curator of the Musée de l'Artillerie in Draguignan, and their collaborators
- *Lieutenant-colonel Jean-Louis Riccioli*, former curator of the Musée de l'Infanterie in Montpellier and present curator of the Musée de l'Emperi in Salon-de-Provence
- *Lieutenant-colonel Antoine Champeaux*, curator of the Musée des Troupes de marine in Fréjus and his collaborators
- *Capitaine Fontaine*, Traditions officer of the ERS 01/091 'Gascogne' in Mont-de-Marsan
- *Jean-Michel Soldi* and *Eric Renoux* of the Musée de la Libération 15 août 1944 in Le Muy.
- Madame *Marc Kosloff* who kindly authorized us to publish the works of her husband, a former member of the 1er Bataillon Médical who had escaped from occupied France through Spain
- *Colonels* (ret.) *Jean-Pierre Berthomieu* and *Jean Houben*
- *Pierre Besnard*, of the 'Le Poilu' Militaria Shop in Paris
- The members of '*Association Provence 44*' and especially *Jean-Patrick André, Caroline André, Olivier André, Vincent Benon, Thierry Janvier, Jean-Michel Poupon, Jean-Michel Touraine, Olivier Vanborre*
- *Frank Bachmann, Alain Chazette, Jonathan Gawne, Grégoire Georges-Picot* from the Amicale du Groupe Marat in Marseilles, *Guy Julien, Claude Majastre, Jean-Yves Nasse, Philippe Charbonnier, Jacques Sicard.*

Design and Layout by Alexandre THERS, Jean-Marie MONGIN and Philippe CHARBONNIER.
Computer graphics by Christophe CAMILOTTE, Antoine POGGIOLI and André JOUINEAU © *Histoire & Collections 2004*

ISBN: 2-915239-50-9

Publisher's number: 2-915239

A book published by
HISTOIRE & COLLECTIONS
SA au capital de 182 938, 82 €
5, avenue de la République
F-75541 Paris Cédex 11 France
Téléphone (33-1) 40 21 18 20
Fax (33-1) 47 00 51 11
e-mail: militaria@histecoll.com

This book has been designed, typed, laid-out and processed by
The Studio A&C, fully on integrated computer equipment

Printed by Zure, Spain, European Union
September 2004